Nefarious Artists: The Evolution and Art of the Punk
Rock, Post-Punk, New Wave, Hardcore Punk and Alternative
Rock Compilation Record 1976 - 1989

© Welly Artcore 2023

ISBN: 9781916864122 (paperback)

Cover and interior graphic design and layout by Welly Artcore
artcorefanzine@gmail.com

10 9 8 7 6 5 4 3 2 1

Published by Earth Island Books
Pickforde Lodge
Pickforde Lane
Ticehurst
TN5 7BN
www.earthislandbooks.com

Printed in the U.K.

"The truth is only known by guttersnipes."

The Clash

TRACK LIST

THANKS LIST

Tina, Kieran and Heidi
David Gamage and Earth Island Books
Jeff Nelson
David Markey
James Cornell
Daryl Buote
Federico Gomez
Dave Brushback
Kip-Xool
Jon Evans

LINER NOTES

I recently saw an advert, or should I say propaganda, from a global corporate music streaming company that read, "Half a billion engaged listeners means your message will be heard." Do you remember when you discovered new music, it didn't discover you? I still think it was easier to get your "message heard" before the internet via the medium of D.I.Y. punk; no middlemen, no manufactured scarcity, no "fear of missing out", no tyranny of the algorithm. You just took a chance, a risk, both buying and releasing music. And that's where the compilation record came in.

With limited knowledge, you chose a compilation in your local record store or a mail order catalogue often based on just one band you'd heard on the record, which in turn led to hearing other bands, labels and scenes. A simple glance at a thanks list, or just the cover art, or a band name you'd read somewhere, each compilation was a door you opened, a gateway to new music, to deeper knowledge, creative inspiration and sometimes even further involvement.

Unimpressed with many of the modern punk history books' habit of splitting up musical history into sub-sub-genres, for a long time I was trying to figure out if there was a way to roughly tell the story of punk rock and its various offshoots holistically in one place, but outside of producing a series of telephone books the task seemed impossible. Then one day I noticed how many compilations were in my collection and it hit me; "To tell the story of punk, look at its compilations. What better way to hear most of the music than to listen to all of the Various Artists?"

Also, what I find lacking more and more in the internet age in regards to music history is context. The connections between music can easily get lost and you can utilise all the sub-genre splicing history books and discography websites in the world and you'll still never be able to see it how it happened, in one picture. This is an attempt to address that.

Now largely regarded as a quaint anachronism largely found in bargain bins the world over, it's hard to believe that once the humble punk compilation was something so intrinsic to the spread and growth of the music, especially of the underground D.I.Y. variety, that they became a fundamental aspect of the international punk rock scene as it developed.

Punk compilations started out as they pretty much ended up; as label samplers or live showcases, but in-between the idea grew from early collections of major label fare to statements on everything from local, national and international scenes to political causes and themes. The D.I.Y. ethos was taken and expanded upon, here was a format you could use to get the word out about four, or twenty or more, bands for the same cost to promote one. This economic idea was then passed on to kids with little money, who when often faced with financial limitations could opt for a cheap compilation to hear new music, and then often go on to release it themselves (including a vast array of compilation cassettes, but that's another book altogether).

Outside of the "Dance Craze" film soundtrack, my introduction to compilations was also my introduction to hardcore punk on the compilation "Let Them Eat Jellybeans". I'd been collecting every record I could find by Dead Kennedys and when I found a book about them that had a discography in the back that included the compilations they were on, suddenly my tiny knowledge of this mysterious new world expanded, and in turn led to more discoveries that expanded it further.

Other compilations in the DK book were; "Can You Hear Me? Music From the Deaf Club", "Not So Quiet On The Western Front", "Rat Music For Rat People", "Flex Your Head" and "Wargasm". I searched high and low for these LPs and pretty soon had a small cache of compilations that all played a significant role in my musical education. Then when international compilations like Pushead's "Cleanse the Bacteria" and R Radical Records' "P.E.A.C.E." came out, they opened up even more new musical horizons, and I never looked back.

Fast forward some forty years and I now have around eight hundred compilation records, and herein I will endeavour to take you chronologically year by year and compilation by compilation (as opposed to a straight A-Z record discography) in an attempt to draw a picture of the evolution of punk rock, post-punk, new wave, hardcore punk and alternative rock between 1976 and 1989, through the medium of the compilation, the subtle changes, shifts and developments that occurred. I'm not going to pretend I know every compilation ever released, or in which order within each year they came out, so within each year each they're alphabetical. I had to draw the line somewhere in regards to what could and could not be included, it's simply impossible to include them all. Sometimes things like one volume of a series will be included as an example but not another.

The wealth of compilations is so vast that I soon realised that I'd opened a Pandora's box and I have since invested a small fortune in compilations I didn't have that needed inclusion. In short, this book took on a life of its own. You may hear some say that compilations are too patchy with too much average material, but that's a glass half empty approach. What has always interested me in compilations is the hidden gems amongst that patchy material. Music is about discovery and what better way to discover new music?

So "Nefarious Artists" is intended as a reference book of sorts, and not one necessarily for the expert who's probably already intentionally sought out a favourite obscurity that's somehow missing. It's also intended as a document for those now or in the future who don't necessarily know every pressing of every record. Something that can be referred to if the reader hasn't heard something, the cover art included to make it more recognisable in that bargain bin. I wrote about each record as I listened to it and painstakingly scanned the covers herein in high resolution, as the sleeve design is also something I feel gets overlooked, so where possible I will mention the artists and designers, again to add some context and highlight the role of graphic design.

Each record has half a page unless I felt the need to extend it to one. Some discipline was needed lest this turned into one of those phone books. I'd rather it something that can be easily referred to, a field guide for the record shop. There's only so much information you can glean on the spot from a website and this wasn't just some cut and paste exercise.

You should be able to find the majority of these records cheaply and easily, as the compilation is now considered largely irrelevant and the expensive ones are usually only rare because they contained one band that went onto bigger things, or if for some particular reason they've been singled out and hyped to death somewhere. It's all included here good and bad, as long as it somehow has a reason for inclusion. Sometimes only one band will have caused it to be featured in the same way that sometimes makes a compilation valuable.

I decided to start in 1976 with the compilation that first bore the word 'punk'. All music is an evolution but I had to start somewhere. The compilations will speak for themselves, and you will read as gradual shifts occur; from punk to new wave, post-punk to hardcore, not only in style of music, but as major label involvement wanes as the independents take over, and a massive creative explosion of underground D.I.Y. compilations takes place.

The book ends at the end of 1989, not because compilations ended then but because I had to stop somewhere. Over the years the punk compilation developed into an art form, some more successfully than others; creatively, critically and commercially, and these records remain as snapshots capturing moments like time capsules that documented a zeitgeist. Records that to this day will hold a place in the memories of countless thousands around the world, and every punk, new wave or hardcore fanatic has a memory of a compilation that connects them to a specific time and place in their life. The wave of creativity documented herein that occurred via the medium of the compilation record hopefully goes some way in telling the story of the music of a generation.

1976-1979: BUSINESS UNUSUAL

In 1976 as the U.S. celebrates two hundred years since its independence from Britain, murmurings of the word 'punk' are coming out of clubs in New York just as Vietnam reunifies and Jimmy Carter is elected president. Taxi Driver, The Omen, and All The President's Men play in theatres while Steve Jobs and friends form Apple and U.S. copyright laws are reformed.

In the U.K. Harold Wilson retires as Prime Minister and is succeeded by a troubled James Callaghan. Queen, Abba and Elton John top the U.K. charts while kids in cinemas watch Rocky, Bugsy Malone and Logan's Run. Meanwhile Stiff Records is setting up their pub rock label in London, and across the pond, Gulcher in Indiana and Mystic in Hollywood are freshly inking their new labels.

The year ends with the Sex Pistols outrageous appearance on Bill Grundy and the Daily Mirror headline "The Filth And The Fury" on December 2nd, before 1976 becomes 1977 and Queen Elizabeth celebrates her silver jubilee, soon to be critiqued by the Sex Pistols. Elvis dies at the age of 42, with 75,000 fans lining the streets of Memphis for his funeral, and Star Wars, Close Encounter Of The Third Kind and Saturday Night Fever open in theatres.

The New York blackout lasts for 25 hours in July for looting of items such as the newly released Commodore PET personal computer and Atari's 2600 video game console, while the series Roots airs and becomes the TV hit of the year. In Los Angeles, new independent labels Dangerhouse and What? Records are firing up the presses, while in London; Illegal, Rough Trade, Beggars Banquet and Raw Records are preparing to document their punk moment, while in the Mid-West, Michigan's Tremor and Ohio's Clone Records are also starting to get in on the independent vinyl action.

Sid Vicious' girlfriend Nancy Spungen is found dead in New York in October 1978 while Superman, Grease and Halloween pack in the crowds at theatres. A Communist regime is installed in Afghanistan and San Francisco Supervisor Harvey Milk and Mayor George Moscone are assassinated by Dan White, sparking riots, around the time that 415 Records begins pressing their first records. Further south in Los Angeles L.A. Weekly goes into publication while the independent record bug begins to bite into the new owners of Slash, Rhino, SST, Posh Boy and Flipside Records. Vietnam invades Cambodia while in Oregon, Greg Sage orders his first run of Trap Records and Minnesota's Twin/Tone records is pressed into reality.

On July 25th the world's first in vitro fertilisation baby, Louise Brown, is brought into the world via a Caesarean section at Oldham General Hospital in Manchester, while nearby Object, TJM and Factory Records are also being born. Around the U.K.; Fast, Heartbeat, Flaccid, Attrix, Mute, Secret and Cherry Red all prepare plans for their new labels, while queues form to see The Deer Hunter, Dawn Of The Dead and Invasion Of The Body Snatchers, while Boney M, Bee Gees and Kate Bush climb high in the charts.

As 1978 makes way for 1979 the Winter of Discontent grips Britain as Rock Against Racism expands their movement with a new label and 2-Tone also joins the fight. Crass Records begins their six year plan set to self-detonate in 1984 as Margaret Thatcher becomes Prime Minister, and over in Cardiff Z Block Records set their sights on the grass roots while Russia invades Afghanistan. Around the U.K.; Fresh Records, Dindisc and Rondelet set the vinyl gears turning as Blondie, The Police and The Boomtown Rats hit the top twenty.

Sid Vicious dies of a heroin overdose in New York just before the Three Mile Island nuclear accident and The Sandinista revolutionaries overthrow the U.S. backed dictatorship in Nicaragua. Alternative Tentacles and Subterranean Records hatch plans for an underground virus in San Francsico, while I.R.S. Records cracks down in Los Angeles just as crowds wait excitedly to see Alien, Apocalypse Now and The Warriors...

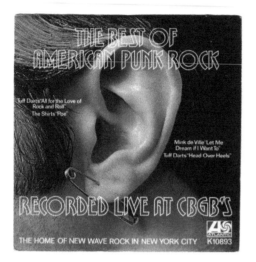

THE BEST OF
AMERICAN PUNK ROCK

Tuff Darts "All for the Love of
Rock and Roll"
The Shirts "Poe"

Mink de Ville "Let Me
Dream if I Want To"
Tuff Darts "Head Over Heels"

RECORDED LIVE AT CBGB'S

THE HOME OF NEW WAVE ROCK IN NEW YORK CITY   K10893

SIDE ONE
ALL FOR THE LOVE OF ROCK 'N' ROLL
LET ME DREAM IF I WANT TO
SIDE TWO
HEAD OVER HEELS
POE

A two record set recorded live at CBGB'S in New York featuring
TUFF DARTS, MINK DeVILLE, THE SHIRTS, THE LAUGHING DOGS,
MANSTER, SUN, STUART'S HAMMER and THE MIAMIS

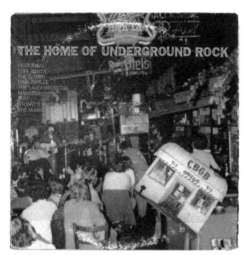

THE HOME OF UNDERGROUND ROCK

FEATURING
TUFF DARTS
THE SHIRTS
MINK DEVILLE
THE LAUGHING DOGS
MANSTRA
SUN
STUART'S HAMMER
THE MIAMIS

LIVE AT CBGB'S

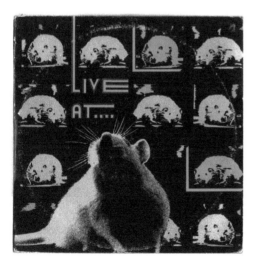

LIVE
AT....

1976
max's
kansas city

WAYNE COUNTY AND THE BACK STREET BOYS
CHERRY VANILLA AND HER STATEN ISLAND BAND
THE FAST ☆ SUICIDE ☆ THE JOHN COLLINS BAND
HARRY TOLEDO ☆ PERE UBU   RAM STEREO 1213

max's
kansas city

1976

(THE) BEST OF AMERICAN PUNK ROCK RECORDED LIVE AT CBGB'S 7" EP (ATLANTIC RECORDS)

Ironically the first compilation to feature the phrase 'punk rock' was merely a promotional EP for the full length "Live At CBGB's - The Home Of Underground Rock" on Atlantic Records, that itself also had a title change for its German release from 'Underground Rock' to 'Punk Rock'. With 7" cover art that depicted a side on view of a catalogue man's head with a safety pin through his ear, the EP featured four songs from the LP, two by Tuff Darts and one each by Mink De Ville and The Shirts. A fairly unremarkable start to the era of punk compilations but fitting that the format started out as a promotional sampler much like it would end up decades later. All three pressings of the 7" were for the burgeoning UK punk market, the final run being in 1977.

LIVE AT CBGB'S - THE HOME OF UNDERGROUND ROCK 2LP (ATLANTIC RECORDS / CBGB & OMFUG RECORDS)

The double full length of the above that kept the title 'Underground Rock' apart from for Germany where it was issued as 'Original Punk Rock' with different cover art. This collection featured all live recordings from the New York club and its legendary acoustics for live recordings, meaning it's high quality. First up was Tuff Darts and then The Shirts, Mink DeVille, The Laughing Dogs, Manster, Sun, Stuart's Hammer and The Miamis. As you can see none of the big names of New York punk were included herein and the compilation as a whole was generally bar rock and amped up rock'n'roll that's not without a few highlights. The cover featured photos of the inside of the club both from the stage and towards it, with a blurry band playing looking like Talking Heads who aren't even on the record, while the inside of the gatefold had the customary band photos. This was also issued in Germany, Canada, the UK and Japan.

LIVE AT THE RAT LP (RAT RECORDS)

Another live album, a theme for the early punk related compilations, 'Live At The Rat' showcased the Boston scene at the legendary venue of the same name. As was normal for 1976 this was a mixed bag of styles, primarily straight up 70s bar/pub rock ranging from pedestrian to atrocious but it took a turn for the better once you hit tracks by DMZ and The Real Kids, the other bands being the ridiculously named Willie 'Loco' Alexander Boom Band, Third Rail, Susan, Thundertrain, Marc Thor, Sass, The Inflictors and The Boize. Housed in a gatefold sleeve that featured rat based cover art that left you guessing the title, with an inside gatefold that featured photos of all ten bands. A one off U.S. pressing, it was reissued in 1978 in Italy on Energy Records as a trimmed down single album and with a few bands omitted, with text 'The Rat' added to the cover of that press to help demystify it, and the added line, "10 of the best from Boston's new wave of rock".

MAX'S KANSAS CITY 1976 LP (RAM RECORDS)

There is validity in New York's claim to the origination of punk rock if for no other reason than simply being the first to start seriously documenting what was happening locally. First up was Wayne County and the Back Street Boys with 'Max's Kansas City' and its lyrics name dropping all the characters of the New York scene. After this suitable intro came The Fast, Harry Toledo, Pere Ubu, Cherry Vanilla And Her Staten Island Band, John Collins Band and Suicide. A mixed bag of pop rock and brooding art rock, like the CBGB album, it doesn't include any of the big NYC names aside from the name drops on the opening song. The front cover sported a Bob Gruen photo of all the scenesters outside the club while the back showed the queue down the block waiting to get in. Released in the US and Japan in 1976 then the UK, Italy and New Zealand in 1978, and again in 1980 as "Max's Kansas City Presents: New Wave Hits For The 80's" on the Max's label with different songs and art.

1977

A BUNCH OF STIFF RECORDS LP (STIFF RECORDS)

"If they're dead - we'll sign 'em". The second LP release on then new London independent Stiff Records (and first compilation, released on April 1st 1977) and in true Stiff style this was a label sampler of their mixed bag roster that featured; Nick Lowe, Wreckless Eric, Motörhead, Elvis Costello, Magic Michael, Graham Parker, Stones Masonry, Jill Read, Dave Edmunds, Tyla Gang and The Takeaways. There were a couple of hits, namely Wreckless Eric and Elvis Costello, and the whole thing came inside a cover that was essentially nothing more than the Stiff Records logo with some Halloween style art on the back, and an inner sleeve with the customary band photos. As well as the U.K. this was released in Germany, Portugal, New Zealand and Australia.

CHISWICK CHARTBUSTERS VOL. 1 - SUBMARINE TRACKS AND FOOL'S GOLD LP (CHISWICK RECORDS)

Another London independent that was straight out the gate with a fistful of singles and a sense of humour: Chiswick Records, run by Ted Carroll and Roger Armstrong of Rock On Records of Notting Hill, and their first collection of 'chartbusters'. Even though this was essentially a set of pub rock 'n' roll standards it warrants inclusion due to the artists involved. Opening with 'Keys to Your Heart' by Joe Strummer's pre-Clash outfit the 101'ers, it also included Count Bishops, the (Hammersmith) Gorillas, Little Bob Story, Radio Stars and Rocky Sharpe and the Razors (later Replays). The twelve songs were handily dated on the back from between 1975 and 1977, with the earliest inclusion being the Count Bishops from December 1975, and the back cover sported the line; "All these titles are still available on 45 r.p.m. Records and can be ordered from your local record shop". The cover featured a photo of some band members selling their gold discs to scrap metal merchants 'Chiswick Waste'.

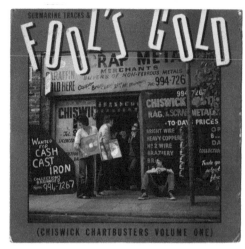

(CHISWICK CHARTBUSTERS VOLUME ONE)

(CHISWICK CHARTBUSTERS VOL. 2)

GEEF VOOR NEW WAVE

NEW WAVE GREATEST HITS

Rubinoos / The Motors / Johnny Moped / Eddie And The Hot Rods
The Adverts / Generation X / Tom Petty & The Heartbreakers / X Ray Spex
Jonathan Richman / Sex Pistols / Motorhead / Dwight Twilley Band
The Radiators From Space / Radio Stars / Earth Quake

THE WASPS MEAN STREET NEO BERNIE TORME
ART ATTACKS SUSPECTS MANIACS

VOLUME ONE

CHISWICK CHARTBUSTERS VOL. 2: LONG SHOTS, DEAD CERTS AND ODDS ON FAVOURITES LP (CHISWICK RECORDS)

Where in the world would you find the likes of MOTÖRHEAD right next to future "white power" exponents SKREWDRIVER? Well look no further. This proper snarling punk and pub rock collection of 'Chiswick Chartbusters' "produced by lots of strange people" also featured THE RADIATORS FROM SPACE, JOHNNY MOPED, RADIO STARS, RINGS, JEFF HILL, COUNT BISHOPS, AMAZORBLADES and THE STUKAS. The cover art featured a group photo of band members under 'Dishonest Ted Carroll' taking bets on their future success, Lemmy pointing at his can of Special Brew. This solid 'hits' compilation also got a pressing in Holland and a Euro cassette version in 1978, as well as two domestic UK runs, one with red Chiswick logo on the label and one in blue.

GEEF VOOR NEW WAVE LP (ARIOLA RECORDS)

In the wake of media hype the major labels of course had to get in on the action and this odd selection of stuff released for the Netherlands market had a title that translated as 'Give For New Wave' that purported to be a charity record with all money apparently going to 'new wave artists' including liner notes espousing this with a 'competition' to visit London. The reality of course was Ariola held licences for the labels that these songs were gleaned from, and as a result had some strange inclusions alongside some genuine punk hits. Within were songs from; The Motors, Johnny Moped, Eddie and the Hot Rods, The Adverts, Generation X, X-Ray Spex, Jonathan Richman, Sex Pistols, Motörhead, The Radiators From Space and Radio Stars as well as the more misfit entries from Rubinoos, Dwight Tilley Band, Tom Petty and the Heartbreakers and Earth Quake. This intriguing mixed bag was also released in France as "It's Not Balls, Here's The New Wave - New Wave Greatest Hits". The cover featured a collage of band photos with a hand holding a collection jar for the starving musicians herein. I wonder how many wide-eyed Dutch kids entered the competition.

HITS GREATEST STIFFS LP (STIFF RECORDS)

For Stiff's second compilation they inadvertently documented the handing off of the baton from pub rock to punk and new wave with this ten band and eleven song collection with an A or mainly a B side from each early 7" release in order from BUY1 to BUY11 (with BUY10 "Neat Neat Neat" by The Damned omitted). The pub rock and blues was mainly handled on side one by Nick Lowe (with "Heart Of The City" and BUY1), Pink Fairies (BUY2), Roogalator (BUY3), Tyla Gang (both sides of BUY4), Lew Lewis (BUY5), The Damned (with "Help" and BUY6), Richard Hell (with "You Gotta Lose" from BUY7), Plummet Airlines (BUY8), Motörhead (with "Leavin' Here" from BUY9 that was released on Stiff later) and Elvis Costello (with "Radio Sweetheart" from BUY11). Judging by the bland garish cover art you'd never have guessed this was punk related in 1977 but the sarcastic liner notes told another story. The heavy printed inner had a Stiff advert side and a side of non-Stiff recommended records.

LIVE AT THE VORTEX - VOLUME ONE LP (NEMS RECORDS)

An authentic snapshot of the legendary short-lived London punk club that lasted only nine months, all recorded live of course at 203 Wardour Street, London, on October 10th and 11th 1977. Starting out with the Wasps and the excellent but immediately dated "Can't Wait 'Til '78", this was followed by more high quality live recordings from Mean Street, Neo, Bernie Tormé, Art Attacks, Suspects and Maniacs. The majority of these being the typical pumped up three chord garage rock'n'roll of the era that owed as much to pub rock as it did to the likes of the Sex Pistols, with pub bands jumping ship onto the new punk trend with each passing week and speeding up their sets. The cover art was a predominantly typographical, stark black, white and red affair with a montage of gig shots underpinning it that ended up looking like a hoarding poster for a Vortex gig you'd have seen on the streets of London in '77. The twelve song album was pressed in the U.K., Germany and Italy.

NEW WAVE LP (VERTIGO)

A showcase of big 'punk' names of the day under the safer 'new wave' tag for the mainstream global market, but it still sported a gobbing punk on the cover. This had all the hits from; Ramones, Patti Smith, Talking Heads, The Damned, Boomtown Rats, Runaways, New York Dolls, Dead Boys, Richard Hell and the Voidoids, as well as the more curious inclusion of the Flamin' Groovies, Skyhooks and Little Bob Story in a "Let's see if we can pass this off as new" tactic that soon became the norm. 'New Wave' didn't try to hide its sampler status by listing the sources of the songs on the back cover, which also featured a strip of studio photos of young people dressed and acting very 'punk'. With its sixteen songs it remains an interesting collection and no doubt an inspiration to many fresh-faced kids back then the world over as it was pressed in the U.K., Netherlands, Germany, Greece, France, Japan, Australia, Portugal, Ireland, New Zealand and Mexico.

NEW WAVE - ROCK'N'ROLL - GET BEHIND IT BEFORE IT GETS PAST YOU 2 X 7" EP (SIRE RECORDS)

A promotional label sampler packaged as a double 7" with two songs per band per side. The four bands included were Dead Boys, Talking Heads, The Saints and Richard Hell and the Voidoids, with one 7" single song for each included ('Sonic Reducer', 'Uh-Oh, Love Comes To Town', 'I'm Stranded' and 'Blank Generation' respectively) as well as one album track. The gatefold sleeve featured a black and white half-toned blob on the outside with photos and the brief liner notes talked about how it didn't matter if you called it punk or new wave for toned down marketing purposes on the inside. The perils of too much time per side of a 33rpm record was very much on display here as the seven and a half minute Saints side couldn't have done them any favours sonically to new ears at near half the volume of the rest. 'New Wave' was pressed solely in the U.S. presumably for radio station and music press consumption.

NEW WAVE

RAMONES
PATTI SMITH
TALKING HEADS
THE DAMNED
THE BOOMTOWN RATS
RUNAWAYS
NEW YORK DOLLS
DEAD BOYS
FLAMIN' GROOVIES
LITTLE BOB STORY
RICHARD HELL &
THE VOID-OIDS

NEW WAVE rock 'n' roll
Get behind it before it
gets past you.

PUNK
COLLECTION

PL 42389

RAW
DEAL!

Twelve "New Wave" tracks
pressed from the Raw
Tapes recorded in the
last year. All bar
one previously
unissued.

Featuring:
The G.T.'s.
The Psycho's.
Acme Sewage Co.
The Sick Things.
The Killjoys.
Zhain. The Bloodclots & The Users.

STREETS

Includes Tracks From

The Art Attacks
Cane
John Cooper Clarke
Arthur Comics
The Dogs
The Doll
Drive
The Drones
The Exile
The Lurkers
The Members
The Nosebleeds
Pork Dukes
The Reaction
Slaughter And The Dogs
Tractor
The Zeros

PUNK COLLECTION LP (RCA RECORDS)

For some reason RCA in Italy was straight off the starting blocks in 1977 with this impressive set of sixteen bands playing the new punk rock style (with a few questionable entries, normal for the majors). Kicking off with "Sheena Is A Punk Rocker" by Ramones followed with "I Don't Care" by The Boys and then "Born To Lose" by "(Johnny Thunders)" Heartbreakers, things went a bit sideways after the first three with the inclusion of the decidedly non-punk Larry Martin Factory of France (and RCA distributed Isadora Records). Side one then continued with Eater, Models, Flamin' Groovies(!) and The Electric Chairs "(Featuring Wayne County)" before side two gave us Iggy Pop, The Police, Warm Gun (again from France and Isadora), Talking Heads, Richard Moore (of The Troggs!), Dead Boys, Richard Hell "(& Voidoids)" and Patti Smith, with hits aplenty. The cover art featured the typical spray paint and band photos with liner notes on the back and a photo of a toilet cistern.

RAW DEAL! LP (RAW RECORDS)

Released in late 1977, the first of the Raw records collections could've just rehashed some of their previously released 7"s onto a sampler collection, but instead all twelve entries apart from "I'm In Love With Today" by The Users were new to vinyl from the 'Raw Tapes'. The Users also appeared incognito as The Bloodclots doing a rendition of "Louie Louie". Acme Sewage Co., Sick Things, The G.T.'s and Psycho's all supplied two snot drenched teenage garage anthems each, while The Killjoys and Zhain submitted one rabble-rousing garage punk song per band. Out of the roster present herein only The Users and The Killjoys saw Raw releases at the time and didn't receive any reissue attention until much later. The black and white sleeve art featured two dark and mysterious photos of a blank mannequin showered in foliage, while the back cover bore the message, "Dedicated to all small labels, who are in it for the fun and glory - not just for the money."

THE Sin

£2.45 AT LIBERATED RECORD SHOPS

PUNKS SEE RED!

'NEW WAVE' ALBUM LEAVES THE WETS BEHIND

RAMONES · NEW YORK DOLLS
RUNAWAYS · THE BOOMTOWN RATS
TALKING HEADS · LITTLE BOB STORY
FLAMIN' GROOVIES · THE DAMNED
PATTI SMITH · DEAD BOYS · SKYHOOKS
RICHARD HELL & THE VOID-OIDS

marketed by phonogram

NEW WAVE

RAMONES
PATTI SMITH
TALKING HEADS
THE DAMNED
THE BOOMTOWN RATS
RUNAWAYS
NEW YORK DOLLS
DEAD BOYS
FLAMIN' GROOVIES
LITTLE BOB STORY
RICHARD HELL &
THE VOID-OIDS

Album 6300 902 Cassette 7199 005

MUSIC PRESS ADVERT IN THE NME FOR THE "NEW WAVE" LP, 23/7/1977

STREETS LP (BEGGARS BANQUET)

Sub-titled "Select highlights from independent British labels" this was put together by the then fledgling Beggars Banquet who up to that point had only put out a couple of Lurkers 7"s. This was as snotty punk as a compilation got at this stage of the game, with a line-up of relative unknowns at the time, it featured; The Art Attacks, Cane, John Cooper Clarke, Arthur Comics (The Snivelling Shits), The Dogs, The Doll, Drive, The Drones, The Exile, The Lurkers, The Members, The Nosebleeds, Pork Dukes, The Reaction, Slaughter and the Dogs, Tractor and The Zeros. With unique cover cartoons by the Savage Pencil (Edwin Pouncey of Sounds), the album's mission statement summed it all up; "1977 was the year that the music came out of the concert halls and onto the streets; when independent labels sprang out of the woodwork to feed new tastes; when rock music once again became about energy and fun; when the majors' boardrooms lost control. Suddenly we could do anything." 'Streets' was only pressed in the U.K. and later Germany in 1979.

THE ROXY LONDON WC2 (JAN - APR 77) LP (HARVEST RECORDS)

Another early live document, this time for a snapshot of this legendary London club between January and April 1977 (it was only open for just shy of four months). High quality but rough'n'ready live performances from Slaughter and the Dogs, The Unwanted, Wire, The Adverts, Johnny Moped, Eater, X-Ray Spex and Buzzcocks. Bonafide punk anthems such as 'Boston Babies', '12XU', 'Bored Teenagers', 'Oh Bondage Up Yours' and 'Breakdown' are all here, while the hilarious intro to Johnny Moped's 'Hard Loving Man' is a definitive moment on this LP ("'ello someone's been stabbed"). The crowd chatter can go on a bit between songs but it did give it an atmosphere. The front cover sported a shot of the gear being set up while the rest is a very punk photo montage with very brief liner notes again calling it 'new wave'. 'The Roxy' was pressed in the U.K., Germany, France, New Zealand, Italy, Portugal, Australia and Japan in 1977.

1978

:30 OVER D.C.-HERE COMES THE NEW WAVE! LP (LIMP RECORDS)

One of the first regional U.S. compilations from Washington D.C. put together by Skip Groff of Yesterday and Today records on his Limp imprint. A simple package with a sheet on the front and back of a plain white sleeve that featured the early brooding and quirky punk wave of the city from; The Penetrators, The Rudéments, Mock Turtle, The Slickee Boys, Chumps, Billy Synth, Jeff Dahl, 1/2 Japanese, White Boy, The Nurses, Mark Hoback, Judies Fixation, Tina Peel, Young turds, Da Moronics and Raisinets. Musically it was all over the place, often rudimentary and frantic with keyboards and saxophones popping up here and there but it had a certain early punk charm. It had three pressings of 500; the first on red vinyl with both numbered and pasted and loose cover sheets, the second on gold vinyl, the third on black.

(THE) AKRON COMPILATION LP (STIFF RECORDS)

Seeing as Stiff was the label to first issue the early Devo 7"s in the UK, they were no doubt inspired to check out what else was happening in the Spudboys' hometown of Akron, Ohio. Featuring some of the output of Nick Nicholis of The Bizarros' Akron based label Clone Records, as well as some that would also appear on Stiff's roster, the album included Jane Aire And The Belvederes, Tin Huey, Rachel Sweet, The Bizarros, The Waitresses, Rubber City Rebels, Sniper, Idiots Convention, Terraplane and Chi Pig. Most of the album was still in the rock and pop department, some with Devo influences and some more mid-western rocking entries from The Bizarros, The Waitresses and Rubber City Rebels. The cover featured the 'Shine On America' mural as seen on Devo's "The Truth about De-Evolution" movie with a scratch and sniff rubber scented tyre in the top corner (mine still stinks 44 years later). The album was released in the UK, Netherlands, Belgium, Spain, France, Germany and Japan.

AYLESBURY GOES FLACCID LP (FLACCID RECORDS)

One of the very first British regional compilations was focused on the unlikely D.I.Y. destination of Aylesbury in Buckinghamshire. The only release on Flaccid Records was put together by Chris France, a local promoter who happened upon the novel idea that if fourteen bands paid for thirty albums each the project would pay for itself. Apparently a newly formed Marillion couldn't guarantee to pay for their copies so didn't make the cut. The album contained a mixed bag of punk, pub rock, new wave and reggae and opened with the great 'No Passion' by the Vice Creems. This was followed by The Speedos, The Man Ezeke, Peter Out and the Faders, The Robins, The Haircuts, Wild Willy Barrett, while side two featured Clumsy, Anal Surgeons, Smiffy, Abbott, Ken Liversausage, Robert And The Remoulds, and Redwood. Housed in a cut-price spineless thin card 12" sleeve, it's sole press remained one of the earliest examples of a true D.I.Y. punk compilation and an early example of "pay-to-play".

BATTLE OF THE BANDS 2 X 7" EP (GOOD VIBRATIONS RECORDS)

The first area compilation out of Northern Ireland was on their legendary homegrown label Good Vibrations of course and was a real D.I.Y. punk offering. This double 7" gave a side each to four bands with a song a piece. The first being Outcasts and 'The Cops are Comin'', followed by Spider with 'Dancing in the Streets' on the flip. Record two featured the Idiots and 'Parents' with Rudi's 'Overcome by Fumes' closing things out. All four songs were of the three chord, catchy and punchy, pop punk variety that Northern Ireland quickly became known for, taking their cues from the likes of Ramones and Buzzcocks. Both singles were wrapped in a D.I.Y. fold-around printed sleeve with photos and liner notes that stated that the Undertones were supposed to be included but 'got signed up to a better company' and were replaced by Spider (poor Spider). The double 7" was pressed multiple times in 1978 with at least seven different sleeve and label variants.

BELFAST ROCK LP (RIP OFF RECORDS)

As the title suggested this was another 1978 collection of talent from Belfast, more specifically of George Doherty's Rip Off Records 7"s. Opening the album up were Pretty Boy Floyd & The Gems with their pub rock 7" A-Side "Spread The Word Around" (featuring Jim Lyttle later of Rogue Male), followed by Blue Steam and their B-Side "Cortina Cowboys" very much in the same pub rock vein. "Looking For A Lady" by Cobra (featuring Nigel Hamilton of The Tearjerkers) then descended into straight up rock as did The Jumpers with "Jimmy Jump" but with added harmonica. No Sweat's B-Side "You Should Be So Lucky" picked up the pace and sounded a bit more like the punk rock of the day, while "Cruisin'" by Detonators (former bassist Ali McMordie had already jumped ship to SLF) went back to hard rock to close the first side. Side two offered another song by each band and the cover art depicted a rocker brandishing a stick of Belfast rock (of course), the songs as illustrated graffiti on the back.

BUSINESS UNUSUAL - THE OTHER RECORD COLLECTION LP (CHERRY RED)

Compiled in conjunction with Zig Zag Magazine by Cherry Red head honchos Iain McNay and Richard Jones, this compilation featured 7" songs from a variety of 1977-78 bands on the then new small independent labels of the day. It opened strong with 'C.I.D.' by the UK Subs followed by Leyton Buzzards, The Outcasts, Dave Goodman And Friends, The Outsiders, The Record Players, Vice Creems, The Dole, The Tights, Skunks, Thomas Leer, Robert Rental, Throbbing Gristle and Cabaret Voltaire. The sleeve simply depicted the fourteen 7" covers from where the songs were gleaned, while the rear had liner notes from Zig Zag's David Marlow. Inside there was a huge 6 x 12" panel foldout poster with the covers reproduced again on one side and in a genuine attempt at spreading the early D.I.Y. punk rock message the flip had a vast 'Small Labels Catalogue' list. 'Business Unusual' was pressed in the U.K., Portugal, Greece, New Zealand, Canada and Japan.

CATCH A WAVE 2 X 10" (NICE RECORDS)

A slightly mysterious mono double 10" collection of 1977
bands that was manufactured in the U.K. but was compiled in
Denmark and distributed primarily in Scandinavian countries.
No label name was present but the catalogue number 'Nice 1'
featured fairly prominently giving the impression that was
the intention. Featuring 19 bands and songs ; Eddie And The
Hot Rods, XTC, The Stukas, The Radiators From Space, Greg
Kihn, Johnny And The Self Abusers, The Table, Blondie,
Little Bob Story, Earth Quake, Radio Stars, Ultravox!, The
Rubinoos, The Motors, Motörhead, Generation X, Skrewdriver,
Jonathan Richman And The Modern Lovers and X Ray Spex. A mix
of punk wave hits with some less obvious entries (and a few
Beserkley pop rockers such as Greg Kihn, Earth Quake and
Rubinoos) presumably licensed from various labels such as
Chiswick, Virgin and Island. The gatefold sleeve featured
a spotty youth spray painting the title on the front,
the rest being street photography with titles overlaid,
and the sleeves and promo posters of the bands inside.

FAREWELL TO THE ROXY LP (LIGHTNING RECORDS)

The second installment of the live documentation of The
Roxy recorded over three nights; December 31st 1977 and
January 1st and 2nd 1978 as a last hurrah of sorts. This
album, recorded when the venue was under new management
and a few months before it closed for good, featured
the immediate second wave of punk bands, and a stack of
lesser known bands delivering their out of tune, charmingly
unrehearsed, buried gems. Out of this roster the UK Subs had
three songs and went onto punk world fame, whereas; Blitz,
Acme Sewage Co., Billy Karloff and the Goats, The Tickets,
The Red Lights, XL5, The Jets, The Streets, Plastix, The
Bears, Open Sore and The Crabs all reside in relative
and undeserved obscurity to this day. The cover was a
relatively uninspiring photo of the venue with a cross
through it and some graffiti on the back. Initially released
on vinyl and cassette and later reissued on vinyl and CD.

FIRST BELGIAN PUNK CONTEST - MARCH 1978 LP (JW'S RECORDS)

Surprisingly powerful for the time, probably due to the high quality live recording at the Old St. Job in Brussels, 'First Belgian Punk Contest' ranged from the primitive punk of P.I.G.Z. to the sloppy approach of a band called Belgium, and it all seemed to be very much influenced by the UK '77 scene ranging from pub rock to a Raw Records style rough and tumble. The bands included herein were; P.I.G.Z., Heavy Capuccino & The Flying Stukas, Modern World, Les Tueurs De La Lune De Miel, Belgium, Cell 609, Juice Heads, Trampolino, Mad Virgins and The Razors, all with a song each apart from P.I.G.Z. and Cell 609. The inclusion of the crowd and applause only added to the "Chaos In Belgium" feel of the record which was full of loose and almost improvised punk performances with no let up in the din from start to finish apart from the "Flemish Reggae" of Juice Heads. The cover depicted some bloke who looked more of a ted than a punk with a customary map on the back.

GUILLOTINE 10" (VIRGIN RECORDS)

Virgin's foray into the world of the punk compilation, or label sampler, came in the form of this eight band, eight song collection of its 7" 'punk' output, first released on a 10" with an inner sleeve and foldout poster. The Motors opened up proceedings with a B-side of their pub rock, followed by Penetration and 'Don't Dictate', Cardiff school kids The Table 'Do The Standing Still' before side one closed with Devon's Avant Gardener (later Gardeners). Side two offered songs by XTC, Roky Erickson, Poet And The Roots and the whole thing ended with 'Oh Bondage Up Yours!' by X-Ray Spex. The inner sleeve sported band info with liner notes apparently by Richard Branson and some cartoons to make it look 'punk', while the poster was much better than the actual 10" cover which was just a dark and mysterious mess. The compilation was expanded to 13 songs for release in France and New Zealand, and later reissued again on 10" in the UK with no inner or poster.

HEROES & COWARDS LP (STIFF RECORDS)

A Stiff collection that was put together purely for the Italian market that featured 7" tracks of their punk and pre-punk hits. Alberto Y Lost Trios Paranoias opened up proceedings with their snotty spoof punk, followed by Ian Dury ("Sex and Drugs And Rock And Roll"), Nick Lowe ("Heart of the City"), The Damned (both sides of the "New Rose" 7"), Elvis Costello ("Alison"), Motörhead, Wreckless Eric ("Whole Wide World"), The Adverts ("One Chord Wonders") and Mick Farren And The Deviants. Some bands had two songs while Albertos and Elvis Costello managed three. The cover depicted a bi-plane dropping a bomb of the band names, presumably on Italy. While 'Heroes & Cowards' was nothing more than a budget price sampler that literally said 'New Wave Rock - Special Price' on the cover, at the time it no doubt introduced some young Italian punks to the hits of Stiff Records, which I guess was the whole point. The album was pressed three times in Italy.

HOPE & ANCHOR FRONT ROW FESTIVAL 2LP (WARNER BROS.)

A double LP continuing the live album theme of early punk and new wave albums, this one recorded at the London pub and legendary venue of the title and was of high quality sound wise. The recordings were at gigs between Tuesday 22nd November and Thursday 15th December 1977 with the album being released in March 1978. The set included an eclectic mix of punk, new wave and of course pub rock and featured; Wilko Johnson Band, The Stranglers, Tyla Gang, The Pirates, Steve Gibbon Band, XTC, Suburban Studs, The Pleasers, Dire Straits, Burlesque, X-Ray Spex, 999, The Saints, The Only Ones, Steel Pulse, Roogalator and Philip Rambow, with quite a few turning in two songs. The gatefold sleeve featured an illustration of the pub and surrounding streets, while the black and white insert filled you in on the band details. The collection was only released in the U.K. and Germany with a handful of reissues later, and reached number 28 in the U.K. albums chart at the time.

JUBILEE CERT. X - SOUNDTRACK LP (POLYDOR)

Sub-titled "The outrageous soundtrack from the motion picture" this was the audio accompaniment to the Derek Jarman punk film "Jubilee". Although scored by Brian Eno (with two pieces at the end here) the film also featured various punk acts including; Adam Ant, Toyah, Jordan and Jayne County, and side one featured two songs by Adam And The Ants ("Deutscher Girls" and "Plastic Surgery"). Unique at the time, both songs were later repackaged in 1982 as a Polydor 7" to capitalise on the Ants later success. Wayne County And The Electric Chairs and Chelsea supplied a legitimate song each, as well as Maneaters, a side-project of Toyah and Adam Ant. Besides Eno, side two featured non-punk soundtrack filler tripe from Suzi Pinns and Amilcar. The cover featured Jordan as Britannia with various other stills from the film adorning the back. This fairly average "cash-in on punk" album was released in the U.K., Germany, Italy, Spain and Australia in 1978.

KEIHARD EN SWINGEND! (LIVE IN PARADISO) LP (EMI)

Recorded at the Paradiso in Amsterdam between 12th and 14th February 1978, "Hard And Swinging" proved that the Dutch weren't about to get left behind in the new punk wave. First up was Sammy America's Gasphetti, the only band to get two songs, who delivered a pounding punk followed by Subway who were very much channelling the London '77 bands after being a hippie band a few years earlier. WhiZZ Guy were almost Cramps like in their minimal rock'n'roll, while Suzannes then Panic looked to Chiswick for their inspiration. Side two saw Captain Coke, The Nits, Sylph, Turf, Cilinders and The Lizards bring forth their new wave wares in more varying styles with a lot more keyboards. A bit of a lost gem of the early punk era, with high quality recording and song writing, the cover featured some great photos front and back with liner notes that captured the punk mood of how we'd all be better off... "In a room with some glass damage than in a hall full of binoculars."

LETHAL WEAPONS LP (SUICIDE RECORDS)

The first Australian punk compilation was the brainchild
of band manager Barrie Earl who'd returned from the U.K.
with the idea of a Stiff Records style label. He talked
Mushroom Records and RCA into investing and the short-lived
Suicide Records was born. 'Lethal Weapons' opened with
Teenage Radio Stars and "Wanna Be Ya Baby" which sounded
suspiciously like a Vibrators song with the word "Baby" in
the title. Each band had two songs apart from The Negatives
who only had one, while The Boys Next Door supplied three.
The Boys Next Door being the band who became The Birthday
Party, with Nick Cave on vocals, here for his first vinyl
appearance with "These Boots Are Made For Walking" and two
great punk originals. Wasted Daze were more of a rock'n'roll
Wild West inspired band while Jab's nervous vocals rode a
poppy synth wave, and The Survivors had a tepid pub rock
feel. The album closed with The brooding Negatives and
dramatic X Ray Z and was originally issued on white vinyl.

LIVE STIFFS LP (STIFF RECORDS)

The vinyl document of the Live Stiffs tour of 1977 as
immortalised in the documentary "If It Ain't Stiff, It Ain't
Worth a Fuck". A showcase of the 'new wave' somewhat comprised
of the old wave playing good ol' rock'n'roll standards.
Regardless, this was a well recorded (at the University of
East Anglia, Norwich) and enjoyable package featuring Nick
Lowe's Last Chicken In The Shop (with other old rocker Dave
Edmunds), Wreckless Eric And The New Rockets, Larry Wallis'
Psychedelic Rowdies, Elvis Costello And The Attractions,
and Ian Dury And The Blockheads, concluded with a version
of "Sex And Drugs And Rock'n'Roll (And Chaos)' featuring
everybody all at once, as can be seen in the documentary,
as a closing cacophony. The five lead performers were
featured on the front cover while a signed leather jacket
adorned the rear. The LP was released in the UK, US,
Germany, Netherlands, Australia, Canada, Belgium, Greece,
Portugal, Spain, Italy, France, Scandinavia and Japan.

MEET THE NEW PUNK WAVE LP (EMI)

It's somewhat ironic that one of the strongest examples
of the first wave of punk compilations was only issued in
the Netherlands. Opening with "Emergency" by 999 followed
by the lesser known but noteworthy Advertising. The Saints
were hot on their heels with "I'm Stranded" before The
Banned and "Little Girl". London supplied album title
track "Animal Games" and then The Blitzz from Amsterdam
added a Dutch punk twist. The Stranglers closed side one
and opened side two with "Straighten Out" and "Peaches",
before Rich Kids performed their eponymous song. Then Wire
with "Mannequin" and The Secret doing "The Young Ones".
More Dutch action followed with The Flyin' Spiderz and
"Movies" before The Flys provided the classic "Love And
A Molotov Cocktail". The album concluded this solid set
with "What Do I Get" by Buzzcocks, while the cover art was
all torn posters on a Wall. Unfortunately the album only
received one pressing in the Netherlands.

NO NEW YORK LP (ANTILLES RECORDS)

Rejecting the rock'n'roll norms of punk and new wave, 'no
wave' was a musical and artistic moment in New York that
attempted to approach things slightly differently to what
was going on elsewhere. The album to document all this
was 'No New York', shared between four bands spanning 16
songs; The Contortions, Teenage Jesus And The Jerks, Mars
and DNA. The resulting sonic assault took the then new
explorations in music on a jazzy tangent with off-beat
rhythms and dissonant guitars, that was essentially what a
lot of post-punk also was becoming, mixed with what some
residents of cities like San Francisco were or would also
soon be doing. The cover art was a blurred image with band
member mug shots on the back, and the appearance of the
name Brian Eno multiple times in the credits suggested that
it wasn't the paradigm-smashing break from the past it was
made out to be. 'No New York' received four pressings in the
year of release and was later reissued in Russia and Japan.

OH NO IT'S - MORE FROM RAW LP (RAW RECORDS)

Sub-titled "The Raw Records First Anniversary Album" this
was round two of Lee Wood's Raw Records' compilations and
this one was a 7" showcase. The trademark snotty punk mixed
with pub rock of Raw was on full display here with some
now classic hits from The Users ("Sick Of You" and "(I'm)
In Love With Today), The Soft Boys, Downliners Sect, Some
Chicken, The Gorillas and The Hammersmith Gorillas, The
Unwanted, The Killjoys ("Johnny Won't Get To Heaven" -
Raw's biggest hit that sold an alleged 18,000 copies) and
Lockjaw, clocking up twelve songs. The cover art depicted
a selection of Raw Records' cover stories in the UK music
press backed by a hard-to-read tracklist that's all in
the wrong order. Around 2,500 copies were pressed in the
UK, mainly for export, and it was much later reissued on
vinyl and CD in 2003. Lee Wood went on to run his own Sound
Publishing and Spiral Scratch magazine, which was set up
to rival Record Collector magazine.

POHJALLA LP (LOVE RECORDS)

Finland was an early entry into the international punk
conversation with "Pohjalla" or "On The Bottom". Opening
with the decidedly punk 1978 with "Electronic Xtasy" and
followed by the more rockin' New York Dolls meets Raw
Records style garage punk of Problems? with "I Want To
Go", and then Sehr Schnell (Very Fast) with the anthemic
punk of "18 V.V.K." After another Problems? song, Pelle
Miljoona & N.U.S. (that featured Petri Tiili also of 1978)
performed the nasal three chord punk of "A Rock Star",
before another Problems? song and then Se with a more
melodic power pop song in the form of "Ei Asfaltti Liiku".
Another Pelle Miljoona & N.U.S. tune concluded side 1 and
side 2 continued with more songs from most of the bands,
with Problems?, Sehr Schnell and Pelle Miljoona & N.U.S.
all having four songs each (with 1978 and Se both only
submitting one), although the opening 1978 is a strong solo
entry. I'm not quite sure what was going on cover art wise.

SATURDAY NIGHT POGO LP (RHINO RECORDS)

Sub-titled "A Collection Of Los Angeles New Wave Bands" this parody of 'Saturday Night Fever' reflected the Hollywood mix of the era of early punk, proto-punk, garage, power pop and glam typical of Rhino Records and the early Los Angeles punk era scene. This set was comprised of The Winos, The Berlin Brats, The Droogs, Needles And Pins, The Motels, Vom, The Low Numbers, The Dils, Daddy Maxfield, The Young Republicans, Backstage Pass, The Dogs, Chainsaw, and The Hebe Geebees doing "Night Fever". Standouts here were The Dils 'Mr. Big' and Vom's "I'm In Love With Your Mom", the rest bringing rock and pop, full of long hair and Rolling Stones Influences, that owed more to the old rock guard than to any kind of new wave... but every label had to get in on the new wave action. The cover featured rock journalist and Vom member Richard Meltzer posing on the dance floor with The Hebe Geebees replacing the Bee Gees, band info on the rear. Three pressings existed with different colour sleeves.

SHORT CIRCUIT - LIVE AT THE ELECTRIC CIRCUS 10" (VIRGIN RECORDS)

The first collection, live of course, from Manchester (with the addition of Birmingham's Steel Pulse). A brief eight song 10" featuring The Fall, John Cooper Clarke, Joy Division, The Drones, Steel Pulse and The Buzzcocks. The quality was high, John Cooper Clark delivered the hilarious "(You Never See A Nipple In The) Daily Express" and "I Married A Monster From Outer Space", Joy Division got all edgy mentioning Rudolf Hess, and Steel Pulse took nearly half a side to "Makka Splaff". The Fall also managed two songs "Stepping Out" and "Last Orders", while The Buzzcocks close proceedings with "Time's Up". The cover art was a circuit diagram (of course) while the rear sported live photos and the insert had liner notes from Paul Morley. The first two presses came on different colour vinyl with a John Dowie 7" and poster, while the subsequent handful of pressings didn't. The 10" was reissued in the U.K. and Greece in the mid 80s and much later on CD in 1991.

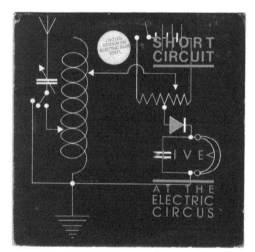

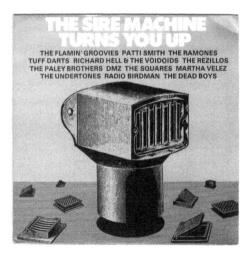

THE BEST OF BOMP - VOLUME ONE LP (BOMP RECORDS)

Sub-titled "A Collection of Highlights from the First Four Years of America's Pioneer 'New Wave' Label", this was the first showcase of Greg (and Suzy) Shaw's Bomp! Records, and extension of his fanzine 'Who Put The Bomp' that evolved into a label in 1974, "for the "hard core" rock and roll fans". Primarily a sixties garage and power pop label this warrants inclusion on the strength of some punk related content from the Weirdos and Zeros ("A Life Of Crime" and "Wimp" respectively). Iggy and the Stooges got two songs, and the collection also included DMZ, 20/20, The Flamin' Groovies, The Poppees, The Wackers, The Choir, The Rockfield Chorale, Venus and the Razorblades, Snatch, Willie Alexander and the Boom Boom Band and Shoes. The sleeve was a garish collage of band photos with back cover text so unreadable that it was reproduced on the white insert. Originally on white vinyl and then pink in the U.S., it was also issued in Canada and Germany with a different cover.

THE SIRE MACHINE TURNS YOU UP LP (SIRE RECORDS)

A showcase of Sire Records punk and new wave for the UK market. A fairly low effort budget sampler with album tracks from the catalogues at the time of; Ramones, Richard Hell And The Voidoids, Dead Boys, The Undertones, Radio Birdman, Rezillos, Patti Smith, DMZ and Tuff Darts, as well as the decidedly less 'new' wave Paley Brothers, Martha Velez, Flamin' Groovies and Squares. More curious still was the short 'Also Available' list on the back which listed two Talking Heads albums and they weren't even on this record, I guess they ran out of vinyl space. It's seems a bit like whichever intern at Warner/WEA that drew the short straw to put this together just couldn't be bothered, had no idea what the music was all about or was too busy holding their nose while putting it together. The cover art was some fittingly abstract thing full of drains and vents and I have no idea what the connection to the title is but I guess that's in keeping with the aimless nature of the LP.

122 LOVELL ROAD • CAMBRIDGE • CB4 2QP • ENGLAND

SOUND PUBLISHING •

TEL 0223 358508/462466 • FAX 0223 358038 • VAT REG NO 432 2499 58 • PROPRIETOR LEE WOOD

30/3/89

Dear J,

   Thanks for your subscription, hope you
continue to enjoy the magazine. Your request about RAW
came to the right place. RAW was a label I ran
between 1977 and 1979. The compilation album (Oh No It's)
MORE FROM RAW was issued in 1978 and about 2500 copies
were made. Most of them went to other countries (export)
so it's very hard to find in this country. I would
say the current value is £10 - 15.

I am currently researching my files and a feature on RAW
is planned for an up-coming issue of Spiral Scratch.

Hope that info helps.

Best Wishes-

Lee Wood.

LETTER FOUND IN MY COPY OF "OH NO IT'S - MORE FROM RAW" LP FROM
LEE WOOD OF RAW RECORDS/SOUND PUBLISHING/SPIRAL SCRATCH, 1989

VAULTAGE 78 - TWO SIDES OF BRIGHTON LP (ATTRIX RECORDS)

Brighton's contribution to early punk, notable for the inclusion of the early Peter And The Test Tube Babies with "Elvis Is Dead". Opening the album though was Nicky And The Dots with a quirky keyboard fare that would soon see them put out a 7" on Small Wonder. The Dodgems offered up two songs including "Lord Lucan Is Missing", which later became a single in 1980. Devil's Dykes provided two brooding keyboard songs while the two Parrots tunes saw them soon record a 12" for Attrix. The Vitamins' only submitted one song and their only vinyl appearance. Finally, the Piranhas three reggae-tinged numbers would soon see them grab a top ten hit for twelve weeks in 1980 with "Tom Hark". The cover featured a silhouette of the Brighton "skyline" with it all lying in ruin on the back. The insert had band info, an explanation of how it was all put together at the local community centre, and a charming piece entitled "How To Make Your Own Record". "Vaultage '78" had three pressings, with two further volumes in '79 and '80.

1979

499 2139 LP (ROCKET RECORD COMPANY)

A set of 'contemporary bands' on Elton John's label gleaned from small ads placed in the back pages of two U.K. music weeklies that bore the contact number above. Bands sent in their tapes following a phone call and the this was the result. Considering these are the band's own submissions (bar one) the recordings were surprisingly consistent. Twelve bands were featured; The Act, The Lambrettas, the Classics, Malcolm Practice, Escalators, The Vye, Wolfboys!!, Wardens, The Brick Wall Band, Les Elite, Reafer and Sinister, with a song each apart from The Act and Malcolm Practice with two. The most punk entry here was Wolfboys!! With the rest being new wave or mod related but with a high level of song writing, probably due to pop svengali Pete Waterman being involved. Husband and wife photography team Carol Starr and Chalkie Davies handled the cover and it was only pressed in the U.K. and Netherlands.

4 ALTERNATIVES 7" EP (HEARTBEAT RECORDS)

A succinct area compilation from Bristol's Heartbeat featuring four local punk wave bands; The Numbers, The X-Certs, Joe Public and 48 Hours, who were all very much in the vein of 1979 U.K. punk in that they were all proficient on their instruments, there were more than a few skinny ties present, and an all around sound that's similar to other U.K. bands of the day such as The Shapes or The Jam. All the songs were memorable and this quality control was probably helped by it being an EP. For the D.I.Y. economic aspect, all four bands were recorded in one day on April 8th 1979 at Crescent Studios in Bath. The front cover art looked like some sort of dirty protest with band photos and info on the back. Cherry Red handled the business end of things and the EP received two pressings in the year of release, one with a glossy sleeve and one without.

20 OF ANOTHER KIND - VOLUME 1 AND 2 LPS (POLYDOR RECORDS)

The two volumes of the Polydor singles showcase, and it
was clear that they'd wasted no time in hoovering up
punk talent for their roster. Featuring one or songs per
band, volume one featured; Plastic Bertrand, The Jam, The
Skids, Otway And Barratt, Sham 69, The Cure, Stiff Little
Fingers, The Adverts, Generation X, 999, The Stranglers,
The Boys, Patrik Fitzgerald, The Jolt, The Heartbreakers
and The Lurkers. Volume two featured further appearance
from The Jam, The Cure, Sham 69, Patrik Fitzgerald and
The Lurkers, and also features Tubeway Army / Gary Numan,
Twist, The Chords, Protex, The Invaders, Purple Hearts, The
Headboys, The Carpettes and Xdreamysts. Wrapped in super
punk artwork these were two of the strongest collections
if you just wanted to spin the punk wave hits of the days,
especially volume one as it was compiled by Polydor A&R man
and Fiction Records owner Chris Parry. Both albums were
never issued again after their initial release.

AK•79 LP (RIPPER RECORDS)

Bearing the description on the back cover, "A collection
of demo tapes recorded by various bands in Auckland city
over a period of about one year, ending in late '79". New
Zealand entered the punk conversation with AK•79, put
together by late night radio DJ Bryan Staff who asked six
new punk bands he'd got to know if they could supply two
songs each, and if the LP sold he'd carry on releasing NZ
bands until the money ran out. The bands in question were
Scavengers, Terrorways, Proud Scum, Swingers, Primmers and
Toy Love. You could hear the strong influence of 1977 U.K.
catchy pogo punk throughout, with most bands taking a
similar approach to bands such as Buzzcocks and The Shapes,
apart from the post Suburban Reptiles/Split Enz band The
Swingers, who were a little more glam rock. Lemonheads
would later make slightly more famous the Proud Scum song
"I Am A Rabbit" on their debut 7" in 1986. The album was
been reissued numerous times in New Zealand over the years.

A MANCHESTER COLLECTION LP (OBJECT MUSIC)

Sub-titled "(Bands of the Manchester Musicians Collective)" this intriguing compilation opened with the jangly new wave of Grow-Up before I.Q. Zero and their spiky post-punk. The more well-known Fast Cars took the stage next for two songs of sharp caffeinated punk with a definite early Devo influence on "I Must Obey" then more of a traditional power pop feel on "Why". Mediaters offered a robotic Fall style post-punk number with parping horns and side one concluded with Fireplace and their Stranglers influenced post-punk. Side two brought us the experimental synthscapes of Picture Chords, while Manchester Mekon then tried their hand at a Rick Wakeman style instrumental before Property Of... made their post-punk statement, Vibrant Thigh offered a highlight with a rapid Buzzcocks style song, F.T. Index then gave us some white reggae before three piece Slight Seconds completed the LP with some engaging and memorable post-punk. The cover photo was by music photographer Kevin Cummins.

AND NOW LIVE FROM TORONTO - THE LAST POGO LP (BOMB RECORDS)

One of the first of two 1979 area compilations from Canada recorded live at the Horseshoe Tavern on December 1st and 2nd 1978, there was also a documentary of the same name by Colin Brunton. The Secrets open proceedings featuring members of the Diodes, Arson and Viletones among others, followed by the horn and keyboard new wave of Drastic Measures. The spirited dark punk of Cardboard Brains' "Babies Run My World" was followed by The Scenics odd post-punk for two songs. Next up devotees of The Jam The Mods brought their parka revival before the power pop of The Everglades closed side one. The second side featured another song by all the bands, bar The Scenics, with the addition of the pulsing punk rock of The Ugly and the reggae of Ishan Band, with The Mods closing proceedings with their single "Step Out Tonight". The front cover depicted punks waiting for the gig to start with band photos on the back, while the insert displayed some charming shots of some local degenerates.

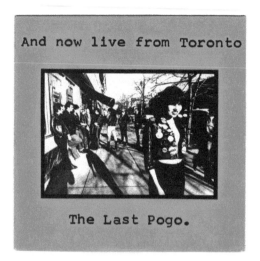

And now live from Toronto

The Last Pogo.

ARE WE TOO LATE FOR THE TREND...

VOMIT PIGS
=CONTROL=
Barry Kooda
NERVE BREAKERS
Blindate
ESR
SMEGMA
Spasm
SUPERMAN'S GIRLFRIEND
PLASTIC IDOLS
THE SKUDS
THE TELEFONES
THE INFANTS

AVON CALLING

THE BRISTOL COMPILATION

Beach Blvd

BIG HITS OF MID-AMERICA VOLUME THREE

ARE WE TOO LATE FOR THE TREND... LP (ESR RECORDS)

Legendary Texan punk compilation (primarily Dallas) that featured Vomit Pigs (Dallas), Plastic Idols (Houston), The Telefones (Dallas), The Infants (Dallas), Barry Kooda (Barry Huebne, Dallas), Blindate, E-MC² (aka Telefones), The Skuds, Control, Smegma, Superman's Girlfriend (Dallas), Nervebreakers (Dallas) and Snakes, thirteen songs by twelve or thirteen bands depending on which way you looked at it (E-MC² were the Telefones). Notably for the time and place, this was a studio and not a live record, as was often the case, especially with early Texas punk compilations. The majority of this was in the power pop and garage rock'n'roll end of the early American punk department, with a few bands utilising sax. "We're Not Here" by Blindate was a catchy stand out as was slow burner "Dead Dogs" by The Skuds, and of course the Nervebreakers turned in a strong entry with "I Love Your Neurosis". The simple cover featured band logos and a high school year book photo of "Dear Boy", chopped up band photos on the back, and an insert with line-up info.

AVON CALLING (THE BRISTOL COMPILATION) LP (HEARTBEAT RECORDS)

Putting Bristol on the punk wave map 'Avon Calling' opened with the post-punk of Glaxo Babies and the new wave of the Europeans (with Jon Klein on guitar who went on to Co-found the Bat Cave in London). Private Dicks followed with their snappy and catchy power pop punk could've-been-a-hit "Green Is In The Red". Moskow from Trowbridge, Wiltshire brought their frantic post-punk with two members going on to The Bolshoi. Essential Bop, Directors and Various Artists then did their own takes on new wave sounds to close side one. The flip showed us the talents of Sneak Preview, The Stingrays (not the psychobilly band), The X-Certs, Apartment, The Numbers, early Vice Squad, Stereo Models and Double Vision. A varied showcase with some great songs 'Avon Calling' had an aerial shot of Bristol on the front with a minimalist rear and a poster of band photos included. With only one press it was reissued on vinyl and CD much later.

BEACH BLVD LP (POSH BOY)

Punk hit the beach in a big way with the second LP release
on Posh Boy that highlighted the effects of the new wave
on surf drenched youth for the first time. No Hollywood art
bands just three coastal acts; Simpletones, Rik L Rik and
The Crowd. Simpletones were up first with a trio of catchy
and sunny pop punk tunes complete with handclaps. Members
of the Simpletones started out in Child Abuse but would
go on to bands such as Stepmothers, Cheifs and The Klan.
Post F-Word vocalist Rik L Rik, although appearing under
his own name, were Posh Boy demo recordings of the third
incarnation of Negative Trend with Tim Mooney (Sleepers
and Toiling Midgets) on drums, Craig Gray (also Toiling
Midgets) on guitar, and Jay Lansford of Simpletones on
bass. The third band were The Crowd, notable for their
Huntington Beach strut and high energy anthems, of which
'Modern Machine' was an absolute highlight here. Go-Go's
manager Ginger Canzoneri handled design with a nifty graphic
of street sign and tyre track with band info on the back.

BIG HITS OF MID-AMERICA - VOLUME THREE 2LP (TWIN/TONE RECORDS)

The title being a homage to the first two volumes of
Minneapolis area compilations of the 1960s, Twin/Tone took
up the baton to showcase the new breed of garage bands of
the late 70s. Featured here were new wavers and early punks;
The Suburbs, The (Suicide) Commandos, NNB, The Swingers,
Curtis A. & The Originals, Buzz Barker & The Atomic Bums,
Robert Ivers & Ice Stars, The Hypstrz, The Jets, Yipes,
The Wad, The Pistons, Fingerprints and The Swan Lake Six.
The majority of the bands included were similar to so many
other scenes of the era; snappy but still firmly based in
rock'n'roll, not that there was anything wrong with that.
Some grittier rockers like Buzz Barker & The Atomic Bums
delivered some memorable tunes. The gatefold sleeve harked
back to a bygone era design-wise, with band member photos
on the inside and an info sheet. Outside of the two U.S.
pressings this was only ever reissued in Germany.

EARCOM - #1 LP, #2 12" & #3 2 X 7" (FAST PRODUCT)

A series of three collections compiled by Bob Last and
partner Hilary Morrison's Edinburgh label Fast Product
with their finger very much on the pulse of the DIY scene.
Earcom 1 (short for 'Ear Comics') was a nine song LP
featuring Edinburgh locals; teens on pots'n'pans The Prats
and post-punk The Flowers, Lancashire's The Blank Students,
Sheffield's Graph supplied a brooding highlight while locals
Simon Bloomfield and Tim Pierce did an unrecognisable
electronic rendition of The Rezillos. The first volume
came with mysterious cover art and a foldout insert.

Earcom 2 was a three band six song 12" notable for its
inclusion of Joy Division as well as Thursdays and Basczax,
with two songs each. Joy Division, although recorded by
Martin Hannett in April '79, were sans the synthetic
drum effect of their albums and these two brooding songs
('Auto-Suggestion' and 'From Safety To Where...?') were
the only songs they submitted to a compilation during their
existence. Thursdays did a plodding version of "(Sittin'
On) The Dock Of The Bay" and some erratic post-punk on
'Perfection', while Basczax offered up some keyboard driven
post-punk with members going onto The Flaming Mussolinis.
Earcom 2 had the widest distribution of the three volumes
with three pressings and came with a printed inner sleeve.

Earcom 3 was a gatefold double 7" that opened up with two songs
by San Francisco's Noh Mercy with the inspired 'Caucasian
Guilt' and 'Revolutionary Spy'. The flip offered up two
plink-plonk pre-school type songs by the five and eight year
old Stupid Babies, of which Adam Tinley would become techno
artist Adamski. More uninspired bedroom 'art' was then
supplied by From Chorley before record two gave us a side of
D.A.F.'s (Deutsch Amerikanische Freundschaft) electronic
plod from Düsseldorf. The record culminated in a surprising
side of two songs by Orange County's Middle Class from their
"Out Of Vogue" 7". The gatefold double 7" came with a colour
postcard that mentioned an upcoming Fast Product film.

40

FAST PRODUCT LP (FAST PRODUCT)

A 7" showcase of Fast Product releases that featured The Mekons ('Never Been In A Riot' and 'I'll Have To Dance Then (On My Own)' 7"s), Scars ('Adult/ery' 7"), The Human League ('Being Boiled' 7"), 2.3 ('All Time Low' 7") and Gang Of Four ('Damaged Goods' 7"). With fourteen songs in total and the cover art reproduced in miniature on the back Sleeve. This remains a great way to get all six 7"s without having to buy them individually or merely play them all without having to get out of your seat repeatedly. The album was updated in 1980 for the U.S. and Canada on PVC and Passport Records for a handful of pressings with a new sleeve and title "Mutant Pop 78/79" with The Flowers 'Confessions' 7" replacing two Mekons songs. The Flowers 7" being on Bob Last and Hilary Morrison's then new Pop Aural label that they started hot on the heels of Fast when it stopped operating. The original 'Fast Product' was only released in the U.K. and Australia on EMI International.

IDENTITY PARADE LP (TJM RECORDS)

A set of Manchester bands who presumably all rehearsed at label owner, Drones manager and local promoter Tony 'T.J.' Davidson's local dank rehearsal rooms (where Joy Division recorded that famous video). V2 opened the album with an instrumental followed by another instrumental by Mellotron, which was a bit of an anti-climax. Direct Hits followed with some new wave before Genocide raised the pulse and Speed carried on the three chord feeling. Side one closed with Eddie Mooney And The Grave who also had a second song on side two, as did Direct Hits and V2, who offered something more interesting on the flip, while the low-key She Cracked featured BBC DJ Mark Radcliffe. Sister Ray bashed through an untuned number while Steroid Kiddies and The Teardrops closed out the album in punk style. Local artist Alan Adler handled the sleeve while the liner notes were penned by then local DJ Pete Baker declaring, "Punk is dead... VIVA LA REVOLUTION!" The LP was only pressed once in the U.K.

42

IS THE WAR OVER? A CARDIFF COMPILATION LP (Z BLOCK RECORDS)

The punk wave compilation entry from Cardiff in South Wales on local label Z Block that all eight bands recorded in the coffee bar of the local community centre 'Grassroots'. Addiction opened the LP with three steady punk numbers, while Mad Dog supplied two songs of riffed up garage punk (Mad Dog guitarist Busby would later start his own P.A. company and man the desk for countless South Wales punk gigs throughout the 80s). One man synth act Test To Destruction made noise for a few minutes before The Riotous Brothers gave us two understated songs. Side two showcased the post-punk talents of Reptile Ranch who also released two 7"s on Z Block, The New Form, the pub rock of Beaver (who featured Dave Dearnaley who would later become a renowned luthier), and the album closed with minimalists Young Marble Giants who soon went onto Rough Trade and a U.S. tour. The album had a simple black'n'white cover with band info on the back with the legend, "It was easy, it was cheap, your turn next."

KROQ FM - DEVOTEES ALBUM LP (RHINO RECORDS)

The first tribute album? Certainly the first new wave one. Los Angeles radio station KROQ directed listeners to submit their own takes on "Are We Not Men?" era Devo songs throughout the summers of 1978 and 1979 and the winners were included on this LP. A variety of clattering and skronky amateur renditions resided herein, 'Bands' who never did anything else such as; Knife Lust, Jupiter, The View, The Firemen, The Deadliners, Lonnie And The Devotions, The Doguloids, The Touch Tone Tuners, Y-22, The Sordes, and Bohonian Plimguins all submitted a song a piece, with 'Mongoloid' and 'Jocko Homo' getting three attempts each. The most curious addition here was by The Bakersfield Boogie Boys who did a version of non-Devo song "Okie From Muskogee" but also coincidentally had a four song 12" put on Rhino that included the song. The album only received one pressing and the cover art was obviously heavily Devo based with a variety of dorks posing in yellow jumpsuits.

43

L.A. IN LP (RHINO RECORDS)

Sub-titled "A Collection Of Los Angeles Rock And New Wave Bands", Rhino at least had the honesty to say it was 'rock' instead of pretending otherwise. Half of this album was pedestrian radio pop rock at its worst and at best the U.S. equivalent of pub rock, or the dog end of glam, that still had one eye fixed firmly on the sixties rather than any kind of "new wave". The Kats, Charm School, Rubber City Rebels, The Low Numbers, Denny Ward, Spock, Surf Punks, The Ravers, The Droogs, Spock, and The Furys all set out looking for radio play and ended up getting swept away by the real new wave, while the album was saved by the quirky and frantic Oingo Boingo, The Twisters thumping pub rock and The Weasels "Beat Her With A Rake" which were pretty much the only attempts at anything resembling 'new' and with a pulse. The title and cover art was a reference to the the new film Alien, with band photos and info on the back, and also included is a Rhino insert asking for $10 to be a 'Rhino Rebel'. Cash in on the new wave!

LABELS UNLIMITED - THE SECOND RECORD COLLECTION LP (CHERRY RED)

For Cherry Red's second collection they really went all out for the hits and we were treated with "Big Time" by Rudi as an opener, "Wot's For Lunch Mum? (Not B***s Again!)" by The Shapes, "Holocaust" by Crisis, "Hypocrite" By Newtown Neurotics, "Cold City" by Spizz, "Jilly" by The Piranhas, and "N.C.B." By early Welsh language punks Llygod Ffyrnig. On top of this lot we got; Spizzoil, Girlschool, Those Naughty Lumps, Scissor Fits, The Piranhas, Staa Marx, Glaxo Babies, Poison Girls, I Jog And The Tracksuits, AK Process, and Second Layer. The cover graphics were a montage of band related images, with liner notes on the back flicking the V's to the major labels talking about the coming 1980s. The inner sleeve was a promo for Cherry Red releases on one side and Bristol's Heartbeat Records on the other. The sixteen song album was also released in New Zealand in 1979, Canada in 1980 and Greece in 1981.

44

L. A. I. N

A collection of Los Angeles rock and new wave bands.

LIVE AT RAUL'S LP (RAUL'S RECORDS)

Austin, Texas, entered the ring with the usual live showcase
at their local new wave friendly and legendary venue Raul's,
captured by the Reelsound Recording mobile truck. Five
early Austin punk wave bands were included with two songs
apiece; The Explosives, Standing Waves, Terminal Mind, The
Next, and The Skunks. All the bands played a similar guitar
based rock'n'roll so typical of the time where catchy tunes
and mid-tempo were still the order of the day, and this LP
sounded just like so many other collections from the period.
The cover featured the standard fare photo of the venue on
the front with band photos and info on the back completed
by some liner notes by Austin journalist, and then self-
confessed groupie in the 'The Texas Blondes', Margaret
Moser, who talked almost posthumously about the club.
"Live At Raul's" had one vinyl pressing of 1,000 on release
and was later reissued on CD in the U.S. and Netherlands
with two songs added featuring Roky Erickson jamming with
The Explosives. It was also much later reissued on vinyl.

MODS MAYDAY '79 LP (BRIDGEHOUSE RECORDS)

Not to be left out, the U.K. punks in parkas had their own
live document six months before the release of The Who's
Quadrophenia, that somehow apparently kick started the '79
mod revival. Opening proceedings, recorded at The Bridge
House, Canning Town in London on May 7th, were Secret Affair
with two songs, followed by Beggar from Mountain Ash in the
Welsh valleys (and the only non-London band), then Small
Hours, The Mods and Squire. The bands were all of a similar
sound; R'n'B based mid-tempo early 60s influenced power pop
with occasional keyboards, trumpet and harmonies. Out of
the set the standouts were the live renditions of singles;
"Time For Action" and "Let Your Heart Dance" by Secret Affair
and "Walking Down The King's Road" by Squire. The cover was
of course a mod on a scooter with the requisite photos and
band info on the rear. The LP received four U.K. pressings
in 1979, with a few reissues in the '80s, '90s and 2000.

NO WAVE LP - U.K. & U.S. VERSIONS (A&M RECORDS)

The U.K. and U.S. versions of this LP were pretty different but were both released on different sides of the Atlantic with the same title in the same year and on the same label, so are essentially different versions of the same compilation. A showcase of A&M's 7" new wave output, the songs common to both were by; (U.K.) Squeeze, The Dickies, The Police, Klark Kent, and Joe Jackson, with additional songs on the U.K. version by all five. The Stranglers didn't have songs on the U.K. version while David Kubinec, Bobby Henry and Shrink only had songs on the U.K. version. This whole Transatlantic mess included some big new wave hits though and came out on a plethora of wild and wacky vinyl as was the norm then, especially for A&M and their "Hey Vinyl Junkies" cover stickers. The U.S. version had 12 songs and was only pressed in the U.S. and Canada, while the U.K. version had 15 songs and was also pressed in the Netherlands, Spain, Ireland, Japan and the er, U.S.

OBJECTIVITY: THE OBJECT SINGLES ALBUM LP (OBJECT MUSIC)

The second compilation and a singles collection from Manchester's Object Music, run by Steve Solamar of the band Spherical Objects, who both opened and closed this album with two songs from both their keyboard enhanced post-punk 7"s "The Kill" and "Seventies Romance". Steve Miro And The Eyes followed with their "Dreams Of Desire" 7" of bouncy new wave that had a hint of ska. Grow-Up continued with the three song A-Side from their self-titled debut EP of snappy post-punk, while side one was closed with the arty post-punk of Alternomen Unlimited (aka Steve Solamar and Steve Miro). Side two opened with The Warriors, a reggae project again featuring Steve Solamar and their "Martial Time/ Martial Law" 7" very much in the early UB40 vein. Steve Miro then rolled out his solo new wave "Up And About" 7", before Spherical Objects concluded the album. The sleeve featured a photo of a dog with an Object record in its mouth and band info on the back. Quirky in a John Peel kinda way.

PÆRE PUNK LP (KONG PÆRE RECORDS)

Danish punk entered the fray with what was initially due to be a live album of a punk festival of the same name that took place in November 1978, Medley Records decided against releasing it and a studio album was recorded instead and released on its subsidiary Kong Pære. With two or three songs each, the album documented; Lost Kids, Sods (fresh from releasing their debut album on Medley), Elektrochok, Slim, Kliche, Brats (guitarist Hank The Wank went on to form Mercyful Fate), Dream Police (featuring Johnny Concrete of No Århus zine) and No Knox. The opening track "Asocial" by Lost Kids was a cover of Devo's "Mongoloid" with new lyrics. The standard was high throughout with bands like Sods and Elektrochok being pretty driving, and what bands like Slim and Brats lacked in ability they made up for in obnoxiousness, while Kilche bordered on pop rock, Dream Police U.K. style punk, and No Knox made a right royal racket. Pære Punk had multiple 1979 pressings and was reissued decades later.

PERMANENT WAVE LP (EPIC RECORDS)

Epic got in on the new wave action with the sub-title; "A collection of tomorrow's favourites by today's bands on yesterday's vinyl" that opened with some awful not-very-new-wave from After The Fire that sounded more like yacht rock. After this audio faux pas came the pub rock of Kursaal Flyers, followed by The Cortinas, New Hearts, The Diodes, The Only Ones, The Vibrators, Masterswitch, and The Spikes, which was a one-off 'new wave' project from Epic executive Bruce Harris, which said it all really. That said, for a bargain bin compilation this had some genuinely good songs on it such as the pre-Secret Affair New Hearts "Just Another Teenage Anthem", "Another Girl, Another Planet" by The Only Ones, and The Diodes rendition of "Red Rubber Ball". The cover photo couldn't get anymore "major label does new wave" and was filled with liner notes by 'The Kid' likening new wave to countercultures of the recent past. "Permanent Wave" was pressed in the U.S., Canada and Australia.

PROPAGANDA - NO WAVE II LP (A&M RECORDS)

Moving away from the straight up 7" showcase for volume two of "No Wave", A&M opted for live recordings, album tracks and even some unreleased. Side one was all live, with Squeeze supplying one song before Joe Jackson and The Police offered two each, all recorded in 1979 and with the latter two definitely capturing their more energetic side, The Police doing "Landlord" and "Next To You". The flip opened with a Joe Jackson album track and then it was Shrink, producer Bobby Henry (who was also on volume one), an 'unreleased' Squeeze tune that also appeared on a 'Smash Hits' promo flexi (although that was probably unplayable), upbeat new wavers The Secret, and it all ended with a slow burning album track by The Reds. Apparently inspired by the inclusion of The Reds, the cover art by Brian Davis depicted Chairman Mao rocking out with his band to the party faithful, with The Reds logo most notably placed. The LP was released in the U.K., Greece, Spain and 'Europe'.

ROCK 'N' ROLL HIGH SCHOOL LP (SIRE RECORDS)

"Music From The Original Motion Picture Soundtrack" so yeah, there was a lot of Ramones on here as this film was essentially a Ramones flick, but, it was still a compilation that also featured; Nick Lowe with "So It Goes", Devo with "Come Back Jonee", Eddie And The Hot Rods with "Teenage Depression", as well as Brian Eno, P.J. Soles, Brownsville Station, Chuck Berry, Todd Rundgren, and Alice Cooper with their various school related songs. Granted, that wasn't a 100% punk/new wave selection, but close enough. As well as a couple of Ramones classics we also got an eleven minute Ramones medley of six songs, and collaborations with The Paley Brothers with central character actor P.J. Soles adding vocals to Ramones songs. The cover featured the movie poster artwork and the record was pressed in the U.S., Canada, Germany, Greece, Spain, Portugal, the U.K., Scandinavia, Italy, Australia, Japan, France, Argentina, 'Europe', Poland, and Brazil. So yeah, pretty much everywhere.

S.F. UNDERGROUND 7" EP (SUBTERRANEAN RECORDS)

The first release on San Francisco's now legendary punk and experimental label Subterranean Records, and one of the first real tastes of actual underground U.S. punk bands with no connection to 70s rock's mulleted past, and from where else but the burgeoning San Francisco punk scene. First up was No Alternative and the brilliantly snotty "Johnny Got His Gun" followed by the world's introduction to Flipper and the grindingly slow belligerence of "Earthworm". On the flip came The Tools with "Asexuality In The 80s" who featured Mike Fox on guitar, who also produced the whole EP at Sauna Studios in Richmond, CA. The EP was concluded by VKTMS with slow burner "Ballad Of Pincushion Smith", and the cover was simply a photograph of local punk friendly club 'San Francisco Club Of The Deaf' with the songs on the back and an inner sheet featuring band photos, info and lyrics. "S.F. Underground" initially received a pressing of 2,000 with multiple represses following thereafter.

STREET TO STREET - A LIVERPOOL ALBUM LP (OPEN EYE RECORDS)

You wouldn't find any Merseybeat on Liverpool's answer to the call of the new wave, that opened with a surf instrumental by Big In Japan who featured future members of Frankie Goes To Hollywood, The KLF, Teardrop Explodes and Siouxsie And The Banshees. After this were The ID, Jaqui And Jeanette, Modern Eon, Activity Minimal, Dead Trout, Tontrix, The Accelerators, Malchix, Fun, The Moderates, and Echo And The Bunnymen. The (unrecognisable here) Bunnymen went onto world fame but also notable was a decidedly punk song by Modern Eon, the post-punk of Tontrix and The Accelerators, who released a solid but overlooked 12" also in 1979, recorded at the Open Eye four track studio four months after this session (guitarist Kathy Freeman went onto London rockers The Birdhouse). The cover featured a street scene with a superimposed illustration of a lady with chest half bared, with liner notes by John Peel on the back. "Street To Street" had two pressings on this non-profit label in 1979.

51

SUBTERRANEAN MODERN LP (RALPH RECORDS)

Four bands with their own industrial art damaged noise
offerings; Chrome, MX-80 Sound, The Residents and Tuxedomoon.
Up until this release, all Ralph Records had only been by
The Residents or Snakefinger so in an attempt to diversify
they had bands submit new material on the theme of San
Francisco (each here doing their own twisted version of "I
Left My Heart In San Francisco") and these four, including
The Residents, made the cut. Side one saw Chrome offer
their patented driving hypnotic soundscapes while MX-80
Sound weaved their way through their unique Bloomington,
Indiana approach. On side two The Residents floated along on
their other worldly repetitive weirdness while Tuxedomoon
closed out the album with their dark pulsating Polymoog
workouts. The sleeve featured art by Gary Panter and with
an "Official Buy Or Die Innersleeve" inside. "Subterranean
Modern" received three domestic pressings in 1979, 1980
and 1983, all with slightly differing colours on the cover.

THE LABEL SOFAR! (SOFA) LP (THE LABEL)

A label showcase of the 'The Label' run by producer Dave
Goodman and Caruzo Fuller. Here they presented their fairly
limited punk era roster from their fairly limited existence
(1977-1979) with six bands; Eater, Dave Goodman & Friends,
Bombers, Front, Tribesmen, and Cash Pussies. Whereas you'd
think this was a label sampler of their 7"s, it wasn't.
Aside from "Outside View" the other two Eater songs were
unreleased and only one of the three Front songs were
previously released as the flip side of their "System" 7".
The Dave Goodman And Friends song was their 7" "Justifiable
Homicide", as was the Bombers and "I'm A Liar, Babe", and
the Cash Pussies "99% Is Shit", whereas the Tribesman
provided a dub version of their 7" "Rockin' Time". The
album with its corny title came wrapped in some equally lack
lustre artwork and was also issued as "The World's First
Punk Picture Disc Album" aka a "Han-O-Disc" that reared
its ugly head again in 1982 for the "The D.I.Y. Album".

THE NOW WAVE SAMPLER PROMO 7" EP (COLUMBIA RECORDS)

If you ever wondered what the soon-to-plug-in hardcore punk bands were railing against with shouts of "New wave sucks!" then it was this. The "Now Wave" being of course a 7" sampler of bearded and poodle-haired top twenty pop rock repackaged as 'new wave' by a major label. The band descriptions here being particularly unconvincing, with The Sinceros described as, "Forerunners of a new trend". Of course The Sinceros were nothing of the sort and Hounds who followed them with their 'new wave' cover of "Doo Wah Diddy Diddy" was even more appalling. The record's only redeeming feature was side two openers The (Paul Collins') Beat, and even that wasn't their strongest effort. Jules And The Polar Bears closed out this well deserved bargain bin fodder with a vocalist singing outside of his range with some over the top keyboards just to make sure you know it's 'new wave'. Pressed in the U.S. and also New Zealand for some reason, presumably so they could use it to scare sheep.

THE RARE STUFF? LP (HARVEST RECORDS)

Harvest records' (aka EMI) entry into the punk and new wave compilation lottery was "The Rare Stuff?" which was essentially a handful of their 7" songs rearranged on an LP as was often the case with so many of these early compilations. The Saints' "One Two Three Four" double 7" was included, as well as Wire's "Dot Dash" 7", both Harvest singles by The Banned, The Flys' "Love And A Molotov Cocktail" 7", as well as one song from another single, and finally The Rich Kids and The Shirts supplied one 7" B-side each. Whereas this may sound quite dull in reality the album was a strong release due to the quality of the majority of the songs, with The Flys, The Saints and Wire standing out from the pack. The cover was an artist's rendition of a leather jacket with the band logos as badges, while the original photographic image was on the back. 'The Rare Stuff?' was released in the U.K., Australia and New Zealand.

TOOTH AND NAIL LP (UPSETTER RECORDS)

A fascinating early document from the emerging Los Angeles punk rock scene from 'Upsetter' set up by Judith Bell of Slash and then boyfriend Chris D. of The Flesh Eaters, essentially to release The Flesh Eaters (this compilation being the anomaly). Three songs each by The Controllers, Flesh Eaters and Germs, and two songs each from Middle Class, U.X.A. and Negative Trend (when they were briefly L.A. based, see: 'Beach Blvd', where these songs also appeared). There were no power pop pretenders here, this could easily have been a Dangerhouse or Slash compilation with much of the mixing occurring at Kitchen Sync. From The Stooges influenced punk of The Controllers to the frenetic proto-hardcore of Middle Class this album stands as a time capsule of this moment in L.A. just before hardcore took over. Along with the label owners, Steve Samiof of Slash and Exene of X were involved on the art of side of things. Only released in the U.S. and reissued once a decade later.

UITHOLLING OVERDWARS LP (STICHTING POPMUZIEK NEDERLAND)

Another 'new wave' era set from the 'Netherlands Pop Music Foundation' with liner notes that declared; "Long live the Dutch language rock!" The album opened with some mulleted rock'n'roll from Toontje Lager followed in a similar pub rock fashion by Jonny Jumbo And The Highjackers. Tedje En De Flikkers and Jong Oranje then threw some keyboards and sax into their pedestrian new wave before Jan Van De Grond Groep turned up the tempo and added some frantic violin, that saw them stand out in comparison to the previous bands. Legendary punks Ivy Green then closed side one with a rockin' and raucous number that pretty much single handedly saved the day. The second side continued the 'new wave' with Dorpsstraat, Doe Maar, Nasmaak, Noodweer, Utang and Braak, pretty much all of which (apart from punk standout Utang) were more amateur pop than anything truly new wave. Wrapped in a curious road sign cover art, with band photos on the back, next to each band's home phone number.

VANCOUVER COMPLICATION LP (PINNED RECORDS)

Inspired by "The Akron Compilation" Quintessence Records employee, and future owner of Zulu Records, Grant McDonagh, along with Stephem Macklam, put their city on the punk map with this area compilation, mainly recorded at one studio (and all finally remixed by Bob Rock and Ron Obvious at Little Mountain Sound). Titled due to the complications it took to get it released, "Vancouver Complication" opened with a Pointed Sticks song followed by the eclectic new punk sounds of; Exxotone, D.O.A., Active Dog, Wasted Lives, The Subhumans, UJ3RK5, Private School, No Fun, Dishrags, The K-Tels, The Shades, Tim Ray & A.V., and [e?], some with two songs, some with one. Notable for the inclusion of D.O.A., The Subhumans and Pointed Sticks, this early Vancouver scene defining LP was originally pressed in a numbered black and white sleeve with a 16 page booklet with band info. It was later reissued in different cover variations; with the black and white flipped and in blue and white with a simple insert.

WAVES - AN ANTHOLOGY OF NEW MUSIC VOL. 1 LP (BOMP RECORDS)

Another Bomp 'new wave' collection that opened with 'new waver' Tommy Rock, who'd started his career on the cusp of new wave in 1964. 20/20 followed with some power pop, before The Human Switchboard supplied some quirky keyboard new wave. Despite forming in New York in 1977 The Flashcubes just sounded like 60s or early 70s wet radio pop. Permanent Wave attempted to raise the stakes but it was still basically just old rock'n'roll complete with chonking piano. The Last were last on side one and managed to submit a song that sounded nothing like The Last. Paul Collins on the other hand provided a catchy thumper that could've been his old band The Nerves. The Marshalls, The Invaders, The Romantics, and Blitzkrieg Bop continued this desperate attempt at convincing everyone that 60s music was in fact 'new wave', while JJ 180 did something resembling garage punk. Pressed in the U.S. on blue and black vinyl in gatefold sleeve full of band info, and also three regular pressings in Germany.

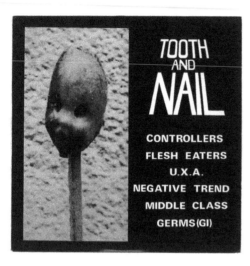

TOOTH
AND
NAIL

CONTROLLERS
FLESH EATERS
U.X.A.
NEGATIVE TREND
MIDDLE CLASS
GERMS (GI)

UITHOLLING OVERDWARS

VANCOUVER

COMPLICATION

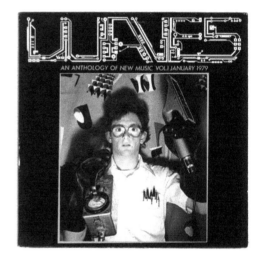

AN ANTHOLOGY OF NEW MUSIC VOL.1 JANUARY 1979

NOT PRODUCED BY BRIAN ENO

Los Angeles

WE DON'T NEED THE ENGLISH
Bags (C. Lee)

NO GOD
Germs (Crash)

YES L.A.
SIDE ONLY
EW-79

LOS ANGELES
X (BJ. Doe)

TOO MUCH JUNK
Alley Cats (Stodola)

DISNEYLAND
Eyes (Nervous Ricky)

DOWN AT THE LAUNDRYMAT
Black Randy (Black Randy)

ALL COMPOSITIONS © 1979
DANGERHOUSE © 1979

YESTERDAY'S SOUND TODAY

VOX

YES L.A. 12" (DANGERHOUSE RECORDS)

Just as much a statement as a compilation, Los Angeles'
answer to "No New York" on a silk-screened, six band, six
song 12" on their own homegrown Dangerhouse Records, the
legendary "Yes L.A.". The EP opened with The Bags and "We
Don't Need The English", that made yet another statement
(you got the impression they were really trying to put
L.A. on the map with this record). The Eyes followed with
"Disneyland", then The Alley Cats brought us "Too Much
Junk" before the strange intermission of Black Randy and
"Down At The Laundrymat". Following this bizarre interlude
X submitted their soon-to-be-released debut album's title
track "Los Angeles" for consideration. The 12" concluded
in fine style with The Germs blazing "No God" from the
"Lexicon Devil" 7". 2,000 copies were pressed in the U.S.
only and came in four colour variations, and the record
stated, "Not produced by Brian Eno" just to twist that "No
New York" knife. An undisputed heavyweight classic.

YESTERDAY'S SOUND TODAY LP (LINE RECORDS)

A collection of primarily Bomp! Records power pop for the
new wave era on Line Records for the German market. Fourteen
songs by fourteen bands that included; The Romantics, The
Last, Permanent Wave, Battered Wives (with an unreleased
song), B-Girls, Shoes, The Poppees, Stiv Bators, Boyfriends,
Nikki & The Corvettes, The Scruffs, 20/20, Willie Alexander
& The Boom Boom Band, and The Crawdaddys. The only non-Bomp
bands were Toronto's Battered Wives and The Scruffs from
Memphis, both of whom had separate Line licensed releases
in Germany. The Last did a rendition of "Be Bop A Lula", The
B-Girls supplied "B-Side" from their sole Bomp! 7" and Stiv
Bators' contribution was of course "It's Cold Outside".
Being essentially a Bomp comp., the material of course owed
more to the 60s than the new wave but at least they didn't
try to hide it what with that title and the Vox amp on the
cover. That said, if you're not averse to catchy tunes then
this is probably the strongest of the Bomp! compilations.

1980-1982:
DECLARATION OF INDEPENDENTS

As a new decade is ushered in, the Cold War heats up with the Carter Doctrine in 1980, seeing the U.S. defend its interests in the Gulf States and withdraw from the SALT II Treaty banning technology sales to the Soviet Union, all as a result of the Russian Invasion of Afghanistan. The Mount St. Helens eruption in Washington State in May kills fifty seven, while south in California; Frontier, New Alliance, Bemisbrain, and Smoke 7 Records all begin their own molten vinyl flow as the U.S. boycotts the Moscow Olympics in further protest at the 1979 Russian invasion, and American theatre attendances swell for Airplane!, The Blues Brothers and Fame. On the East Coast Dischord Records forms in Washington D.C. as Ronald Reagan is elected, and Modern Method comes to life at Newbury Comics in Boston.

In the U.K., the fourteen week British Steel strike begins in January, while MI6 begins covert operations in Afghanistan to support the Mujahideen, before Clay Records and Riot City start their own dispute. In May as the Iranian Embassy siege unfolds Ian Curtis ends his life on the cusp of a U.S. tour while Secret and Statik Records begin their own. The singer of The Ruts, Malcolm Owen, dies of a heroin overdose in July as The Clash movie Rude Boy is released and The Jam, Madness and Blondie hit the top twenty just as Statik and Secret Records press their first records.

The European Commission backs the U.S. grain Embargo against the Soviet Union as New Rose Records in France and Rock-O-Rama Records in Germany begin. Yugoslavian Communist dictator Tito dies and the Gdansk Agreement is signed forming the Polish trade union Solidarity. Iraq invades Iran while Azaria Chamberlain disappears at Uluru (Ayers Rock) and Australian label Cleopatra gets its first handful of releases. 1980 ends with Darby Crash of The Germs committing suicide hours before John Lennon is murdered.

As 1981 begins in the U.K., the Yorkshire Ripper is arrested and Rupert Murdoch buys The Times and Sunday Times while Spiderleg and Pax, begin their own plans to take over the press. The first London Marathon takes place and soon after Brixton is rioting, spreading to a handful of other cities. No Future and Xcentric Noise begin operations while the Specials "Ghost Town" tops the charts just as Prince Charles marries Diana Spencer and the riots hit their peak. Meanwhile, British cinemas are packed out for An American Werewolf In London, Chariots Of Fire and Time Bandits.

Meanwhile in the U.S., Ronald Reagan becomes president and suffers an assassination attempt as Epitaph, Enigma and R Radical plan to release their first vinyl. By the time the 18 month global recession begins, Henry Rollins is on his way to join Black Flag in California where Thrasher is firing up the printing presses for the first time. MTV starts airing on 1st August while in Michigan, Touch And Go morphs from a punk zine into a record label and theatres sell popcorn for The Evil Dead, Scanners and Escape From New York.

Ozzy Osbourne gets 1982 off to a bloody start by biting the head off a bat on stage in Iowa, while Letterman goes on air in February and Reagan announces sanctions against Libya in March. Meanwhile, the Better Youth Organization in Los Angeles begins forming its Youth Brigade, while Affirmation in Ohio, No Core in North Carolina and Incas in Connecticut all begin releasing records, and U.S. theatres throw back the curtains for Poltergeist, The Thing and E.T.

In the U.K. unemployment rises above 3 million, Argentina invades the Falkland Islands and CH4 goes on air, while Bluurg, Rot and Fallout Records begin their anti-war message as Crass squat the Zig Zag in London and Bucks Fizz, Culture Club and Eddy Grant race up the charts. U.K. cinemas show Blade Runner, First Blood and Tron while Spain joins NATO, Yuri Andropov becomes General Secretary of the USSR, and Helmut Kohl becomes Chancellor of West Germany just as Weird System begins pressing records in Hamburg...

10-29-79

415 MUSIC

JO ALLEN
AND THE SHAPES
THE DONUTS
THE OFFS
THE MUTANTS
THE READYMADES
SUDDEN FUN
SVT
THE SYMPTOMS
391
TIMES 5
THE VIPs

SUPERMUSIC P.A. HIRE

BACK·STAGE PASS

BOB DE VRIES

SLF

U.K. SUBS   COCKNEY REJECTS

VICE   ANGELIC UPSTARTS   SLAUGHTER
AND THE DOGS

Manufactured   THE EXPLOITED   ANTI-
Romance   PASTI

SLICKEE
BOYS
NIGHTMAN   JUKE BOX JURY
D.CEATS
NURSES
TEX
RUBINOWITZ
THE RAZZ
SHIRKERS
PENETRATORS
BAD BRAINS

THE BEST OF
(...REST OF
LIMP)

LIMP 1004

BLACKPOOL
ROX
E.P.

SYNTAX · SECTION 25 · THE MEMBRANES

KENNETH TURNER SET ·

BOUNCING IN THE RED
A BIRMINGHAM COMPILATION

20 10 7 5 3 0 3
0   50   100%   +

VU

UB40 / STEEL PULSE / STEVE GIBBONS BAND / WIDE BOYS / FASHION / DANGEROUS GIRLS
DENIZENS / RAINMAKER / RICKY COOL AND THE ICEBERGS / FERRARI / MEAN STREET DEALERS / QUADS

1980

10-29-79 LP (TRAP RECORDS)

As the title suggested this set of Portland punk was recorded live on both audio and video on Monday 29th October 1979 at a seven hour all ages gig at the Earth Tavern in Portland, the door proceeds financing this LP on Greg Sage of The Wipers' imprint. Sado-Nation opened proceedings with "Johnny Paranoid" followed by two songs each by Lo Tek and the all-female post-punk of Neo Boys. Smegma then offered up two strange songs to close side one while side two opened with The Wipers and "Same Old Thing", unique to this release. Stiphnoyds upped the pace with two punk songs; "Meat Is Rotten" and "Jimmy Carter" before Rubbers offered two songs; "Bug" and "Riot Squad" (later re-worked on the "Who Cares" compilation when Rubbers vocalist Bob Glassley moved to L.A. soon after this recording and formed The Cheifs). Bop Zombies closed the LP with some rock'n'roll. The cover depicted records as UFOs attacking the people of Portland.

415 MUSIC LP (415 RECORDS)

San Francisco new wave showcase from local label 415 Records that was set up by Howie Klein, Chris Knab and Butch Bridges (415 being the U.S. police code for disturbing the peace). This was a collection of original material (rather than just a rehash of 7"s) that opened with "415 Music" by The Readymades to set the mood. Following that was one song each by; Times 5, The Mutants (who were due to support Joy Division on their cancelled U.S. tour in May of this year), 391 (with Jeff Olener of The Nuns), Sudden Fun, The Donuts, SVT (featuring Jack Casady), The Symptons, The VIPs (featuring Jennifer ('Miro') Anderson and Pat Ryan of The Nuns), Jo Allen And The Shapes, and the album concluded with "I've got The Handle" by The Offs. The cover art concept went for the police reference of course and the album only received one solitary pressing in the U.S.

BACK-STAGE PASS LP (SUPERMUSIC RECORD CO.)

Put together by the 'Supermusic P.A. Hire' company run by
tour manager and studio engineer Dave Leaper of Yorkshire,
"Back-stage Pass" featured bands they'd worked live sound
and studio work for. The line-up on this one read like a
who's who of 1970s U.K. punk with; Slaughter And The Dogs,
Cockney Rejects, Cyanide, U.K. Subs, Manufactured Romance,
Angelic Upstarts and Stiff Little Fingers, all with two
songs each, and one song each for The Exploited, Bob De
Vries, and Anti-Pasti. There were hits aplenty here (all
studio) with songs you don't need paired with the band name
to know such as; "Where Have All The Boot Boys Gone?",
"Emotional Blackmail", "Police Car", "Police Oppression",
"Crashed Out" and "No Government"... the list went on. The
cover art was simply the band logos surrounded by barbed
wire with a P.A. stack on the back cover. "Back-stage
Pass" was pressed in the U.K. and licensed for release in
Portugal in 1980, New Zealand in 1982 and Poland in 1986.

THE BEST OF LIMP (...REST OF LIMP) LP (LIMP RECORDS)

The second installment of early D.C. bands from Skip
Groff's Limp Records that was originally put together prior
to 1980 but didn't make it beyond test pressing stage.
Notable for album closers and the first vinyl appearance
of Bad Brains in the form of "Don't Bother Me". This was
very much a continuation of ":30 Over D.C." (although only
two songs here were previously unreleased) and the line-up
was; The Slickee Boys, Nightman, D. Ceats, The Nurses, Tex
Rubinowitz, The Razz (featuring Tommy Keene), The Shirkers
(with "Drunk And Disorderly" later covered by Black Market
Baby), and The Penetrators. The majority of this was new
wave pop with 60s influences and apart from Bad Brains'
rough and ready clatter there was little indication of what
was to come out of D.C. a year later. "The Best Of Limp" came
in a plain white jacket with a sheet of blue paper front
and back containing album info (printed in red and black)
and it was later reissued in simply black on yellow paper.

BLACKPOOL ROX 7" EP (VINYL DRIP RECORDS)

The first release on John Robb of The Membranes label and in keeping with the times it was a local collection of Blackpool bands. First up of course were The Membranes with slow post-punk burner "Ice Age". Next came Factory Records artists Section 25 with "Red Voice", a rumbling post-punk instrumental. The flip picked up steam with The Kenneth Turner Set and "Overload", an instantly memorable early Buzzcocks style song. The EP concluded with "Dot Dot" by Syntax which was very much in the early Joy Division vein with punch. The cover art depicted a broken Blackpool Tower along with some doodling, and the inside of the foldout sleeve was simply typewriter text that explained how all the bands pulled an all-nighter for £100 at Cargo Studios in Rochdale and that the record cost £430 to press, "Now that you know this information you may be able to make your own record" as well as, "Help shift product. Buy this record. If you can't afford it, tape it." D.I.Y. by example.

BOUNCING IN THE RED - A BIRMINGHAM COMPILATION LP (ODEON/EMI)

As the title suggested this was a collection of bands from Birmingham in the English Midlands with a mixed bag of punk, new wave, post-punk, pop, rock and reggae so typical of the time in urban Britain. Twelve bands and songs "recorded at breakneck speed over a period of ten months, August '79 to May '80" from; Steel Pulse, Wide Boys, Fashion, Dangerous Girls, Denizens, UB40, Steve Gibbons Band, Ferrari, Ricky Cool And The Icebergs, Rainmaker, Mean Street Dealers, and Quads. After the initial reggae numbers Fashion turned things full synth before Dangerous Girls and Denizens headed in a spiky post-punk direction. UB40 then gave their first compilation appearance with "25%" from "Signing Off" closing side one. Side two turned more pop and reggae until the upbeat rock of Mean Street Dealers and the maximum R'n'B of the Quads. With a cover graphic of an audio volume unit tipping into the red, the back sleeve featured a photograph of the track list as flyers in a shop window.

BOUQUET OF STEEL LP (AARDVARK RECORDS)

Steel City Sheffield and its satellites made themselves
known with this set of bands with the locale hinted at in the
title. Compiled by Marcus Featherby soon to be running Pax
Records, Artery opened up with a marching pots 'n' pans jam
followed by B Troop with a more poppy new wave approach not
unlike San Francisco's Mutants, then Comsat Angels brought
some pulsing atmospheric post-punk. After this; Disease,
Flying Alphonso Brothers (a snappy mod-punk standout), I'm
So Hollow (spooky goth), Musical Janeens (And Other Party
Games), Negatives, Repulsive Alien, Scarborough Antelopes,
Shy Tots, Veiled Threat, Vendino Pact, De Tian, and Y? Two
versions were released in the year of release; blue vinyl
with black and white cover and then on black with yellow
cover text. The first version came with a nicely designed
16 page booklet which was expanded to 28 for the second
press with further info on other bands from the area such
as Cabaret Voltaire, The Human League, and Def Leppard(!)

BOWLING BALLS FROM HELL LP (CLONE RECORDS)

Ohio entered the conversation for a second time with a
collection of quirky new wave and strange synth pieces
possibly inspired by the success of locals Devo, or maybe
just something in the Ohio water. The album opened with The
Waitresses with "Wait Here I'll Be Right Back..." which was
an early version of "I Know What Boys Like", soon picked up
by Polydor, when the band relocated to New York, to become
a club hit that was much later covered by U.K. pop outfit
Shampoo. After The Waitresses, a series of one-off projects
with names like Haff Notz and Hurricane Bob paled beneath
the limelight of Denis DeFrange and Ralph Carney (of Tin
Huey) who took up majority of the album collaborating
with other artists such as David Thomas of Pere Ubu and
Mark Frazier, with sonic experimentation that sounded like
twisted movie soundtrack work for the neon cyberpunk era.
Perhaps unsurprisingly, "Bowling Balls From Hell" was only
pressed once on Nick Nicholis of the Bizarros Clone Records.

BULLSHIT DETECTOR LP (CRASS RECORDS)

Crass put their money where their mouths were with this set of bands who'd submitted their demos and were selected for inclusion for this real D.I.Y. Snapshot of the U.K. anarcho punk scene. Those that made the cut were; Andy T, Counter Attack, Alternative, Clockwork Criminals, Reputations In Jeopardy, Crass (with a suitably biscuit tin rendition of "Do They Owe Us A Living"), Amebix, Sceptics, The Sinyx, Frenzy Battalion, Icon, The Speakers, A.P.F. Brigade, Fuck The C.I.A., Caine Mutiny And The Kallisti Apples Of Nonsense, The Sucks, Porno Squad, S.P.G. Murders, Eratics, Red Alert, The Snipers, Armchair Power, Disruptive, and Action Frogs. The quality varied from bedroom shouting to good quality studio recordings, with those who didn't know how to tune up falling somewhere between. "Bullshit Detector" came in the Crass house style six panel poster full of teenage protest art submitted by the bands, for a couple of pressings, and all for the pay-no-more-than price of £1.35.

BUY OR DIE '1980' & '1980 1/2' 7" EPs (RALPH RECORDS)

"Buy Or Die!" was the slogan of The Residents' Ralph Records and the name of its bi-annual mail order catalogue between 1977 and 1989. A series of sampler 7"s were also sometimes issued whereby a coupon in a music magazine advert would be cut out and mailed into Ralph to receive a catalogue and a free "Buy Or Die" record with tracks from some of their then current releases on the label, as well a $1 coupon off any release, what a great idea! "Buy Or Die 1980" featured four tracks by four artists; MX-80 Sound, Snakefinger, Tuxedomoon, and The Residents, while "Buy Or Die 1980 1/2" had six tracks by; The Residents, Snakefinger, Yello, and Fred Frith. If you're familiar with Ralph Records then you'll know it was the home for the weird, unique and artistic end of things, that listened to now reminds you of a time when experimental meant just that, some artists being more accessible than others - prepare to be challenged. Each record also came with great cover art by Gary Panter.

CAN YOU HEAR ME? MUSIC FROM THE DEAF CLUB LP (OPTIONAL MUSIC)

The San Francisco Club for the Deaf had existed since the 1930s as a clubhouse for the deaf on Valencia Street in San Francisco, but in late 1978 it came to host punk gigs for a little over 18 months after The Offs manager Robert Hanrahan discovered it. The first gig was on 9th December 1978 with The Offs, Mutants, and On the Rag (who became Noh Mercy) and the club ended up hosting over 100 bands from up and down the West Coast. This high quality live album documented by Jim Keylor (also of Army Street Studios) on a mobile eight track featured two or three songs each by; Dead Kennedys, K.G.B. (who turned into No Alternative), The Offs, Mutants, Pink Section, and Tuxedomoon. Each side was introduced by exiled-from-the-BBC and regular Deaf Club DJ Johnnie Walker. The cover art was by Diana Miami and the insert had liner notes by Vale of Search And Destroy, photos by Sue Brisk, along with quotes and a list of bands. "Music From The Deaf Club" was reissued on PVC Records.

CASH COWS LP (VIRGIN RECORDS)

Your typical label sampler cash-in from Virgin with a mash up of musical styles packaged for the gullible. Thirteen acts and songs from; XTC, The Human League, Mike Oldfield, Japan, The Ruts, Skids, The Professionals, The Flying Lizards, Fingerprintz, Captain Beefheart & The Magic Band, Gillan, Kevin Coyne, and Public Image Limited. A predictable 'new wave' collection featuring some decidedly not very 'new wave' artists. The most significant thing about this was the Canadian press (pictured) which looked the same but was a significantly different record, completely removing six artists; Mike Oldfield, The Ruts, Skids, The Professionals, Kevin Coyne and PiL, replacing them with; Valerie Lagrange, Magazine, Canadians Nash The Slash and Martha And The Muffins, OMD and Tangerine Dream, and then switched out the songs from Fingerprintz, Captain Beefheart and Gillan... so nine of the thirteen songs were totally different. Clad in some fittingly tacky cover art.

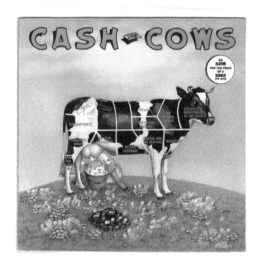

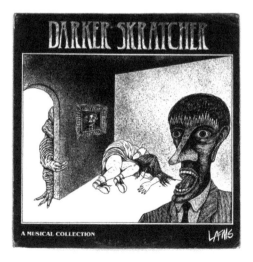

CRACKS IN THE SIDEWALK 12" (NEW ALLIANCE RECORDS)

The first release on D. Boon and Mike Watt of the Minutemen's label (along with Martin Tamburovich of their previous incarnation The Reactionaries). A six band, six song 12" that featured hardcore punk on side one and something more arty on side two (a style mix theme that would run through the label's releases). The bands on the first side; Minutemen with "9:30 May 2", Black Flag with "Clocked In", and Saccharine Trust with "Hearts And Barbarians" steered the punk course. While the second side had Kindled Imagination featuring Greg Hurley, George Hurley of the Minutemen's brother, before it was time for the record's producer Spot and his Artless Entanglements cacophonous jazz project. Finally, Sharp Corners closed the nine minute EP with more jazz noise and side two was essentially people in the label's circle making a noise that sounded like so much of what would come later on SST and New Alliance. Cover art by Raymond Pettibon, the EP had numerous U.S. pressings.

CRUISING SOUNDTRACK LP (LORIMAR / CBS RECORDS)

The soundtrack to the Al Pacino film about a cop sent deep undercover to track down a serial killer stalking New York's gay leather bar community is notable for the inclusion of "Lion's Share" by Germs (G.I.) for Germs completists. Aside from that energetic punk interlude the soundtrack included Willy Deville (of Mink DeVille), The Cripples, John Hiatt, Madelynn Von Ritz, Mutiny, and Rough Trade, and is all pretty much sleazy rock and pop with a little funk thrown in. With sleeve art depicted stills from the film and the album was released in the U.S., Europe, Canada, U.K., Spain, Italy, Australia and Japan, and as a result was probably the widest audience the Germs received during their existence. The production of the film was hampered by protests from the gay community who feared being depicted in a negative light and as such had to be largely overdubbed but still somehow made a profit at the box office. It was reissued in 2019 with all five Germs session songs.

DAMN STRAIGHT - PHOENIX'S BEST NEW ROCK '80 LP (NANXIETY)

Radio station KUPD and Nanxiety Records, whose only other
release was by Phoenix punks Red Squares, compiled this
local compilation of Phoenix for the then new decade. A
mixed bag of standard rock and pop on side one from the likes
of Sky Harbour (the city's airport), Fax, Llory McDonald,
Rampage, Ultrasapiens, Captain Trips, and Cazmorai. But
things got interesting on side two with The Nervous and
"T.V. Static", a lost punk classic if there ever was one.
This was followed by the power pop of The Spiffs, and then
"Pretty Punk" by the quirky new wave band The Untouchables
(not the L.A. band) that blatantly ripped off the "buzz buzz
buzz" line from The Cramps "Human Fly". Jack Alves followed
before the hectic punk of Cicadas, before Ultrasapiens and
Sky Harbour got second songs before Cosmo Topper completed
the album. "Damn Straight" came with a KUPD bumper sticker
and inner sleeve of adverts for local businesses; attorney,
cinema, and venue The Mason Jar (now The Rebel Lounge).

DARKER SKRATCHER LP (LAFMS)

The "Los Angeles Free Music Society" had been around since
1974 to promote the improvisational side of local music and
this compilation blended the people involved with LAFMS
with some newer post-punk artists. The album was notable
on the punk-related side of things for featuring the first
vinyl appearance by 45 Grave with "Riboflavin-Flavored,
Non-Carbonated, Polyunsaturated Blood", as well BPeople,
Human Hands, and Monitor. The album also had a variety
of experimental outbursts from the likes of; Boyd Rice &
Daniel Miller (soon to start Mute Records), Jad Fair (of
Half Japanese), The Rick Potts Band, Doo-Dooettes, NON,
Foundation Boo, Airway, Dennis Duck, and Le Forte Four,
all connected to the same people involved in LAFMS. The
majority of the album was a Ralph Records style repetitive
and experimental din that wouldn't sound out of place on a
David Lynch soundtrack, and even the bands here explored
their weirder side. The LP was also issued in the Netherlands.

DECLARATION OF INDEPENDENTS LP (AMBITION RECORDS)

Sub-titled; "13 Tracks Of U.S. Rock 1980", Washington D.C.'s Ambition Records licensed all the songs herein for this eclectic snapshot of American rock in the post-punk era. Everything was covered from power pop to surf to rock'n'roll and the album opened with SVT's "Heart Of Stone" followed by Jim Wunderle's only single, a cover of The Seeds "Pushin' Too Hard". Then D. Clinton Thompson served up a surf rock instrumental before Pylon perambulated awkwardly through their own brand of post-punk. The Razz took the stage next with their new wave pop partly powered by Tommy Keene, and so on... The other artists presented were; Kevin Dunn, Robin Lane And The Chartbusters, Luxury, The News, Ragnar Kvaran, Tex Rubinowitz, Root Boy Slim And The Sex Change Band, and finally Bubba Lou And The Highballs. "Declaration Of Independents", with its art depicting George Washington having a meltdown was issued in the U.K. by Stiff Records and Canada by Basement Records.

DETROIT DEFACES THE EIGHTIES LP (TREMOR RECORDS)

For their first long player this Detroit label put together a showcase of local talent paid for via a series of benefit gigs that also featured the bands. Cinecyde opened the record with a some catchy new wave, followed by The Cubes with their female vocal-led and synth twiddling new wave. The Ivories then ironically had none to tinkle but offered instead a working man's Detroit bar rock, before The Twenty-Seven jerked back and forth in a Devo style before bursting into high energy punk on stand out "Break The Ties", before Rushlow-King Combo added some jangle and harmonica to the new wave proceedings. Mark J. Norton concluded side one with a slow and maudlin live number. Five of the bands had a further song on side two while two had one; Rushlow-King Combo, and Service with "Overboard", a snappy and quirky new wave song with an underwater bass effects pedal. The cover art was so typical of the time, the rear featured band photos, info and liner notes.

DINDISC LP (DINDISC)

An introductory showcase of releases of the then new Virgin subsidiary Dindisc with a handful of its signings. Toronto's Martha And The Muffins opened the album with their hit "Echo Beach" and other single "Suburban Dreams". London's Monochrome Set also delivered two 7"s with "405 Lines" and "Apocalypso", while the debut single by hard rockers Dedringer "Sunday Drivers" closed side one. The flip gave us the post-Rezillos Revillos with 7" A-side "Hungry For Love" and album track "On The Beach". The final band was synth duo Orchestral Manoeuvres In The Dark with two singles and a VU cover, two of which were re-recorded versions. A mixed bag that looked more towards what would become indie pop, although wasn't quite yet. "Dindisc" came in an embossed sleeve with minimalist design by Peter Saville and included a foldout poster which was a board game where you were required to make your way around the U.K. to various gigs. The album was only issued in the U.K. and New Zealand.

EAST LP (DEAD GOOD RECORDS)

"East" being Lincolnshire, this area compilation also took in bands from Nottingham, Mansfield and Leicester, all within a comparative stone's throw from Lincolnshire, and on the Company Records affiliated Dead Good Records. A charming and consistent, but somehow lesser known, second wave punk collection featuring; The Cigarettes, The Fatal Charm, Whizz Kids, B-Movies, Pseudo Existors, Sincere Americans (members went on to play in 2-Tone's The Apollinaires), Half Life, and the charmingly named Vick Sinex And The Nasal Sprays, which wasn't a band but a minimalist solo project. The whole album was recorded on 4-track at Studio Playground in Wragby, Lincolnshire, but didn't sound like it. Most of the bands featured herein had their own releases on either Dead Good or Company Records and "East" came in a textured sleeve with artwork that just screamed, "Here come the 80s", with an insert featuring band info. "East" only received one pressing in the U.K.

EXPERIMENTS IN DESTINY 2LP (BOMP! RECORDS)

A beast from Bomp! This double opus featured one song each
from; Stiv Bators, The Real Kids, The Dadistics, Blake Xolton
& The Martians, Jimmy Lewis & The Checkers, The Nuns, Gary
Charlson, Rodney (Bingenheimer) & The Brunettes, The "B"
Girls, The MnM's, Paul Collins, Nikki & The Corvettes, Kathy
& The Lawnmowers, Prof. Anonymous, The Sonics, The Weirdos,
The Zantees, Jon & The Nightriders, The Lipstick Killers,
The Hypstrz, The Last, The Dead Boys, The Crawdaddys, The
Martians, Pete Holly & The Looks, The Wombats, Rainbow Red
Oxidizer, Cheek, and The Romantics. Being Bomp the emphasis
was on power pop with 60s influences but the inclusion of
bands like The Nuns ("Wild"), The Weirdos ("Jungle Rock")
and The Dead Boys ("3rd Generation Nation" live) gave it
an edge. "Experiments In Destiny" only received one U.S.
pressing and came in a gatefold sleeve nicely designed by
Frontier Records' designer Diane Zincavage (see: Circle
Jerks, T.S.O.L. and Adolescents LP sleeve designs).

FOUR STARS (****) LP (SAUSAGE RECORDS)

The second New Zealand compilation after "AK•79" veered
into the Rough Trade style post-punk direction with 4-track
recordings made at Sausage Studios/records proprietor
Robbie Duncan's studio in October 1980. Four bands from
Wellington's "Terrace Scene" (that gravitated around the
old flats near Victoria University) and thirteen songs
from; Life In The Fridge Exists, Wallsockets, Naked Spots
Dance, and Beat Rhythm Fashion, with all the bands seeming
to have a strong female presence. Beat Rhythm fashion
featured drummer Caroline Easther later of The Chills,
while Nick Swan of Life In The Fridge Exists played in Riot
111. Reminiscent of the compilations that were coming out
of the post-punk U.K. at this time, the cover art by Brett
Carstens depicted the title as simply the stars from the
New Zealand flag "****" while the record labels explained
the title. An original run locally of only 250 rendered
this almost completely obscure until a reissue in 2020.

GROETEN UIT AMSTERDAM LP (NO LABEL: RCS 443)

"Greetings From Amsterdam" was a showcase of twelve punk
and new wave bands from said city that was recorded and
mixed at the punk related Oktopus Studios in Amsterdam
during May and June 1980, during the 2-Tone ska revival in
the U.K. Tante Libido kicked of the album with their jerky
ska punk followed by Heat with some male/female vocal new
wave, again with a hint of ska. The ska theme continued with
De Bunkers, this time with some sax and keyboards, before
The Clinch took things a little more in the direction of
the lounge. The Dutch were fairly pedestrian in approach
while Presse Papier supplied some truly weird new wave to
conclude side one. The second side documented the musical
existence of Rollende Zelfdestruktie Revue (reggae/ska),
Bullet (funky/reggae), Brown Jenkin (dramatic music hall
new wave), Rock Bottom (hard rock, of course), Infantile
(Sabbath meets punk) and Workmates (punk and the album
standout). Only 3 bands had their own releases at the time.

HAPPY SQUID SAMPLER 7" EP (HAPPY SQUID RECORDS)

The fourth release on the Urinals imprint with a one-off
numbered press of 500 that featured Happy Squid bands on the
first side and Neef on side two. First, of course, Urinals
banged, crashed and walloped through a sub-minute punk
rattler "U" before Danny And The Doorknobs mixed Sixties
garage harmonies with an actual recording in their garage.
Arrow Book Club, aka John Talley-Jones of Urinals, made
some disconnected noises that sounded like a band tune-up
entitled "Get Down, Part 4" followed by stand out "Laurie's
Lament" by Vidiots that featured Rik L Rik on vocals, that
you may know from the first "Rodney On The Roq" compilation
LP. Finally on the Happy Squid side "experimental synth
musician" Phil Bedel made farting bubble noises entitled
"No Title". The Neef side titled "Atrophy Of The Sporting
Spirit" was so experimental it wasn't an actual song,
rather another improvised band tune-up with a title. The
7" came in a foldover sleeve with info on the inside.

the HAPPY SQUID sampler

URINALS

DANNY AND THE DOORKNOBS

ARROW BOOK CLUB

VIDIOTS

PHIL BEDEL

HAPPY SQUID RECORDS HS 004

HICKS FROM THE STICKS

International Record Syndicate, Inc.
GREATEST HITS Vol. 1
★ ★ ★ ★ ★
A sampler of tunes you want
to hear over and over again.

COMSAT ANGELS   EXCEL   INVADERS   PROTEX

Made in Britain

MINT SAUCE FOR THE MASSES

CLUB OF ROME
FLEXIBLE RESPONSE
FUN CITY
TWISTED NERVE

HICKS FROM THE STICKS LP (ROCKBURGH RECORDS)

An album compiled by rock writer Nigel Burnham (pseudonym: 'Des Moines') with the mission of presenting 'provincial' bands who he thought were being ignored by the London-centric music industry to the south. With a map on the back sleeve pointing out the location of the bands; Airkraft from Halifax, Radio 5 from Bradford, Music For Pleasure and The Expelaires from Leeds, Ada Wilson And Keeping Dark, The Distributors and Stranger Than Fiction from Wakefield, I'm So Hollow, Clock DVA and They Must Be Russians from Sheffield, Medium Medium and Art Failure from Birmingham, Nightmares In Wax, Wah! Heat, and Modern Eon from Liverpool, and finally Section 25 from Blackpool. "Hicks From The Sticks" presented a mix of throbbing post-punk and what would become indie with a wide variety of accessible songs mainly gleaned from obscure 7"s, with many of the artists going on to bigger things. The album was also issued in the U.S., Germany, Canada, New Zealand and Scandinavia.

I.R.S. GREATEST HITS VOLUME 1 LP (I.R.S. RECORDS)

Even though it was released a year before it's offspring "I.R.S. Greatest Hits Vols. 2 & 3", within that double LP came a coupon to order this extra promo LP for $2. So it was kind of a precursor and part accompaniment. Either way this is a solid LP of the I.R.S. punk wave roster in its own right with; Vancouver's The Payola$ (featuring Bob Rock), Klark Kent (Stewart Copeland, brother of I.R.S. owner Miles Copeland), Oingo Boingo, Berlin, The Stranglers, Henry Badowski, Buzzcocks, and Chelsea. A stand out was Berlin's cold war paranoia new wave single "Matter Of Time" recorded years before chart success with "Take My Breath Away". Two of the most well known Oingo Boingo songs were included in the form of "Only A Lad" and "This Is The Life", while the Stranglers offered up "The Raven" and "Vietnamerica". Buzzcocks gave us "Are Everything" while Chelsea closed the album with "No Escape". The LP received one pressing and came in a white die-cut sleeve with hype sticker.

LIVE AT TARGET LP (SUBTERRANEAN RECORDS)

Recorded live at Joe Rees' Target Video studio on February 24th 1980, this gig was also available as a VHS video from Target. The Target warehouse was three floors of video (Target), audio recording (Subterranean Records) and publishing (Damage) as well a venue located at 678 South Van Ness Avenue in San Francisco. "Live At Target" offered a glimpse into the art and experimental side of the post-punk era with throbbing compositions from; Factrix, Los Angeles' Nervous Gender, and Uns (aka Z'EV) as well as Flipper's particular brand of punk existentialism. The level of D.I.Y. involvement and creativity on this record was impressive, originally coming with two sheets for a front and back cover and five inserts, from all four artists and one with a mission statement from Subterranean by Steve Tupper and Mike Fox. It was later reissued in a regular sleeve. The Target Video building suffered extensive damage in the Loma Prieta earthquake of 1989 and was vacated.

MADE IN BRITAIN LP (POLYDOR)

Four bands who'd signed to Polydor between 1978 and 1980 given the promo treatment with four songs each from various Polydor releases. Invaders opened proceedings with their dramatic new wave. Originally from West Yorkshire they relocated to London and added Soo Lucas (punk icon Soo Catwoman) on backing vocals (and lead vocals on "Backstreet Romeo"). Bradford's Excel were up next with their power pop that wouldn't have sounded out of place on Rhino Records. Side two kicked off with Sheffield's Comsat Angels with their rhythmic post-punk, and Belfast's Protex closed the album with four rock'n'roll power pop songs that included their three Polydor A-Sides and the then unreleased "All I Wanna Do (Is Rock'N'Roll)". Each band was introduced by a posh male voice in the style of an old radio announcer and the cover featured a cartoon of a crowd outside a disco drawn by Paul Sample of the "Ogri" cartoon strip. The back cover featured photos and liner notes over a Union Jack design.

MINT SAUCE FOR THE MASSES 7" EP (PLAYLIST RECORDS)

A four band, six song set of bands from Edinburgh, Scotland. Club Of Rome started things off with a slow reggae-tinged number that was standard fare for this time period, their second song a slow dull post-punk song with saxophone. Flexible Response was next with a sloppy instrumental, "The Shortest War". Side two started off with Fun City featuring Gary McCormack of The Exploited on bass and Ronnie MacKinnon of The Valves on guitar, and their song "Avalanche" was very much in the '77 punk category with a Rotten rolled 'R' on the vocals and rot'n'roll guitar solo. Twisted Nerve completed the EP with two songs; "Neutral Zone", an anti-National Front anthem and "Vertigo", both of which sound like lost Partisans songs, and as a result side two really made this EP. The green sheep-adorned cover folded out into a six panel 'sleevezine' with a poster featuring photos of all the members on one side and loads of info on each band, a band shot and lyrics on the other.

MUTANT POP 78/79 LP (PVC/PASSPORT RECORDS)

A reworking of 1979's "Fast Product" for the U.S. and Canadian markets on PVC and Passport Records that warrants inclusion for the changes made. A similar 7" showcase of Fast Product 7" releases that featured; The Mekons, Scars, The Human League, 2.3, Gang Of Four, and The Flowers. Still with fourteen songs in total, Edinburgh's The Flowers "Confessions" 7" replaced two of the five Mekons songs. The Flowers 7" an addition to this amended set as the first 7" on Bob Last and Hilary Morrison's then new Pop Aural label that they started hot on the heels of Fast Product when it closed shop. The original "Fast Product" had only been released in the U.K. and Australia on EMI International, whereas this LP was intended to harness interest in U.K. post-punk in North America. The new cover art was accordingly more fitting, depicting a pixelated U.K. map with arrows from the three cities where the bands hailed from (Leeds, Sheffield and Edinburgh) directed at the Statue Of Liberty.

NEW WAVE - O ROCK DOS ANOS 80 7" EP (WEA)

"New Wave - 80s Rock" was a 33rpm promotional only 7" EP released only in Brazil featuring full songs from Gary Numan ("Cars") and The Pretenders ("Brass In Pocket") on side one, and sub one minute snippets of six bands and songs on side two featuring; The Inmates and "Dirty Water", The B-52's with "Rock Lobster", Elvis Costello playing "I Can't Stand Up For Falling Down", Ramones and their movie theme "Rock 'N' Roll High School", The Cars with "Double Life", and Dave Edmunds doing "Girl's Talk", essentially each clip giving you one verse and one chorus of each song. The EP came wrapped in an eight panel foldout 7" sleeve that opened to reveal a poster, with Gary Numan claiming the majority of the limelight, the other panels featured photos and band info in Portuguese, and for some reason post-Motors band Bram Tchaikovsky had their own panel and two of their album sleeves were featured leaving you wondering if they were originally supposed to be included.

N.O. EXPERIENCE NECESSARY LP (OBLIQUE RECORDS)

The "N.O." being New Orleans with a front cover graphic featuring the newspaper advert the label placed to attract talent, and seeing as Oblique's only other release was the Manic Depressives 7" I guess the aim here was this compilation. Backstabbers set the stage with a catchy U.K. punk style song "Lunatic Fringe", then Driveways gave us some keyboard led new wave with sax. The album continued with some high quality Louisana punk of the day from Room Service, Men In Black, Mechanics, Contenders (a big stand out here being The Clash inspired "Drug City"), Mandeville Mike & The Mental Block (another rockin' standout), and the first vinyl appearance from The Shitdogs (Baton Rouge) with memorable number "Not Responsible". Considering the quality here it's surprising that you can still pick this up cheaply, possibly due to the lack of other N.O. bands such as The Normals and Skinnies, who were later included on an alternative reissued different version of the album.

NO PEDESTRIANS LP (CHAMELEON RECORDS)

Following 1979's "The Last Pogo" this was the second collection of Toronto bands and it was a mixed bag of styles that opened with the catchy rock of The Sharks and "Get Off The Radio", followed by the power pop of Winston Hancock (who along with 60s garage influenced The Secrets had two songs to everyone else's one). The Secrets, featuring members of The Viletones and The Diodes, played "All The Words", followed by Arson and their unique rendition of The Animals' "We've Gotta Get Out Of This Place", then the dodgily named S.S. Concluded side one with "Working Girl". Side two opened with the punk rock of Tyranna, Zro4 (a standout) and True Confessions. The cover had a pedestrian theme that was continued on the red hexagonal stop sign insert with band line-up info. The back cover featured a photo collage as well as a photo of each band with a logo made to look like their own record cover. A nice job all around and a one-off Canadian pressing for this obscurity.

NO QUESTIONS, NO ANSWERS LP (VINYL SOLUTION RECORDS)

The second New Orleans area compilation from 1980 and this one is more sought after now possibly as it featured a new more urgent breed of bands such as Red Rockers who went onto Columbia Records. Aside from the Clash city Red Rockers the other players here were Aces 88, RZA, The Hostages, The Models (with the anthem "Fire Patrol"), the mod revival punk of The Wayward Youth, the synth wave of David Oh!, the snappy The Fugitives, Mandeville Mike, The Swingin' Millionaires (with the great "The Cannibals Next Door"), The Cheaters and The Manic Depressives. Three of these bands already had 7"s on Vinyl Solution, the label run by Larry Holmes of The Manic Depressives. The quality was high and whole album was recorded at BB Recording Studio in Belle Chase, Louisiana, and "No Questions, No Answers" was actually the album from where the majority of the content for the later alternative version of "N.O. Experience Necessary" was gleaned that was mentioned in a previous entry.

OI! THE ALBUM LP (EMI RECORDS)

If there's one thing music journalists love is to coin a
name for a new genre. Enter Garry Bushell and the 'new punk'
that he coined "Oi!" in Sounds Magazine (who claimed to
'present' this album for street level label EMI). Of course
Oi! was all just second wave U.K. working class punk bands
but thanks to Bushell it served as a new soundtrack for the
often dodgy skinhead element at punk and 2-tone gigs that
then splintered off as a new warring faction in the punk
wars. The majority of "Oi! The Album" though consisted of
mainly sussed punk bands chosen for this new 'movement';
Cockney Rejects, Peter And The Test Tube Babies, Angelic
Upstarts, Slaughter And The Dogs, The Exploited, glam pub
rockers Cock Sparrer and Rejects spin-offs Terrible Twins,
and Postmen, as well as possibly the only actual Oi! band
here, the 4-Skins. There was also some 'comedy' provided by
Max Splodge/Desert Island Joe, and Barney And The Rubbles.
The LP was unsurprisingly only ever pressed in the U.K.

ROCK AGAINST RACISM - RAR'S GREATEST HITS LP (RARECORDS)

Invoking Newton's third law, "for every action there is an
equal and opposite reaction" came "Rock Against Racism",
the record, the label and the movement that stood against
the idiotic rise of the far right in the latter half
of 1970s Britain that was also infecting its music. The
album featured bands involved in the various RAR gigs and
carnivals; The Members, The Piranhas, Steel Pulse, The
Mekons, X-Ray Spex ("Oh Bondage Up Yours!" of course),
Matumbi, Tom Robinson Band (with "Winter Of '79"), Elvis
Costello And The Attractions, Stiff Little Fingers (with
"Law And Order"), Barry Ford Band, Carol Grimes Band, Gang
Of Four, Aswad, and The Clash (with an exclusive alternative
mix/version of "White Man In Hammersmith Palais"). The
cover featured the RAR icon with band photos on the rear
and liner notes inside by Andy Xerox. All proceeds went to
RAR and the LP was issued in the U.K., Sweden, Netherlands,
New Zealand, Finland, Portugal, France and Israel.

ROCK AGAINST RACISM

RAR's GREATEST HITS

BARRY FORD BAND
X-RAY SPEX
ELVIS COSTELLO & THE ATTRACTIONS
ASWAD
CLASH
PIRANHAS
MEKONS
STEEL PULSE
CAROL GRIMES BAND
STIFF LITTLE FINGERS
TOM ROBINSON BAND
MEMBERS
GANG OF FOUR
MATUMBI

DO NOT PAY MORE THAN £3·99

FRONT   R.   O.   R.

SECOND CITY STATIK a glasgow compilation

THE ALLEGED
POSITIVE NOISE
RESTRICTED CODE

SENT
FROM
COVENTRY

County of West Midlands
Coventry

URGE
SQUAD
THE END
THE MIX
MACHINE
PROTEGE
HOMICIDE
RIOT ACT
THE CLIQUE
THE V. BABIES
SOLID ACTION
THE WILD BOYS

S.F.
Underground
2

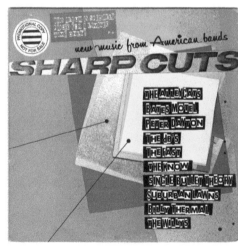

PROMOTIONAL COPY
NOT FOR SALE

new music from American bands

SHARP CUTS

THE ALLEY CATS
BATES MOTEL
PETER DAYTON
THE JB'S
THE LAST
THE KNOW
SINGLE BULLET THEORY
SUBURBAN LAWNS
BILLY THERMAL
THE WIGS

RODNEY ON THE ROQ LP (POSH BOY RECORDS)

The hardcore punk kids from Southern California's beach communities and Orange County really began to put their engineer boot stamp on proceedings with this showcase of Rodney Bingenheimer's radio show on L.A.'s KROQ station. With an introduction by Brooke Shields, side one was a run through of now punk classics from L.A.; Agent Orange, Adolescents, Circle Jerks, UXA, The Klan, Black Flag and Rik L Rik, with side two being a little more mainstream but also offering; The Crowd, The Simpletones, Vidiots, and San Francisco's The Nuns alongside the synth pop of David Microwave, the quirky post-punk of Fender Buddies, and Cristina with "Is That All There Is?". The sleeve was typically 'groupie' themed, as you'd expect from Rodney, and the album came with a special issue of Flipside Fanzine (#21) with a page on each band and a family tree of the bands. The album was issued in the U.S. and Finland and reissued domestically a few times between 1981 and 1986.

SECOND CITY STATIK - A GLASGOW COMPILATION 12" (STATIK RECORDS)

The first release from Laurie Dunn's Statik Records (the label spelling of Static or Statik as yet undecided here) with a three band and six song showcase of Glasgow post-punk talent. Opening up the record was Restricted Code and "The New Messiah", a 60s-tinged hyperactive garage punk song. Following this was Positive Noise and "Refugees", a smart synth-infused Joy Division style post-punk. The third of the three bands came in the form of The Alleged and "2 Out Of 3", a bouncing and catchy new wave song with a Buzzcocks feel. The Alleged continued onto side two with "Despair" and the Manchester comparisons continue as it reminded me of The Distractions. Restricted Code followed with the choppy "Seeing Much Better (With Your Eyes)" and Positive Noise closed the record in a cold and dramatic Joy Division fashion with "The Long March". This somewhat historically overlooked record came in a typically arty sleeve with the back cover featuring band shots and info.

SENT FROM COVENTRY LP (KATHEDRAL RECORDS)

Coventry put itself on the punk wave map with this collection of twelve bands, all with one song apart from The Wild Boys, former band of Roddy Radiation of The Specials, with his brother Mark on guitar (Roddy wrote both these songs). The Clique offered a bouncy alternative image of new wave, The End played some strong keyboard-led new wave on "Panic In The Night", while The Mix were equally impressive with "With You". The album continued with Machine (ska), Urge (new wave), Protégé (mod edged), Solid Action (more mod edge), Squad (Terry Hall's punk band prior to this record), Homicide, Riot Act, and V. Babies. It's surprising that hardly any of these bands achieved notoriety but I guess Coventry's other output may have faded in the shadow of 2-Tone. The LP came with a special issue of zine "Alternative Sounds" with 12 pages on all the bands. The cover featuring photos and liner notes by Horace of The Specials on the back. The LP was pressed once and reissued 20 years later.

S.F. UNDERGROUND 2 7" EP (SUBTERRANEAN RECORDS)

Hardcore punk had started to take hold of Northern California by 1980 and these early nihilistic musings draped in chains and leather were of course documented by Subterranean Records. First up were Spikes from Santa Cruz with slow burner "Life Is Hell" featuring the charmingly named Vic Drano on guitar and David Delinquent on vocals. Seattle imports The Lewd followed them in great style with their sneering working class anthem "Mobile Home", while the flip gave us Society Dog and "Title Role". The EP closed with The Undead and their rudimentary punk on "Hitler's Brain". Bob Noxious of The Undead and Joe Dirt of Society Dog would go on to form Fuck-Ups, while Jonithin Christ of Society Dog would soon front Code Of Honor. The back to front two colour cover featured a photo of S.F. club the Sound Of Music while the foldout sheet insert had photos of all four bands, all lyrics and line-up info. 'S.F. Underground 2' had just one pressing of 3,800.

SHARP CUTS LP (PLANET RECORDS)

Sub-titled "New Music From American Bands" the atrocious cover art of 'Sharp Cuts' alone should be enough to put anyone off from actually listening to it, but I'm going in. Herein were songs by two real punk and post-punk bands; The Alley Cats and Suburban Lawns, alongside a whole host of 'new wave bands' who were that breed of poodle-haired and waist-coated 70s rock bands such as; Single Bullet Theory, Billy Thermal, Bates Motel, The Know, The Willys, The Fast and The dB's, as well as a 'solo' band project by Peter Dayton of La Peste, which didn't save proceedings, the entire album only rescued by the inclusion of The Alley Cats and Suburban Lawns. Even the back cover of Polaroids of the bands with barely readable info is a complete mess. I'm not so sure it should've been called 'Sharp Cuts', maybe 'Blunt Instruments' would've been more fitting. Even the Planet Records logo looks like some sci-fi disco shit. Issued in U.S., Canada, Europe, Italy, Greece and Japan: Why?

STREET LEVEL (20 NEW WAVE HITS) LP (RONCO RECORDS)

Keeping up with the trends, telemarketing label Ronco (similar to Music For Pleasure) that was known for churning out cheap compilations, issued this 'As Seen On TV' new wave hits collection. As it turned out this 20 band set was full of hits for your punky new wave party featuring; Sex Pistols, The Stranglers, Pretenders, Ian Dury, The Skids, The Buzzcocks, Magazine, The Plasmatics, Public Image Ltd., Blondie, Boomtown Rats, Tom Robinsons Band, Gary Numan, John Foxx, Nick Straker Band, XTC, Generation X, The Members, The Dickies, and Jona Lewie. This many chart smashers in one place had its drawbacks and it was a little quiet in places with the statement, "To ensure the highest quality reproduction the running times of the some of the titles as originally released have been changed". With suitable new wave cover art in an underpass, one pressing came as a Levi Strauss promotion with different cover art featuring simply their denim button on the front.

AS SEEN ON TV

↑ STREET LEVEL ↑

20 NEW WAVE HITS

PRETENDERS   SEX PISTOLS
BOOMTOWN RATS   GARY NUMAN
IAN DURY
BLONDIE   TOM ROBINSON BAND
STRANGLERS

Ronco

SURF CITY UNDERGROUND

SWISS WAVE THE ALBUM

FEATURING LiLiPUT GRAUZONE RUDOLPH DIETRICH + KDF
MOTHERS RUIN THE SICK LADYSHAVE JACK + THE RIPPERS

INCLUDING ORIGINALAUFNAHME

EISBÄR • GRAUZONE

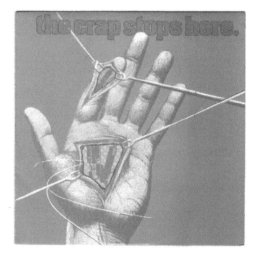

the crap stops here.

THE DECLINE

Alice Bag Band   Black Flag   Catholic Discipline
Circle Jerks   Fear   Germs
and X

The Insane....Darrell   Wayne.......

SURF CITY UNDERGROUND LP (BLUEBEAT RECORDS)

A sixteen song area showcase of new wave bands from Santa Cruz, California. The album opened with The Humans and their version of instrumental "Telstar" (they were signed by I.R.S. around this time). The Drivers followed with the standout punk of their 7" made rare by a "Bloodstains" compilation song "Johnny's Dying" and featured drummer Michael Litton soon of hardcore band The Scapegoats. Tao Chemical took things in a new wave direction before The Satellites played their rock standard that also featured a future Scapegoats member in the form of Henry Hample. The album continued with mainly standard bar rock in the era of new wave fare from; Joe Richards Group, Small Nambas, Doug Springs, David Larstein, The Prisoners, Lol Halsey, The Newtrons, Bari Boswell, and JJ 180, with further songs from; The Drivers (with their 7" B-side "I'm No Moron"), Tao Chemical and The Satellites. The cover art featured a surf image with basic band info on the back cover.

SWISS WAVE THE ALBUM LP (OFF COURSE RECORDS)

Switzerland joined the punk wave conversation with this collection of bands. The album opened with the synth post-punk of Grauzone which almost seems muted in comparison to The Sick who grabbed the mic in a more punk fashion straight after. Jack & The Rippers then took the stage with their catchy '77 punk before Liliput (the band Kleenex after a name change that followed a legal threat from Kleenex manufacturer Kimberly-Clark) closed side one with their Slits style jerky post-punk. Side two began with the power pop punk of Rudolph Dietrich & KDF (Kraft Durch Freude) followed by more of the catchy punk of Jack & The Rippers, the then modern take on old rock 'n' roll of Ladyshave, and in closing the jerky post-punk of Mother's Ruin featuring the English tinged punk vocals of Sylvia Holenstein. Grauzone's "Eisbär" (Polar Bear) ended up being a hit in Germany and Austria (this fact soon added to the LP cover). The LP had six pressings and was issued in Italy, Germany and the U.K.

THE CRAP STOPS HERE LP (RABID RECORDS)

"The Crap Stops Here" was essentially a one press farewell 7" collection of Manchester label 'Rabid' that opened with the first Slaughter And The Dogs 7" "Cranked Up Really High", followed by The Nosebleeds with the A-side "Ain't Bin To No Music School". John Cooper Clarke then got a good chunk of side a with "Psycle Sluts 1 And 2" and "Bronze Adonis" (live) before Gyro's "Central Detention Centre" 7" got an airing. The flip gave us Jilted John's eponymous hit song before The Out's "No One Is Innocent" 7" was added before it returned inexplicably to Jilted John for "Mrs. Pickering". Freshies vocalist Chris Sievey then gave his B-side a blast before The Freshies themselves threw in a demo only song "Yesterday/Tomorrow". Slaughter And The Dogs roadie Ed Banger aka Edmund Garrity showed us his A-side before finally Prime Time Suckers closed the LP with an unreleased song. I'm not sure what the cover art represented but I like it, and the back cover features band images and info.

THE DECLINE OF WESTERN CIVILIZATION LP (SLASH RECORDS)

The classic soundtrack to the legendary film that documented the Los Angeles scene's transition from early punk into the hardcore era, that also acted as taster for the film that didn't actually come out until July 1981. High quality live recordings taken between December 1979 and May 1980 interspersed with many quotable soundbites and live banter from the film. The album opened with three Black Flag songs with Ron Reyes on vocals, followed by two solitary offerings from Germs and Catholic Discipline, before X gave us three of their rockin' rollers, and then Circle Jerks blasted through four songs from "Group Sex" like there was no tomorrow. The Alice Bag Band acted as a mere interlude before Fear stole the show with six and a half minutes of the most incendiary punk rock and crowd abuse ever committed to vinyl. The album was housed in stills from the film along with a lyric sheet, or inner sleeve, and was reissued many times but was only issued outside of the U.S. in Italy in 1983.

THE INSANE DARRELL WAYNE'S NO DISCO ALBUM LP (BOMP! RECORDS)

Bomp overload! This was an anti-disco compilation put together by KROQ DJ Insane Darrell Wayne and by submission in much the same way as the previous 'Devotees' album. As a result quite a few of these artists only ever appeared here with their anti-disco screeds and you won't find any records out there by; Farbo & The Cheeseheads, Homecookin', Cap'N Crisco & The Disco Ninnies, Dim Dandy & The Dolts, Ground Zero, Sgab From The Planet Zed, Cindy & The Gidget Haters, Madfox, or Ubuibi, whereas you may find 7"s by The Tokyos, The Vectors, Cliche, The Press, Zilch or Flash Boyancy. Musically it was a mixed bag from folk to punk to spoof disco, but with song titles like; "Death To Disco", "Pogoin's For Me", "Disco Sucks", "Discoectomy", "Disco's Dead" and "Disco Defecation" you really can't resist the stupidity of it all and marvel at a time when this kind of nonsense would come out on LP and people would buy it. The album had one U.S. press and a German issue on Line Records.

THE LAST STIFF COMPILATION LP (STIFF RECORDS)

"...Until the next one" but I think I'll stop with this hits collection on the short-lived Stiff Records U.S. based in New York. The album opened with "Dance Stance" by Dexy's Midnight Runners followed by pub rockers Lew Lewis Reformer. "Jumping Someone Else's Train" by the Cure was followed by "Bed And Breakfast Man" by Madness before; Any Trouble, Mo-Dettes, John Otway, and Lene Lovich filled out side one. The flip opened with the curious inclusion of composer Anthony Moore with some new wave before Lori & The Chameleons, Wreckless Eric, The Chords ("Maybe Tomorrow"), John Cooper Clarke ("Chicken Town"), Motörhead ("No Class"), Cockney Rejects ("Flares 'N' Slippers"), and The Damned ("Smash It Up") heated up side two. With a sleeve that was a mess of 7" sleeves, the LP came with an insert with info on this eclectic mix of U.K. artists. There were two versions: one with 16 songs and one with only 14 omitting Lene Lovich and John Cooper Clarke presumably for contractual reasons.

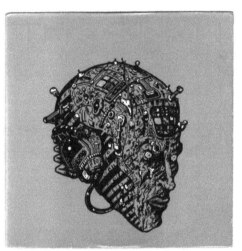

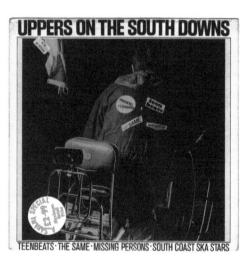

THE MOONLIGHT TAPES LP (DANCEVILLE RECORDS)

One of only two releases on Danceville recorded at Decca
Studios, live from The Moonlight Club between 27th April
and 2nd May 1980. The album began with London power pop
punks Sore Throat with 7" B-side "Complex". Next was The
Members with "Rat Up A Drainpipe", another 7" B-side of
their punky reggae. The Lightning Raiders then delivered
a strong song with yet another 7" B-side in the form of
"Views", before Local Operator from Denmark finally gave
us an A-side in "Law And Order" with an anti-Thatcher intro
and a ska feel. These were followed by; The Edge (formerly
Jane Aire And The Belvederes but without Jane), The Q.T's,
then The School Bullies (aka The Damned incognito "Machine
Gun Etiquette" line-up) who gave us the blazing "Lookin'
For Another" which was released nowhere else. After this
it's time for the stabby post-punk of The Passions, The Soul
Boys and The Kameras. The cover was a Sgt. Peppers homage
with The Damned front and centre and lyrics on the back.

THE SIREN LP (POSH BOY RECORDS)

A three band compilation LP from Los Angeles' Posh Boy
Records (that followed "Beach Blvd") that opened with three
songs from 391 who featured Jeff Olener and Jeff Raphael
of San Francisco's The Nuns. These three songs would later
form a 12" EP on Posh Boy with their other song from the
session that had appeared on "415 Music". Their approach
was similar to The Nuns but with a more 70s rock edge.
Next up was the debut vinyl appearance from L.A. teen punks
Red Cross with six snotty outbursts that would later be
reissued in a different order as their classic 12" on Posh
Boy. Finally, Salt Lake City, Utah's, Spittin' Teeth with
their brooding punk closed the album with slow burners
"Prostitute" and "Destruction" that really should've seen
them more remembered than they are, no doubt because they
were the only band here not to have this material reissued
as a 12". The LP featured some odd robot art by British
designer David Allen/Artrouble and received one pressing.

TIMES SQUARE - ORIGINAL SOUNDTRACK 2LP (RSO RECORDS)

The soundtrack of the film about two girls who ran away
from a mental institution for the streets of New York
City to form a band called The Sleez Sisters that starred
Trini Alvarado, Robin Johnson and Tim Curry. Whereas the
soundtrack was as varied as you'd expect, the punk and new
wave inclusions were enough for it to be notable, and the
whole thing ended like a snapshot of the musical zeitgeist
of 1980. The punk and new wave era bands in question
being; The Ruts, Ramones, The Cure, Talking Heads, Patti
Smith Group, XTC, Joe Jackson, Gary Numan, The Pretenders,
as well as Suzi Quatro, Roxy Music, Marcy Levy (later of
Shakespear's Sister), and Barry Gibb (Bee Gees). Also the
lead actors Robin Johnson and Trini Alvarado, D.L. Byron,
Lou Reed, Desmond Child & Rouge (disco), Garland Jeffreys,
and David Johansen (New York Dolls). The double album was
pressed in countless countries upon release in a bright
gatefold sleeve with graphics that scream "the 80s are here!"

TROUBLEMAKERS 2LP (WARNER BROTHERS RECORDS)

Opening and closing with Sex Pistols songs live from their
last gig at Winterland in San Francisco ("Anarchy In The
U.S.A." and "No Fun (Excerpts)", this Warner Brothers
collection of punk and new wave mixed in with some decidedly
not new artists was the final release in Warners' "Loss
Leaders" series that were mail order only records they'd
been putting out since 1969. Also appearing were; Urban
Verbs, Robin Lane & The Chartbusters, Wire, Marianne
Faithfull ("Working Class Hero"), John Cale, Gang Of Four,
The Modern Lovers, Devo, PiL, The Buggles, Pearl Harbor And
The Explosions, Nico, and Brian Briggs, with most having two
songs from Warner releases. With very 'new wave' art from Gary
Panter and Ronn Spencer (also of White Noise Records) in a
gatefold sleeve with band photos and info. An above average
major label set and something to look out for if you're a
Pistols completist. 'Troublemakers' had two pressings with
alternate coloured new wave candy stripes on the cover.

UPPERS ON THE SOUTH DOWNS LP (SAFARI RECORDS)

A compilation of four mod revival bands from the south coast of England. First up came The Teenbeats from Hastings, who took up most of side one with five songs very much in keeping with other mod revival maximum R&B stuff of the day, with some some songs bordering on pub rock. The South Coast Ska Stars concluded side one with "South Coast Rumble" (I detect a theme here) a ska instrumental. First up on side two came The Same with two songs that were more spiky new wave than mod but in keeping with the theme with song titles like "I Am A Face". Missing Persons followed with three mod songs, including the highlight "Forever Young" and the LP closed with another South Coast Ska Stars song. The cover art depicted a parka wearing mod on a 50cc Vespa with miniscule liner notes by Ray Fenwick of The Syndicate, The Spencer Davis Group and Ian Gillan Band. It was reissued a year later adding three songs by The Purple Hearts and removing one by South Coast Ska Stars.

WAITING ROOM LP (OBJECT MUSIC)

Another collection from Manchester's Object Music, previously responsible for the "A Manchester Collection", with more songs from three of the bands from that LP. First up was a full side by Stockport three piece Slight Seconds with nine well recorded and executed songs of brooding catchy post-punk, not unlike Wire or Magazine, who somehow to this day still manages to languish in obscurity. Two members of Slight Seconds had previously been in punk band Elite during 1977-78 before forming this new band after about a dozen gigs. Side two offered five songs by The Mediaters of loud and quiet highly developed post-punk with parping saxophones, and the last thirteen minutes of side two was simply one song by Picture Chords of jarring post-punk but with the addition of a synthesizer. The sleeve art was simply text and three band photos of all the sixth form looking lads exuding 1979 in a variety of parkas, scarves and extra large glasses. John Peel must've played this.

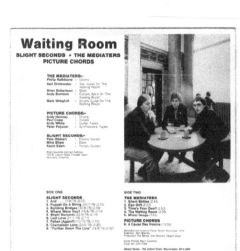

WANNA BUY A BRIDGE? LP (ROUGH TRADE)

Honestly sub-titled "A Rough Trade Compilation Of Singles" this is literally that; Rough Trade's hits between 1978-1979 compiled for U.S. release to promote its catalogue at the same time as the likes of Cabaret Voltaire and Young Marble Giants were venturing to California to tour in 1980. Featuring A-side punk indie hits from; Stiff Little Fingers, Delta 5, The Slits, Essential Logic, T.V. Personalities, Swell Maps, The Pop Group, Spizz Energi, Kleenex, Cabaret Voltaire, The Raincoats, Young Marble Giants, Scritti Politti, and Robert Wyatt. The album ended up as a kind of unofficial guide to post-punk, the quality of songs being high with no filler. "Wanna Buy A Bridge?" Was pressed in different colour sleeves (blue, green and brown) in the U.S. with a fourth on a different brown in Finland for luck. The back cover had the customary map guide to where the bands were from with an inner sleeve featuring all fourteen 7" covers with info.

WAVES - AN ANTHOLOGY OF NEW MUSIC VOL. 2 LP (BOMP! RECORDS)

Sub-titled "Spring 1980" this Bomp follow-up to its previous "new music" collection was yet more; "Documentation of the growing grassroots music scene across America", that being Bomp of course all still somehow managed to be good old 60s music with some early 70s pop rock tripe thrown in. Bands included were; The Martians, The Singles (for Nerves fans), The Toasters (for fans of The Dickies), Gary Charlson (70s pop rock tripe), Billy Hancock (rock'n'roll), Jeff Stacy & The National Debt, Pointed Sticks (saving the day here with their Vancouver pop punk), Psycotic Pineapple, The Dadaistics, The Lonely Boys, The Jumpers, Toy Love, and Oho. The majority of the album was sunny British invasion style power pop, with the emphasis on the pop, with harmonies and keyboards, but made the grade as it had an unreleased Pointed Sticks song on. The cover depicted the Easter Island statues as guitar heads and was a gatefold with band info inside. The LP was pressed in the U.S., Canada and Germany.

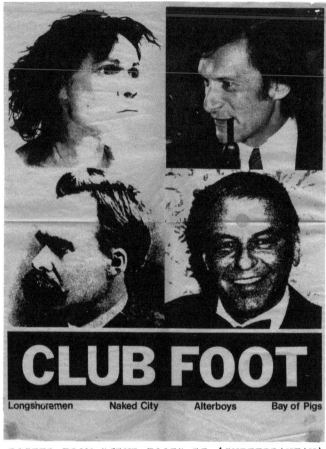

POSTER FROM "CLUB FOOT" LP (SUBTERRANEAN)

COVER/INTRO: "ALTERNATIVE SOUNDS" FROM "SENT FROM COVENTRY" LP

WE DO 'EM OUR WAY LP (MUSIC FOR PLEASURE)

It didn't take long for the punk rock revolution to have
its very own collection on household name cheesy reissue
label Music For Pleasure (MFP). That said, at least some
effort went into this, the theme being new wave bands (and
some long haired chancers) covering songs from previous
decades. The album opened with Sex Pistols and "Rock Around
The Clock" followed by Devo's take on "Satisfaction" and
continues with The Golant Pistons, Sex Pistols (again,
with "Stepping Stone"), Those Helicopters, Hollywood Brats
("Then He Kissed Me"), The Flying Lizards ("Money"), The
Slits ("I Heard It Through The Grapevine"), The Stranglers
("Walk On By"), The Hammersmith Gorillas ("You Really
Got Me"), U.K. Subs ("She's Not There"), and The Dickies
("Nights In White Satin"). With its cover art re-working of
the Mona Lisa with punk hair, all this LP was missing was
some wacky coloured vinyl to have made it more noticeable
in the history of punk related cheesy compilations.

YES NUKES - 14 ATOMIC POWERED CUTS LP (RHINO RECORDS)

Sub-titled "A Collection Of Los Angeles Rock Bands" this
album continued the Rhino annual showcase compilation that
carried on from "Saturday Night Pogo" and "L.A. In" with;
The Pop, The Twisters (power pop), Cliche (with the then
topical "I Ran From Iran... when the shooting began"),
The Nu Kats (70s pop rock tripe), The Naughty Sweeties,
Bakersfield Boogie Boys (a joke band with a 12" On Rhino
promoted here as 'new wave' who somehow got a song on the
Rhino 'Devotees' LP that wasn't a Devo song - I guess they
knew someone), The Soul Dads (James Brown style), The
Weirdos (with "Helium Bar"), The Makers (imagine having
your sole shot at a record appearance and choosing a Kinks
cover), Quiet Riot (yes, really), The Runaways ("Take
Over"), The Wedge (surf), Sumner, and Malibooz. The cover
art was some loud 'new wave' futuristic rubbish with bands
on the back and an inner sleeve promoting all the then
current Rhino releases. The album was pressed once.

"a wicked good time!"

the modern method compilation

MODERN METHOD VOLUME 2

BACKLASH!

THREATS
END RESULT
FACTORY POEMS
VICTIMS OF WHAT ?
& SIGNIFICANT ZERØS

ABANDONING ALL COMMERCIAL SANITY,
SIXTEEN OF AMERICA'S WILDEST NEW
PSYCHEDELIC BANDS MEET
ON ONE ALBUM FOR THE
ULTIMATE SHOWDOWN...

BATTLE OF THE GARAGES

BLITZ

SECRET RECORDS IN CONJUNCTION WITH THE REINDEER MEAT MARKETING BOARD PRESENT...2

Bollocks to Christmas

featuring
THE 4 SKINS
MAX SPLODGE
THE BUSINESS
THE GONADS

1981

A WICKED GOOD TIME! VOLUME 1 & 2 LPS (MODERN METHOD RECORDS)

First to document the Boston area punk bands was Modern Method, the record label of record store Newbury Comics with these two LPs put together in conjunction with radio station WBCN. Punk rock, post-punk and new wave from; Pastiche, The Outlets, Future Dads, Boys Life, La Peste (their only compilation appearance with "Army Of Apathy" and standout "Lease On Life" sounding like a lost Agent Orange song), Swingers Resort, Young Snakes, Vacuumheads, Suade Cowboys, Bound & Gagged, Someone And The Somebodies, Bird Songs Of The Mesozoic (the Mission Of Burma side project), and The Loners with one or two songs apiece. Hot on its heels "Volume Two" featured November Group, The Freeze (with with an early version of "American Town"), Future Dads, Leper, Vitamin, Pastiche (The Mini-Band), Boys Life, Someone And The Somebodies, Limbo Race, CCCP-TV, The Stains, The Trademarks and Vinny.

BACKLASH! 7" EP (PLAYLIST RECORDS)

The second compilation from this Edinburgh based label that followed on from "Mint Sauce For The Masses" the year before. Five Scottish bands with a song each starting with Significant Zer0s and the pacey '77 style punk of "Stiff Citizens". Factory Poems followed this with the decidedly post-punk "Passion Dance". Near future Rondelet recording artists Threats then concluded side one with "Pacivity", a sharp Killing Joke inspired song with a spiky guitar. The flip gave way to the intricate post-punk of Victims Of What? and the more Ultravox! meets post-punk of End Result. The EP came in a hand stamped inner with a six panel foldout sleeve with graphic design that was very much above average for the U.K. at the time. Some copies were given away with Glasgow fashion magazine, "Instant Whip" #1. A surprisingly overlooked EP considering its quality.

BATTLE OF THE GARAGES LP (VOXX RECORDS)

Bomp subsidiary Voxx took submissions for this set of 'psychedelic bands' that ended up with a few punk entries. Three more volumes followed but this one had a few notable inclusions; Deniz Tek of Radio Birdman recorded in Houston in 1981 with Really Red's Jean-Paul Williams and Bob Weber, a cover from the session of The Four Speeds' "RPM" (see: 'Pebbles Vol. 4') appeared here, and the other; "100 Fools", came out on a split 7" with Radio Birdman in 1983. L.A. rock punks Stepmothers supplied an unreleased song with "Let Her Dance", Kansas post-punks The Embarrassment contributed a cover of The Seeds "Pushin' Too Hard", and DC's Slickee Boys offered up "Glendora/Going All The Way". The other bands on this enjoyable LP were; United States Of Existence, The Vertebrats, Pete Holly & The Looks, Eddy Best, Brad Long, The Dark Side, The Wombats, The Crawdaddies, The Unclaimed, The Chesterfield Kings, Billy Synth & The Turn-Ups, and Plasticland. All with 60s influences. The sleeve featured quality artwork by Diane Zincavage (see: Frontier, Posh Boy and other classic covers) and was also issued in Germany.

BLITZ LP (RCA VICTOR)

One of those major label 'new wave' compilations again, with acts from their already existing roster, that had any kind of tenuous link whatsoever to whatever was in at the time, thrown together with some artwork that looked in this case 'new wave'. One or two songs each by; Bow Wow Wow, Slow Children, Robert Ellis Orrall, Sparks, Shock, Polyrock, and Landscape. The vast majority of this was synth pop that had an obvious eye on the charts and was an indicator a new move towards 'New Romantic' by the major labels. Sparks of course were very much pre-new wave, and aside from them, only Bow Wow Wow and Landscape ever did any top forty worrying, and that's probably why "Blitz", wrapped in some very Devo-esque 'new wave' art (about the best thing about it), was only issued once in the U.S. and even then only mainly as a promo. The album included an inner sleeve with liner notes and the bands' record covers.

BOLLOCKS TO CHRISTMAS 7" EP (SECRET RECORDS)

The first punk Christmas compilation was of course Oi! because when I think of Christmas the first things to spring to mind are skinheads. The 4 Skins got the booze flowing with a cover of Slade's "Merry Christmas Everybody", and somehow played a cover version better than their own songs, before Max Splodge offered some fake drunk studio out-take of "The 12 Days Of Christmas", with Gaz Bushell making an appearance at the end just to remind you that it's all a joke, honest guv. The flip side began with The Business doin' Elton John's "Step Into Christmas" with altered lyrics all about beer and drinking, and they somehow managed to get through it without threatening any students. Finally, the ever hilarious Gonads fell sideways through "White Christmas" and thankfully didn't make it all about race (just mentioned it). Cheesy Xmas card cartoon art adorned the cover and Garry Bushell rambled through his usual side-splitting liner notes on the back. A must for fans of a good old British Xmas knees up and tone deaf vocals.

BOWLING BALLS II LP (CLONE RECORDS)

Volume two of this showcase of Ohio new music from Nick Nicholis' (of The Bizarros) Clone Records and unlike volume one that descended into freeform synth art hell this album opened with some new wave pop from Susan Schmidt and Debbie Smith (of Chi-Pig and Friction), followed by the similar catchy female-led new wave of Unit 5. The Bizarros brought their wave punk and then Hammer Damage entertained with the seemingly Devo inspired "Noise Pollution". Tin Huey closed side one in a quirky Pere Ubu style while side two featured two more Unit 5 songs, another Susan Schmidt & Debbie Smith, and one each by the repetitive beats of Totsuzen Danball (with a slight departure from the Ohio theme seeing as they were from Japan), and the album closed with the funky space age new wave of The Waitresses. I have no idea what's going on with the front cover but the back had band photos and info. "Bowling Balls II" was only issued once in the U.S.

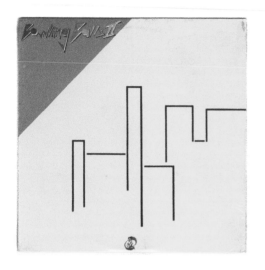

Bud Luxford Presents:

"13 fine bands playing and singing the finest music that this world has ever known."

Bud Luxford Presents:
..ON SALE INSIDE..

"If it wasn't for me these bands would hafta play for free!"

BUSTED AT OZ

GARRY BUSHELL PRESENTS FOR YOUR PENULTIMATE STIMULATION, RELAXATION AND EXULTATION – Oi 3!
CARRY ON Oi!!

BUD LUXFORD PRESENTS LP & ON SALE INSIDE LP (GRANT RECORDS)

Two spoof albums of Vancouver 'fuck bands', all playing under pseudonyms with fictitious band member names such as 'Tony Baloney', that arose from Bud Luxford's revue style showcase 'Budstock' gigs that inspired many of these improvised outfits. You can guess from the band names and recognise some of the players in the photos on the insert with volume one or the photocopied zine in volume two but for the most part it's all a mystery. Volume one had; Los Radical Popularos (later dropping the 'Radical'), Sasquatch, Melody Pimps, Jimbo And The Lizard Kings, Raisinettes, Snuggle Bunnies, Buddy Selfish (Ian Tiles), Rude Norton, Snow Geese, Tots In Bondage, Sgt. Nick Penis Band, Pino Rogeletti And The IUDs, and Mrs. Luxford's Fish. While volume two had Melody Pimps, Wrecking Crew, Handsome Brutes, Young Winstons, Sawhorse, Corsage, Buddy Selfish, Puckhead, Mrs. Luxford's Fish, Thirsty Souls, Rude Norton, Pino Rogeletti And The IUDs, and The Masons. Irreverent fun but historically now not much more than an amusing footnote.

BUSTED AT OZ LP (AUTUMN RECORDS)

Chicago entered the punk rock ring with this now classic live document of its early venue OZ recorded between March 9 and 11th, 1981, not long before it closed. Naked Raygun got the album started with some of their early more art punk work in the form of "Bomb Shelter" and "When The Screaming Stops". Following this Strike Under supplied the thud with "Fucking Uniforms" and featured Pierre Kezdy who would later join Naked Raygun. The Subverts did their "March Forth" before The Effigies brought the tension with "Quota". After DA performed "Fish Shit", Silver Abuse concluded side one with three songs, starting with Skrewdriver piss-take "Anti-Hot Dog" and concluding with another version of "Bomb Shelter". Side two brought more; Effigies, Subverts, Naked Raygun, DA, Strike Under, and Silver Abuse. The recording quality was high and gave you a real feel for the performances. The cover and inner were all photos of the bands and audience all expertly designed by Ann T. Brumbach.

BUY OR DIE... 1981 7" EP (RALPH RECORDS)

The descent into weirdness continued with Ralph Records' mail order freebie sampler "Buy Or Die", this the 1981 edition featuring four songs by four artists; Fred Frith, MX-80 Sound, Renaldo And The Loaf, and Tuxedomoon. Fred Frith supplied an overloaded instrumental called "A Spit In The Ocean" from the "Speechless" album. Next was MX-80 Sound with "Why Are We Here", a stabbing jazz punk song from the "Crowd Control" LP. The flip gave us the verbosity of Renaldo And The Loaf with "Honest Joe's Indian Gets The Goat On The Way To The Cowboys' Conga", an instrumental incantation from the "Songs From Swinging Larvae" album. Finally Tuxedomoon gave us "Incubus (Blue Suit)" from the "Desire" LP, a pulsating synth wave song reminiscent of early Ultravox. The cover art was as usual colourfully executed by Gary Panter (see: Screamers, The Plugz covers etc.) The 7" received a singular pressing to promote the then current releases on the label.

CARRY ON OI! LP (SECRET RECORDS)

"Garry Bushell presents for your penultimate stimulation, relaxation and exultation"... the third Oi! album (the second comes later in this chapter) continued the theme of living up to the working class yob stereotype, so much so even the liner notes were written in a Cockney accent. Gone was EMI and Deram, this release shifted to indie Secret. 'Punk Poet' Garry Johnson 'kicked' this off with the poem "United" (don't forget to drop the 't'). JJ All Stars (4 Skins) then did a ska instrumental before The Business railed against middle class trendy wankers. Infa Riot followed as well as; The Partisans, The Ejected, Peter & The Test Tube Babies, Blitz, and Last Resort ("No mess, no fuss, just pure impact"... pffft) closing side 1. Side 2 had more from most of that lot as well as The Gonads, 4 Skins, Red Alert, more 'punk poetry' from "Oi The Comrade", and finally some unintelligible drivel from Oi The Choir. Also issued in Scandinavia and Finland to rocketing glue sales.

CHUNKS LP (NEW ALLIANCE RECORDS)

The second collection from the Minutemen's label and "Chunks" was fleshed out to a full LP. In keeping with a style that would become fairly normal for Californian punk compilations, the more hardcore stuff was on side one while the artier stuff was on side two. The first side here had early Descendents ("Global Probing") along with Cheifs, Minutemen, Black Flag (with Dez), and Stains for a scorching whole seven minutes. The flip veered off with a hard left turn into the post-punk and experimental; Peer Group, Vox Pop, Ken (Starkey), Slivers, Saccharine Trust, Artless Entanglements (producer Spot's project), and Nig-Heist (Black Flag roadie Mugger's "wind up the punks" band). The result was a patchy but interesting snapshot into this little micro scene of bands, most of whom would later becoming legendary. With cover art by Raymond Pettibon ("Guns don't kill people. Songs do"), "Chunks" was reissued on CD, cassette and vinyl in 1988.

CLUB FOOT LP (SUBTERRANEAN RECORDS)

The album of the Club Foot, which was located at 2520 Third Street in San Francisco, and was created by a collective of five artists from New York who'd recently relocated to the city; Richard Kelly, JC Garrett, Cindy Buff, Katherine Robinson, and Richard Edson (Sonic Youth's first drummer). the intention was to combine "high art values" with the "vitality of underground performance art". This was not a live album though, recorded at Subterranean Studios with a revolving door of musicians, and featured; Longshoremen (with three members of Pink Section), Alterboys, Club Foot Orchestra, Naked City, and Bay Of Pigs (with Joseph T. Jacobs of Factrix), and it showed the city's connection to the beat generation in that it mainly consisted of jazz art instrumentals with obscure poetry, in places. Not unlistenable, Naked City's "Modern Jazz" was like driving around the city with Dirty Harry. Club Foot Orchestra would go onto score silent films. It was reissued in 2010.

CHUNKS

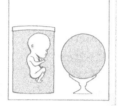

CLUB FOOT

THE D.T.s
TOY DOLLS
ALLERGIC TO CATS
RED ALERT
ZILCHO BABES
GENOCIDE EXIT

COMPILATION N.E.1

THE CRIME
THE FASHIONABLE IMPURE
PRESENTED BY
RHYTHM METHODISTS
THE CULT

DURHAM BOOK CENTRE

24 HOURS
HIGH SPEED HEROES
REMNANTS OF WARSAW
THE SUSPECTS
ZULU 'N' THE HEARTACHES
NEGATIVE THROB

CONNECTED

WITH BLACK MARKET BABY-
THE DARK-TOMMY KEENE
NIGHTMAN-THE NURSES
THE SLICKEE BOYS
THE VELVET MONKEYS

2 TONE

BAD MANNERS
THE BEAT
THE BODYSNATCHERS
MADNESS
THE SELECTER
SPECIALS

DANCE CRAZE

THE BEST OF BRITISH SKA...LIVE!

DO THE MARU

COMPILATION N.E.1 LP (GUARDIAN RECORDS N' TAPES)

A showcase of local talent from Sunderland in England's North East from the "Sunderland Musicians Collective". Sixteen songs from sixteen bands; 24 Hours, Allergic To Cats, Zilcho Babes, Rhythm Methodists, Suspects, Remnants Of Warsaw, Red Alert, The Fashionable Impure, Toy Dolls, D.T.'s, Negative Throb, Zulu 'n' The Heartaches, Genocide Exit, The Crime, The Cult, and High Speed Heroes. Notable from a punk perspective for early rare recordings from Red Alert ("In Britain") and Toy Dolls ("Worky Ticket"), but also a source of interest was the inclusion of Frankie Stubbs (of Leatherface) early band Remnants Of Warsaw and their only vinyl output in the form of "Arctotis Sloath Part 1 & 2", a brooding post-punk entry. The rest of the compilation was a mixed bag of styles so typical of post-punk Britain. The cover featured the band names pasted over a photo of Durham Book Centre in Sunderland that was run by Ann Dumble, apparently also responsible for the sleeve.

CONNECTED LP (LIMP RECORDS)

The third and final compilation from Washington DC's Limp Records run by Skip Groff of Yesterday & Today Records showcasing local bands and songs from his label. With two songs each by seven bands, the album was opened by Tommy Keene with the title song from his debut power pop album "Strange Alliance". More of the same followed with a more rock edge from Nightman, who were the majority of Tommy Keene's band on his aforementioned record. Next up were The Slickee Boys with "Connected" (see title) with their catchy new wave rock. The Dark followed with duo female vocals over a 60s influenced power pop, while The Nurses and Velvet Monkeys both kept things in the same vein. Closing side one was Black Market Baby, by far the most punk rock band on the record with "World At War", which didn't appear elsewhere until much later, and on side two they supplied "America's Youth" from their first 7". "Connected" had two pressings with different colour schemes.

DANCE CRAZE LP (TWO-TONE RECORDS)

The soundtrack to the film of the same year that documented
the energetic live performances of the 2-Tone movement.
Filmed around the U.K. in 1980 by American director Joe
Massot, the film was originally going to be about Madness
but was expanded to also feature; The Specials, The Beat,
Bad Manners, The Selecter, and The Bodysnatchers. It only
aired in theatres for what seemed like a few days on release
but somehow I managed to see it in that short window in an
almost empty cinema. The hits-aplenty recordings on the LP
were high quality and really captured the energy, and each
song also segued into the next to enhance the feeling of
urgency. The cover art was a striking graphic of dancing
legs in dogtooth trousers and tassled loafers, while the
back cover featured stills from the film. Early copies
came with a six panel foldout poster of all six bands.
"Dance Craze" was released globally on all formats and has
been reissued numerous times since.

DO THE MARU 12" (OBJECT MUSIC)

For its last compilation, and one of its last releases,
Manchester's Object music delved into the experimental synth
direction with this four song mini 12". First up was Steve
Solamar, Object's founder and of band Spherical Objects,
with "Forewarned", a jarring instrumental soundscape. Next
up was 41 Degrees aka Kevin Eden of Object recording
artists Slight Seconds with "Just...My Crazy Mind", two
songs, one with more of a funky mesmerising feel, the other
a sort of flamenco space rock instrumental. The flip gave
us Roger Blackburn with "In Memory", another hypnotic knob
twiddling synth instrumental and a hypnotic stand out.
Finally The Noyes Brothers aka Steve Solamar and Steve Miro
with "Good Question", an instrumental full of synth noise,
violins and dogs barking. Soon after Solamar needed to end
the label, and failing to find a successor, discarded the
master tapes, underwent gender reassignment surgery and
moved to London for a career as a computer programmer.

FRANK JOHNSON'S FAVORITES LP (RALPH RECORDS)

For a label with a distinct anti-commercial sound to their
releases Ralph had to be one of the most promotion heavy
labels of the post-punk era and here was yet another label
sampler. The back cover stated that the songs for this
collection were chosen by Ralph Records' computer Frank
Johnson but whether they actually even had an office computer
was anyone's guess. This LP mainly contained songs from
7"s, with one unreleased song. The artists were the usual
Ralph suspects; The Residents, Snakefinger, Tuxedomoon,
MX-80 Sound, Yello, Fred Frith, Art Bears, and Renaldo And
The Loaf. If you're not familiar by now by even reading this
book you'll know that Ralph specialised in experimental art
bands and projects who created their own unique pieces, some
listenable, some unbearable and "Frank Johnson's Favorites"
was as good a place to start as any. The LP had a fairly
unimaginative sleeve and the trademark "Official Buy Or
Die innersleeve" with info on other releases on the label.

FUTUREROCK LP (FUTUREROCK RECORD)

A showcase of unsigned bands and "fresh material" from
Orange County gleaned from a competition run by music
store La Habra Music Center in conjunction with KROQ's
'Futurerock' radio show. After the opening poodle-haired
pop rock of Teeze came the baritone dark new wave of Exits
with "Nuclear Love". The Light and Dunham And Heard Band
then gave us some more pop rock before side one closed with
City Lights doing The Zombies' "Time Of The Season". The
second side began in new wave power pop territory with The
Reverbs and Bungie Chords before Scooter And The Big Men
and The Strohlers then made their sole vinyl appearance
with their new wave pop, before the reason for this album's
inclusion came in the form of RF7 who'd been picked for
the final slot on the album after vocalist Felix Alanis
submitted their debut 7" to the store for consideration and
they selected slow rocker "No One to Trust". The cover art
featured classic 'new wave' art with band info on the back.

RALPH RECORDS
presents
FRANK JOHNSON'S FAVORITES
featuring
THE RESIDENTS
SNAKEFINGER
TUXEDOMOON
MX-80 SOUND
YELLO
FRED FRITH
ART BEARS
RENALDO and the LOAF

FUTUREROCK

ha! ha! funny polis

defiant pose
the fegs
urban enemies
xs discharge

GROUCHO MARXIST

HELL COMES TO YOUR HOUSE

hemisbrain records

INTERNATIONAL RECORD SYNDICATE, INC.
I.R.S. GREATEST HITS VOLS. 2 & 3

ALTERNATIVE TV   THE FALL   WAZMO NARIZ   BUZZCOCKS
FLESHTONES   SECTOR 27   THE HUMANS   JOHN CALE   KLARK KENT
BRIAN JAMES   SQUEEZE   PATRICK D. MARTIN OXAFISH   CHELSEA
HENRY BADOWSKI   JOOLS HOLLAND   THE STRANGLERS   FASHION
                                       OINGO BOINGO   THE CRAMPS
                                                         THE DAMNED

KEATS
RIDES
A
HARLEY

HA! HA! FUNNY POLIS 7" EP (GROUCHO MARXIST RECORD CO:OPERATIVE)

The second release and compilation on this short-lived label that followed 1979's "Spectacular Commodity!" 7" EP. "Groucho Marxist", run by printer Tommy Kayes from Paisley in Scotland, to the west of Glasgow, was a member of a Clydeside Anarchist group. With a title designed to have a go at their local constabulary, the EP made the front cover of their local paper the "Paisley Daily Express" bearing the legend, "Police boss slams 'hatred' disc by Paisley anarchists." The anarchists in question were four local bands; The Fegs with "Mill Street Law And Order", X-S Discharge and "Lifted", "Fight" by Defiant Pose, and Urban Enemies with "Who Do You Hate". Musically very much still in the 1977 punk camp with rock and roll riffs and a snotty spirited bounce throughout, the cover featured a still of James Cagney from 1938's "Angels with Dirty Faces", track list on the back, along with the address of Rock Against Racism in London. Two EPs followed by Defiant Pose and X-S Discharge.

HELL COMES TO YOUR HOUSE LP (BEMISBRAIN RECORDS)

The murmurings from the dark hardcore corners of Southern Californian punk began to slowly seep out from the various 'burbs in the form of LPs like "Hell Comes To Your House", with its trick or treat theme aimed at scaring your parents, on Jimmy Bemis of Modern Warfare's label. The album, mainly recorded at O.C. Recorders between July and September 1981, opened with two early Social Distortion songs followed by the driving punk of; Legal Weapon, Red Cross, Modern Warfare, and the raging Secret Hate and Conservatives, and that was just side one. The flip took a darker turn to match all that smeared eyeliner and brought us three distinctly punk 45 Grave songs and then a lurching Christian Death before 100 Flowers, Rhino 39 and Super Heroines fleshed out side two. An updated LP was issued in the U.K. by Riot State (Riot City) a year later with a scrambled song list, the Red Cross song removed, the two Modern Warfare songs replaced with a different one and an Outer Circle song added.

I.R.S. GREATEST HITS VOLS. 2 & 3 2LP (I.R.S. RECORDS)

Following the mail order only volume 1 came this who's
who of I.R.S. bands with mainly singles, but also some
B-sides and album tracks by; Fleshtones, Brian James, Henry
Badowski, Alternative TV, Squeeze, Skafish, The Damned,
Klark Kent, The Stranglers, Chelsea, The Cramps, The Humans,
The Police, Sector 27, John Cale, Jools Holland, Payolas,
The Fall, Patrick D. Martin, Oingo Boingo, Buzzcocks,
Klark Kent, Wazmo Nariz, and Fashion, all with a song each.
Familiar punk favourites such as "Action Time Vision",
"Wait For The Blackout" and "Straighten Out" sat alongside
the lesser known, but the no less quality; "Sodium Pentathol
Negative", "I Live In The City" and "Jukebox". Issued in
a deluxe gatefold sleeve depicting I.R.S. records smashed
all over the floor, with printed inners with; photos, the
record sleeves in question, and band info. The double
album was only issued in the U.S. and Canada on release
but was reissued two years later with a different sleeve.

KEATS RIDES A HARLEY LP (HAPPY SQUID RECORDS)

The first full length LP release from The Urinals' label
where they collected like-minded bands, mainly from
Southern California, to produce a unique collection of
post-punk and experimental music that featured nine bands;
Earwigs, Toxic Shock, S Squad, Gun Club, Meat Puppets,
Leaving Trains, Tunneltones, Human Hands, and 100 Flowers.
Toxic Shock would later become Slovenly, Human Hands
featured members of the "Los Angeles Free Music Society"
as mentioned in the previous "Darker Skratcher" entry,
while 100 Flowers was the new name for The Urinals when
they changed musical direction. The Gun Club, Meat Puppets
and Leaving Trains songs were later re-recorded on their
own albums. A challenging listen at times, the LP was
issued with minimalist art and little information. It was
much later reissued on CD with an extra song by all nine
bands from the same sessions, plus most of their earlier
compilation "The Happy Squid Sampler" 7" EP.

LET THEM EAT JELLYBEANS! LP (ALTERNATIVE TENTACLES)

Sub-titled "17 Extracts From Americas Darker Side", this was arguably one of the most important of the early American hardcore compilations. With this and other early releases Jello Biafra of Dead Kennedys and his label Alternative Tentacles almost single-handedly introduced the U.S. and Europe to the U.S. punk underground. With side one handling hardcore and side two, the more artistic side of post-punk. The impressive line-up included; Flipper, D.O.A., Black Flag, Bad Brains, Dead Kennedys, Circle Jerks, Really Red, The Feederz, The Subhumans, Geza X, Bpeople, Wounds, The Offs, Anonymous, 1/2 Japanese, Christian Lunch, and Voice Farm. With striking cover art by Winston Smith (of Reagan as Marie-Antoinette referencing his favourite sweet treat), a foldout poster supplied photos, lyrics, info and a list of other bands to seek out both real and imagined (a hobby of Winston Smith was to flyer S.F. with flyers for fictitious bands). The album received over a dozen pressings.

LIFE IN THE EUROPEAN THEATRE LP (WEA/ELEKTRA RECORDS)

An anti-nuclear benefit where 50% of the artists' royalties were donated to a fund for projects opposing nuclear arms and power allocated by four anti-nuclear organisations, with the other 50% to directly to those organisations. Thirteen songs and bands featuring a host of familiar names and hits that opened with The Clash and "London Calling" (of course). The Jam continued the theme with "Little Boy Soldiers" before "I Am Your Flag" by The Beat and "Man At C&A" by The Specials. More paranoid chants followed from; XTC, Peter Gabriel, Ian Dury And The Blockheads, Madness, Bad Manners, The Stranglers ("Nuclear Device"), The Undertones, Echo & The Bunnymen, and The Au Pairs. A real zeitgeist record, even the small print on the back contained existential messages; "Handle your records carefully, they will then be playable up to, but like yourself, not outlast nuclear contamination." Ian Dury was replaced by The Doors(!?) for the U.S. version with different cover art (also pictured).

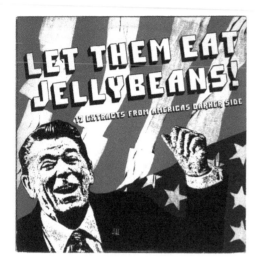

LET THEM EAT JELLYBEANS!
17 EXTRACTS FROM AMERICAS DARKER SIDE

THE JAM – THE CLASH – BAD MANNERS
SPECIALS – PETER GABRIEL – MADNESS
ECHO AND THE BUNNYMEN – THE BEAT
XTC – IAN DURY & THE BLOCKHEADS
STRANGLERS – UNDERTONES – AU PAIRS

LIFE IN THE EUROPEAN THEATRE

LIFE IN THE
EUROPEAN
THEATER
THE JAM
THE CLASH
BAD MANNERS
SPECIALS
PETER GABRIEL
THE DOORS
MADNESS
ECHO AND THE
BUNNYMEN
THE BEAT
X T C
STRANGLERS
UNDERTONES
AU PAIRS

MANDATORY MUSIC

PROCESS OF ELIMINATION E.P.

PROPAGANDA

EP

MANDATORY MUSIC LP (TREMOR RECORDS)

The second set from this Detroit label of local bands and this was an 8 band and 12 song collection that were originally intended as 7" releases but ended up compiled herein. The album began with The Boners and the deranged rock'n'roll punk of "Cool Teenager From The Planet X" that was like a mix of The Cramps and B52's. Cinecyde followed with "Enemy Man", a hard rocking punk hit that was like a Midwest Lewd. Former Creem associate editor and film maker Mark J. Norton then gave us his dark keyboard new wave before Service delivered their power pop on "Follow Me". Pre-Boners 1976 garage outfit The Pigs then got dragged from the vault for "Stay Away From Me Janet". The Cubes then closed side one with one of two of their synth new wave entries. Side two saw another song each from Cinecyde, Mark J. Norton, The Boners and The Cubes as well as Natasha, a new wave band fronted by rock violinist Sarana VerLin, and Burning Bibles with the rockin' "Johnny And The Jets".

PROCESS OF ELIMINATION 7" EP (TOUCH AND GO RECORDS)

One of the earliest of the D.I.Y. hardcore punk compilations and this 7" EP on Touch And Go that sprang out of the punk fanzine of the same name run by Tesco Vee and Dave Stimson, with Corey Rusk of Necros coming on board with Vee for the label side. "Process Of Elimination" showcased Michigan and Ohio bands with; Necros' "Bad Dream", the Meatmen's "Meatmen Stomp", "Lost Cause" by Negative Approach, Youth Patrol's "America's Power", Toxic Reasons with "Riot Squad", "I Can't Take It" by Violent Apathy, "Miniature Golf" by spoof band McDonalds, and concluded with The Fix with the roundhouse kick of "No Idols". As if to highlight how the small the hardcore scene was then, a few of the bands shared members. The EP with cover photograph of a jet fighter flying over the Egyptian desert during the Six Day War in 1967, with bodies laying on the floor on the back. The EP came with two inserts; one with lyrics and one with photos. Two thousand copies were pressed in total over three pressings.

PROPAGANDA 7" EP (PROPAGANDA RECORDS)

The first release on Finland's fanzine turned label "Propaganda". Before Finnish punk took a more hardcore approach this EP provided a snapshot into the more '77 influenced bands early on. First up was Opium with a slow number bordering on standard rock, and their only vinyl appearance. Nato then sped things up a little but remained very much in the garage punk department with a Clash style chorus. 013 then took the reins with a pacey pub rock punk that wouldn't have sounded out of place on Raw Records. The flip brought us the snappily named Aapeli Kissala Ja Antipatia with a slow folk meets anarcho sounding tune before Elastic Boredom and a plodding '77 style punk song. Finally Viimeiset Kiusaukset sped things up a bit in a hard rock meets punk way with an anthemic chorus. With its basic sleeve art and little info this is more interesting as a historical document than anything else. It was reissued in 2013 by Finnish label Svart Records.

PROPELLER PRODUCT 7" EP (PROPELLER PRODUCT)

The first compilation from Propeller Product of area Boston college bands recorded in late 1980 and 1981. The 7" EP opened with the first vinyl appearance from Neats with "Six" a post-punk song with swirling keyboards and repetitive vocals. Neats would soon to go on to record for Ace Of Hearts Records. People In Stores followed this with "Factory", a more robotic post-punk number with short clipped vocal lines. People In Stores released one 7" for Propeller directly after this release. CCCP-TV were first up on the flip side with more rhythmic post-punk with sharp stabbing guitar, keyboards and wandering vocals in the form of "Fear That Mindless". Finally Wild Stares gave us the layered and staggering post-punk meets college rock of "Moving Targets". Wild Stares released two 7"s for Propeller before relocating to Los Angeles. The cover depicted a simple graphic of a propeller with an aerial shot on the label as if looking down from a plane.

PUBLIC SERVICE LP (SMOKE SEVEN RECORDS)

The first LP from Felix Alanis of RF7's label from Canoga Park in Los Angeles. A five band collection of early Southern California hardcore bands, four of which recorded at Reels Of Sound in Ventura, CA by Mike Smith. Red Cross started proceedings with three songs that would also appear on their then upcoming LP "Born Innocent" for Smoke Seven. RF7 were up next with four songs, three of which soon appeared again on their LP "Weight of the World". Circle One saw out side one with two of their dramatic songs that were never released elsewhere. The earliest Bad Religion recordings opened side two, and even though all three also appeared on their debut 7", they were played here with far more energy and recorded with more clarity by Jim Mankey at Track Record. Disability, the only band here to not release anything else, gave us three songs of Red Cross style punk, with guitarist Gene Lipin soon forming Red Scare. Circle One returned to conclude the LP with two more rapid fire blasts.

RED SNERTS - THE SOUND OF GULCHER LP (GULCHER RECORDS)

The state of Indiana entered the punk wave conversation with this ambitious collection compiled by Jamie X. Jetson of The Jetsons that featured 16 bands with a song apiece; Amoebas In Chaos, the Gizmos, The Panics (with the snotty "Punks Are For Thugs"), The Jetsons, Mr. Science (Brad Garton of Dow Jones & The Industrials being experimental), The Defekts (great synth punk), A. Xax, E-In Brino (Paul Mahern with members of The Slammies and Truckadelics doing "Indianapolis"), Phil Hundley, Zero Boys, Dow Jones & The Industrials, Post Raisin Band, Last Four (4) Digits, Freddy & The Fruitloops, Bay-Root, and The Dancing Cigarettes. An eclectic mix of Mid-West punk era bands that contained some catchy and memorable songs, a lot of which were unique to this release. Zero Boys' early version of "New Generation" was notably the pre-Tufty "Livin' In The 80's" line-up and The Gizmos song "The Midwest Can Be Allright" was the musical answer to Dow Jones' "Can't Stand The Midwest".

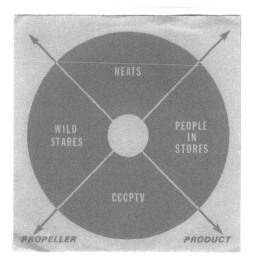

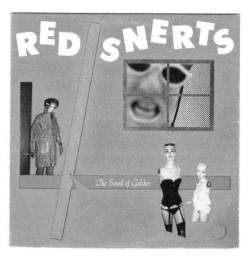

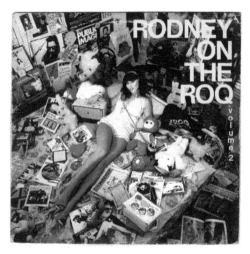

RED SPOT LP (SUBTERRANEAN RECORDS)

San Francisco's Subterranean Records continued their
campaign to document the artier side of S.F. post-punk as
well as the hardcore punk side, and 'Red Spot' was another
example of the artier side, featuring Minimal Man (with the
disturbing 8 minutes and 20 seconds of "Shower Sequence"),
Research Library, Micon (featuring Mike Fox of Tools and
Code Of Honor), Fried Abortions (a.k.a. Lennonburger with
the 48 second rant of "Joel Selvin", featuring Metal Mike
Saunders of Angry Samoans on drums, aimed at the San
Francisco music journalist, and very much in keeping with
the Saunders approach), Jed Speare (of Ultrasheen) & Eazy
Teeth, Animal Things ("Wanna Buy Some... fucking heroin?"),
The always great post-punk of Woundz, and finally Arsenal
(aka Amerikan Arsenal, later on the "Bullshit Detector 2"
2LP, who featured Dave King of Sleeping Dogs and designer
of the Crass logo). Pressed once (2,816 copies) on white
vinyl with a booklet that had a page each by the bands.

RISING STARS OF SAN FRANCISCO LP (WAR BRIDE RECORDS)

Sub-titled "Featuring 12 new sounds on the street", San
Francisco was a boomtown for music at this time and this
compilation centred more on the new wave end of things.
First up was Holy Stanton with the title track of her
synth new wave album. The rock'n'roll meets power pop
of Kingsnakes followed before Barry Beam attempted some
robotic pop wave and Roy Loney & the Phantom Movers managed
to totally kill momentum before New Romans injected some
keyboard back into the new wave. Side one ended with 415
recording artists The Impostors and "Sounds On The Street"
(see above), a pure power pop number in the vein of The
Nerves. The flip side started with The Readymades and the
first song from their 12" "Runnin' Too Fast". Then Holly
Stanton was back for a cover of "Black Is Black" before Eye
Protection chimed in with vocalist Andy Prieboy later of
Wall Of Voodoo. Fun Addicts (pop rock), Timmy Spence (synth
wave), and Pushups closed play with some sharp power pop.

RODNEY ON THE ROQ VOL. 2 LP (POSH BOY RECORDS)

This second installment of Rodney Bingenheimer's KROQ showcase of local talent showed that hardcore punk was very much in the ascendency in L.A. What better way to get on the radio than write a theme song for the show in question. Well that's what Target 13 did and kicked the album off with "Rodney On The Roq". Following them it was hits all the way from; Social Distortion rattle through "1945" then comes Shattered Faith, Black Flag ("Rise Above"), Minutemen, Red Cross, CH3, Agent Orange and "Dead Heroes" by Red Rockers... and that was just side one. The second side took the usual pop and new wave turn with Unit 3 With Venus (an 8 year old girl and her family), and then Stepmothers brought things back to the rock before Gleaming Spires and Little Girls did their synth pop, while Levi & The Rockats did a rock 'n' roll interlude before Twisted Roots and Geza X closed the LP in fine style. The LP came with Flipside fanzine 28 and was pressed a handful of times.

SAVOY SOUND WAVE GOODBYE LP (GO! RECORDS)

The first release on Go! Records was to commemorate the demise of the short-lived San Francsico club The Savoy Tivoli on 1434 Grant Avenue just up the road from the label. The S.F. art-punk scene was at its peak at this time and this was a live album that featured the moody Tuxedomoon, the marching post-punk of Cipher from Los Angeles, while the Sleepers closed side one with two atmospheric songs from their "Painless Nights" LP "Zenith / Theory". Side two kicked off with Earl Zero bringing the reggae before Snakefinger spin-off Skankin' Babylonians followed this with Prince Buster's "Rough Rider". Ultrasheen parped and clanked their way through two songs before Charles McMahon did a stint on the didgeridoo. Snakefinger got repetitious before Mutants stole the show, and Eazy Teeth made some noises. The cover was as artistic as you'd expect from label co-owners Olga Carpmill-Gerrard and her husband Gerry Gerrard, while the back sleeve and insert had band and crowd shots and band info.

SEATTLE SYNDROME - VOLUME ONE LP (ENGRAM RECORDS)

The title gave the game away here as to which part of the
world we're talking about on this collection of Seattle
area bands. First up was X-15 with the long-winded new wave
of "Vaporized" followed by the chunky punk of The Pudz.
Student Nurse ska'd it up with "Discover Your Feet" before
The Beakers did their spiky new wave and Jim Basnight (of
the Moberlys) played his smooth power pop. The Fastbacks
led by Lulu and Kim were up next featuring Duff, later
of Guns'n'Roses, and Kurt, later of Young Fresh Fellows,
before The Refuzors gave us the easily misunderstood "White
Power" before The Fartz delivered their "Campaign Speech"
and The 88's closed side one with some old rock'n'roll.
Side 2 took a left turn as usual with the new wave of The
Blackouts, The Macs (the stand-out synth slow burner "I'm
37"), Phillipo Scrooge fell all over the place on "Love Is
A Tractor", while Savant, Body Falling Downstairs, and K7SS
synth-off the album. Volume two followed two years later.

SOUNDTRACKS ZUM UNTERGANG LP (AGGRESSIVE ROCKPRODUKTIONEN)

"Soundtrack to the Downfall", the first release on
Aggressive Rock Productions and one of the first German
punk compilations to reach beyond its borders, featuring;
Middle Class Fantasies, Offensive Herbst 87, Hass, Aheads,
Slime, ZK, Razors, M.D. Blitz, Daily Terror, and Störtrupp,
all playing their own version of rapid fire hardcore based
on the U.K. punk model. There was some post-punk in the mix
from bands like Aheads, but seeing as all of the album was
German language it gave it its own distinct sound. 3,000
copies of the initial run were pressed but in 1983 the
Amtsgericht Tiergarten court in Berlin ruled that this and
the first Slime LP were "media harmful to young people" and
banned them with the second press of this LP beeped on the
first song "Helden" by Middle Class Fantasies and "Polizei-
SA-SS" by Slime. With a cover typically depicting war, being
pre-international hardcore punk scene, the "Soundtracks
Zum Untergang" came with a lyric sheet all in German.

SAVOY SOUND
WAVE GOODBYE

TUXEDOMOON CIPHER SLEEPERS
EARL ZERO SKANKIN' BABYLONIANS ULTRASHEEN CHARLES McMAHON SNAKEFINGER
MUTANTS EAZY TEETH

Seattle
Syndrome

VOLUME ONE

fifteen bands

erste
aggressive
rockproduktion

slime
middle class fantasies
hass
störtrupp
razors
zk
daily terror
aheads
offensive herbst
87
m.d.blitz

soundtracks
zum
untergang

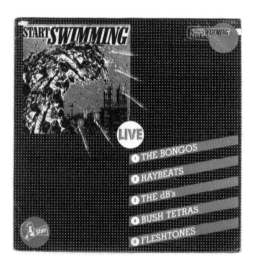

START SWIMMING

LIVE

1 THE BONGOS
2 RAYBEATS
3 THE dB's
4 BUSH TETRAS
5 FLESHTONES

sounds presents for your further inebriation
titillation and emancipation Oi 2

STRENGTH THRU
Oi!

featuring
SPLODGE
4-SKINS
INFA-RIOT
THE STRIKE
TOY DOLLS
COCK
SPARRER
LAST RESORT
+MANY MORE

TEST PATTERNS

RMA RESOLUTION A CHART 1946

THE FELONS · THE MOPEDS · THE STRIKERS · SWIFT KICK
· THE OOZKICKS · TRAINED ANIMAL · THE ZANTI MISFITS

START SWIMMING LP (STIFF AMERICA)

The vinyl document of a five U.S. band showcase called "Taking Liberties" recorded live at The Rainbow in Finsbury Park in London on 20th February 1981, that you could've attended for the princely sum of £2.99. Released on the short-lived New York branch of Stiff Records, all the bands were affiliated with Stiff, Fetish, Don't Fall Off The Mountain or I.R.S. Records, all labels in the business of promoting U.S. bands in the U.K. The gig and album both featured; the stomping new wave of The Bongos, the twanging guitars and keyboards of the surf-edged Raybeats and their instrumentals with titles like "Rise And Fall Of Flingel Bunt", the power pop of The dB's, who formed in New York but were all from Winston-Salem in North Carolina, the jarring post-punk of Bush Tetras and finally garage rockers The Fleshtones with their retro rock'n'roll with keyboards. With sleeve art very much of its time "Start Swimming" was pressed only once with just as many promo stamped copies.

STRENGTH THRU OI! LP (DERAM/DECCA RECORDS)

Although alphabetically the third album came earlier in this chapter, this was the second installment with infamous dodgy skinhead Nicky Crane on the cover and the edgy title borrowed off the Nazis. Of course by volume two there were actual 'Oi!' bands and most of the first LP's punk rabble were long gone with only two bands remaining from the first. The "Oi!" mythology was further solidified here with three underdog class conscious 'poems' by Garry Johnson rhyming yobs with jobs and someone going by the name of Barney Rubble. The music was noticeably more primitive and plodding than the first LP from the likes of; 4-Skins, The Strike, Infa Riot, The Last Resort, Criminal Class, The Toy Dolls, Cock Sparrer, Splodge, and the Shaven Heads, with an average of two 'songs' each. Bushell's liner notes with tripe like, "The Union Jack is our flag not theirs" make it all make sense that he joined UKIP years later, and the back cover sported a variety of bald goons being hilarious.

Produced by
Robbie Fields
℗ & © 1981
Posh Boy Records
An SST/Posh Boy
Co-Production
Release Date:
August 1, 1981

33⅓ RPM
PBS-120-A
Covina High
Music (BMI)

THE FUTURE LOOKS BRIGHT
SHATTERED FAITH: 1. ANOTHER DAY PASSES 2. THE VERDICT
3. TRILOGY; TSOL: 4. PEACE THROUGH POWER
5. ABOLISH GOVERNMENT/SILENT MAJORITY
SOCIAL DISTORTION: 6. PLAYPEN 7. JUSTICE FOR ALL
CH 3: 8. WAITING IN THE WINGS 9. MANZANAR
NOT FOR SALE/STRICTLY FOR
PROMOTION ONLY
AVAILABLE TO PUBLIC AS
PBC 120 CASSETTE

1-11 Produced
by Spot
12-14 Produced
by Spot & Geza X
℗ 1981
SST Records
An SST/Posh Boy
Co-Production

33⅓ RPM
PBS-120-B
1-8 New Alliance
Music (BMI)
9-15 SST Music
(BMI)

THE FUTURE LOOKS BRIGHT
MINUTEMEN: 1. THE PUNCH LINE, WARFARE, STRAIGHT JACKET,
TENSION; DESCENDENTS: 2. HEY, HEY, MY DAD SUCKS,
I LIKE FOOD, DER WIENERSCHNITZEL
℗ 1981 NEW ALLIANCE RECORDS
SACCHARINE TRUST: 3. WE DON'T NEED FREEDOM,
MAD AT THE COMPANY, SUCCESS AND FAILURE;
BLACK FLAG: 4. SIX PACK 5. I'VE HEARD
IT BEFORE 6. AMERICAN WASTE;
STAINS: 7. PRETTY GIRLS
FOR INFORMATION ON SST RECORDS
WRITE P.O. BOX 1
LAWNDALE, CA 90260

TEST PATTERNS LP (HI-TEST RECORDS)

An eclectic mix of new wave bands from St. Louis, Missouri, put together by John Korst (aka John the Mailman) of St. Louis' Jet Lag fanzine (with Steve Pick). The pair went about spreading the word about their local scene by first setting up a phone line the "New Wave Information Line" where people could find out about upcoming events, but then John the Postman set about compiling this document. "Test Patterns" opened with the ska of The Felons, followed by the power pop of The Zanti Misfits. Trained Animal played some synth new wave and featured members who soon went onto spoof far right band White Pride. The Mopeds continued the new wave theme with the catchy "Woe Is Me" before a kicking theme kicks in with three bands; The Oozkicks, Swift Kick (with the catchy "Crushin' Russian Girl"), and The Strikers (with "Kick Around"), each with a unique punk wave approach. The seven bands all contributed two songs each and the LP with a TV theme came with an insert with band info and photos.

THE FUTURE LOOKS BRIGHT LP (POSH BOY RECORDS / SST RECORDS)

A promotional LP with Posh Boy bands on one side and SST bands on the other that only received a one-off pressing of 500 for promotional mail outs to radio stations and music mags, that was also officially released on cassette at this time. The Posh Boy material was a blend of released and unreleased material and first up was Shattered Faith with three then unreleased early songs, before T.S.O.L. With "Abolish Government/Silent Majority" and the then unreleased "Peace Through Power". Social Distortion then gave us "Playpen" and the then unreleased "Justice For All" before CH3 closed side one with two songs from their debut 12". On the flip all of the SST material was released; Minutemen (from "The Punch Line"), Descendents (songs from "Fat E.P." That sounded like a different mix), Saccharine Trust (from "Paganicons"), Black Flag (the "Six Pack" 7") and Stains ("Pretty Girls"). The LP was re-worked as a Posh Boy only LP in 1987 as "The Future Looks Brighter".

TRAP SAMPLER LP (TRAP RECORDS)

Following on from 1980's "10-29-79" compilation this was the second and last compilation from Greg Sage of Wipers' Trap Records recorded at Wave Studio in Vancouver, Washington between February and March 1981. A four band, all Portland, Oregon affair from; Wipers, Napalm Beach (originally from Longview, Washington), Pell Mell, and Drum Bunny. Two songs from the slow burning and hypnotic Wipers began proceedings with; "My Vengeance" and "The Story". Following this Napalm Beach brought us three songs including the great surf-edged song "The Angels Ride" where you can hear how Napalm Beach and Wipers were mutually influential to each other. Side two brought us two each from Pell Mell and Drum Bunny, Pell Mell supplying two long post-punk instrumentals while Drum Bunny gave us their only recording of a more jerky post-punk with female vocals. The "Trap Sampler" was housed in a simple fold-over piece of paper with arty new wave cover art and track list.

THE UP ANOTHER OCTAVE TRANSMISSION LP (UP ANOTHER RECORDS)

An O.C. showcase of local talent in conjunction with radio station KNAC 105.5 sub-titled, "A Compilation of Orange County Nu Music Artists". Side one began with Fahrenheit supplying a synth instrumental from members of Berlin, during an early hiatus, along with future Der Stab vocalist Keith Walsh. Craig Sibley followed them with more of the same before Berlin then offered "Talk Talk Video" from their first album long before chart fame. Null And Void, Nu Beams, and Videos filled out side one with more synth new wave. Side two got more interesting with The Barbies with some poppy new wave then The Vectors (known for "Death To Disco") with some snotty punk rock before the most notable aspect of the record; The Detours, featuring Rikk Agnew and Casey Royer, later of Adolescents and D.I., doing a great early version of "Hang Ten In East Berlin". The rest of the side featured a variety of catchy and memorable punk wave O.C. sounds from Beat-E-O's, Removed, Finesse, Tactics and The End.

URGH! A MUSIC WAR 2LP (A&M RECORDS)

The double live album soundtrack to the live footage film
of the same name that was like a who's who of 1981 new wave;
The Police, Wall Of Voodoo, Toyah Wilcox, OMD, Oingo Boingo,
XTC, The Members, Go-Go's, Klaus Nomi, Athletic Spizz '80,
The Alley Cats, Jools Holland, Steel Pulse, Devo, Echo And
The Bunnymen, The Au Pairs, The Cramps, Joan Jett & The
Blackhearts, Pere Ubu, Gary Numan, Fleshtones, Gang Of
Four, John Otway, 999, X, Magazine, and Skafish. The movie/
album was recorded in very high quality at various gigs in
Los Angeles (Santa Monica and Hollywood), New York, Paris,
San Diego, London and Portsmouth, and really captured the
mood and music of the day and helped put a cinematic moving
image to the sounds in a time long before the internet.
Whereas the record had 27 songs the film had 37 and;
Dead Kennedys, Chelsea, John Cooper Clarke, Surf Punks,
Invisible Sex, Splodgenessabounds, and UB40 (as well as two
more Police and a Klaus Nomi songs) did not make the LP.

VANCOUVER INDEPENDENCE LP (FRIENDS RECORDS)

The only compilation on Vancouver's Friends Records, home
to D.O.A. and Subhumans, with a collection of mainly obscure
and short-lived bands. The usual set of eclectic sounds
from Vancouver opening with "Behind the Smile" by the most
well known band here; Subhumans, followed by the new wave
pop of Metros and the synth weirdness of Si Monkey. No Exit
then ran through the sloppy punk of "No Excuse" featuring
a young J.J. Pearson later of Toxic Reasons, before The
Droogs (not the L.A. band) did their 60s influenced keyboard
new wave. Vancouver's resident ska band B-Sides then gave
us "Spy Vs Spy" based on the James Bond theme and clearly
influenced by The Selecter's version of "James Bond".
M.E.C. (Melodic Energy Commission) closed out side one
with their synth and theremin laced hippie space rock. All
the bands got a second song on side two apart from M.E.C.,
replaced by Singing Cowboys, who did a spaced out synth
instrumental. The LP came with a small insert with info.

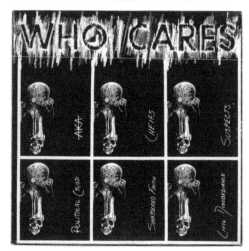

FLIPSIDE
FANZINE
ISSUES
#21/#28/#35

FROM "RODNEY
ON THE ROQ"
VOLUMES 1-3
(POSH BOY)

WAKE THE DEAD FLEXI (TAKE IT! MAGAZINE)

The fifth flexi that came with the fifth issue of Boston's Take It! punk wave magazine (a large format newsprint paper like the U.K. music weeklies) but the first that was a compilation as opposed to a split. Featuring; Dead Kennedys, Flipper, and Angry Samoans in line with the issue's content. Dead Kennedys were up first with a different mix of "Nazi Punks Fuck Off" that wasn't available elsewhere. Flipper then gave us "The Game's Got A Price" that sounds like the music from "Ha Ha Ha" sped up with garbled and unintelligible computer vocals. Angry Samoans then supplied two different takes of "Steaknife" and "Lights Out" to the versions on their belligerent California hardcore classic "Back From Samoa", with F-words fully bleeped out all over the place. The short and sharp flexi concluded with an unknown eleven year old kid banging on guitar singing the "Take It!" theme song, presumably the editors younger brother. An interesting obscurity.

WHO CARES LP (AMERICAN STANDARD RECORDS)

An excellent showcase from American Standard (who later released The Joneses "Criminals" 12") that centred around the Orange County beach punk bands. First up was AKA with their catchy punk that featured Steve Houston of The Joneses and Greg Zellner later of Radio Head (not the U.K. band) on vocals. The Cheifs (sic) followed with a similar beach sound with Bob Glass(l)ey fresh from Portland, as well as Jerry Koskie and Rabbit from the Simpletones. Shattered Faith stepped up next with their signature Huntington Beach punk followed by Suspects who picked up the pace before Civil Disobedience then upped the ante into hardcore even more before Political Crap, featuring skater Duane Peters on vocals, slowed things back down with a tuneful but no less sneering punk. All bands supplied three songs recorded in March 1981 at Sound Off Studios in Compton, apart from AKA with one song and Suspects with four. The cover featured some existential foetal art with band info on the back.

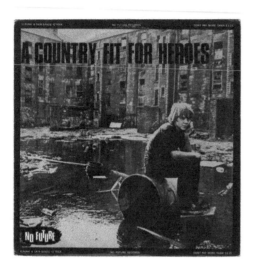

1982

A COUNTRY FIT FOR HEROES LP (NO FUTURE RECORDS)

Swamped in demo tapes from their new found success, No
Future from Malvern in Worcestershire put together this
cut price sampler of emerging talent from the U.K. opened
by Southport's Blitzkrieg with their anthemic punk before
The Violators from Chapel-en-le-Frith offered two songs;
one in the Vice Squad model, the other a primal brick wall
pounder. Hostile Youth's fast offering became their only
released song, while Worcester locals The Samples showed
enough promise that they soon had a 7" on No Future. Side
one closed with an early slow version of "Jerusalem" by One
Way System. Attak from Derbyshire started side two followed
by; Protest from Manchester, Nuneaton's Crux, Distortion
from Cumbria, Swansea's Pseudo Sadists, and Chaotic Youth
from Ayrshire, all showcasing how a definitive sound was
emerging across the U.K. in 1982. The LP was issued in a
budget 12" sleeve sporting a typical urban decay cover theme.

A FRESH SELECTION LP (FRESH RECORDS)

Sub-titled "A Compilation of Fresh Records Singles", Fresh
started life in Alex Howe's "Wretched Records" stall in
London's Soho Market, and some of the resulting releases were
documented a few years later on this eclectic Collection.
Side one was mix of new wave and rock'n'roll with Dumb
Blondes, Cuddly Toys (the only band with two songs), The
Igloos, Family Fodder, Wilko Johnson (playing Dr. Feelgood's
"Back In The Night" from a bonus 7" issued with Fresh LP "Ice
On The Motorway" in 1980), and Bernie Torme (covering The
Kinks' "All Day And All Of The Night"). Side two featured
the label's more punk entries with; UK Decay, Manufactured
Romance, The Dark, The Wall, J.C.'s Mainmen, Menace, and
The Art Attacks (see also the 1977 compilations: "Live at
the Vortex" and "Streets"). The sleeve had a freshening up
theme with song info and the label's discography on the rear.

AMERICAN YOUTH REPORT LP (INVASION RECORDS)

Southern California Youth Report to be more precise. This collection from the short-lived Invasion Records, a Bomp subsidiary, gave us a snapshot into the new hardcore goings on from this neck of the woods with sixteen bands and songs, seven of which were then unreleased. "American Youth Report" boasted an impressive roster of talent; Modern Warfare, Bad Religion, Channel 3, Adolescents, Lost Cause, Legal Weapon, Flesheaters, Rhino 39, Hypnotics, Descendents, M.I.A. (from when they were still a Las Vegas band), T.S.O.L., Shattered Faith, Minutemen, RF7, and Red Kross. Whereas some of this was like a best of L.A. hardcore, there were also some less obvious songs from the likes of Lost Cause and Hypnotics. The Diane Zincavage designed cover depicted a mocked up newspaper with photos by Glen E. Friedman and Ed Colver (his work throughout on the great insert), although lorem ipsum replaced actual text. Bruce Pavitt of Sub Pop fanzine supplied the liner notes.

AMUCK LP (PLACEBO RECORDS)

The first of the Placebo Records compilations out of Phoenix, Arizona. After the weird intro by Dali's Daughter, JFA gave us the unreleased "Bouncer" before Meat Puppets ran through the also unreleased and chaotic "Unpleasant". Paris 1942 then offered a punk cover of The Modern Lovers' "She Cracked", while Killer Pussy dashed through a frantic B-52's style number. Sun City Girls were remarkably straight up punk, then Victory Acres were on the 45 Grave side of things (featuring two Meat Puppets), Happy People supplied the synth, Soylent Greene took us back to hardcore, while Precious Secrets' "I Wanna Know" was a stand out punk number, and Teds (with Greg Hynes of Mighty Sphincter on drums) supplied some catchy new wave. As was the style of the day, side two went more esoteric with experimental, art rock and even jazz from; International Language, Knebnagauje, Tone Set, Poet's Corner, Mask, and Destruction. This somewhat overlooked gem came with a typed insert with band info.

AUTO GLAMOUR SOUND 2 X 7" EP (HOSPITAL RECORDS)

The only compilation from this label from Cincinnati, Ohio, and it was a double 7" that began with a two song side of B.P.A. (Bowling Pros Of America, later By-Products Of America) with some art-damaged jazz punk with free form guitar and a persistent rhythm section. The flip then gave us three songs from Cointelpro, which was essentially the same band with the same jazzed out post-punk that seemed to be simultaneously channelling earlier Ohio art bands and also pointing to underground music that was yet to come. Disc two was entirely dedicated to the band 11,000 Stitches, that featured label owner David Lewis, with four songs of a similar marching but broken ear irritant, not totally dissimilar to locals Pere Ubu, and also sharing members with the other bands here. The 29 minute long double 7" came in a screen printed six panel single-sided foldout sleeve with minimalist art and lyrics. It was reissued as an expanded CD in 2005.

BACK ON THE STREETS 7" EP (SECRET RECORDS)

What with having too much outstanding material for "Oi! Oi! That's Yer Lot!" (see page 148) Ol' Gaz Bushell and Secret Records were forced to release an accompanying 7" as an extra special treat. Venom opened up the plod with a song about the plod, "Where's Dock Green?" followed by The Strike with "Victim", a low IQ terrace sing-along about havin' a dust up and havin' a larf. Side two kicked off with the East End Badoes and "The Way It's Got To Be", which picked up the pace a bit but they still sounded like they were struggling, and just as you were starting to think this was all a parody of Oi! the highlight of the EP arrived in the form of members of anarcho band Chumbawamba masquerading as Oi band "Skin Disease" and playing a basic riff and shouting "I'm Thick" 72 times, which pretty much summed it all up. The EP was concluded by Angela Rippon's Bum and "Fight For Your Lives" which sounded like a high school band's first practice trying to work out a Cockney Rejects song.

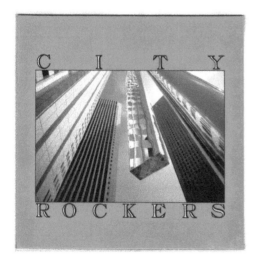

BEST OF RALPH 2LP (RALPH RECORDS)

The highlights of the Ralph Records house of bands to date all in one place over two albums, as the cover states; "Selections on sides one and two are the result of a poll of our mail order customers favorites. Selections on sides three and four were chosen by the staff of Ralph Records". Snakefinger began proceedings with a faithful cover of Kraftwerk's "The Model". After this; The Residents, Fred Frith, Tuxedomoon, Yello, Art Bears, Mx-80 Sound, and Renaldo & The Loaf, all with varying amounts of entries totalling twenty seven. If you're not familiar with the label then this was probably the best place to start as it offered a broad insight into the Residents' label's output from the seventies on. Ralph Records was a label to approach with an open mind as no two artists were the same and the results were often of a mind-melting artistic nature. The cover art was suitably nondescript and the package came with two "Buy Or Die" inner sleeves.

BRITANNIA WAIVES THE RULES 12" (SECRET RECORDS)

A fairly pointless three band and three song 12" at the height of the 1982 UK punk cash-in from Secret Records. Side A was simply a two minute Exploited song "Y.O.P." (about the then government scheme the "Youth Opportunities Program") and the flip side had two more; Chron Gen with the studio version of "Clouded Eyes", the melodic stand out here. Finally, closing this blink-and-you've-missed-it EP was Infa-Riot and "Feel The Rage" who sounded more like the Angelic Upstarts here. The 12" came wrapped in some typically cheesy 'punk' art of the day depicting a young punk lady as Britannia in attire fitting for a drooling mob of studded glue bag youth. A skull and crossbones featured on the front and back purely as sales device, along with hidden male genitalia on the front just to keep the tone suitably base for the target demographic. Three live band photos on the reverse completed the picture of this EP that must've been thrown together in an afternoon.

BULLSHIT DETECTOR TWO 2LP (CRASS RECORDS)

Volume two of Crass' demo tape D.I.Y. showcase opened
with the irritating Waiting For Bardot, as if to warn you
that you're about to be subjected to double punishment of
bedroom tape hell. After this though, things looked up with
Omega Tribe, before Suspects who sounded like John Cooper
Clarke fronting a reggae band. The following 36 bands and
songs were a hit and miss selection of U.K. anarcho punk,
some of whom went onto be punk rock household names. The
rest of the bands were as follows; Your Funeral, Deformed,
Krondstadt Uprising, No Label, The Rejected, Boffo, XS,
Polemic Attack, A. Gardener, Toxic, 1984, Unknown Artist,
Toxik Ephex, Sic, Molitov Cocktail, Naked, Endangered
Species, Pseudo Sadists, Total Chaos, Dougie, St. Vitus
Dancers, Stegz, Metro Youth, Normality Complex, Youth In
Asia, Riot Squad, Destructors, The Pits, The Bored, Toby
Kettle, Chumbawamba, Passion Killers, and Amerikan Arsenal.
The standard six panel foldout poster supplied the info.

BURNING AMBITIONS: A HISTORY OF PUNK 2LP (CHERRY RED)

For some like me who were a little younger than the '77
punks, this double album served as a good education about
what had come before. Running chronologically through 38
bands and songs the collection included; Buzzcocks, The
Fall, Wire, Alternative TV, 101'ers, 999, Adverts, Dave
Goodman And Friends, Slaughter And The Dogs, Stranglers,
Generation X, Vibrators, X Ray Spex, Swell Maps, The
Saints, Heartbreakers, Eater, Lurkers, Adam And The Ants,
The Damned, Boomtown Rats, Spizz Energi, The Ruts, Sham
69, UK Subs, Cockney Rejects, Killing Joke, Anti-Pasti,
Dead Kennedys, The Exploited, Vice Squad, The Business,
Partisans, Blitz, GBH, Disorder, Attila The Stockbroker,
and Angelic Upstarts. Even though key bands such as; Sex
Pistols, The Jam, The Clash and The Banshees weren't here,
it was still a good cross-section of mainly U.K. punk. The
gatefold sleeve featured a punk Sgt. Peppers theme while
the inside was a collage with liner notes by Chris Salewicz.

CITY ROCKERS LP (CITY ROCKER RECORDS)

The first compilation from Tokyo punk label City Rocker featured four Japanese bands starting with the debut vinyl appearance from legendary hardcore band Gauze, with ten pounding songs that spanned nearly all of side one, none of which breached the two minute mark and taking a similar approach to Dead Kennedys and Discharge. This brevity allowed the post-punk of Isolation to provide three songs, two of which totalled nearly eleven minutes in the melancholy vein of Joy Division, with a short stabbing instrumental "Play Loud" sandwiched in-between. Side two gave us three songs of the blend of post-punk and death rock of Radical who played in the style of Christian Death meets Part One. Nursery Rhyme concluded the LP with two songs that continued the post-punk theme (making Gauze the odd band out here) in PiL style with their self-titled closing theme song clocking in at seven and a half minutes. The sleeve featured gleaming city buildings with photos on the rear.

CLEVELAND CONFIDENTIAL LP (TERMINAL RECORDS)

Mike Hudson of the Pagans with his Cleveland, Ohio showcase following on from the 1980 7" of the same name. The album opened with Womanhaters who exuded a Stooges feel before Severe hit us with some memorable punk rock with "Her Name Was Jane" and then Menthol Wars with more stabbing keyboard punk. The first three bands all featured members of the Pagans. After this trio Defnics delivered some nihilistic belligerence before the Dark made their vinyl debut with slow burner "I Can Wait". Styrenes (sloppy), Invisibles (live lo-fi) and Lab Rats ("Cover Song End Of Side One" aka Shocking Blue's "Venus") closed out side one. Side two brought us Keith Matic and some frantic Sixties garage sounding punk, Jazz Destroyers with a short, damaged fuzzed up tune entitled "Love Meant To Die" and Offbeats with the fast and snappy "I'm Confused". Pagans then took the stage with "Boy Can I Dance Good" followed by more art by Red Decade, John Lovsin and Easter Monkeys. The LP had basic artwork with no info.

EASTERN FRONT

SATURDAY JULY 25   11 AM to 6 PM   SUNDAY JULY 26

D.O.A.	THE SLITS
FLIPPER	SNAKEFINGER
T.S.O.L.	THE OFFS
THE LEWD	EARL ZERO
WAR ZONE	MIDDLE CLASS
THE FIX	THE WOUNDS
7 SECONDS	TOILING MIDGETS
SIC PLEASURE	TANKS
ANTI-L.A.	

AQUATIC PARK BERKELEY   3rd St & BANCROFT WAY

tickets available at bass

©PEPE MORENO

POSTER FOR EASTERN FRONT FESTIVAL

EASTERN FRONT

D.O.A.   FLIPPER
THE OFFS   T.S.O.L.
TOILING MIDGETS   THE LEWD
                THE WOUNDS
WAR ZONE   TANKS

The EASTERN FRONT: produced by Wes Robinson   Mastered at Quad-Tech, Hollywood, Calif., by Mike Zeltner.
SOUND AMPLIFICATION: Third Ear Sound Co.   K2 SANOBLAST RECORDS, 1755 North Hollywood, CA 90028.
STAGE MANAGER: Rodney Readie   Distributed through: JEM, GREENWORLD, ROUGHTRADE,
PHOTOGRAPHY: Steve Harris, Nancy Nadel   SKY DISC and DISC TRADING CO.
ASSOCIATED PRODUCER: East Bay Ray   MUSIC RECORDED, PRODUCED AND MIXED by Tom Mallon
ASSOCIATE EXECUTIVE PRODUCER: Chris Peiser   COLLAGE: Wes Robinson
Album Design: Pepe Moreno; and Thanks to Ron Blakeman and Suzanne Odeanon

DJ Promotional
Copy

Extracts from
WARGASM (PAX 4)

Side 1   45 rpm

HEY JO : CAPTAIN SENSIBLE
(Burns - Rock Music Co. Ltd) 3'10

KINKY SEX MAKES THE WORLD/
GO ROUND : DEAD KENNEDYS
(Dead Kennedys -
Virgin Music) 4'17

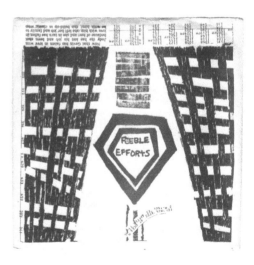

FEEBLE
EFFORTS

EASTERN FRONT LP (ICI SANOBLAST)

The album to document the "Eastern Front" matinee Festival
that took place on Friday and Saturday July 25th and 26th 1981
at Aquatic Park at 3rd Street and Bancroft Way, Berkeley,
California. The LP opened with two D.O.A. songs; "Unknown"
and "Fucked Up Baby". T.S.O.L. followed with "Love Story"
and The Lewd with "Suburban Prodigy". Jeff Bale's (of MRR)
War Zone then delivered two short, sharp hardcore songs
before Flipper concluded side one with "Ever" that falls
apart in glorious fashion over an audience bully, with the
band abusing the individual in rhyme; "Alright, let's have
a fight, beat on his ass with a piece of broken glass". Side
two saw The Offs bring the ska with "One More Shot" then The
Wounds, Tanks, and Toiling Midgets rounded out the album in
post-punk style. The sleeve depicted a Kamikaze pilot as
featured on the festival poster drawn by Pepe Moreno. The
festival also included The Fix, 7 Seconds, Sick Pleasure,
Anti, The Slits, Snakefinger, Earl Zero and Middle Class.

FEEBLE EFFORTS 7" EP (NEW ALLIANCE RECORDS)

The third compilation and eighth release from this label
founded by D. Boon and Mike Watt of Minutemen, along with
friend Martin Tamburovich, and this was a nine song set
from some of their friends with D.I.Y. home "recordings
made on cassette tape recorders" with varying degrees of
success. All of this project was art experimentation in its
rawest form and featured; Ken Starkey (Plebs), Jack Brewer
(Saccharine Trust), Plebs, D. Boon (Minutemen), Invisible
Chains, Fluid, Sec, Gary Jacobelly, Tony Platon, and Debt
Of Nature. Jack Brewer's song "A Need" was a listenable
Minutemen style song, whereas D. Boon's effort was machine
noise with him singing in the background, sounding more
like something from the Eraserhead soundtrack. Invisible
Chains was a full band in a practice room situation as were
Plebs with their jazz jam "A Day At The Track". The cover
was suitably artistic with typed track list on the reverse,
all in keeping with the 'New Alliance' house style.

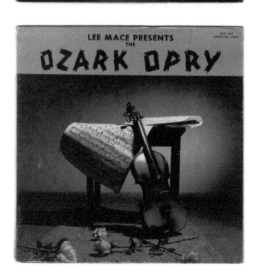

FLEX YOUR HEAD LP (DISCHORD RECORDS)

Washington D.C. hardcore announced itself to the world with this legendary LP featuring 11 bands and 36 songs; The Teen Idles, Untouchables, State Of Alert, Minor Threat, Government Issue, Youth Brigade, Red C, Void, Iron Cross, Artificial Peace, and Deadline all pounded their way through this compilation that soon became a punk rock household name. The LP came in four different sleeves, the first two on over-printed stock sleeves usually used by gospel and country artists, the first press featuring a violin, the second a wheat field. I asked Dischord co-owner, designer and Minor Threat drummer Jeff Nelson about the stock sleeves;

"We chose the first two covers for "Flex Your Head" because we thought they were funny (mostly the violin cover) and because they were all we could afford. These were among the stock covers offered by Nashville Record Productions where we got our records pressed. This was in the days when LP jackets where made of unprinted, stiff cardboard with paper "slicks" glued first onto the front (which wrapped around the spine, top, and bottom) and then secondarily onto the back. You can easily see this secondary slick on the first two pressings of "Flex Your Head." And this method of fabricating an LP jacket is how the Beatles "Butcher Cover" came to be here in the USA. After the original cover (showing the Beatles in white butcher smocks, holding hunks of meat and baby dolls) was considered too shocking, all the unsold records were recalled from stores. They destroyed most of them, but some of the records merely had a new front slick applied over the old one. Carefully peeling off the front slick of the Beatles gathered around a steamer trunk reveals the original cover."

"Flex Your Head" was issued a year later in the U.K. on Alternative Tentacles in a DC flag 'XXX' sleeve and in 1985 with a blurred head photo that was in keeping with the Dischord house style at that time. The first issue came with a booklet and thereon after a poster with all the bands.

GRITO SUBURBANO LP (PUNK ROCK DISCOS)

The Brazilians announced their entry into the international punk conversation with this no frills three band compilation, with each band supplying four songs; OLHO SECO with a barrage of UK '82 inspired hardcore, INOCENTES with a slightly more restrained but no less snarling punk rock, while CÓLERA sounded like they'd recently visited Bristol with buzzsaw guitars and shouted choruses. As if to emphasise the urgency the album was pressed on 45RPM, rattled along at a hell of a pace, and was over in the blink of an eye. The rapid fire blasts and simple structures made this seem like the Brazilian bands really had their shit together, and showed how the punk rock disease had spread far and wide across the planet. Featuring a ripped up black and white cover collage of various punks and the bands on the back (as well as a simple lyric sheet), "Grito Suburbano" was reissued in 1984 on Pogar in Germany and New Face Records in Brazil, who also reissued it again a decade later.

HUDSON ROCK LP (MCE RECORDS)

Rock Hudson, geddit?! "Fifteen bands from Albany, New York" recorded at MCE studios. A mixed bag that opened with the showtune rock of Blotto before The A.D.'s delivered a Stooges style groove and then The Morons kept it up with their belligerent keyboard punk. The Rockin Dakotas did some rock'n'roll before the funky new wave of Faulty Products artists Fear Of Strangers. Hot Lobsters and Standing Offer concluded side one with more new wave while side two began with The Verge and their upbeat post-punk before Bow Wow Wow inspired The Weekenders. The Extras then turned the punk up to eleven while The X-Istentials and Lumpen Proles took it back to darker new wave. Capitle then provided a short blast of hardcore before The Crude flung some real punk snot and The Young Reptiles with their rock'n'roll. This lost gem, with more than a few standouts, concluded with a hidden four second Capitle song "All My Friends Are In Bands And They Suck". Volume two followed in 1987.

LIFE IS UGLY WHY NOT KILL YOURSELF LP (NEW UNDERGROUND)

The first compilation on New Underground Records, the label run by Danny Dean Phillips and Gary Kail of the band Anti, that was very much aesthetically similar to Minutemen's New Alliance Records. In keeping with New Alliance and other Southern Californian compilations of the day, this was a mix of straight up hardcore punk and the more arty end of things. Opening with early Red Cross, Descendents and Anti, and continuing with the lesser known but no less able Ill Will and Civil Dismay, side one ended with two China White songs. The flip offered up Danny Dean Phillips' other band Mood Of Defiance before Minutemen gave us two typically short blasts with "Shit You Hear At Parties" and "Maternal Rite". 100 Flowers took their spot followed by their previous incarnation Urinals, before Gary Kail's other project Zurich 1916 continued. New Alliance artists Plebs gave us "Payday" before Saccharine Trust concluded the album with the unreleased elsewhere "Disillusion Fool".

LOCOS POR LA MÚSICA LP (PISTA LIBRE)

An early Spanish entry featuring bands who appeared on the "Crazy For The Music" section of youth TV series "Pista Libre" that broadcast on TVE (Televisión Espanola) on 20th June 1982 (the series ran from January 1982 - September 1985). A mix of punk, new wave, post-punk and pop, this ten band and song album featured; Paralisis Permanente, Espasmodicos, Esclarecidos, Glutamato Ye-Ye, Derribos Arias, La Banda Del Tren, Zoquillos, Telegrama, Pistones, and WAQ. Paralisis Permanente and Espasmodicos opened up the album in a pacey distorted punk fashion (Espasmodicos bordering on hardcore speed, and a stand out here), while La Banda Del Tren and Zoquillos offered a more sunny power pop style. The rest of the album highlighted the ubiquitous post-punk and new wave styles of the day. With very Spanish cartoon cover art by Victor Aparicio (also of the band Los Coyotes), the back featured liner notes from noted Spanish music journalist Diego A. Manrique.

147

NOT SO QUIET ON THE WESTERN FRONT 2LP (ALTERNATIVE TENTACLES)

Sub-titled "Deprogramming by 47 Northern California and Nevada bands", this impressive debut compilation from Maximum Rock'n'Roll fanzine boasted the following mainly S.F. Area hardcore bands; Intensified Chaos, Social Unrest, Naked Lady Wrestlers, M.A.D., Killjoy, Fang, Capitol Punishment, Ribsy, Crucifix, Square Cools, Los Olvidados, Code Of Honor, 7 Seconds, Unaware, Frigidettes, 5th Column, Ghost Dance, Dead Kennedys, Rebel Truth, Pariah, Lennonburger, Impatient Youth, Bad Posture, Demented Youth, MDC, Karnage, Domino Theory, NBJ, Whipping Boy, Angst, Free Beer, Flipper, Vengeance, Juvinel Justice, Section 8, Tongue Avulsion, Maniax, Vicious Circle, UXB, Scapegoats, Church Police, Deadly Reign, No Alternative, Wrecks, Urban Assault Bent Nails, and MIA. Tim Yohannan famously expanded the geography of the LP to include MIA due to their song "New Left", which was in keeping with his agenda for punk. The double LP came with issue zero of nowlegendary fanzine Maximum RocknRoll.

OI! OI! THAT'S YER LOT! LP (SECRET RECORDS)

The fourth and final installment of the Oi! series, well there were many spin-offs later but I'll be stopping here. The Business landed the first punch with "Real Enemy" before Five O clattered their way through "Dr. Crippens". Cardiff anti-fascist skinheads The Oppressed then submitted "White Flag" from a time when they were still just singing about violence rather being anti-fascist. Cambridge skins Sub-Culture bashed the toms through a common Oi! theme of "Stick Together" before Crux handled another common theme on "Liddle Towers". Post-Last Resort band The Warriors struggled through some plod and Attak did their bit before side one closed with the surprise entry of Black Flag and "Revenge" which saw skinheads everywhere think they were Oi!, buy their records, then sell them again. Side two featured; Arthur & The Afters, Frankie & The Flames, The Magnificent (!) Gonads, Attila The Stockbroker, Judge Dread, Skin Graft, Attila The Stockbroker, and Coming Blood (The Blood).

OUTSIDER LP (CITY ROCKER RECORDS)

The second City Rocker compilation was a raw mix of live
and studio recordings from the then latest Japanese punk
crop. Opening the album on the "Hard "Metal" Core Side"
was Tokyo's Gism with a rough and ready hardcore holocaust
spanning five songs recorded at Shinjuku Loft, Tokyo on
22nd September 1982. The Comes, also from Tokyo, continued
in a similar frantic fashion at the same gig before the
amusingly named Laughin Nose from Osaka continued the theme
for two songs with raw and throttled bass lines. Gauze then
closed out side one with four blazing songs including the
romantic ballad "Children Fuck Off". The "New "Block" Punk
Side" featured the less thrashing but no less pounding
punk of Mastervation from Kyoto, Fullx, the rockin' '77
style punk of Route 66, as well as the more goth edged punk
of Madame Edwarda. "Outsider" came housed in an impressive
six panel Crass style poster sleeve by Sakevi of Gism and
has never been officially reissued.

PILLOWS & PRAYERS LP (CHERRY RED RECORDS)

Sub-titled "Cherry Red (1982-1983)", if you'd like to hear
the moment when post-punk turned into indie pop then look
no further than this Cherry Red budget compilation released
for Christmas 1982. Featuring seventeen artists and songs
from; Five Or Six, The Monochrome Set, Thomas Leer, Tracey
Thorn, Ben Watt (Thorn and Watt would soon emerge below as
Everything But The Girl and years later married), Kevin
Coyne, Piero Milesi, Joe Crow, Marine Girls, Felt, Eyeless
In Gaza, The Passage, Everything But The Girl, Attila
The Stockbroker, The Misunderstood, The Nightingales, and
Quentin Crisp. An Eclectic mix of varying styles it did
sound like ground zero for indie music as any rough edges
of post-punk could be heard drifting away into a smoother
pop. The cover art was a photo of a kid blowing bubbles with
photos on the back and more on the inner sleeve. The 99p
pay no more than price helped the album hit number one in
the U.K. indie chart for five weeks selling 120,000 copies.

PROPAGANDA - RUSSIA BOMBS FINLAND LP (PROPAGANDA RECORDS)

Finland's Propaganda Records followed their first release, the 1981 compilation 7" EP simply titled "Propaganda EP", with this eleven band and thirty five song album. Fast, raw and ripping hardcore mainly in the Discharge vein but also with some lingering 1977 and emerging U.S. hardcore influences. With five songs each from Bastards and Riistetyt, four songs each from Antiheko and Nato, three songs each from Kaaos, 013 and Sekunda, and two songs each from Terveet Kädet, Maho Neitsyt, Appendix, and Dachau. "Russia Bombs Finland" gave the world a better understanding of what Finnish hardcore punk was all about in 1982. The title always seemed to simply have been gleaned from the central text of the back cover chaotic punk montage art with "Propaganda" taking the centre of the front. It was initially pressed on red vinyl with a booklet, as well as cassette and black vinyl, and has been reissued and bootlegged numerous times since.

PROPELLER - LAUGHING AT THE GROUND 7" EP (PROPELLER PRODUCT)

Across the Atlantic a similar thing was happening to the U.K. and college town Boston played a significant role in post-punk morphing into college rock, and labels like Propeller Product were there to document its inception. The four band EP opened with three piece 21-645 and their melodic Mission Of Burma style post-punk with "Babble" (before they became The Flies with the addition of Nat Freedberg). The all-female Dangerous Birds followed with the jangly art rock of "Emergency" who featured vocalist/guitarist Thalia Zedek later of Uzi, Live Skull and Come. The flip offered V; with "Schitzed", more of their shimmering yet jagged post-punk with the spiky vocals of Susan Anway. The EP concluded in a clear college rock direction with Christmas and the chanting "Close My Eyes". Issued in a basic sleeve with little info with a graphic depicting a propeller and the b-side aerial label photo as if you are falling from a plane. The third and final Propeller compilation.

PUNK AND DISORDERLY & FURTHER CHARGES LPS (ANAGRAM)

Capitalising on the success of UK '82 punk Cherry Red subsidiary Anagram issued two volumes of this in the same year. With singles licensed from other labels this will take you back on your stereo time machine. Volume one featured; Vice Squad, The Adicts, UK Decay, Disorder, Peter And The Test Tube Babies, Disrupters, Red Alert, Blitz, Dead Kennedys, The Partisans, Demob, The Insane, Abrasive Wheels, Chaos UK, Outcasts, and GBH. "Further Charges" featured five of the same bands; GBH, The Insane, Abrasive Wheels, Disorder, and Vice Squad, as well as; The Expelled, One Way System, Court Martial, Action Pact, The Dark, Violators, Channel 3, The Enemy, Riot/Clone, The Wall, and Erazerhead. As you can see these were strictly all UK affairs apart from DK and CH3 who both had U.K. issues of their material on the labels this was all licensed from. Both with cover photos of various punks in the street, volume one was issued in the U.S. on Posh Boy Records.

RAT MUSIC FOR RAT PEOPLE LP (GO! RECORDS)

Go! Records was an early label version of CD Presents, the gig promotion company run by notorious San Francisco impresario David Ferguson, and this was a live document of gigs both in the hardcore and early punk era of gigs put on by promoter Paul Rat and Ferguson. The album featured one or two songs each by; D.O.A., Flipper, Circle Jerks, Bad Brains, Crucifix, Dead Kennedys, Black Flag, T.S.O.L., Avengers, and The Dils. The last two bands were recorded in 1979 and 1977 respectively while the D.O.A. and Flipper songs were at the same gig with Black Flag, Saccharine Trust and Overkill at the Elite Club, Halloween 1981. The Bad Brains, Dead Kennedys and T.S.O.L. songs were recorded at the same gig, again at the Elite Club, on March 20th 1982, with 7 Seconds and Domino Theory. The Black Flag song was their opening number on the second of two nights at the On Broadway on July 24th 1982 with Meat Puppets, Descendents and Angst. "Rat Music" came with a large foldout poster.

RIOTOUS ASSEMBLY LP (RIOT CITY RECORDS)

Riot City, the label put together by Heartbeat Records boss Simon Edwards along with Dave Bateman and Shane Baldwin from Vice Squad with their first compilation of UK '82 punk, and it wasn't just a singles collection. One song each (with two from Vice Squad of course) from fourteen bands; Vice Squad, Organized Chaos, Abrasive Wheels, Court Martial, Chaos UK, Dead Katss, Resistance 77, Havoc, Mayhem, Expelled, T.D.A., Undead, Lunatic Fringe, and Chaotic Dischord. With eight of the bands hailing from Bristol and surrounding hamlets, the album had a strong west country accent and a whiff of cider. Journalist Garry Bushell famously described Riot City as "The Dustbin of Punk" and considering he put together four Oi! albums it's best we say no more about that. The cover art to this pounding slab of council estate plod and drunk crusty thrash couldn't be any more punk with its leopard skin background, photos of various punks, spiky writing, and of course it came on red vinyl.

RODNEY ON THE ROQ VOL. 3 LP (POSH BOY RECORDS)

Round three of Rodney Bingenheimer's largely Southern Californian punk showcase based on his KROQ radio show. As per usual side one was hardcore punk opening with the sing-along "Radio Moscow" by Kent State, before the Vandals wanted be cowboys with "Urban Struggle", Ill Repute got out the milk and cookies with "Clean-Cut American Kid") and then JFA (from Arizona) took aim at the "Preppy". CH3 steamed through "Separate Peace" before Catch 22 plead to "Stop The Cycle", then Pariah said it was "Up To Us", before Red Scare served up some "Streetlife", and No Crisis proclaimed "She's Into The Scene", before Belfast's Rudi concluded side one with "Crimson". Side two was an eclectic new wave mix with; Unit 3 With Venus, Bangles (with surf instrumental "Bitchen Summer"), Action Now, Signals, Gayle Welch, Radio Music, and David Hines. The cover followed the teen theme of the previous two, and the LP came with issue 35 of Flipside fanzine with interviews and photos of all the bands.

154

SOMEONE GOT THEIR HEAD KICKED IN! LP (B.Y.O.)

For their first release the Better Youth Organization, formed by the brothers Stern of Youth Brigade, put together this classic compilation of Southern California bands. Featuring eighteen songs by eight bands that included three songs each by; Youth Brigade, Agression, Battalion Of Saints, and Blades, two each by Adolescents and Joneses, and one song each from Social Distortion and Bad Religion, this became one of the pivotal compilations of Southern Californian hardcore punk. Five of the bands, with the exception of Bad Religion, Adolescents and Social Distortion recorded at Doug Moody's Mystic Sound in May 1982. With cover art by Pushead that depicted punk "violence" on the front, and a shot of the bands on the tour bus soon to be seen in the movie "Another State Of Mind" on the rear. The LP also included a twelve page booklet with a page for each band, a photo centre spread and an "Introduction to the BYO". The booklet became a folded insert for subsequent pressings.

SOUNDTRACKS ZUM UNTERTANG 2LP (AGGRESSIVE ROCKPRODUKTIONEN)

Sub-titled "New German punk underground" this was the second installment of the "Soundtrack to the Downfall" of Deutsch punk with eight bands; Sluts, Normahl, Marionetz, Blitzkrieg, Notdurft, Böhse Onkelz, Canalterror, and Neurotic Arseholes. With nineteen songs in total from a time before the influence of U.S. hardcore had crept into the music and German punks were still in awe of the sounds of the U.K. The result was mainly mid-tempo 1977, UK '82 and Oi! Sounding songs from pretty much all the bands with occasional German Oompah sections. Standouts being Neurotic Arseholes (with three early songs), and Normahl (who pick up the pace significantly). The album came with fittingly apocalyptic cover art and an insert with lyrics on one side and an Aggressive Rockproduktionen advert on the other, with the first nine releases on the label (this being the eighth). "Soundtracks Zum Untertang" was reissued on the same label ten years, and then forty years later.

SUDDEN DEATH LP (SMOKE SEVEN RECORDS)

The sixth release on Felix Alanis of RF7's label imprint
and their second compilation after 1981's "Public Service".
"Sudden Death" contained eleven bands and twenty eight
songs from; J.F.A., Sin 34, Moral Decay, Crankshaft, Sadist
Faction, The Sins (guitarist Tony Bramel aka Fate of The
Reactors also later played in The Grey Spikes, Symbol Six
and The Bellrays), The Demented, Redd Kross, Youth Gone Mad,
Naughty Women, and Dead Youth. All from Southern California
with the exception of J.F.A. from Phoenix. While being no
classic of the genre "Sudden Death" serves as a snapshot
of hardcore punk in 1982 with around half of the bands
such as; Dead Youth, Naughty Women, The Demented, Sadist
Faction, Crankshaft, and Moral Decay doing very little
else apart from compilation tracks during their existence.
Eight of the eleven bands were recorded at Reels Of Sound
Studios in Moorpark, California by Mike Smith. The sleeve
depicted a scene of mass murder with lyrics on the back.

THE BIG APPLE - ROTTEN TO THE CORE LP (S.I.N. RECORDS)

As the title suggested this was a collection of New York
bands put together by Ism's label S.I.N. Records. The album
began with the belligerent punk of Ism and "John Hinckley
Jr. (What Has Jodie Foster Done To You?)" Featuring Greg
Psomas later of Georgia's DDT on drums. Squirm, then Butch
Lust And The Hypocrites, both followed in a similar snotty
vein before The Mob then upped the pace with their early
New York hardcore. Killer Instinct then stole the limelight
with their 3/4 female menacing punk that pulled no punches.
The Headlickers completed the six band line-up with a very
Dead Boys style approach. All the bands then got more
tracks each with all songs spread out in a random order
with Ism offering four in total, Squirm five, Butch Lust
And The Hypocrites four, The Mob and Killer Instinct only
two each and The Headlickers with three, all totalling
twenty songs. A true diamond in the rough from a time just
before New York hardcore became codified in its approach.

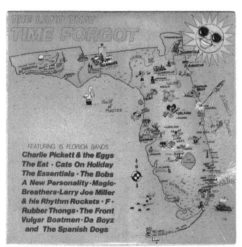

THE D.I.Y. ALBUM LP (JW PRODUCTIONS)

An obscure compilation put together by Jim Warsinske of
D.I.Y. magazine of Los Angeles using a vinyl production
technique called "Han-O-Disc" which was essentially the
two sides of the record being joined together so that
holographic images or even liquids could be encapsulated
within (curiously, this album was just clear vinyl). The
pressing technique also apparently made it warp proof and
sounded better (although this copy doesn't). All in all
it sounded like Mr. Warsinske was invested in this new
pressing process that, like most of the bands, clearly
never took off. The compilation itself was a curious mix
of styles, notably including "Six Pack" by Black Flag,
"Can You Hear Them" by Red Rockers and Slickee Boys "Here
To Stay" alongside the more mainstream acts; Enemies, And
And The Rattlesnakes, Mikel Japp, Lorelei, Dreamers, Treva
Spontaine & The Grafics, and A.K.A./Etc. The album came in
a plain white or PVC sleeve with sticker and press release.

THE LAND THAT TIME FORGOT LP (OPEN RECORDS)

A state wide collection of Florida bands from Fort Lauderdale,
that label Open Records slimmed down 60 demos to 15 they'd
received after declaring their intent to release this
record. The album opened with The Eat of "Communist Radio"
fame followed by a slow burner from The Bobs. Rubber Thongs
from Coconut Grove then went all wacky new wave with "Mondo
Condo" before Cats On Holiday served up some rock'n'roll.
The legendary "F" continued with "I Saw Your Vision" while
The Essentials gave us some catchy punk with "Turn Off Your
Radio". Da Boyz and Charlie Pickett And The Eggs rounded out
side one in a fairly pedestrian rock fashion. Side two gave
us Larry Joe Miller And His Rhythm Rockets (rock'n'roll),
Breathers (power pop), Magic (country rock), The Spanish
Dogs (radio rock), The Vulgar Boatmen (art school new
wave), A New Personality (post-punk), and The Front (synth
new wave). The cover featured a postcard style cartoon of
Florida with liner notes, band photos and info on the rear.

THE MASTER TAPE LP (NIMROD/AFFIRMATION RECORDS)

The legendary mainly Mid-West compilation featuring 11
bands and 24 songs compiled by Paul Mahern of Zero Boys and
all recorded by him in Indiana, apart from Boston's finest
The F.U.'s. First up was Toxic Reasons (OH) with two killer
first album era songs before Slammies (IN) with three.
Battered Youth (IN) then blasted through two tunes featuring
three future members of Honor Role before Delinquents (OH)
gave us another two rippers that sounded a lot like the
Zero Boys (IN), who then saw out side one with three snappy
classics. The flip began with two from Articles Of Faith (IL)
before two more from Repellents (IN, featuring Jackie later
of Musical Suicide) and Learned Helplessness (IN) before
two thrashers from The F.U.'s. The Pattern (IN) followed
with two more before the legendary Die Kreuzen (WI) closed
the album in fine style. The album art depicted an x-ray
master tape on a silver background and came with a foldout
poster. It received two pressings of 2,000 copies each.

THE ONLY ALTERNATIVE LP (RONDELET RECORDS)

A lively showcase of Rondelet Records talent at the height of
UK '82 that opened with the brick wall anthem "No Government"
by Anti-Pasti (and they had two more 7" songs throughout).
After this came the oompah-plod of Special Duties with the
squawking singalong of "Violent Society" (and they also
have two more songs later on). Scottish louts The Threats
followed with "Afghanistan" and deeper into the album "Go
To Hell". Then came the strange interlude of Catwax throwing
their instruments down the stairs before more Anti-Pasti
and Blackpool's shouty The Fits. Side one closed with Riot
Squad and their charmingly titled dole queue hit "Fuck The
Tories". Side two opened with more Special Duties before
Dead Man's Shadow and the classic "Bomb Scare". The rest
of side two featured more Anti-Pasti, Threats, Fits, Riot
Squad and Special Duties. The cover art featured a torn,
chopped up and updated version of Adam And The Ants "Prince
Charming" album. One of the better UK '82 compilations.

THE SECRET LIVES OF PUNKS LP (SECRET RECORDS)

As the title subtly suggested this was a mainly singles compilation of Secret Records with hits aplenty to cash in on the wave of popularity of UK '82 punk. It kicked off with "Dogs Of War" by The Exploited followed by "One Law For Them" by 4-Skins (that a lot of people thought was about the class system due to the cover art but was actually about Asian immigrants in the 1981 riot in Southall following a 4-Skins gig). Infa Riot continued with "Kids Of The 80s" before The Partisans supplied "No U Turns" and The Business delivered "Employers Black List". The Gonads, Blitz ("Youth"), Chron Gen ("Jet Boy Jet Girl"), The Last Resort, and Peter And The Test Tube Babies ("Maniac") all got one song apiece while The Exploited ("Army Life"), 4 Skins ("Yesterdays Heroes"), Infa Riot ("Catch 22") and The Business ("Harry May") all had another bite. The cover featured a cartoon of a punk couple by Art Dragon, who were also responsible for The Business and Infa Riot albums.

THIS IS BOSTON NOT L.A. LP (MODERN METHOD)

The album that put Boston, Massachusetts, on the hardcore map was a seven band rapid fire set put together by record store Newbury Comics for their label Modern Method, and the third compilation on the label following the two volumes of "A Wicked Good Time" in 1981. Jerry's Kids opened proceedings with six songs in as many minutes and next came three songs from The Proletariat who really stood out from the speed pack with their politically charged Gang Of Four style attack. Next up were Groinoids for a whole minute in the sun with the song "Angel" (members later going onto Kilslug and Upsidedowncross). The F.U.'s closed out side one with four blasts of their tongue in cheek hardcore. Side two offered up seven thrashers from legends Gang Green, one Decadence song; the pit themed "Slam", before finally The Freeze gave us eight great songs concluding with the album theme "Boston Not L.A." The cover featured a photo of the local slam pit taken by photographer Phil In Phlash.

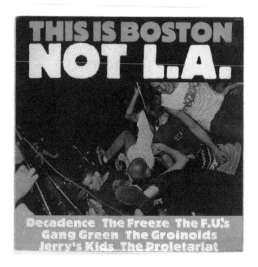

THIS IS BOSTON NOT L.A.

Decadence The Freeze The F.U.'s
Gang Green The Groinoids
Jerry's Kids The Proletariat

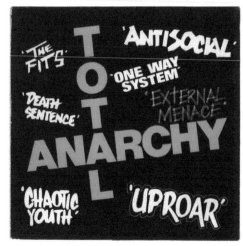

'THE FITS' 'ANTISOCIAL'
TOTAL 'ONE WAY SYSTEM'
'DEATH SENTENCE' 'EXTERNAL MENACE'
ANARCHY
'CHAOTIC YOUTH' 'UPROAR'

TOTAL NOISE #1

STARRING

THE BUSINESS THE GONADS
TOT 1 BLITZ DEAD GENERATION

NUMBER ONE IN A SERIES OF SINUS-SCORCHING
ADVENTURES INTO OVERKILL AURAL EXTREMITIES!

UNDERGROUND HITS I

BLACK FLAG
ANGRY SAMOANS
BAD BRAINS
SACCHARINE TRUST
CHAOS-Z
TOXOPLASMA
RAZZIA
NEUROTIC ARSEHOLES

UNSAFE AT ANY SPEED

WARGASM

ANGELIC UPSTARTS   INFA RIOT
CANKER OPERA   MAU MAUS
CAPTAIN SENSIBLE   POISON GIRLS
the DANSE SOCIETY   QUITE UNNERVING
DEAD KENNEDYS   RAT SCABIES
FLUX OF PINK INDIANS   the SYSTEM

TOTAL ANARCHY LP (BEAT THE SYSTEM/LIGHTBEAT RECORDS)

A showcase of this Blackpool label (two names, one label) of predominantly bands from the North of England and Scotland. A mix of 7" and unreleased songs from seven bands on the label with two songs each, making a total of fourteen from; External Menace, One Way System, Uproar, Antisocial, The Fits, Chaotic Youth, and Death Sentence. The style was of the UK '82 variety throughout with fist-in-the-air sing-along songs and a tenuous grasp of guitar tuning. The back cover stated, "This album is dedicated to all the punks and skins who came to the Blackpool Punk Festival on 20th September to find it cancelled due to 'local herberts'". This must've been the second part of the "Up Yer Tower" punk festival that was in August 1982 at The Venue featuring Abrasive Wheels, The Adicts, One Way System, Peter and the Test Tube Babies, and GBH. The album came wrapped in unimaginative cover art that gave the impression of bland major label sampler with very little information on the bands.

TOTAL NOISE 7" EP (TOTAL NOISE RECORDS)

A four song showcase of the U.K. Oi! punk crop compiled by Garry Bushell that was due to be a series but turned out to be only one. Opening with The Business and "Loud, Proud & Punk" all about the punk scene with a football chant chorus, "Voice Of A Generation" by Blitz continued the terrace anthem theme. Side two switched from 45rpm to 33rpm for The Gonads and "TNT" that bordered on heavy metal replete with ridiculous guitar solo that went off like a damp squib. The EP closed with Dead Generation, aka Cockney Rejects in disguise, and more dull hard rock with the song "Francine" that opened with some kind of misguided piss-take in a northern English accent. A bit like "Bollocks To Christmas" you were left with the feeling that this was all recorded in one day with a slab of cans all paid for by some label or other. The standout aspect of this was the cover graphics by Graham Humphreys, and art direction by Vermilion Sands formerly of Search & Destroy magazine of San Francisco.

The Dils.
The Eyes.
The Germs.
The Controllers.
The Skulls.
Kaos.

UNDERGROUND HITS 1 LP (AGGRESSIVE ROCKPRODUKTIONEN)

As if to usher in the American hardcore influence on German
punk, "Underground Hits" featured one side of four German
bands and one side of four American bands, for the third
compilation on AGR following the two volumes of "Soundtracks
Zum Untergang". The "Deutsche Seite" featured; Toxoplasma,
Razzia, Neurotic Arseholes, and Chaos Z, all with three
songs each apart from Razzia with two, and all showing a
faster more aggressive approach to previous efforts with
better production. The "Ami Seite" consisted of; Angry
Samoans, Black Flag, Bad Brains, and Saccharine Trust, the
first two having German licensed versions of their records
on Aggressive Rock. The Angry Samoans notably had two
unreleased songs; "Posh Boy's Cock" ("Steak Knife" with new
lyrics), that got them banned from Rodney On The Roq for its
offensive attack on Rodney and Posh Boy owner Robbie Fields,
as well as a cover of "Pictures Of Matchstickmen". The Black
Flag "Nervous Breakdown" 7" was included in its entirety.

UNSAFE AT ANY SPEED 7" EP (MODERN METHOD)

A few months after "This Is Boston Not L.A." Modern Method
issued this companion 7" featuring six bands from the LP,
but with songs unique to this release. Far from being
a leftovers record Gang Green opened with the blazing
"Selfish" before Groinoids then gave us stomper "Empty
Skull" which was a stronger song than the one on the actual
album. The Proletariat then supplied "Voodoo Economics",
again one of their stronger songs lambasting the then new
Neoliberal economic policies of the Reagan era. On the flip
came Jerry's Kids with the rapid fire assault of "Machine
Gun", The F.U.'s with the snotty "CETA Suckers", and Cape
Cod's The Freeze again closed the record in fine style with
creepy slow burner "Refrigerator Heaven", that showcased
Clif Hanger's almost Stephen King'esque dark lyrics. More
slam pit photography by Phil In Phlash adorned the fold over
cover, along with the unmistakable Block font that gave
both records a distinctive house style all of their own.

WARGASM LP & EXTRACTS FROM WARGASM 7" EP (PAX RECORDS)

The fourth release on Pax Records and their second compilation, this being an anti-war themed album with striking cover art that also came with a large poster of the same. The album itself was a mix of arty post-punk, anarcho and hardcore punk with each artist donating to a different charity. The goth of The Danse Society opened the album followed by the anarcho of Flux Of Pink Indians. These were followed by Canker Opera and then Dead Kennedys with the then unreleased "Kinky Sex Makes The World Go Around". Rat Scabies closed side one in an artistic fashion. On side two Poison Girls made their "Statement" before Captain Sensible offered a Stranglers style song in "Hey Jo". The LP then turned more punk for Maus Maus, Angelic Upstarts, The System, The Insane, and Infa Riot before Quite Unnerving closed the LP with the title track. A "DJ Promotional" 7" was also issued in plain sleeve with the; Sensible, DK, Infa Riot and Flux songs (pictured under 'E' for 'Extracts').

WAVE NEWS 1 & 2 LPs (INTERCORD)

Sub-titled "The New Generation Of Music" and "Independent Smash Hits" respectively, "Wave News" comprised of two volumes for the German market licensed from a variety of labels of punk, post-punk, new wave and synth pop, both well known and obscure. The first was decidedly more 'wave' with; Depeche Mode, The Damned, Max Meldau, Lovely Previn, Eyeless In Gaza, Jo Broadbery & The Standouts, China Doll, Medium Medium, Au Pairs, Fad Gadget, Dead Kennedys, Thomas Leer, The Exploited, Eddie Maelov And Sunshine Patteson, Bloodless Pharoahs, and UK Subs. While volume 2 leaned a little more into UK82 more with; The Exploited, Chron Gen, The 4 Skinds, UK Subs, The Damned, Infa Riot, The Business, The Gonads, Girls At Our Best, The Klones, Eddie Maelov And Sunshine Patteson, Fad Gadget, Brian Brain, and Jo Broadbery & The Standouts. Both LPs were on coloured vinyl (purple and orange) in printed PVC sleeves with 6"x12" foldout inserts featuring info in German on all the bands.

WESSEX '82 7" EP (BLUURG RECORDS)

This was the first vinyl release on Wiltshire label Bluurg run by Dick of Subhumans and it was a local area compilation named after the ancient Anglo-Saxon kingdom in the South of England and featuring bands all from Warminster in Wiltshire. First up was Subhumans and "No Thanks" about the music industry, followed by Pagans and "Wave Goodbye To Your Dreams", who shared members and a similar sound to Subhumans. On the flip Organized Chaos sped things up with "Victim" and again had the same geographical sound. Finally A-Heads changed things a little with "No Rule" and that classic British anarcho punk with female vocals sound. The cover featured a photo of the Westbury White Horse on Salisbury Plain in Wiltshire with the band logos on the bottom and the customary pay no more than price of 99p. The back sleeve featured a detailed and intertwined family tree of all the bands that stretched all the way back to 1978 with members all playing in each other's punk combos.

WHAT IS IT. LP (WHAT RECORDS?)

A collection of Chris Ashford's What Records that had helped document early Los Angeles punk, largely on 7". Containing a mix of released and then otherwise unreleased early L.A. punk gems it started with "Forming" by The Germs of course as it was their first release. This was followed by Kaos and "Top Secret" from the "Product Of A Sick Mind" 12". "I Hate The Rich" by The Dils was followed by The Skulls "Victims" from the 1978 three way split 7" with the Controllers and The Eyes (all three songs from that 7" were included here), The Controllers "Neutron Bomb" followed to conclude the first side. Side two contained the three unreleased songs starting with an alternative "Forming" by The Germs. The Controllers "Killer Queers", the flip of their "Neutron Bomb" 7" followed before The Eyes and "Don't Talk To Me" from that three way split. Two more unreleased songs completed the ten song album; Kaos with "Auto Pilot" and The Skulls with "On Target". Only one pressing exists.

INSET: MAXIMUMROCKNROLL #0
FROM "NOT SO QUIET ON THE
WESTERN FRONT" 2LP, 1982
(ALTERNATIVE TENTACLES)

EASTERN FRONT

JULY·AUG·SEPT

SATURDAY JULY 31ST 11AM/8PM
AQUATIC PARK 3RD ST & BANCROFT WAY, BERKELEY.

FROM ENGLAND CHRON·GEN

WASTED YOUTH · BATALLIONS OF SAINTS

THE LEWD · JODY FOSTER'S ARMY

CIRCLE·ONE · CHANNEL THREE

HUSKER DÜ · SHATTERED FAITH

FREE BEER · DEADLY REIGN

· RANDY TUTEN ·

"EASTERN FRONT" FESTIVAL POSTER 1982 (VOLUME 2 LP)

WHO'S LISTENING LP (GOVERNMENT RECORDS)

A showcase of San Diego bands on red vinyl that was recorded live at Spirit in San Diego over three nights in late November 1981. The album opened with the funky post-punk of DFX2 before The Penetrators with their slow burning keyboard surfy new wave on "Let's Talk" (titled "We Can Talk" on their album of the same year). Trowsers then picked it up with a 2-Tone ska inspired song before Solid State took the album on a synth and sax jazzy new wave turn with male crooning, before by Girl Talk concluded side one in a similar fashion but with female vocals. The second side got going with the standard new wave rock fare of Four Eyes and "Life After High School" before the amusingly named Claude Coma & The I.V.'s gave us more of the same with "The Will To Survive". Prolific rockabillies The Paladins then took the stage for "Lonesome Train" before Land Piranha did a rendition of The Stooges "T.V. Eye", and Puppies concluded proceedings in a slow ska style with "Slang Lingo".

YOU CANT ARGUE WITH SUCKSESS LP (MYSTIC RECORDS)

The first punk compilation on Mystic compiled by Roger Rogerson of Circle Jerks featured nine bands and twenty three songs with most bands having three songs apiece. First up was F Troop from Long Beach with some rapid fire hardcore, followed by more of the same from The Crewd, who for some reason decided to get involved in the politics of Northern Ireland. Red Beret followed with more yelping hardcore for one song, then Nuclear Baby Food slowed things down in a more post-punk style. Mad Society saw out side one with their early teen hardcore (vocalist Stevie Metz would've been eleven at this time, the rest fourteen). Secret Hate opened up side two with more Long Beach hardcore followed by one No Crisis song and then Conservatives (see: "Hell Comes To Your House") rattled through their brand of anger. Red Beret got another song, concluding with Even Worse (from New York!) with two songs. The album featured the photography of the ubiquitous Ed Colver front and back.

1983-1986:
THE BLASTING CONCEPT

Ronald Reagan declares the Soviet Union an "Evil Empire" in March 1983 and proposes the "Star Wars" Strategic Defence Initiative just as Toxic Shock, Homestead and Big City Records turn their ideas to start labels into a reality. American audiences watch Flashdance, Trading Places and Scarface as Michael Jackson's "Thriller" tops the charts.

American Cruise missiles arrive at Greenham Common in Berkshire in the U.K. and an over one million people join an anti-nuclear weapons march in London just as Conflict begin pressing their first records on Mortahate, and Culture Club, UB40 and Billy Joel hit radio rotation.

In Russia, Stanislav Petrov identifies a false alarm on the USSR early warning system and prevents a nuclear war as Starving Missile presses its first release in West Germany. As 1983 turns into 1984, X-Port Plater in Norway and Uproar Records in Sweden put plans in place for a vinyl assault, while in Canada Psyche Industry fires up the presses for the first time.

A year-long strike by 150,000 coal miners in the U.K. gets underway as Mortahate Records spin-off Fight Back begins, and audiences queue in the rain for This Is Spinal Tap, Footloose and Beverly Hills Cop. Band Aid shifts units to help with the famine in Ethiopia while Frankie Goes To Hollywood and Wham create their own pop chart excitement.

The summer Olympics gets underway in Los Angeles to limited screenings of Youth Brigades' "Another State Of Mind" before Ronald Reagan jokes, "We begin bombing in five minutes" and Pusmort, Positive Force, Taang! and Maximum Rock'n'Roll become record labels. Prince, Tina Turner and Kenny Loggins get mass U.S. airplay while theatres swell for Terminator, Ghostbusters and Gremlins.

As 1985 begins Ronald Reagan starts his second presidential term and Mikhail Gorbachev becomes leader of the Soviet Union as "Revolution Summer" takes place in the punk scene of Washington D.C. Meanwhile Foreigner, Hall & Oates and Chaka Khan top the Billboard charts, and audiences are captivated by Back To The Future, The Breakfast Club and The Goonies.

1984's Band Aid single "Do They Know It's Christmas?" gives birth to Live Aid in July 1985, with over 160,000 in attendance in London and Philadelphia, and millions watching worldwide. Just as Earache, Hybrid and One Little Indian put plans in place for their first vinyl releases, British teenagers buy records by Madonna and Paul Hardcastle, while their parents watch Out Of Africa, Brazil and Fright Night.

U.S. Army military intelligence officer Major Arthur D. Nicholson is shot to death by a Soviet sentry in East Germany and just to the west; X-Mist and We Bite in West Germany, Konkurrent in the Netherlands, Ataque Frontal in Brazil and 77KK in France, all begin releasing records.

1986 gets off to an explosive start with the U.S. space shuttle Challenger exploding after lift-off just as Sub Pop and Amphetamine Reptile start releasing records. The U.S. bombs Libya and the Iran-Contra affair heats up as Alchemy and Phantom Records begin their relatively short lives. American audiences are glued to Top Gun, Crocodile Dundee and Platoon, as Survivor, Whitney Houston and Lionel Richie all grace the American hit parade.

The Chernobyl nuclear plant explodes in Russia, Mad Cow Disease hits the news, and Argentina win the World Cup in Mexico, as British Gas is privatised in the U.K. and print workers strike at Wapping. Strange Fruit, Loony Tunes, Words Of Warning, and Meantime Records all celebrate their inaugural releases while cinemas are witness to the flickering celluloid of Stand By Me, Pretty In Pink and Aliens, as The Communards along with Cliff Richard and the Young Ones both scale the charts...

A BOSTON ROCK CHRISTMAS

Del Fuegos
Native Tongue
Jeff & Jane
Christmas
SSD

a country
fit for heroes

VOLUME 2

Attack Of The Killer B's

The Most Flipped Sides From The Nation's Leading Waxworks Including: Laurie Anderson, The Blasters, T-Bone Burnett,
Marshall Crenshaw, Peter Gabriel, Gang Of Four, John Hiatt, Pretenders, Ramones, Roxy Music, Talking Heads, The Time
Volume One

BARRICADED SUSPECTS

BIG CITY

AINT TOO PRETTY

CHAOS PRODUCTIONS présente

CHAOS EN FRANCE
VOLUME N°1

CAMERA SILENS
COLLABOS
TROTSKIDS
DREI OKLOK
BLANK SS
DE CONTROL

KOMINTERN SECT
KIDNAP
REICH ORGASM
SUB KIDS
NO CLASS
FOUTRE
SNIX

1983

A BOSTON ROCK CHRISTMAS 12" (BOSTON ROCK)

As the title suggested this was a Boston based Christmas
album put together by Boston Rock Magazine around the time
they put out issue 47 that featured Proletariat on the
cover as best band from their annual readers poll. Opening
with SSD (yes, really) with a slow rock, almost Oi! version
of "Jolly Old Saint Nicholas", and presumably an out-take
from "How We Rock" as all the recording credits are the
same. After this Jeff & Jane played a synth pop rendition
of "Jingle Bells" before the aptly named Christmas did a
college rock run through of "O Holy Night". The flip offered
Sonny Columbus & His Del Fuegos with "That Punchbowl Full
Of Joy", a roots rockabilly number, before Native Tongue
concluded proceedings with the post-punk meets college
rock meets reggae "Do You Hear What I Hear?". The cover art
was of course Christmas themed in green and red.

A COUNTRY FIT FOR HEROES VOLUME 2 LP (NO FUTURE RECORDS)

The second installment of the No Future demos collection
featuring "9 bands 12 trax" and first up was Patrol from
Leven in Scotland with two typical UK 82 sing-along anthems
before Mania from Sheffield picked up the pace a little
on "Blood Money". Government Lies (Bedford), On Parole
(Livingston) and Criminal Damage (Eastbourne) filled out
the rest of side one with three more songs that sounded
exactly like everything else. Side two featured; A.B.H.
(Lowestoft), Cadaverous Clan (Birmingham, featuring Damien
Thompson later of Warwound, Sacrilege and Varukers), Impact
(Cwmbran) and Intensive Care (Crawley) who all came from
a very similar musical place. Perhaps unsurprisingly only
two of the bands here went on to release anything on vinyl
during their existence and one of them was the novelty
single "Punk Christmas" by Impact. The LP was pressed as 12"
on 45rpm in a cheap sleeve with a pay no more than £2.50.

172

ATTACK OF THE KILLER B'S (VOLUME ONE) LP (WARNER BROTHERS)

An intriguing concept for a compilation, this was compiled
by Warner exceeutive Bob Merlis to highlight the oft ignored
B-side and presented this apparent set of flip sides for
our consideration, from a mixed bag of artists and musical
styles, in conjunction with Sire, Geffen, Slash and EG
Records. The curious thing is that despite the liner notes
by Merlis talking about B-sides, while some are indeed
B-sides, some of the songs are also album tracks or even
A-sides so ultimately it leaves you scratching your head in
the same way as how major labels used to dress up certain
bands to be 'new wave' on these compilations. Side one
featured; Marshall Crenshaw, The Pretenders, The Blasters,
Ramones ("Babysitter"), John Hiatt and Roxy Music. While
the B-side offered; Peter Gabriel, The Time, Talking Heads,
Gang Of Four ("Producer"), T-Bone Burnett, and Laurie
Anderson. The cover art depicted a graphic storyboard of a
strongman with a bee's head breaking a record.

BARRICADED SUSPECTS LP (TOXIC SHOCK RECORDS)

The first LP compilation from California label Toxic Shock
Records of underground hardcore bands from the U.S. and
Canada, that contained some gems mixed in with the more
forgettable. Of course the album opened with the label
owner Bill Sassenberger's own band Peace Corpse in a death
rock style before Human Therapy gave us their quirky
Southern Californian punk. Red Tide from British Columbia
changed things up with some all-over-the-place hardcore
before; Killroy, Romulans, Knockabouts, Abscess, Suburban
Mutilation, Septic Death (their first vinyl appearance), and
The Dull filled side one with varying styles of U.S. punk.
Side two continued in very much the same vein with; Massacre
Guys (featuring Karl Alvarez later of Descendents), Decry,
Roach Motel, Bonded In Unity, Mad Parade, The Hundredth
Monkey, Vision/Decay, and Hue And Cry. The LP featured cover
art by Pushead and came with an issue of Brainstorm zine
with a page on each band and Vince Ransid art on the back.

BIG CITY - AIN'T TOO PRETTY 7" EP (BIG CITY RECORDS)

The first of many great gritty D.I.Y. releases on the New York hardcore label and fanzine "Big City" run by Javi Savage aka John Souvadji of Vance Street, the Bronx. XKI (formerly Killer Instinct) opened proceedings with some three-quarters-female primitive hardcore on "I Hate Everything", followed by Betrayed and the hectic "Self Oppression". U.V. (Ultra Violence) continued with the frenetic hardcore of "I Don't Wanna Work" and side one closed with Javi's own Savage Circle and "We Don't Have To" with a searing guitar. No Thanks opened up the side two pit with more thrashing on "Are You Ready" before Armed Citizens and "Thrill Of It All" had a more controlled punk edge. "The Masses" by Fathead Suburbia supplied more of that dirty bass throttling New York hardcore and finally Savage Circle supplied a second song with the frantic "Kill Corps". The cover art depicted a graffitied wall and the EP also came with a small 12 page booklet with a page on each band.

CHAOS EN FRANCE - VOLUME NO. 1 LP (CHAOS PRODUCTIONS)

For some reason the French always seemed to have a penchant for Oi! so it's not surprising that this country's earliest foray into the hardcore punk era compilation would be centred around all thing boots and braces. Thirteen bands with a song each; Camera Silens, Collabos, Trotskids, Drei Oklok, Blank SS, Decontrol, Komintern Sect, Kidnap, Reich Orgasm, Sub Kids, No Class, Foutre, and Snix. Pretty much all badly played and barely in tune skinhead rock but with all the requisite sing-along Oi! Oi! Oi! choruses. As far as I'm aware the only band known to be politically dodgy here were Snix. The whole album was just dull and uninspiring plod, all seemingly based around the balder bands of U.K. '82 but with even less practice. Maybe glue was cheaper in France, who knows? The cover art was a cartoon by Punky dit Stephane of Komintern Sect depicting their crazy skinhead antics with the tricolour behind, of course. Some copies came with a 16 page "Chaos Fanzine No. 1". Oi! Le Album.

COTTAGE CHEESE FROM THE LIPS OF DEATH

A TEXAS HARDCORE COMPILATION

Disturbing the peace

415 RECORDS

RadioShow

ROMEO VOID
TRANSLATOR
RED ROCKERS
NEW MATH
POP'O'PIES
WIRE TRAIN

NOT FOR SALE
FOR PROMOTION ONLY

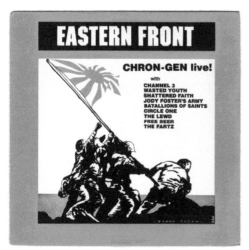

EASTERN FRONT

CHRON-GEN live!

with

CHANNEL 3
WASTED YOUTH
SHATTERED FAITH
JODY FOSTER'S ARMY
BATALLIONS OF SAINTS
CIRCLE ONE
THE LEWD
FREE BEER
THE FARTZ

ORIGINAL MOTION PICTURE SOUNDTRACK

Get Crazy

SPARKS
"GET CRAZY"

RAMONES
"CHOP SUEY"

LOU REED
"LITTLE SISTER"

MARSHALL CRENSHAW

LORI EASTSIDE & NADA
"HOT SHIMA MEE II" "YOU CAN'T MAKE ME"

MALCOLM McDOWELL
"NOT MINE"

'ISM

LAUGHIN NOSE

THE EXECUTE

B-Z ET

THE CLAY

ABURADAKO

GREAT
PUNK
HITS

HARD CORE TAKES OVER

DIRT

Compilation #Two

COTTAGE CHEESE FROM THE LIPS OF DEATH LP (WARD-9 RECORDS)

Pretty much the definitive Texas hardcore era compilation on Ward-9 out of San Antonio that featured; Really Red, D.R.I. (Dirty Rotten Imbeciles), The Offenders, Mydolls, Not For Sale, Big Boys, Prenatal Lust, Stick Men With Rayguns, Hugh Beaumont Experience, Marching Plague, Butthole Surfers, Bang Gang, The Dicks, and Watchtower. Side one rattled along at a hell of a clip for the first three songs before Mydolls, Not For Sale and Big Boys pulled the reins and Prenatal Lust ended side one fast. The second opened darkly with Stick Men With Rayguns, before Hugh Beaumont Experience and Marching Plague delivered the hardcore. "The Shah Sleeps" by Butthole Surfers then appears (on the second press it was replaced by "I Hate My Job" presumably as by that point "The Shah Sleeps" was the opener on their debut 12"). Bang Gang then returned to hardcore before The Dicks delivered their strangest song and Watchtower concluded in a metal style. Cover art (and probably title) was by Gibby Haynes.

DISTURBING THE PEACE - RADIO SHOW LP (415 RECORDS)

A unique not for sale promo only LP of a radio show to promote San Francisco's 415 Records, recorded by label head Howie Klein at local station KUSF 90.3FM where he was also a DJ. The show began with three songs by Romeo Void (including the hit "Never Say Never") followed by Translator with three songs (featuring their post-punk cold war paranoia anthem "Sleeping Snakes"), three from Red Rockers (with "Dead Heroes" that also featured a band intro), and then one song each from; New Math, Pop-O-Pies (for some reason the repetitive "Truckin'"), and Wire Train. There was plenty of informative spiel from Howie between songs, as well as radio jingles and interludes aplenty, a spoof movie advert for "Exene's Bongo Party" and non-featured band members chime in such as; Hugo Burnham from Gang Of Four, B-Team, Richard Butler of Psychedelic Furs, and even Johnny Ramone. Howie even checks the clock and gives out the phone number for you to call in. An excellent yet unknown compilation.

EASTERN FRONT (VOLUME TWO) LP (ENIGMA RECORDS)

The second live installment to document the second of Wes Robertson's Eastern Front hardcore festivals in Berkeley that took place on Sat July 31st 1982 at Aquatic Park. Headliners Chron Gen opened the album with two songs "Clouded Eyes" and "Reality" before Channel 3 blazed through "Mannequin" and Free Beer gave us "My Money Or My Car". Wasted Youth continued with "We're On Heroin" before Battalion Of Saints closed side one with "Fighting Boys". Side two brought us more Chron Gen with "Breaking Down" followed by locals The Lewd and "M-17". "Final Conflict" by Shattered Faith, "Low Rider" by JFA (Jody Foster's Army), Circle One's "Red Machine" and a great version of "Buried Alive" by The Fartz concluded the LP. Hüsker Dü and Deadly Reign played but didn't make the LP cut for some reason. The festival poster art by San Francisco designer Randy Tuten (known for his work for Bill Graham at The Fillmore) became the cover art for the album that received only one press.

GET CRAZY - SOUNDTRACK LP (MOROCCO RECORDS)

The soundtrack to the rock'n'roll comedy flick that starred Malcolm McDowell as Reggie Wanker, Lee Ving of Fear as Piggy and Lou Reed as Auden. Opening with the title track as performed by Sparks, then spoof movie band Lori Eastside (of Kid Creole And The Coconuts) & Nada, and it hit 80s synth pop overload at this point but then Ramones turned up with the unreleased elsewhere "Chop Suey". Marshall Crenshaw put in a country rock appearance before Lou Reed closed out side one with the six minute "Little Sister" (Nico). Side two had another Lori Eastside & Nada song before Malcolm McDowell did "Hot Shot" (also with Nada) and Bill Henderson supplied a version of Muddy Waters' "The Blues Had A Baby And They Named It Rock & Roll". The album then piqued punk interest with the then unreleased version of "Hoochie Coochie Man" by Fear, before Michael Boddicker and Howard Kaylan & Cast completed the picture. Along with the lurid cover art this is pretty much peak eighties cheese.

GREAT PUNK HITS LP (JAPAN RECORD)

Six Japanese bands and twelve songs and first up was Gism
with a slower trudging metal punk song and a faster number
both with trademark Sakevi's guttural vocals. The Execute
were up next with two pacey metallic thrashers (the Japanese
really were ahead of the curve with the metal influence
in punk), and Aburadako concluded side one with two more
snotty punk songs that sounded right out of Bristol 1982.
Side two opened with the amusingly named Laughin Nose with
one Oi! influenced thumper and a faster more abrasive
thrasher, again that seemed to have a little Bristol cider
influence. The Clay let rip with two galloping Discharge
style rippers before G-Zet follow with one U.K. style throaty
punk belcher, and a slower instrumental closed play. Out
of the early 80s Japanese compilations this was the most
consistent for my money. The cover art depicted a spiky
punk that was later reworked for "Killed By Death #6 - Great
Punk Shits". The Japanese insert had photos and band info.

HARDCORE TAKES OVER (DIRT COMPILATION # TWO) LP (DIRT RECORDS)

An 8 band 16 song set from New Jersey bands recorded live at
the Dirt Club in Bloomfield, NJ. TMA set the tone by blasting
through two power rippers, "I'm In Love With Nancy Reagan"
and "Herpes II" before the Phil Scalzo Band supplied the
snarling "Savage Truth" and "Death House Riot". Mourning
Noise took things down a darker path with "Progress For
The People" (written by two members of Adrenalin O.D.) and
"Radical", followed by Mad Daddys who rocked it up in a
Cramps style with "Cool And Wild" and "Acid Rain Dance".
Stetz opened up the second side rattling through "East
Coast Slamming" and "Ain't Gonna Be In No Army" before Sand
In The Face gave us the reverb vocals of "Auschwitz" and
"Laughing At Me". Hardcore rippers 13 Day Vacation then
served up the charmingly titled "She Fucks For Drugs" and
"Tear Down The Walls" before Genocide (of the split LP with
M.I.A.) belted through "Stillborn" and "Never Nothing".
Some nice hand-written graphic design tops off the package.

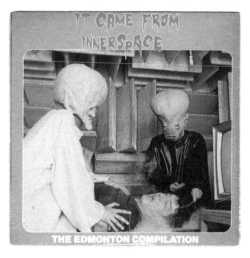

HELL COMES TO YOUR HOUSE - PART II LP (BEMISBRAIN RECORDS)

For the second installment Bemisbrain veered away from the hardcore and death rock of volume one and tilted towards the roots rock'n'roll that had splintered off in L.A. when hardcore rose its ugly head. First up came The Joneses with two of their more rock'n'roll numbers followed by two Stooges style Mau Maus songs (this being their only vinyl appearance during their existence). Cambridge Apostles also only ever appeared here (featuring Bruce and Mike Atta of Middle Class with Alice Bag and Tiffany of Castration Squad) with a long winded dance song. Blood On The Saddle concluded side one with two rockin' country numbers while side two delivered three Tex And The Horseheads tunes before Minutemen gave us "Corona". Two rock'n'roll meets the Go-Go's songs by Screamin' Sirens were next before the album closed with Lotus Lame And The Lame Flames. Incredible cover art by Shawn Kerri (Germs, Circle Jerks) adorned the front cover with a photo collage on the back.

IT CAME FROM INNERSPACE LP (RUBBER RECORDS)

Sub-titled "The Edmonton Compilation", this of course was a showcase of Edmonton, Alberta, bands all recorded in June 1983 at The Funhouse and notable for the first appearance of the now legendary SNFU. The first three bands; The Touch, The Thieves and Route 66 all had a jerky and jangly mod feel to them, while Facecrime slowed things down in a bass-driven post-punk way with a catchy poppy chorus. Down Syndrome then turned the punk rock burners on before Malibu Kens supplied a little harmonised Beach Boys style pop punk. SNFU then made their vinyl debut with "(Real Men Don't Watch) Quincy" (all three of their songs here ended up on a bootleg 7" of the same name). The Standards then closed side one with their only choppy mod style song while all the other bands got to have another song on side two. A reenactment photo of sci-fi series Outer Limits adorned the front and back covers, and the album also came with a small eight page glossy booklet with liner notes espousing D.I.Y.

(I'VE GOT THOSE...) DEMO-LITION BLUES! LP (INSANE RECORDS)

A collection of eighteen U.K. bands who submitted demo
tapes (and most of whom did very little else), with a song
each compiled by the Middlehurst brothers of The Insane
on Insane Records of Wigan. Side one featured the thumping
U.K. '83 punk sounds of; The Deceased, Epidemic, The
Secluded, Solvent Abuse, The Drill, A Few Tears, Diabolists,
Obsessed, and Youthanasia PX. Side two afforded more noise
and distortion with; Aborted, Picture Frame Seduction, Act
Of Defiance, Seizure, Social Outrage, Devoid, M.W.A.B.,
and the LP concluded with two Welsh bands; Mutilated Jelly
and The Oppressed. As you can probably imagine, the vast
majority of this was fairly similar in approach at a time
when there was a huge wave of U.K. bands pretty much all
emulating the likes of The Exploited, GBH or Chaos U.K.,
and you could hear it throughout this collection. The front
cover typically features a bulldozer with, presumably, the
Middlehurst brothers on the reverse wielding sledgehammers.

KEINE EXPERIMENTE! LP (WEIRD SYSTEM)

West Germany turned up the heat again with the standard
Weird System formula of nine bands with two songs each,
totalling eighteen tracks, recorded at various studios
in Essen and Berlin between January and September 1983.
Featuring; Razzia, Boskops, ZSD, The Buttocks, Upright
Citizens, Blut & Eisen, Deutsche Trinkerjugend, Razzia, and
Daily Terror, who all put in a good showing with some high
energy crunchy and pacey punk with no filler. The charmingly
named The Buttocks stood out with their ripping hardcore
with breakneck and piercing hi-hat and of course Upright
Citizens with "Gift to Europe" and "Stand Up". Razzia and
ZSD also delivered the goods with searing guitars while
SS Ultrabrutal even dabbled in bass-driven spiky post-
punk stand out "You Could Be Me". The cover predicted the
future with a photo of three grannies in wheelchairs done
up as punks/bikers, a photo of young German punks on the
rear, and an LP sized insert supplied all the band info.

LIFE IS BEAUTIFUL SO WHY NOT EAT HEALTH FOODS? LP
(NEW UNDERGROUND RECORDS)

The second installment of the "Life Is..." Collections
from Anti's label and for this one they upped the ante
with fifteen bands and twenty four songs. Side one kicked
off in raucous style with; Bags "We Will Bury You" before
two Anti songs, three by Shattered Faith, one from China
White, and then two each from M.I.A. (not the Las Vegas
band), while Ill Will and Germs (live) to concluded side
one. As was the case with most of the compilations, side
one was for the hardcore while side two headed into artier
territory, so the flip here brought us Minutemen, Bpeople,
(the Anti related) Mood Of Defiance, Invisible Chains,
Marshall Mellow (not actually included due to technical
difficulties), Zurich 1916, Vox Pop, and Powertrip. The
hippie mocking front cover art was of course by Raymond
Pettibon, while the back simply had a hand-written track
list, with lyrics and info on the photocopied insert.

LIFE IS BORING SO WHY NOT STEAL THIS RECORD LP
(NEW UNDERGROUND RECORDS)

The third and final installment of the "Life Is..." series
and this carried on the yellow and red cover art theme
of the first with Pettibon artwork depicting a group of
skinheads; "The violence is, to me, more exciting, more
thrilling, more sensationally sexy... than Black Flag"
signed by Pettibon. The album itself also continued the
theme of bands; Germs (live), Minutemen, Redd Kross, Modern
Warfare, Shattered Faith, Anti, Mood Of Defiance, Hari-
Kari, Sin 34, Artistic Decline, Modern Torture, Invisible
Chains, Slivers, Vox Pop, Marshall Mellow, Carl Stone,
Doo-Dooettes, Zurich 1916, Tone Deaf, and Debt Of Nature.
An 8.5" x 11" pink insert was included and, due to the
screw up omitting Marshall Mellow on the previous volume,
one side is dedicated to them with typed info on the rest
on the reverse. All three albums in the series provided an
insight into the Southern California punk scene of the day.

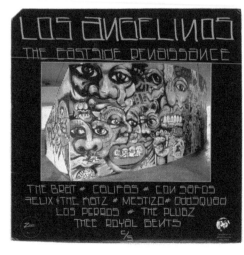

The Texas music scene is as eclectic as that of any region in the world today. **Moment Productions** is Texas' largest new music record label. The Lone Star State's tradition as a breeding ground for innovative music can be traced from **Bob Wills** to **Buddy Holly** to the **Thirteenth Floor Elevators** to the modern Texas sounds that Moment represents. Moment's artists roster exemplifies the best new Texas music ranging from avant-garde electronic to hardcore. The following information serves only as an introduction—there is much, much more to come.

LIVE AT THE HOT KLUB LP (VVV RECORDS)

"Made in Texas by Texans"... Recorded live at the Dallas club in June 1982 on Neal Caldwell of Non Compos Mentis' label and record store VVV. First up was the new wave of the Doo (formerly of Tulsa, OK), followed by the white reggae of The Telefones. The Ralphs then showcased their dark synth punk with "Drug Induced State" before The Fort Worth Cats did a Shadows style surfy rock'n'roll instrumental, and side one closed with The Ejectors (also from Fort Worth) with a scratchy new wave song. Side two opened with the raucous punk of Non Compos Mentis (NCM) and "Mental Case", before Hugh Beaumont Experience offered two snotty teenage hardcore blasts that were worth the price of admission alone. Stickmen With Rayguns then took things down a dark path before The Devices delivered some basic punk rock. The Frenetics supplied some nervous new wave followed by NCM who closed the album with "No Can Do". The cover featured a live shot with photos of the venue on the back.

LOS ANGELINOS - THE EASTSIDE RENAISSANCE LP (ZYANYA RECORDS)

On the Rhino subsidiary Zyanya came this showcase of the Chicano new wave era bands of East Los Angeles. Opening with an early 1979 version of the brilliant later 7" "Achin'" by El Paso imports The Plugz, and followed by the equally excellent The Brat with "The Wolf", a critique of American democracy. Felix & The Katz then delivered a ska tinged new wave with a Latin identity imported from Tecate, Mexico. The Brat followed this again with the punk rock "High School" before Odd Squad took it all in a dancey new wave direction featuring Eddie Ayala, the original Los Illegals vocalist (Los Illegals noticeably absent from the LP). Con Safos closed the side in a funk style, featuring Ruben Guevara who ran Zyanya. Apart from "Electrify Me" by The Plugz side two took a more traditional Hispanic turn with trumpets, flute, congas and timbales from; Thee Royal Gents, Califas, Mestizo, and Los Perros. The cover featured barrio graffiti with band photos and information on the back. A lost gem.

LUNG COOKIES - A NATIONAL COLLECTION LP (SMOKE 7/YOUR FLESH)

Originally planned as a cassette compilation but switched
to vinyl to "get more attention". A collaboration between
Felix Alanis of RF7 from Canoga Park, California, and Peter
Davis of Your Flesh fanzine of Minneapolis, Minnesota.
"Lung Cookies" opened with 3 songs from Seattle's 10 Minute
Warning, featuring Fartz and Accüsed members (two of these
songs later adopted by those bands). Final Conflict and
Ground Zero (both from Minneapolis), followed with 3 and
2 songs respectively, before Seattle's Rejectors blasted
through 3 more hardcore outbursts. Otto's Chemical Lounge
from Minneapolis grungily closed side one featuring Tom
Hazelmeyer, later of Amphetamine Reptile Records. Side two
brought us the punk of Boy Elroy (Minneapolis) and the hardcore
of RF7 (L.A.), Willful Neglect and Red Meat (Minneapolis),
Sacred Order (Milwaukee), and No Thanks (NYC). The cover
featured a still from 1958 flick "The Cyclops", and the LP
came with a 12 page Xerox zine with a page on each band.

MIGHTY FEEBLE LP (NEW ALLIANCE RECORDS)

Following on from "Feeble Efforts" came the full length
"Mighty Feeble" on the Minutemen's label New Alliance,
that delved into the art and experimental side of the
underground, as well as some one-off projects by their
friends. Tape loops, random shouts and offbeat drum beats,
sometimes bordering on proto-industrial was the order of
the day from the following artists; Misguided Population,
Debt Of Nature, Marshal Mellow, Elevator (Bill Stevenson,
Greg Ginn and Mike Watt), Jimmy Smack, James B. Slayden
Jr., Autistic Divinity, Los Luies, Modern Torture, Gary
Jacobelly Ensemble, Severed Head In A Bag, Spot (the
engineer), Kamikaze Refrigerators, Buffalo Gals, Mr. Epp &
The Calculations (featuring Mark Arm and Steve Turner who
went onto form Green River and Mudhoney), Turds From Space,
Gino Pusztai, Sec, Epedermal Refractions, and Zurich 1916
(Gary Kail of Anti). With a total length of 48 minutes this
is not totally unlistenable and comes in an arty sleeve.

MIXED NUTS DON'T CRACK LP (OUTSIDE RECORDS)

While Dischord Records quickly took over the punk landscape of Washington D.C. there were other bands who, for whatever reason, didn't see releases on the label. First on this alternative to "Flex Your Head" was Media Disease with six songs of HarDCore not unlike early Dischord EPs by the likes of Youth Brigade. The all-female band Chalk Circle then changed the tempo to a more subdued marching post-punk for two songs before Social Suicide saw out side one blasting through four hardcore songs and featured Danny Ingram of Youth Brigade (and many others) on drums. Side two began with four typically blistering whirlwind hardcore songs from United Mutation, who were like Void's even more disturbed brother, then four songs from the strange Nuclear Crayons before three from Hate From Ignorance featuring Monica Richards later of Madhouse. The sleeve featured two etchings from Albrecht Dürer and the album came with two large lyric sheets and six smaller inserts for each band.

MOMENT PRODUCTIONS 8" FLEXI (MOMENT PRODUCTIONS)

An oversized promotional flexi to promote this Austin, Texas, label that was run by Alisa Erin O'Leary and Anne Goetzmann, and existed between 1979 and 1985. Opening band D-Day played a very pop new wave with a hint of ska and female vocals on "More Than That", followed by two songs from the legendary Big Boys in the form of "Lesson" and "Funk Off" from their Moment album "Lullabies Help The Brain Grow". The flip of this double sided heavy duty flexi gave us Standing Waves and more ska infused new wave with "Crash And Burn" from their Moment 12". The showcase concluded with The Pool and the synth pop of "Dance It Down" ("...in Austin town"), again from their Moment 12". The packaging was quite unique in that it was a sort of 8"x10" foldout featuring a Moment record playing on the cover and a pocket for the flexi. The inside of the foldout featured photos and info on the bands, as well as their record covers reproduced, and mini-discographies on the back cover.

NEWWAVE/ULTRAWAVE - BOSTON ROCK-N-ROLL ANTHOLOGY LP (VARULVEN)

As the title suggests this was a double A-side showcase of
Boston bands from Count Viglione's "Varulven" imprint that
had started as a zine in 1969. The Spores opened the "New
Wave" side with a pounding 80s rock anthem with lead sax,
before Ava Electra followed with two female-vocal rock
thumpers, and then the Count Viglione Band took things in
a hypnotic rock direction. Future City then went the synth
rock route before Joe Mazzari Of The Daughters did their
classic rock. The more interesting "Ultra Wave" side began
with Relentless Cookout with the catchy and political
almost-ska new wave of "Poverty", before IC4 offered two
jerky synth new wave songs. The New Race then gave us some
standard new wave before Disarray were a little heavier in
the dramatic synth new wave department. Concluding the LP
was the first vinyl appearance of legendary Boston thrashers
Psycho with the blazing "How Much Longer?" presumably
recorded at Radiobeat along with their debut "8 Song E.P."

NOISE FROM NOWHERE 7" EP (TOXIC SHOCK RECORDS)

"This is not L.A. or Boston or nowhere!" The first Toxic
Shock 7" release opened with Kent State and "Breakout
Breakfree", one of their two vinyl appearances (the other
being "Radio Moscow" on the third "Rodney On The Roq"
compilation LP from 1982), this being the less anthemic of
the two. Modern Industry followed this with the chiming
melodic punk of "Out Of Focus" and featured two members
who went onto Abandoned and Flower Leperds. Moslem Birth
on the flip slowed things down into a nihilistic dirge with
"Horror Snores" that was all the Peace Corpse members with
Toxic Shock's Bill Sassenberger on vocals. Manson Youth
closed play with the snappy beach punk sound of "Penis
Brain" that featured Corey Miller on drums who later became
a famous tattooist on Kat Von D's "L.A. Ink" TV show (his
own studio being "Six Feet Under" in Upland, California).
The sleeve was adorned with hideous Pushead artwork, with
band photos and info on the inside.

PHILLY HARDCORE COMPILATION - GET OFF MY BACK LP (RED MUSIC)

As the title stated this was Philadelphia putting itself on
the hardcore map with a ten band and twenty song set. First
up was YDI (Why Die?) with two of their signature hardcore
songs (one fast, one slow). F.O.D. (Flag Of Democracy) was
up next with two of their deranged DK style thrashers,
before Blunder Boys offered three scrappy polka hardcore
tunes, while Little Gentlemen slowed things down to a
shouty punk tempo. Autistic Behavior closed side one with
two twisted teenage outbursts. Side two began with two
catchy Ruin numbers (one slow, one fast), before Informed
Sources gave us a couple of frantic youth blasts and Seeds
Of Terror attempted high school hardcore with what sounded
like an out of tune toy guitar and a few shoe boxes. Skate
rock legends McRad followed this with some reggae-into-
hardcore, before The Heathens ended things with snotty
hardcore. Wrapped in black and white adolescent punk art
this was oddly pressed by a CBS subsidiary in Holland.

POSH HITS VOL. 1 LP (POSH BOY RECORDS)

"I would like to introduce you to 16 California groups with
which I've worked since 1979". Following on from "Rodney
On The Roq", Robbie Fields' Posh Boy released this all-star
Californian punk (with some synth pop) collection that was
a logical continuation of that three record series (and
containing some of the same songs). Featuring underground
hits by; Circle Jerks, Agent Orange, Social Distortion,
Crowd, U.X.A., Red Cross, Baby Buddha, F-Word!, Los
Microwaves, Channel 3, Black Flag, Simpletones, Shattered
Faith, T.S.O.L., Stepmothers, and Nuns, this remains a
classic compilation of the era. With liner notes by Al
Flipside, punk-mocking cover art by Raymond Pettibon and
graphic design by Diane Zincavage, "Posh Hits" was reissued
as "God Bless America" in the U.K. by Fallout Records (a Jungle
subsidiary) in 1985 with different cover art (pictured),
and the U.K. version of the cover was then later colourised
in 1987 and reissued in the U.S. under its original title.

PROPAGANDA - HARDCORE '83 LP (PROPAGANDA RECORDS)

While the U.K. was still largely mired in a council estate plod, the Finnish weren't messing around and this 18 band and 35 song album was testament to that. Of those songs only 7 breach 2 minutes so I'm sure you can imagine what style these bands were going for. Featuring a line-up of many soon-to-be Finnish punk bands of note; Kansan Uutiset, Riistetyt, Jakke & Lateri, Äpärät, Rattus, Tampere SS, Protesti, alamaailma, Kuolema, Bastards, H.I.C. Systeemi, Fucking Finland, Destrucktions, Marionetti, Maanalainen Pelastusarmeija, Sekunda, Takuu, and Varaus. The vast majority of the bands here modelled themselves on the hugely influential Discharge (mixed with some lingering '77 influences) but this was before big production and metal-creep so it was all raw and unfiltered (Tampere SS being a good example). The cover art was a black and white collage of photos of Finnish punks formed into a map of Finland with a skull and crossbones montage on the reverse.

PUNK AND DISORDERLY III - THE FINAL SOLUTION LP (ANAGRAM)

The final installment in this series of U.K. punk indie chart busters that was hit after hit of the old Evo-stik compiled by Phil Langham of The Dark, with songs licensed from the likes of Riot City, No Future, Secret and Fallout Records. Sixteen songs from sixteen bands that kicked off with; Abrasive Wheels ("Burn 'Em Down"), One Way System ("Give Us A Future"), Newtown Neurotics ("Kick Out The Tories"), and a similar roster of 7" songs from; U.K. Subs, The Destructors (what the hell was "Jailbait" all about eh?), The Expelled, The Samples ("Dead Hero"), Angelic Upstarts, The Adicts ("Viva La Revolution"), The Vibrators, The Exploited ("Computers Don't Blunder"), Urban Dogs, The Ejected, Chron Gen, Action Pact, and The Violators. The cover depicted a group of punks facing a firing squad outside No. 10 Downing Street while Hitler and Thatcher looked on, although it has to be said that the punks photographed on the floor were more likely to have been drunk than dead.

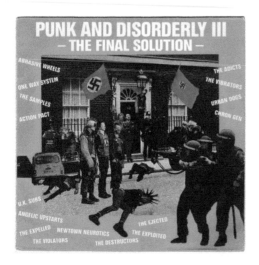

PUNK AND DISORDERLY III
— THE FINAL SOLUTION —

ABRASIVE WHEELS
ONE WAY SYSTEM
THE SAMPLES
ACTION PACT

THE ADICTS
THE VIBRATORS
URBAN DOGS
CHRON GEN

U.K. SUBS
ANGELIC UPSTARTS
THE EXPELLED   NEWTOWN NEUROTICS   THE EJECTED
THE VIOLATORS   THE DESTRUCTORS   THE EXPLOITED

PUNK DEAD – NAH MATE, THE SMELL IS JUS SUMMINK IN YER UNDERPANTS INNIT

PUNK QUE? PUNK

REVENGE OF PERMANENT WAVE

SF Sound OF Music Club Live

Stereo   Vol.1

PUNK DEAD - NAH MATE, THE SMELL IS JUS SUMMINK IN YER UNDERPANTS INNIT LP (PAX RECORDS)

The somewhat adolescent title belied some of the more serious intent of some of the content contained on this Pax Records compilation that followed on from Wargasm. If the passionate liner notes on the reverse were anything to go by, label owner Marcus Featherby was mainly inspired to release this record by one less-than-inspiring Garry Bushell article. The bands herein were mainly from the label's home town of Sheffield, although Bradford, Huddersfield and Chesterfield were also represented. The bands in question were; Mau Maus, Xtract (featuring Karl Morris of Exploited and Broken Bones on guitar), Anti-System, Mania, Xpozez (featuring Tez later of Instigators), and Septic Psychos, all with two songs each. The cover art depicted a grid of photos of various punks (proving punk's not dead?) With liner notes on the back, lyrics, and even more photos on the inside of the gatefold sleeve.

PUNK QUE? PUNK LP (DRO)

Another early entry into the Spanish punk conversation on DRO (Discos Radioactivos Organizados) and this one removed any new wave in favour of straight up punk rock. Fourteen songs from eight artists; P.P. Tan Solo, Urgente, Espasmódicos, No (5), N.634, KGB, Seguridad Social, and Carne De Psiquiatrico, with two songs each apart from P.P. Tan Solo who also played in Carne De Psiquiatrico so those two had one song each. The opener by P.P. Tan Solo "I Want To Be The Guitarist Of Siniestro Total" was interesting as it was a song he recorded after being impressed by the band Siniestro Total and sent it into a radio station, receiving airplay in a competition where he was voted up to 26th place. As a result Siniestro Total credited him on their 1982 debut LP "¿Cuándo Se Come Aquí?" ("When do you eat here?"). The style throughout is anthemic 1982 style punk with the more hardcore Espasmódicos standing out from the crowd. The cover art featured a very punk dead rat.

REALLY FAST VOL. 1 LP (REALLY FAST RECORDS)

The first volume in a series of ten Swedish hardcore punk compilations that spanned the Eighties and Nineties, with the first four falling within the dates of this book. Thirty one songs from twelve bands; Missbrukarna, Anti-Cimex, Kurt I Kuvös, Product Assar, Hidden Industrials, Terror Pop, Asta Kask, Huvudtvätt, Nasty Boys, DNA, Destroy, Sune Studs Och Grönlandsrockarna, Ernst And The Edsholm Rebels (E.A.T.E.R.), and P-Nissarna. For the most part this set was made up of rapid fire hardcore blasters in the Discharge vein that would go on to influence many as Käng Punk. That said, side one concluded with the more tuneful punk of Terror Pop and Trall Punk of Asta Kask. Side two opened with Huvudtvätt aka Headcleaners that set the album back on its noisy course and this style continued with E.A.T.E.R. being a stand out. The sleeve was a D.I.Y. foldout poster with a photo collage on the front, track list on a plain back cover and band graphic sections on the reverse.

REVENGE OF THE PERMANENT WAVE LP (EPIC RECORDS)

Four years after "Permanent Wave" Epic compiled this ten band and song follow-up at the back end of "new wave" in 1983. First of the set was; New Musik from London with their synth pop new wave (their other band was 'fusion' funk outfit the Nick Straker Band). Mi-Sex from New Zealand followed this with more synth (more older bearded types who'd emerged out of various prog bands). Then came The Quick (not the L.A. band) with more funky synth rock hell, before The Photos brought back the guitars and drums with the somewhat older "I'm So Attractive" and Susan Fassbender closed side one with more synth pop. "Video Killed The Radio Star" co-writer Bruce Woolley then presented his version of the song with his Camera Club before T.V. Smith's Explorers briefly took a different direction. L.A. power pop band 20/20 then gave us older song "Yellow Pills" before synthy Australians Flash & The Pan and then this odd album closed with The Tourists (Annie Lennox) from 1979.

SF SOUND OF MUSIC CLUB LIVE, VOL. 1 LP (SOM RECORDS)

Another live document and hidden gem of the artier side of the San Francisco punk era. Recorded at the club of the same name that was situated on Turk Street in the Tenderloin district, and owned by Filipino Celso Ruperto who started booking punk as an alternative to drag shows. The ten song and ten band album opened with the overlooked all-female new wave trio The Contractions with the menacing "Life & Death". Following this were Repeat Offenders and the Nicaragua themed political reggae of "Somoza Is Dead". ELF warbled their way through their keyboard post-punk before Arkansaw Man did their understated post-punk, and Boy Trouble ended side one in a disturbing fashion. Defectors dark offering opened the flip before Ibbilly Bibbily went all smoke-filled lounge. Dogtown then did the chiming, marching post-punk of "Nightmare" followed by the shimmering "Punk" of Katherin, and Farmers concluded the album with the "Blade Runner" style synth/sax wave of "Torch Song".

SLASH: THE EARLY SESSIONS LP (SLASH RECORDS)

A budget hits sampler collection of early material on L.A.'s Slash Records from between 1980-1983. Opening side one came The Blasters and the steady rock'n'roll of "Border Radio", before Gun Club pounded "Sex Beat" into your skull. Post-Dils country punk outfit Rank And File followed this with "The Conductor Wore Black", followed by Violent Femmes' indie anthem "Blister In The Sun". The Blasters returned to conclude the first half with "Long White Cadillac". The second side began with X and debut album title song "Los Angeles" before Fear and "New York's Alright If You Like Saxophones" and "Caught In My Eye" by Germs. The slightly square-peg feel of The Dream Syndicate then played their jangly college rock with "Tell Me When It's Over" before X returned to close play with their single "White Girl". A religious etching of Gustave Doré featured on the cover, put together by designer Lou Beach that depicted Moses delivering the Ten Commandments, updated to feature an LP.

THE BEST OF

LOUIE, LOUIE

The Greatest Renditions of Rock's #1 All Time Song

The Sandpipers The Kingsmen Richard Berry Rice University Marching Band

The Stains The Last Black Flag

AND MORE!

THE
BLASTING CONCEPT

BLACK FLAG   HÜSKER DÜ   SACCHARINE TRUST   WURM
MINUTEMEN   MEAT PUPPETS   STAINS   OVERKILL

AN SST COMPILATION

THE DEFIANT POSE

THE LORDS OF THE NEW CHURCH • THE CRAMPS • THE ALARM • CROWN OF THORNS • WALL OF VOODOO • THE FALL • COMETIES

HOLY WAR • DRUG TRAIN • MARCHING ON • GONE ARE THE DAYS • ON INTERSTATE 15 • FIERY JACK • THE CRACK

THE KIDS ARE UNITED

Sham 69 · Exploited · Cockney Rejects · Splodge

UK Subs   4 Skins   Angelic Upstarts   + more

THE MASTER TAPE VOL. 2

THE BEST OF LOUIE, LOUIE LP (RHINO RECORDS)

Did the world need ten versions of the song "Louie Louie"? Probably not. But Rhino Records was happy to oblige anyway on this album compiled by label head Richard Foos in conjunction with L.A. radio station KFJC. First was Rice University Marching Owl Band doing a brass band instrumental version which acted as an intro of sorts before Richard Berry's original 1956 doo-wop version with The Pharaohs. The first rock'n'roll version from 1961 by Rockin' Robin Roberts followed this before The Sonics 1966 fuzzed up garage version continued the chronological theme. Closing the first side, The Sandpipers did their 1967 harmonious Laurel Canyon style take. Back to 1963 on side two for The Kingsmen's version that popularised the song before it all went back up to date with The Last and their slower, darker 1983 take before Black Flag took it by the throat in 1981 (the reason for this LP's inclusion). Les Dantz And His Orchestra and The Impossibles then supplied filler versions for this LP.

THE BLASTING CONCEPT LP (SST RECORDS)

The first compilation from SST was a label sampler with songs from the first 11 releases plus a bolted on Hüsker Dü song from the 20th. Minutemen opened up with 4 of their short signature blasts, 2 from "Paranoid Time" and 2 from "The Punch Line". Meat Puppets followed this with 2 songs from their first album, "Tumblin' Tumbleweeds" and their theme, before Saccharine Trust closed side 1 with "A Human Certainty" from their "Paganicons" 12". Side 2 saw Black Flag offer 3 songs from 3 releases and 3 vocalists; "Nervous Breakdown", "Jealous Again" and "I've Heard It Before", then came Overkill's "Hell's Getting Hotter" from their 7", "Get Revenge" from the Stains LP, Würm's "I'm Dead" from their 7" and Hüsker Dü's "Real World" from later "Metal Circus". The cover art of course was by Raymond Pettibon while the liner notes were by Harvey Kubernik dated September 1983. Presumably the release was delayed as the first 20 SST releases are featured while the catalogue number was SST013.

THE DEFIANT POSE LP (ILLEGAL)

A budget sampler of some of the talent on Miles Copeland's U.K. based label (he also founded I.R.S., Faulty Products, Step-Forward, Total Noise and Deptford Fun City among others) that he'd started to release the first 7" from his brother's band The Police. This compilation was a sixteen band mix of material from releases on Illegal, Step-Forward and I.R.S.; The Lords Of The New Church, The Cramps, The Alarm, Crown Of Thorns, Wall Of Voodoo, The Fall, Cosmetics, Chelsea, Chron Gen, The Business, Major Accident, Menace, The Cortinas, Sham 69, The Models, and Circle Jerks. As you can probably imagine this was all over the map style-wise from '77 punk to UK '82 to all manner of post-punk, despite its punk cover image of an attack dog. The art department must've misread the tracklist as only the songs for side two appear on the back sleeve and it looks as if they thought the song titles for the side two bands were the band names for the bands on side one.

THE KIDS ARE UNITED LP (MUSIC FOR NATIONS)

Every label it seems had a punk compilation and metal label Music For Nations was no exception with this collection nestled between Tank and Virgin Steele as one of its early releases. With a lengthy waffle on the back cover by Garry Bushell who, as usual, was banging on about how these bands were due to replace that tired old '77 punk with their "street level rock'n'roll". That said, this centred around the Oi! side of things and was pretty much like another in the Oi! set of albums with some songs from "Oi! The Album", featuring; Sham 69, Cockney Rejects, Angelic Upstarts, The Exploited, 4 Skins, Toy Dolls, Peter And The Test Tube Babies, Max Splodge, U.K. Subs, and Cock Sparrer. Most of the bands supplied two songs apart from; 4 Skins, Test Tubes, Splodge, U.K. Subs, and Cock Sparrer (with the atrocious "Sunday Stripper") who all only had the one. The front cover featured a crowd shot of some fittingly aggressive looking youth in stark black and white.

THE MASTER TAPE VOL. 2 2LP (AFFIRMATION RECORDS)

Following on from volume 1, Paul Mahern went all out with a double album of 19 bands and 43 songs that alongside volume 1, stood as documents of how the hardcore punk infection had spread far from the coastal cities and deep into the suburbs of the heartland. Violent Apathy (MI), Malignant Growth (KY), Idiot Savants (OH), Sand In The Face (NJ), Poison Center (IN), Sacred Order (WI), No Labels (NC), Front Line (VA), End Result (IL), Repellents (IN), Killing Children (IN), The Fetish (IN, formerly Vibrato Fetish, and featuring Randy Ferguson, bassist of Latex Novelties and The Jetsons), Mecht Mensch (WI), Gynecologists (IN), Zero Boys (IN), Delinquents (IN), Tar Babies (WI), Wasted Talent (PA), and Anti-Bodies (IL). Pretty much all U.S. hardcore, but from a time when there was a level of uniformity, but also still individuality and geographic nature to the sound. With similar artwork to the first on silver the LP came with a 24 page newsprint booklet with a page on each band.

THE NEW HOPE LP (NEW HOPE RECORDS)

An overlooked set of eleven young Ohio bands that opened with the outstanding hardcore of The Guns, who were around 13-14 when they recorded their two opening songs. Positive Violence followed with three oompah hardcore songs, before Spike In Vain took us down a darker road for two. Agitated then ripped it up with three hardcore shredders featuring members of Starvation Army, Offbeats and Plague among others. No Parole then blasted through three songs with throaty female vocals before The Dark finished of side one in desperate style. Zero Defex kicked off side two with "Drop The A Bomb On Me", and three more erratic one minute blasts, before Outerwear offered two slower, stabbing songs featuring members of Spike In Vain. Then Offbeats ripped through two songs before P.P.G. slowed things down into a dirge (featuring members of Zero Defex and Plasma Alliance). Starvation Army then ended the album in a frantic fashion. This DIY punk album came with a 12 page Xeroxed booklet.

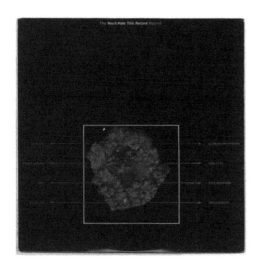

THE RADIO TOKYO TAPES LP (EAR MOVIE RECORDS)

Sub-titled "A Compilation Of 17 Los Angeles Bands", all recorded at the Radio Tokyo studio by Ethan James. First up was The Last with their 60s influenced power pop, and the general theme of the album was definitely the new sounds that were happening adjacent to the apex of Los Angeles hardcore punk that were steering their own course away from that, such as the "Paisley Underground" bands who were known to frequent the studio. Following The Last were; Jane Bond & The Undercovermen, The Long Ryders, The Bangles, Choir Invisible, The Three O'Clock, Rain Parade, The Spoiler Project, Minutemen, Savage Republic, Alisa And The Nomads, Michael James, Wednesday Week, 100 Flowers, Würm, Action Now, and Harvey Kubernik's Attention Getting Device. The cover featured a photo of actor Brinke Stevens (of horror comedy flicks such as "Sorority Babes in the Slimeball Bowl-O-Rama") eating master tape with chopsticks at the mixing desk. The back featured band line-up info.

THE SOUND OF HOLLYWOOD - DESTROY L.A. LP (MYSTIC RECORDS)

The second in the series (following the "Girls" album next) and compiled in conjunction with Destroy L.A. fanzine. Opening with the hardcore punk of S.V.D.B. (St. Vitus Dance Band) and Shattered Faith this quickly deteriorated into the pop of Still Life and the rock'n'roll of F-Beat. Bobbi Brat's Red Scare then saved proceedings with "Drag The Lake" before the first of two acoustic Bad Religion songs that were recorded before the release of "Into The Unknown" and featured Greg and Brett, as well as Paul Dedona of that line-up on the bass. Red Scare came back for another with the great "America The Beautiful", before Circle One closed side one with their biblical hardcore. Side two featured the hardcore of Battalion Of Saints, the punk of 10,000 Hurts and Würm as well as more from; Bad Religion, F-Beat, S.V.D.B., and Shattered Faith. The album came in basic Mystic artwork with the liner notes rendered almost unreadable in the background of the back.

THE SOUND OF HOLLYWOOD - GIRLS LP (MYSTIC RECORDS)

The first in the series of Doug Moody's Hollywood showcases and this one was a curious mix of hard rock and punk with a female theme. Kicking off with L.A. Girls, who were very much in the Runaways vein, before Soloman Kane gave us some 70s style pop rock. The Skirts were up next, an all female hard rock band featuring Linnea Quigleyon on vocals who went on to be the "Queen of the Bs" starring as redhead Trash in Return of the Living Dead, as well as Night of the Demons and Hollywood Chainsaw Hookers. All-girl roots rockers Screamin' Sirens followed, before hard rockers Butch and De De Troit (of UXA) with a synth-punk song "He Hit Me". Things went full metal on side two with Hellion and Bitch, before Sin 34 brought us some hardcore, and I.U.D. with some scrappy punk featuring the Barrie sisters. The rock of Hot Food To Go followed, fronted by Ruth Less, before Toxic Fumes closed the album (a.k.a. The Fumes) with some new wave. The cover featured a cheesy lipstick kiss and the band logos.

THE "YOU'LL HATE THIS RECORD" RECORD LP
(THE ONLY LABEL IN THE WORLD)

A collection of the most obnoxious Maximum Rock'n'Roll baiting punk that Mykel Board could find all on one LP. Opening with GG Allin & The Jabbers followed by ART, The Only Band In The World, Furry Couch, Fuck Ups, German Shepherds, Tina Peel, Psychodrama, and Shockabilly. Most of the bands got two songs and Board seemed to go out of his way to try to be clever and stupid all at the same time with songs like, "Rock Against Racism / Smash The Nazis", claiming (of course) that anti-fascists are the real fascists long before it became trendy. The GG Allin material was before his descent into pathetic rape rock, while he snotty punk of Fuck Ups was interspersed with experimental synth filler from German Shepherds. The basic graphic design featured a piece of joke shop sticky plastic puke (with lyrics on the back) like a kind of softer version of the sandpaper on The Feederz first LP, the idea itself from Guy Debord.

THIS ARE TWO TONE LP (TWO-TONE RECORDS)

Almost as an afterthought, this document of the 2-Tone
label was released when most of the bands had moved on into
pop, and the original roster of bands had largely split
up, their 'Dance Craze' as Trojan horse to a British anti-
racist youth revolution seemingly successful (or so it
seemed at the time). That said, this sixteen song collection
featured top twenty radio hits aplenty with six of the songs
being by Specials alone. Madness, Selecter, The Beat, The
Bodysnatchers, Swingin' Cats, Rico, and Rhoda Dakar did get
a look in though (although "The Boiler" was released with
the Special AKA). The sleeve depicted the 7" record labels
in fairly generic fashion with liner notes on the reverse by
Adrian Thrills of NME, who was the journalist who travelled
to Coventry for the BBC's Arena in 1980. Three songs were
removed from the U.S. version (including "The Boiler",
probably for sensitive types) and initial U.K. copies
came with a poster of the various bands and musicians.

UK/DK - THE ORIGINAL VIDEO SOUNDTRACK LP (ANAGRAM RECORDS)

The album of the book of the movie; "UK/DK" was the straight
to VHS documentary of the U.K. punk scene of 1982 and here
we had its' vinyl interpretation. The Exploited set the
high-brow tone with "(Fuck The) U.S.A." before The Adicts
(who for some reason had two songs to everyone else's one)
and their repetitive nursery rhyme punk. Chaos U.K. and
Disorder then showed the world what Bristol cider-fuelled
hardcore was all about, while The Business were up next for
a dose of London Oi!, before Action Pact and the slightly
out-of-place 1977 band The Vibrators saw off side one. The
Damned then opened the second side in similar fashion with
"Ignite" before a new wave band called Pressure replaced
"New Age" by Blitz for contractual reasons, yet more
Adicts, the underground hit "Jerusalem" by One Way System,
The Varukers, Angelic Upstarts, and then Vice Squad called
time on the collection. The sleeve design depicted the U.K.
splattered in red and blue paint with very little information.

UK/DK
THE ORIGINAL VIDEO SOUNDTRACK

UltraHardcore Power

NoRMAhl
Chaosz
HERBÄRDS
Bluttat
Inferno

UNDERGROUND HITS 2

ANGRY SAMOANS
YOUTH BRIGADE
FU'S
GOVERNMENT ISSUE
CANAL TERROR

HÜSKER DÜ
SPUX
MEATMEN
ADRENALIN O.D.

NINE MORE LA BANDS... WHEN YOU THOUGHT YOU'D HEARD THEM ALL

WAREE RAT TALES

THE LAST
100 FLOWERS • THE RAIN PARADE
THE POINT • THE QUESTION • CLOCKWATCHERS • WEDNESDAY WEEK • EARWIGS

WE CAN'T HELP IT
IF WE'RE FROM
FLORIDA

MYSTIC RECORDS   presents

WE GOT POWER

party or go home

MLP33125

ULTRA HARDCORE POWER LP (MÜLLEIMER RECORDS)

The first compilation on Thomas Ziegler's Mülleimer, with probably the first use of the word hardcore in German punk. Hardcore for the most part, but essentially sped up brick wall punk like a lot of the U.K. '82 bands (mixed with some beer hall chanting) rather than the U.S. all-out approach. Opening the album was Normahl, who very much fitted this model of faster Deutsch punk with a total of six songs. Bluttat followed (four songs in total) with much of the same, and again Herbärds (with a mere two songs) of Oi! inspired thud. Chaos Z were next with four longer more dour tunes spread over the two sides. The final of the five bands Inferno were the highlight of this album, and the only band who could truly be described as 'hardcore' here as they seemed to have abandoned the rock'n'roll punk and moved into frantic drums and ripping guitars, and a song about Reagan. Naive art adorned the sleeve with skinheads on the back and it came with a 12 page zine/booklet and promo inner sleeve.

UNDERGROUND HITS 2 LP (AGGRESSIVE ROCKPRODUKTIONEN)

The second volume of the American/German band mix out of Germany, although this time only two German bands made the cut with seven American bands. Two Angry Samoans songs opened the record, with two suitably snotty songs from "Inside My Brain". Youth Brigade followed this two more, one from the aborted "Sound & Fury", and compilation song "Care" making its first appearance. Meatmen picked up where the Samoans started in the obnoxious department with two from "Crippled Children Suck", before The F.U.'s with two off "Kill For Christ". Canalterror and Spux then held up the German side of things, which was also Spux's only vinyl appearance. Three Government Issue songs, two by Hüsker Dü, and two Adrenalin O.D. tunes then completed the U.S. hardcore showcase for the German market. The sleeve featured horror art with the tracklist on a gravestone on the rear and the customary promotional inner sleeve featuring some of the relevant releases licensed to Aggressive Rock Productions.

WARF RAT TALES LP (WARFRAT GRAMMOPHON)

Sub-titled "Nine More L.A. Bands... When You Thought You'd Heard Them All", this was the second 1983 compilation of the more Sixties influenced bands coming out of the Los Angeles post-punk and "Paisley Underground" scenes, recorded by Ethan James at Radio Tokyo Studios in Venice. The Last, The Leaving Trains, 100 Flowers, Earwigs, Wednesday Week, The Rain Parade, The Question?, The Point, and Hector And The Clockwatchers, all recorded one or two songs each and all have a distinct, "It's 1983 yet this isn't L.A. hardcore" feel about them. There are some strong songs here, like the all-female three piece Wednesday Week, and post-punk Earwigs, and the album is not only like a continuation of "Radio Tokyo Tapes" but also compilations like "Keats Rides A Harley". The cover art featured a photo of a gas manhole cover, with band logos and info on the reverse, as well as liner notes by Leaving Trains front man Falling James. The album also came with a foldout lyric insert.

WE CAN'T HELP IT IF WE'RE FROM FLORIDA 7" EP (DESTROY RECORDS)

The running joke with Florida punks was always how behind the times they were, but this 1983 EP of straight up hardcore didn't seem to be lagging too far behind the crowd. The blazing hardcore of Hated Youth from Tallahassee opened proceedings with "Hardcore Rules" and the immortal line, "I am God, fuck you". Sector 4 also from Tallahassee were up next with a mid-tempo punk based on the DK model, followed by Morbid Opera from Ft. Lauderdale, a predominantly female punk band. Side two offered Roach Motel from Gainesville with three hardcore blasters with titles like "My Dog's Into Anarchy" and featured George Tabb on guitar. The EP closed with two songs from Rat Cafeteria from Tampa, with a slightly murkier hardcore angle, and included Dorsey Martin later of Pink Lincolns. The cover art featured a photo of a fat guy on the beach, with a simple tracklist on the back, and a foldout insert with band supplied info and scrawls. Two pressings exist with red (first) or blue (second) labels.

WE GOT POWER - PARTY OR GO HOME LP (MYSTIC RECORDS)

Initially intended as a 14 band 7" of one minute songs, by Jordan Schwartz and David Markey of "We Got Power" fanzine, this was the first to enter into the "over forty songs on an LP" stakes. But that was in no way an indicator of poor quality as there were some great songs herein from; The Authorities, Nip Drivers, J.F.A., Dr. Know, White Flag, White Cross, Fuck-Ups, Putrid Girls, Ill Repute, Stalag 13, Rebel Truth, Willful Neglect, Tar Babies, Mecht Mensch, Graven Image, The Vacant, Adrenalin O.D., The Clones, Big Boys, Sin 34, El Duce, Minutemen, Dayglo Abortions, Caustic Cause, Don't Know, S.V.D.B., Patriots, Hated Principles, Crank Shaft, Urban Assault (SF), Urban Assault (Tahoe), 7 Seconds, Jack Shit, Romulans, No Labels, Armed Response, Deranged Diction, False Confession, Manimals, and Red Cross.

Essentially a compilation tape on an LP, the cover was pretty basic (a photocopy of Jordan's face) with track list on the back along with some of the "We Got Power" fanzine covers. Merely fresh-faced punk teenagers, Markey and Schwartz were not yet wise to cut throat operators of the music industry such as Mystic, as David Markey explained;

"Mystic took our compilation and company moniker and ran with it, much to my chagrin. I walked away after the first one as I saw the writing on the wall. They tried doing it again in the 1990's and 2000's with CD reissues and I had to have a lawyer step in and stop them from using "We Got Power". The thing is, at the time, there were limited options for getting your stuff out. And everyone involved had pretty low expectations for the compilations. We just wanted it out and heard. But there was an unexpected by-product from the "We Got Power - Party Or Go Home" compilation. We helped launch that label and put them on the map. None of the bands were compensated (the worst thing that happened) and we were never given sales statements. Learning the hard way as teenagers that it's better to do it yourself, even although we were not equipped to be a record label, already had our hands and hats over extended as it was."

WHAT SURF LP (WHAT? RECORDS)

Following on from 1982's "What Is It" that documented
Chris Ashford's What? Records' early punk years (Germs,
Dils, Skulls, Controllers, Kaos etc.), on this collection
he branched out into surf, but this LP was mainly included
here for the inclusion of two Agent Orange instrumental
surf songs; "Surf Beat" and "Out Of Limits"(the former
not available elsewhere). Aside from Mike Palm's surf
punks the album also included mainly (then) contemporary
surf instrumentals from; The Pyramids, The Halibuts (from
1963), Davie Allen And The Arrows, and The Surf Raiders.
This was by no means wimpy stuff though with songs like
"Polyurethane" and "James bond Theme/Goldfinger" by Davie
Allan And The Arrows really thumping along at a punk rock
pace. A bikini clad female adorned the cover (of course)
with liner notes by Jim Dunfrund of KXLU's "Surfwave" radio
show that ran for over 28 years. An LP for Agent Orange
punk completists? There's definitely more to it than that.

WHY ARE WE HERE? 7" EP (NO CORE RECORDS)

North Carolina announced its presence on the American
hardcore compilation scene with this area showcase that
featured four bands and eleven songs. Bloodmobile kicked off
the EP with three songs of teeth rattling polka hardcore,
with a dash of character, mainly due to the slower sections
with spoken vocals. Corrosion Of Conformity (C.O.C.) then
made their vinyl debut with three of their early blistering
hardcore songs that only hinted at a Southern metal future
on the intro of "Indifferent". Stillborn Christians began
the flip with three muddy and gruff hardcore blasts
beginning with "New Right" that featured Jon McClain later
of Ugly Americans, and multi-instrumentalist Jeb Bishop.
No Labels closed play with two scratchy hardcore numbers
that featured Woody and Reed of C.O.C. in their number.
"Why Are We Here?" Came in a six 7" panel folded sleeve
fronted simply with question marks, with a panel for each
band, and an inside poster sized foldout of live photos.

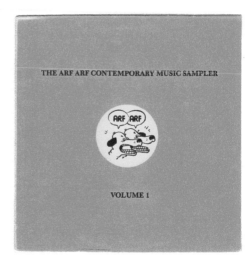

1984

1984: THE FIRST SONIC WORLD WAR LP (NEW WAVE RECORDS)

The first compilation from "New Wave" and it was a primarily French affair with a couple of exceptions. New Wave Records and zine was based in Paris and run by later writer and film maker Herr Sang (a.k.a. Patrice Lamare) and journalist Aline Richard. With one song from each band; Human Being, Le Cadavres, Angry Rats, Abject, Stakhanov S.S., K.B.T., Sub Kids, Los Toreros (Spain), Heimat-Los, Electronaze, R.A.S., Les Collabos, L'Infanterie Sauvage, Hurt, Panik, Ricdu's Chaos, Kremlin Kontingent, and Deadlock (Poland). Being French there was a definite emphasis on Oi! with tribal drumming, but there was also some hardcore punk (Heimat-Los, Electronaze, Les Collabos), post-punk (Abject) and straight up catchy punk rock (K.B.T.) thrown in. Also being French there was a definite graphic style to the black and white sleeve and accompanying 20 page zine/booklet with a page on all the bands as well as label info.

ARF ARF CONTEMPORARY MUSIC SAMPLER LP (ARF! ARF! RECORDS)

A collection of eclectic New England acts from this label that was run by Erik Lindgren, who was in a few of the bands herein, in fact a lot of them seem to be connected in some way. The album opened with the doo-wop of Three Torches before a funky instrumental from harmonica player Richard Hunter. The Mission Of Burma adjacent Birdsongs Of The Mesozoic were up next with another instrumental and things continued in a similar jazzy art damaged way from Poetry And Motion, David Boyer, The Original Artists, The Fugitives, The 2x4's, Willie 'Loco' Alexander, Magic Mose & His Royal Rockers featuring Blind Sam, Bob Suber, Russ Smith, and The Shop Coolies. The simple cover art featuring two dogs barking was backed by extensive liner notes on the rear and a label insert. A collection for fans of Ralph Records and the more challenging side of the post-punk era.

BANDS THAT COULD BE GOD LP (CONFLICT/RADIOBEAT)

A legendary set of Massachussetts bands put together by
Gerard Cosloy, then of Conflict fanzine, later of Homestead
and Matador Records. Opening up the album came Busted
Statues and their hypnotic college rock before Moving
Targets took the vinyl stage for the first time with
their melodic punk, albeit still developing their sound
at this time. Deep Wound continued with a slow number for
them followed by Sorry with their frantic and under-rated
hardcore punk. The Outpatients followed that with their
brand of hardcore before; Beanbag, Christmas, Salem 66,
and Flies changed down the gears into college rock and
post-punk territory. Most of the bands supplied two songs
(mainly recorded at Radiobeat Studios throughout 1983) with
Moving Targets managing three, while Salem 66 and Flies
only managed one each. With striking cover art supplied by
Andrew Burstein of Sorry this eclectic hardcore punk meets
college rock album only received one solitary pressing.

BEATING THE MEAT LP (XCENTRIC NOISE RECORDS)

After a handful of cassette only compilations (as well as
seven 7" releases) Andy "Shesk" Thompson made the transition
to the vinyl compilation LP with this "An Xcentric Punk
Compilation", and one of the very first international
D.I.Y. compilation albums. A whopping twenty six songs
by thirteen bands; Huvudtvätt / Headcleaners (Sweden),
Cult Maniax (U.K.), S.I.B. (Italy), Neos (Canada), Upright
Citizens (West Germany), Olho Seco (Brazil), Suicide
(U.K.), Colera (Brazil), Plastick (U.K.), Powerage (South
Africa), Protest (U.K.), Terveet Kadet, and Rattus (both
from Finland). An impressive roster with many songs that
would later become more well known such as ""Swastika
Rats" and "Nada". With cover art by Pushead at his peak
of his ubiquity on hardcore punk record sleeves, and band
info with liner notes on the back. It was also impressive
that Shesk had organised U.K. and European distribution
this early in the D.I.Y. game.

BIG CITY DON'T WANT NO PITY! 7" EP (BIG CITY RECORDS)

The third compilation on Big City from the Bronx (the second comes later in this chapter) documenting New York Hardcore from a time before it became more uniform in its approach. First up was Ultra Violence and a steady-paced straight forward punk stomper "No One Rules", before Armed Citizens and the chunky hardcore of "Make Sense". On the flip came The Unjust with that charming reverb on the vocals over a snotty but driving punk song "In Shape". Finally the 50/50 male band No Control with one of the two songs they ever recorded (the other also comes later) "Suicide", a strong sneering song that sounded like it could've come out of the early San Francisco punk scene. The sound quality made it seem like these were just taken straight off demo cassettes and put on vinyl. In a fold over sleeve with a half flap on the back, the cover depicted the usual New York landmarks with the songs in correction fluid on the rear and also came with a folded insert with band info.

BLAZING WHEELS & BARKING TRUCKS - SKATE ROCK VOL. 2 LP (THRASHER)

The first excellent compilation from Thrasher to make it to vinyl and the first I heard. McRad opened up with their frantic Philly hardcore, followed by post-Jack Grisham T.S.O.L., and then Austin's Big Boys with their thrasher "Lesson" before Anvil Chorus changed the mood completely with some metal for almost five minutes, and one of the earliest indications of what was to come. The Faction then got things back in the drainage ditch with "Friends And Enemies" before another curveball in the form of the rockabilly of The Kingpins. Los Olvidados then supplied a high point of the record with "Something New" before Borscht and Free Beer saw out side one. JFA opened side two, and the other bands not on side one with additional songs were; Tales Of Terror, Ancestors: Gods Of Sound, and Drunk Injuns (Los Olvidados' alter-ego). The cover featured some sharp cover graphics with photos of Steve Caballero (of The Faction) skating, while a foldout poster supplied band info.

BOLLOX TO THE GONADS - HERE'S THE TESTICLES LP (PAX RECORDS)

The first of two 1984 international hardcore compilations from Marcus Featherby's Pax Records, and along with "Daffodils To The Daffodils Here's The Daffodils" these were pretty much the last releases on the label. Thirteen bands and thirty songs from; Mau Maus (U.K. with three songs), Savage Circle (U.S. with five songs), P.S.A. (Italy with four songs), Legion Of Parasites, Anti-System, Xtract, Riot Squad, Skeptix, Instigators (U.K. with two songs apiece), Subversion (Belgium with two songs), Crude SS (Sweden with two songs), and finally Repulsive Alien and Canal Terror (U.K. and West Germany respectively with one song each). This hefty compilation ranged from UK '82 hangover bands to U.S. hardcore, but was all pretty much straight forward Punk rock. The cover art featured some punks, one with his pants down so a "do not peel this label off!" sticker could cover his "bollox", its removal revealing a photo of Margaret Thatcher covering his "gonads".

BOUNCING BABIES LP (FOUNTAIN OF YOUTH)

The only compilation on this Washington D.C. label run by Derrick Hsu, vocalist of Exiled. Originally this was planned to be an all-hardcore compilation with one side of D.C. bands and one side of Midwest bands put together with the help of Bob Moore of Version Sound from Ohio. This plan fell apart and Hsu instead expanded the sound to a wide variety of mainly unknown D.C. area bands, and quite a few who did little else. "Bouncing Babies" ended up with 19 bands with a song each and opened with Dove followed by; Crippled Pilgrims, Body Count, Lucky Pierre, Underground Soldier, Artificial Peace, Exiled, Scream, Glee Club, Black Market Baby, Reptile House, 9353, The Last Minute, Beaver, Assault & Battery, Braille Party, Void, Government Issue and the unlisted Death Camp 2000. With a "Water Babies" cover theme and hand written liner notes on the rear, "Bouncing Babies" offered a unique glimpse into the non-Dischord activity of the Washington D.C. area in 1984.

BULLSHIT DETECTOR THREE 2LP (CRASS RECORDS)

The third and final installment of collections of demos sent into Crass and pressed onto vinyl, and a whopping 41 bands and one-off bedroom recordings were featured, all very much in the anarcho punk vein; Avert Aversion, Awake Mankind, A Nul Noise, Animus, Peroxide, (Untitled), Xtract, Verbal Assault, Fifth A Column, Potential Victim, 7th Plague, Rebel A, Alienated, Barbed Wire, Rob Williams, Reality Control, Youthanasia, Sammy Rubette & Safety Match, Politicide, Markus Abused, One Man's Meat, Direct Action, Crag, Attrition, Napalm Death (their vinyl debut), The Impalers, Health Hazzard, Phil Hedgehog, Malice, Michael Kingzett Taylor, Brainwashed Pupils, No Defences, A.N.E.E.B., Carnage, Warning, State Of Shock, Neale Hammer, Dead To The World, Dandruff, Richard III, and Funky Rayguns. The recording quality had noticeably improved on much of this and it came in the customary six panel foldout Crass poster with band info and featured artwork by Squeal on the back cover.

CRUISIN' ANN ARBOR II: LIVE AT THE U-CLUB LP (SCHOOLKIDS)

The second in the series of Ann Arbor (Michigan) talent compiled by the "Ann Arbor Music Project" recorded live at the U-Club in September 1984, and co-released with local store Schoolkids Records. This was an eclectic mix of local rock'n'roll, surf, new wave, hard rock/metal and even jazz bands featuring; The Watusies, The Slang, Map Of The World, Steve Nardella's Rock & Roll Trio, Azreal, The Lunar Glee Club, The Evaders, Aluminum Beach, The Buzztones, Ron Brooks Trio Plus One, and Kathy Moore/Stephanie Ozer Quartet. The reason for inclusion though, and notable for punk interest; it was the only compilation appearance from legendary hardcore band The State, only a year after the release of their "No Illusions" EP, and this LP saw them swap hardcore for some dirty Stooges style rock. In keeping with the majority of the content the cover graphics had a retro 50's feel with band photos on the rear and an inner sleeve full of band info, lyrics and classic cars.

DESPERATE TEENAGE LOVE DOLLS LP (GASATANKA RECORDS)

The soundtrack to the Dave Markey (Sin 34) punk flick. The film starred Jennifer Schwartz (sister of Jordan of We Got Power zine) as well Hilary Rubens and Janet Housden (Redd Kross). First up were Redd Kross with two songs (the second with their manager Joanna on vocals, who also joined White Flag for a two songs) exploring their glam influences. Greg Greg (Graffin and Hetson of Bad Religion) then supplied an acoustic song "Runnin' Fast" recorded during the period between "Into The Unknown" and "Back To The Known". White Flag, Sin 34, Nip Drivers, Black Flag, Darkside, and Redd Kross also provided songs. The cover featured cover art by Shawn Cowart (Flipside Vinyl Fanzines 1&2). David Markey explained the move to Gasatanka; "Mystic were going to put out the Lovedolls first soundtrack too, but I snatched that back and ran. They were the sleaziest. Bill Bartell stepped in and offered his label. He had a promotion and distribution deal with Enigma. It was somewhat more straight up."

FLIPSIDE VINYL FANZINE VOLUME 1 LP (GASATANKA RECORDS)

Flipside fanzine of Los Angeles first jump from paper to vinyl and one of the best all-time hardcore punk compilations. Featuring strong songs from; Dickies (live), Government Issue, The Freeze, White Flag, Kraut, F, Plain Wrap!, F.O.D., TSOL (with a version of "Suppose They Give a War and No One Comes", the 1967 psychedelic protest song by The West Coast Pop Art Experimental Band), A.O.D., Scream, The Undead, F.U.'s (live on WERS FM), Black Market Baby, Psycho, Gay Cowboys In Bondage, Borscht, Anti-Scrunti Faction, and Charged G.B.H. (live). To add an extra layer of uniqueness Flipside got the bands to send in intros for their songs and this gave it the feel of a D.I.Y. compilation tape, and bearing in mind that this was in the era of old master tapes in the mail, a nineteen band collection from all over the U.S. was no mean feat. Featuring a cover photo of Flipside on a turntable, with back cover art by Shawn Cowart, the insert supplied band info and photos.

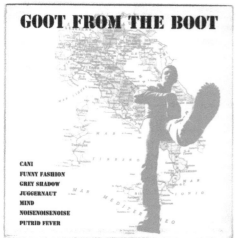

FOUR OLD 7"S ON A 12" LP (DISCHORD RECORDS)

The first four Dischord Records 7" EPs from 1980-1981 that
weren't Minor Threat (those two were reissued at this time
on their own 12"). Side one featured the two first Dischord
releases; The Teen Idles and their "Minor Disturbance EP"
of rough and ready hardcore, followed by the "No Policy EP"
by Henry Rollins' first band S.O.A. (before he joined Black
Flag) with ten short hardcore blasts and some of the best
stuff he was part of. Side two featured Dischord's fourth
and sixth releases; the "Legless Bull EP" by Government
Issue, a yelping polka-punk affair that merely hinted at
the greatness to come, while Youth Brigade's "Possible
EP", named after (their annoyance at) a previous Dischord
advert that said there was only a "Possible Youth Brigade
EP" to come, and yet one of the stronger EPs featured here.
Two sleeve versions of the four covers exist, with the usual
price change and addition of the Black Flag bars to Henry's
arm. Two poster variations of the inserts also exist.

FROM THE VALLEY WITHIN 7" EP (LOST RECORDS)

Four bands from San Jose, California, released by skater
Steve Caballero and his label's only release. Two songs
each that got started with Grim Reality featuring the
highly recognisable Jason Honea, later of Social Unrest,
on vocals (as well as Nico and Ron later of Whipping Boy),
their two songs being mid-tempo chugging punk with some '77
punk and rock influences. Ribzy followed this with snotty
and erratic hardcore that you may remember from Maximum
Rock'n'Roll's "Not So Quiet On The Western Front" from
1982. The Faction kicked off side two with their ripping
skate punk that featured Steve Caballero on the four string.
Concluding proceedings were Mistaken Identity with two
songs of muddy and slightly metallic influenced hardcore.
The cover art featured a photo of someone in a Halloween
mask trying to escape the valley, a skull and crossbones
sporting a bandana on the back. A folded blue insert fleshed
out the band info, photos and lyrics. 1,000 were pressed.

GOOT FROM THE BOOT LP (SPITTLE RECORDS)

A collection of seven punk bands from Northern Italy and differing styles recorded during May and June 1984, and the first release for Spittle. Grey Shadow opened up the album with two spirited early Joy Division meets Fall style post-punk songs, followed by Noisenoisenoise with one driving post-punk song followed by the ska-tinged "Moral Suicide". The simply named Mind followed with keyboard enhanced dramatic post-punk. Due to the song lengths there were only five songs on side one compared to nine on side two and the flip offered Cani with some shouty but jazzy punk followed by a faster hardcore song. Juggernaut came next with three songs of rapid fire hardcore with personality before Putrid Fever took things to another level with their intricate stop and go hardcore. Funny Fashion closed the album in a funny fashion (minimal electronic post-punk). The cover featured someone giving you the boot over the map of Italy with lyrics and credits on the back cover.

GREETINGS FROM SUNNY BEACH - BEST OF CLOSER LP (CLOSER)

These days you'd be forgiven for thinking that in 1984 everyone listening to anything 'alternative' was into hardcore punk, well this is one compilation that disproves that idea. As the title suggested this was a showcase of Closer Records from Le Havre, France, that leaned less on punk and more on garage and power pop. As a result we had this set of twelve bands and songs featuring; Bruce Joyner, Barracudas, Dream Syndicate, Nomads, Bad Brains (French band), Eyes Of Mind, Paul Collins' Beat, Richard Barone, Dickies (with the title track from "Stukas Over Disneyland" that Closer licensed from PVC), Pandoras, Only Ones, and Fixed Up. The overall feel of this collection was bright, guitar pop with a 60s influence. Initially it came in a reverse board gatefold sleeve fronted by a suitably retro photograph and a very minimal amount of information (see labels for track list). Even the two inserts were simply a label catalogue and for some reason the other was a calendar.

HALF SKULL 7" EP (INSANE INDUSTRIES)

One of only two releases on this label (the other being
the Decry debut 7") run by engineer, guitarist, vocalist
(Olivelawn/Fluf) and photographer (Flipside/Thrasher) "O"
out of Arcadia, California, all recorded under his watchful
eye at Casbah Studios in Fullerton. Four bands from Orange
County with a song each and first up was Basic Math with
"Onward", a typically energetic hardcore song of the time
and place. Decry followed this with "Warlords", a song
unavailable elsewhere of their local Arcadia punk. The flip
offered up Love Canal and "Greatest Sports Legends" with the
memorable chorus, "We hate skateboards and skateboarders" on
their stop and start hardcore. Finally, M.I.A. (originally
from Las Vegas) supplied the belting and intelligent
"Turning Into What You Hate". The EP was essentially
untitled but came to be known as "Half Skull" due to the
cover art, which folded over with a simple track list on
the back, the insert supplying the lyrics, photos and info.

HARDCORE POWER MUSIC PART 2 LP (MÜLLEIMER RECORDS)

Following on from 1983's "Ultra Hardcore Power" came this
collection from Mülleimer Records of German hardcore punk
which had picked up the pace significantly from a couple
of years previous. Seventeen songs from ten bands; Razzia,
Ausbrach, Inferno, Kommando Schwarzer Freitag, Maniacs,
Idiots, Lustfinger, Schluckspechte, Tin Can Army, and Mottek.
Four bands offered two songs each while, five supplied
only one and Kommando Schwarzer Freitag (K.S.F.) delivered
three of their more melodic songs. Like the previous volume,
Inferno were a standout here with their frantic hardcore,
Maniacs and Tin Can Army provided the oompah thrash,
Ausbruch delivered a more traditional melodic German punk,
while Razzia came somewhere in between with both power and
melody. With what was becoming somewhat customary, the cover
featured horror cover artwork (lifted from "Creepshow")
reminiscent of the "Underground Hits" compilations, and
the LP came with an 8 page A5 booklet and label insert.

LIMITED EDITION PUNK COMPILATION

HAVE A ROTTEN CHRISTMAS

VARUKERS · RIOT SQUAD · SKEPTIX
ANIMAL FARM · PARANOIA
ENEMY · RESISTANCE 77 · NO CHOICE

Ghetto-Way.

IT CAME FROM SLIMEY VALLEY

DRKNOW
THE GRIM
ILL REPUTE
UNDER CITY KINGS
SLAUGHTERHOUSE
FALSE CONFESSION
REIGN OF TERROR
FLOWER LEPERS
AMERICAN HARDCORE
RIGOR MORTIS
MAX NIX
CIRCLE ONE
CRANKSHAFT

Keine Experimente! Vol. II

NEUROTIC ARSEHOLES
CHAOS-Z
TORPEDO MOSKAU
AGEN 53
PORNO PATROL
CRETINS
TIN CAN ARMY
VØLXFRØNT
EA80

LET'S BREED!
PART TWO OF THE THROBBING LOBSTER SAGA

LIFE IS A JOKE

A Collation of Punk Rock, Hardcore and Hard Energy Noise
from around this planet

CIVIL DISSIDENT (Australia)
RAZZIA (Germany)
PERVERT KADET (Finland)
SANC (USA)
CACOPHONY (Brazil)
RIOT SQUAD B.A. (South Africa)
(England)
SAVE US DIE (Italy)
FASIT S.A. (Spain)

METAL mo COW

HAVE A ROTTEN CHRISTMAS LP (ROT RECORDS)

The third of four 1984 budget compilations on the prolific
Rot Records run by members of Riot Squad out of Mansfield
in Nottinghamshire. This one was intended as a thank you
to people who bought their other releases with many of
the songs unreleased elsewhere at that point. Animal Farm
opened the album with some traditional U.K. punk rock,
followed by Varukers and some standard Discharge homage.
Cardiff's No Choice then slowed things down with their
melodic anarcho punk. Skeptix then took things back to full
throttle with their sweeping metallic guitars and pounding
drums. The "patriotic" band Resistance 77 from Nottingham
then supplied a sing-along Oi! Tune that wasn't on their
1984 debut LP on Rot, while Enemy then closed side one with a
long-winded Rot album track. Riot Squad kicked off side two
while No Choice, Skeptix and Animal Farm had further songs
and the Vice Squad style punk of Paranoia with one song.
The cover art looked like a Xerox of Xmas wrapping paper.

IT CAME FROM SLIMEY VALLEY LP (GHETTO-WAY RECORDS)

A collection of Los Angeles area bands on this Mystic
subsidiary, with very strong full-bodied and bassy production
for Mystic. Piledriving performances from; Dr. Know, Crank
Shaft, Rigor Mortis, Flower Leperds, The G.R.I.M., Mox
Nix, America's Hardcore, Ill Repute, False Confession(s),
Slaughterhouse 5, Reign Of Terror, Circle One, and Undercity
Kings. Sixteen songs in total with that signature Nardcore
area sound. All the bands had one song apart from Flower
Leperds, Dr. Know and Crank Shaft, who all had two. Flower
Leperds particularly put in a strong showing with their
less than politically correct "Preacher's Confession"
and "Prophesy". With loud cover art by horror stipple
enthusiast Mad Marc Rude (Misfits, Battalion Of Saints) this
LP was a stand out for this label and Southern California
hardcore of this time. The back cover featured a tracklist,
credits and a punk collage of the bands while Mystic owner
Doug Moody looked on clutching a glass of green fluid.

KEINE EXPERIMENTE! VOL. II LP (WEIRD SYSTEM)

No experiments! The second and final round of this great West German punk series from Hamburg's Weird System that followed their usual pattern of nine bands with two songs each. Opening with the powerhouse hardcore of Torpedo Moskau followed by Agen 53 and Cretins who both slowed things back down to melodic punk. Tin Can Army then delivered their three chords in a U.K. '82 style before Volxfront had more of a snarling '77 feel. Porno Patrol upped the stakes to fast hardcore just in time for Neurotic Arseholes to add their highly unique melodic plaintive punk to the conversation, followed by EA80 with an even more dramatic baritone punk approach. Chaos Z were the last of the nine bands in a Gothic post-punk style dripping in chorus pedal and Killing Joke. The initial press came on black and purple vinyl with a numbered cover that depicted a chair flying above a crowd. The customary German inner sleeve supplied the lyrics and the covers of what else was on offer from the label.

LET'S BREED LP (THROBBING LOBSTER)

Due to the perils of alphabetisation "part two of the throbbing lobster saga" appears here before part one in this chapter, but this volume came out in the autumn of 1984. A set of Massachusetts bands compiled by Chuck Warner (later of Messthetics fame); Scruffy The Cat, Chain Link Fence, Noonday Underground, Christmas, The Odds (ex-DMZ), The Outlets (featuring future members of Dropkick Murphys and Gang Green), The Unattached, Blackjacks, Busted Statues, The Underachievers, Flies, The Edge, Dumptruck, and Prime Movers. Ranging from roots rock'n'roll (Scruffy The Cat), punk (Noonday Underground - pre-Last Stand), college rock (Christmas, Busted Statues) to garage psych (the excellent Prime Movers). The cover art depicted each band with a corresponding image, tracks and credits on the back. Two pressings totalling 5,000 copies were made, the album hit "#1 on dozens of college radio stations". A varied and fun compilation with some strong songs (Outlets).

LIFE IS A JOKE LP (WEIRD SYSTEM)

"A collection of Punk Rock, Hardcore and High Energy Noise from around this planet", the first installment of this series of international compilations on West German label Weird System with 9 bands and 18 songs with two songs each. Fang (U.S.), Savage Circle (Italy), Inocentes (Brazil), Hysteria (U.K.), Civil Dissident (Australia), Riot Squad S.A. (South Africa), Razzia (West Germany), Terveet Kadet (Finland), and Shit S.A. (Spain). Covering a variety of punk rock approaches of the time, from old fashioned punk to faster hardcore this is one of the earliest of the international compilations and is very evocative of the era. The cover featured a black and white photo of people fleeing an explosion, with band info, lyrics and graphics on the usual West German printed paper inner sleeve. Each sleeve was numbered with no indication of how many were actually pressed and there's a "No Fangks! indeed to the Subhumans (UK) and mental hippies all over" for some reason.

METAL MOO COW LP (MATAKO MAZURI RECORDS)

An eleven band Texas punk collection on Jeff Smith of Hickoids label and his second release. Fearless Iranians From Hell opened proceedings with their America baiting hardcore on "Burn The Books", and their first time on vinyl. Napalm followed with some rapid-fire hardcore before the three Garza sisters' Hispanic metal band Heather Leather "came to destroy". Offenders then got all "Fed Up" before The Jeffersons featuring Buxf Parrot and Glen Taylor of The Dicks sludged things up with "Ya Gotta Walk Ya Dog". Hickoids opened side two with their disturbed cowpunk on "Animal Husbandry" before Scratch Acid got the cramps with a dark psychobilly on "The Greatest Gift". Feast Of Fools' only offering to the world came next with a female vocalist yelling over abrupt post-punk. The Technicolor Yawns, Toejam (great hardcore) and Meat Joy closed play with their unique Texas takes on punk. The cover featured a copper cow of course while the insert supplied the lyrics.

MYSTIC SAMPLER #1 LP (MYSTIC RECORDS)

The first version of this Mystic LP of Southern Californian hardcore era bands was initially released as a cassette only sampler in 1983 simply titled "Mystic Sampler". It contained eight of the bands featured here and seven of the songs (Ill Repute having a different song here). Red Scare and Eleven Sons from the original cassette version didn't make the album, and the final line-up of thirteen bands became; S.V.D.B., Sin 34, Ill Repute, Minutemen, Kommunity FK, Manifest Destiny, Even Worse, Suicidal Tendencies (their first comp. appearance with an alternate version of "I Saw Your Mommy" recorded at Mystic), Acidhead, Noise God, Vox Pop, Mentors, and Powertrip. A solid collection of mainly hardcore but with some death rock and old '77 style punk remnants thrown in. Available on red or black vinyl with red and black sleeve, featuring the Mystic skull and info on the back. Each side ended in a locked groove with a dog barking on side one to ensure you got up to turn it over.

NARDCORE LP (MYSTIC RECORDS)

"A compilation of hardcore bands from Oxnard and neighbouring lands". 1984 saw Mystic Records at the peak of their powers as Southern Californian hardcore punk era label, that was especially prolific for compilations. So much so that owner Doug Moody began moving on from the "Sound Of Hollywood" into other scenes and area showcases, inviting bands to his recording studio in Hollywood for recording. As such, this was the hardcore document of Oxnard, California, a beach community that had developed a strong identity and hardcore sound. The eleven bands here were split up into blocks for the running order; Ill Repute (three songs), Scared Straight (two), Rat Pack (two), Habeas Corpus (one), Agression (two), R.K.L. (three), False Confession (one), the Rotters (two), Dr. Know (one), A.F.U. (one), and Stalag 13 (two songs). Then resident local punks-as-Peanuts artist Brian Walsby covered cover art duties, and initial copies came with a 12 page booklet on all the bands.

NEIGHBORHOOD RHYTHMS (PATTER TRAFFIC) 2LP (FREEWAY RECORDS)

A curiously fascinating collection of mainly spoken word
and acoustic beat style poetry, some only a few second
long, compiled by Freeway owner and writer Harvey Kubernik.
The third in the series after 1982's "Voices Of The Angels
(Spoken Words)" and 1983's "English As A Second Language
(Talking Package)". With one hundred and six tracks over
four sides, and a list far too long to list all the artists
herein, but the SST family as well as original Los Angeles
punks feature heavily; Henry Rollins, Chuck Dukowski, Mike
Watt, D. Boon, Charles Bukowski, Joe Nolte, Jack Brewer,
Michael Steele, Phast Phreddie, Exene Cervenka, Skip Engblom,
James Moreland, Jeffrey Lee Pierce, Susan Gardner, Therese
Covarrubias, John Doe, Dave Alvin, Chris Desjardins, Rodney
Bingheimer, Kim Fowley, Kid Congo, Tequila Mockingbird,
and many more. The tracks were cut tight together so it was
like a succession of poetry. The cover featured a collage
by Drew Steele (Surf Punks) with track list on the rear.

NICE AND LOUD 7" EP (BIG CITY RECORDS)

The second compilation on New York's Big City that came
before "Big City Don't Want No Pity!" that came earlier
in this chapter, and for this they broke the pattern of
having "Big City" as part of the title due to it being a
six band and song set with New York bands on side one and
Connecticut bands on side two. First up was the 50/50 male/
female No Control and one of three hardcore songs they ever
committed to vinyl. Disorderly Conduct and Ultra Violence
followed with more examples of pre-sportswear New York
Hardcore with that trademark muddy production and frantic
stop and go attack. The flip gave us three from Connecticut
featuring; Reflex From Pain, Vatican Commandos and C.I.A.,
with an early version of "I Hate The Radio" (later recorded
by a few of the members' later band 76% Uncertain), Reflex
From Pain also being connected to C.I.A. The sleeve art
depicted an angry looking fella penned by Cripes and it came
with a small insert featuring lyrics and very little else.

NOBODY GETS ON THE GUEST-LIST! LP (THROBBING LOBSTER)

The first in the series of three compilations (that came right before the second one, "Let's Breed!" earlier in this chapter) released by Chuck Warner of Massachusetts in the summer of 1984, it featured fourteen bands and songs that ranged from local college rock to punk to Sixties influenced garage. The Flies opened up with their brand of indie jangle followed by The Underachievers with a stomp not dissimilar to X. The Hopelessly Obscure pounded out some garage rock followed by The Prime Movers in a similar catchy Sixties style. Christmas, Wild Kingdom, 21-645, The Turbines, Classic Ruins, Johnny & The Jumper Cables, Chain Link Fence, Holy Cow, Noise Pencil, and Baby's Arm, all put in spirited performances with little in the way of filler. Selling around 4,000 copies the album reached #1 on some college radio stations and the cover featured a lobster (of course) with a nod to Spinal Tap's "Smell The Glove" on the back along with track list and credits.

NUKE YOUR DINK 7" EP (POSITIVE FORCE RECORDS)

Sub-titled "Nevada Hardcore Sampler E.P." This was the debut release on 7Seconds vocalist Kevin Marvelli's then new label "Positive Force", so of course he started with an eight band compilation of local Nevada bands (more precisely; Reno, Las Vegas, Carson City and South Lake Tahoe). Opening with a raw version of 7Seconds' "In Your Face" and followed by Subterfuge, No Deal, Urban Assault, Jackshit, The Remains, The Expelled and The Yobs, the EP was a rough and ready set of hardcore with low rehearsal room style 'production values' and sounded more like a traded cassette compilation of old, so if you're looking for that authentic raw and tinny teenage hardcore then look no further than this 33 1/3 RPM EP. Housed in a suitably D.I.Y. fold-over sleeve with info, lyrics and a list of "other Nevada bands" on the inside. Despite two pressings with different colour sleeves this EP quickly became impossible to find, no doubt due to 7Seconds completists.

PRIMITIVE
AIR-RAID

MONTREAL '84

LIMITED EDITION PUNK COMPILATION

ROT
IN
HELL

The Varukers
Resistance 77
Freshly
Oi! Polloi
Out Of Order
Overdose
The Filth
No Concern
Angry Rats
Constant State
—X X X—
Bleed
D.O.S

22 TRACKS FOR 3·49 MAXIMUM

P.E.A.C.E. 2LP - (R RADICAL RECORDS)

Arguably one of the most important hardcore punk collections
ever released, this ambitious project featured 55 bands from
13 countries (U.S., U.K., Japan, Denmark, Holland, Canada,
Italy, West Germany, Sweden, Argentina, Australia, Spain
and South Africa), and was put together by Dave Dictor of
MDC and R Radical Records to benefit anti-war causes. The
title was slightly ambiguous as the cover simply stated
'P.E.A.C.E.' while the back cover said 'War' and the spine
read, "International P.E.A.C.E. Benefit Compilation".
P.E.A.C.E. now acts as a kind of time capsule for me and
probably many others, transporting me back to when it came
out and hearing it for the first time with its band list
that read like a who's who of 1984 hardcore punk, that also
introduced me to so many bands at the time...

Articles Of Faith, G.I.S.M., Neon Christ, Kalashnikov, Cause
For Alarm, Local Disturbance, Unwarranted Trust, Wretched,
O.D.F.X, Afflicted, Declino, Dicks, B.G.K., Crass, Upright
Citizens, False Prophets, Mob 47, Offenders, Contrazione,
Scum, Los Violadores, Deadlock, P.P.G., Trash, Vicious
Circle, Condemned To Death, Negazione, D.O.A., Dirty Rotten
Imbeciles, Porno Patrol, Treason, Shit S.A., Septic Death,
Cheetah Chrome Motherfuckers, Peggio Punx, The Proletariat,
Conflict, Iconoclast, Pandemonium, Dead Kennedys, Boskops,
Subhumans, White Lie, Wargasm, Slaughterhouse 4, The Execute,
Reagan Youth, Impact, Butthole Surfers, Kangrena, Porcelain
Forehead, Barely Human, R.A.F. Punk, Zenzile, and MDC.

P.E.A.C.E./WAR also contained a 72 page newsprint magazine
with a page each for all the bands, as well as writing
on the politics behind the release, that you could tell
was done with some help from legendary Berkeley punk zine
MaximumRocknRoll. The album received three pressings in
1984; U.S., U.K./Europe and another North American press
with "Jacket Made In Canada" on the rear. A few CD reissues
occurred later including a UK version in 2002 that I
somehow had the honour of penning some liner notes for.

PRIMITIVE AIR RAID - MONTREAL '84 LP (PSYCHE INDUSTRY)

A fascinating insight into what was going on in Montreal, Canada, and as usual the hardcore punk was on side one with an eclectic selection on side two. Compiled by M.P.A.S. ("Musicians Promotional Assistance Society") and Psyche Industry, Asexuals opened with "Contra-Rebels" before Fair Warning followed with more hardcore, and Vomit And The Zits pumped out some DK style punk. Porcelain Forehead then offered their unique approach before Absurds provided some engaging hardcore. Genetic Control's "Suburban Life", the hardcore classic of the album, came next and side one concluded with Direct Action's crushing attack. Side two offered American Devices (a bit Meat Puppets), The Nils (a highlight), Red Shift (Posh Boy style synth), Iago Neon (computer noise), Morbid Fiesta (ditto), No Policy (great punk) and ≠ (?). The album featured a punk on a roof attempting radio communication and a foldout poster featured a panel on each band as well as liner notes.

RADIO TOKYO TAPES - VOLUME TWO LP (EAR MOVIE RECORDS)

The second in the series recorded at the studio of the same name in Venice, California, and a shift towards the then popular death rock scene in L.A. at the time. The album opened with Shadow Minstrels with some engaging post-punk song before Outer Circle with their new wave, and Kommunity FK with their Goth tinged post-punk. 17 Pygmies took things into a Blade Runner synth direction before Animal Dance and their lively post-punk pop. Alex Gibson & Passionel followed, Gibson formerly of BPeople and later of film work supplied a great song that sounded a lot like his score for Suburbia. John Trubee then closed side one with some dark synth ranting. Side two saw Fibonnacis, Psychobud, Red Wedding (featuring the two other members of Hey Taxi who weren't George Hurley), Food And Shelter, Chill Factor, Pleasure Mask, and Bay Of Pigs all provided their own visions (mainly with synth). The cover art depicted a shrine with band photos with extensive liner notes by Craig Lee (Bags).

RAT MUSIC RAT PEOPLE VOL. 2 LP (CD PRESENTS)

The year of second volumes and Rat Music was no exception.
Compiled by promoter Paul 'Rat' Bachavich and recorded live
by Spot (of SST, and others) at his gigs in conjunction with
infamous CD Presents owner David Ferguson. You would've
never known it was live though as opener Butthole Surfers
"Theme Song" sounded like it was recorded in a studio,
as did the two songs from Texas' Big Boys and Canada's
Personality Crisis, recorded on one of their visits to the
Bay Area. Minutemen, J.F.A. and Tales Of Terror filled out
side one in fine hardcore style, while side two offered
"They Sent Me To Hell C.O.D." by Fang, two by MDC (with the
then unreleased "Pay To Come Along" and "(R)evolution In
Rock"), The Dicks, two by D.R.I. ("Madman" and "Sad To Be")
and the album closed with the MDC affiliated The White Lie.
The cover featured "The Cat and the Old Rat" illustration
by Gustave Doré from 'Fables' by La Fontaine (1868). The
album came with a lyric and label mail order sheets.

REPO MAN - SOUNDTRACK LP (SAN ANDREAS RECORDS)

The soundtrack to Alex Cox's cult punk flick that followed
the exploits of repo men Otto (Emilio Estevez) and Bud
(Harry Dean Stanton). Iggy Pop supplied the opening theme
song accompanied by Steve Jones (Pistols) on guitar as
well as Nigel Harrison and Clem Burke (Blondie) on bass and
drums. Black Flag then provided an alternate version of "TV
Party" before "Institutionalised" by Suicidal Tendencies.
"Coup D'Etat" by Circle Jerks and Latino punks The Plugz "El
Clavo Y La Cruz" (The Nail And The Cross) closed side one.
The flip offered the Burning Sensations version of Jonathan
Richman's "Pablo Picasso" before Fear and "Let's Have A
War", and then Circle Jerks notable lounge version of "When
The Shit Hits The Fan". The only movie-band Juicy Bananas
featuring actor Zander Schloss (later of Circle Jerks) on
bass and actor Sy Richardson (Lite in the film) on vocals
then did "Bad Man" before The Plugz closed with film closer
"Reel Ten". The cover of course featured the movie poster.

ROT IN HELL LP (ROT RECORDS)

The third budget "limited edition punk compilation" from Rot Records (run by members of Riot Squad) and this one featured twenty two songs by thirteen bands; The Varukers, Resistance 77, Freshly, Oi Polloi, Out Of Order, Overdose, The Filth, No Concern, Angry Rats, Constant State, - XXX -, Bleed, and D.O.S. "Rot In Hell" suffered from far too much content and a distinct lack of mastering and as a result you really needed to turn it up loud just to even hear it. A cover sticker stated that it is over an hour in length and contained mainly demo tracks and it really sounded like a fifth generation compilation tape transferred straight to vinyl. Most of the bands were from the U.K. with only - XXX - (Belgium), Angry Rats (France) and Freshly (Denmark) coming from overseas. Most of the content was therefore U.K. '82 style with some Goth thrown in. The cover art was relatively plain with a drawing by 'Pip' of a punk/metal Statue Of Liberty, track list and band addresses on the back.

SOMETHING TO BELIEVE IN LP (B.Y.O. RECORDS)

The second hardcore punk compilation from B.Y.O. following on from "Someone Got Their Head Kicked In", and for this they expanded their attention to across the U.S. and the Stern brothers' homeland of Canada, with sixteen bands and songs. Kicking off with "Scratches & Needles" by Montreal's Nils, which signalled a coming change in the hardcore scene, the album then bounced around North America; Rigor Mortis (L.A.), Big Boys (Austin), Unwanted (Winnipeg), Tourists (L.A.), Kraut (N.Y.), Youth Brigade (L.A.), Youth Youth Youth (Toronto), SNFU (Edmonton), Personality Crisis (Calgary), Channel 3 (L.A. - and the great "Indian Summer"), Young Lions and Zeroption (Toronto), D.O.A. (Vancouver), 7 Seconds (Reno), and Stretch Marks (Winnipeg). With murky cover art of a conquering army, the back featured the bands under their city flags with some typically ambitious liner notes. The album also came with a foldout poster including lyrics, line-ups and even more flags. An essential classic.

SUBURBIA - ORIGINAL SOUNDTRACK RECORDING LP (ENIGMA RECORDS)

The soundtrack to Penelope Spheeris' cult punk film that followed on from "Decline Of Western Civilization" but was a fictional account of a crew of squat punk kids, played by real punk kids, filmed largely in Downey, California. Side one featured the three bands in the film; D.I., T.S.O.L. and The Vandals, all four songs from the film recorded live interspersed with soundbites from the flick. Side two featured the movie score by Alex Gibson of BPeople (see: "Let Them Eat Jellybeans") who went on to work on many films and won an Oscar for sound editing on "Dunkirk" in 2018. His atmospheric and very 80s sounding echoey score was in eight parts, featured chronologically as they appeared in the film. Of the original cast; Flea (Razzle) went onto Red Hot Chili Peppers, Wade Walston (Joe Schmo) went onto play bass for U.S. Bombs, Chris Pedersen (Jack Diddley) went onto films such as Platoon and Point Break, Jennifer Clay (Sheila) went onto be an executive at Skechers shoes, and Timothy O'Brien (Skinner) passed away in 2021 while Bill Coyne (Evan Johnson) died in 2011 in Hot Springs, Arkansas, aged 44 when a gun he was cleaning fired accidentally.

THE BEAT GENERATION AND THE ANGRY YOUNG MEN LP (WELL SUSPECT)

With its title taken from the book on the beat poets, this was a mod revival compilation; "the end result of five weeks hard slog in a dingy Soho basement. A compilation of some fifteen demos and unreleased singles". The album featured; Long Tall Shorty, Small Hours, Purple Hearts, Les Elite, Merton Parkas, and Directions. All the bands either had two or three songs featured and most bands took the maximum pub rock 60s approach with good song writing. Of the bands, Long Tall Shorty featured Tony Morrison of Angelic Upstarts, Small Hours were formed by original Saints bassist Kym Bradshaw, Mick of Merton Parkas of course went onto Style Council and three members of stand outs Directions went onto Big Sound Authority. The cover photo was taken from 60s series "77 Sunset Strip" with liner notes on the back.

THE MIDDLE OF AMERICA COMPILATION LP (H.I.D. PRODUCTIONS)

Compiled by DJ Doug Conn of the "Fast'n'Loud" radio show on WNUR of Evanston and Northwestern University, Illinois, a show that dished out the punk rock on Saturday nights between midnight and 2am for nearly two decades from 1983. Wrapped in strange artwork by Mark Hejnar, "Middle Of America" ended up becoming the Chicago hardcore era compilation of note opening with two Naked Raygun songs followed by two from Savage Beliefs, two from Nadsat Rebel and two from Out Of Order. Side two offered up one from Articles Of Faith, three from Rights Of The Accused, two from Big Black, and closed with a remix of "Security" by The Effigies. The Iain Burgess recorded album was definitely "Fast'n'Loud" and full of your typical tough but catchy Chicago punk. Steve Albini was at Northwestern University at the time and connected DJ Doug Conn up with studio engineer Iain Burgess, as well as contributing himself with Big Black. Doug Conn got the idea for the compilation from a trip to California as he recalled to "This Station Could Be Your Life";

"I went up to Berkeley, cause I have relatives up in San Francisco, and that's where Maximumrocknroll Radio was, which would be called a podcast now, but it was just a tape system back then where people would get copies of their tapes at different record stores or from the mail or listen to them on the Berkeley station. What was interesting about it was that they had also done some compilations and so I kind of realised that they were kind of acting as a funneling point where people can bring their music and they're going to distribute it out to a wider audience. So, when I came back after that trip to Evanston, I thought that's kind of what we are doing in Chicago. I didn't want to be presumptuous, but I was like no-one is really doing this, why don't we try to put a record out of the local bands that we are getting tapes from and you know some of the more established ones and as soon as I came up with the idea, we now knew enough people in the local scene that it started progressing from there."

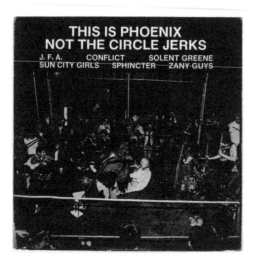

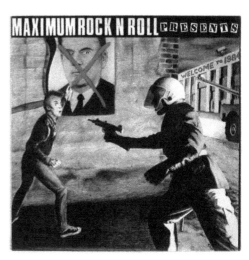

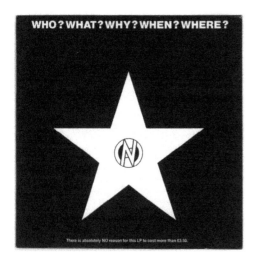

THERE IS NO FUTURE - THE HISTORY OF NO FUTURE LP (NO FUTURE)

The final release and compilation from "UK 82" label No
Future with a greatest hits featuring sixteen 7" glue bag
era U.K. indie chartbusters from; Blitz, Partisans, Peter
And the Test Tube Babies, Red Alert, Violators, Channel 3,
Blitzkrieg, Attak, Insane, The Crash, The Samples, and The
Blood, with one song each apart from; Blitz, Test Tubes,
Partisans and Violators, with two. After 29 singles and 9
LPs label founders Chris Berry and Richard Jones decided
to call it a day three or so years after advertising in
Sounds for punk and Oi! demo tapes and releasing the "All
Out Attack E.P." By Blitz in 1981. The fittingly post-
apocalyptic punk cover graphics with a character borrowed
from "Punk And Disorderly - Further Charges" as a central
figure were backed by liner notes by Berry explaining all
this. There was some cross over with the other 1984 No Future
compilation "Angels With Dirty Faces" here and Channel 3 were
the only non-U.K. to be featured on the label and herein.

THE SOUND OF HOLLYWOOD - COPULATION LP (MYSTIC RECORDS)

Genius level hardcore concept album of cop themed songs
compiled by Doug Moody highlighting the L.A. punk scene's
ongoing relationship with hating cops to the max. 18 songs
and bands, some with pre-existing work and some made for
the album, from; Dr. Know, Sado Nation, S.V.D.B., The
Authorities, Government Issue, Ill Repute, Mentors, Black
Flag, White Flag, Agression, The Stain, America's Hardcore,
Würm, Manifest Destiny, Aryan Disgrace, Grim, Crank Shaft,
and New Regime. White Flag's hilarious pro-cop song
"Shattered Badge" placed knowingly next to Black Flag to go
with their alternative take on the "Police Story" t-shirt is
a standout, as well as The Authorities, whose "I Hate Cops"
went down in history for people mishearing "They're all
fucking piggers" as something else. "Copulation" came with a
lyric insert and some came wrapped in police tape. The cover
photo was taken by Ed Colver on the opening night of "The
Decline of Western Civilization" on Hollywood Blvd in 1980.

THIS IS PHOENIX, NOT THE CIRCLE JERKS LP (PLACEBO RECORDS)

Putting Phoenix, Arizona, on the hardcore map came Tony
Victor's Placebo Records with their second collection of
six Arizona bands and sixteen songs, and a title nod to
"This Is Boston Not L.A." Opening with three exercises in
dark cacophony from Mighty Sphincter followed by three
peacecore tunes from Tucson's Conflict (U.S.), both
recorded at Desert Sounds in 1983, the side then concluded
with three hardcore blasters from Solent Greene, recorded
in the same studio in 1981. The flip was recorded live at
two venues, with three excellent Zany Guys and two Sun City
Girls jazz assaults put to tape at Whiskers in Phoenix, and
two closing J.F.A. songs recorded at the DeVry Institute
Of Technology, Phoenix. The cover featured a live shot of
Mighty Sphincter taken at local Placebo-promoted punk venue
"Mad Garden" (Madison Square Garden) a 1929 wrestling and
boxing arena on 7th Avenue and Van Buren Street where the
bands would play in the wrestling ring between 1981-84.

THIS IS THE CENTRAL COAST (DAMNIT) LP (BOPP N' SKIN RECORDS)

The first and the only release on this label run by the band
Wimpy Dicks out of San Luis Opispo that wasn't a Wimpy Dicks
record. Compiled to promote the hardcore scene along the
Central Coast of California, that featured eleven bands and
a whopping twenty nine songs, you knew this isn't going to
be a laid back affair with; Assault and Los Cremators from
Santa Maria, Corruptors and X-Tortion from Lompoc, Death
Of Glory, Users, Wimpy Dicks and Mood Room from San Luis
Obispo, Group Sex from Nipomo, Pedestrian Abuse from Arroyo
Grande and Pyramod from Atascadero. With the exception of
Mood Room and Pyramod this was all essentially fast teenage
hardcore, and with the exception of Wimpy Dicks none of the
other bands did any other records at the time, although
Assault did release a demo in 1985. Standouts included
Death Of Glory and Corruptors with the theme song "This Is
The Central Coast Damnit!". With its simple cover art, the
rear looked much better and the insert supplied the info.

WE GOT POWER PART II - PARTY ANIMAL LP (MYSTIC RECORDS)

Volume two in the series that, apart from a guest appearance
from Jordan of the zine on the final track by SWA, seemed
to have very little to actually do with We Got Power. 41
hardcore bands and songs from all over the U.S. but primarily
Southern California, with short, sharp blasts from; Ill
Repute, Don't No, Stukas Over Bedrock, Incest Cattle, Scared
Straight, Hated Principles, Juvenile Behavior, Mox Nix,
Manic Subcidal, Sado-Nation, V.O.A., 2nd Thoughts, A.F.U.,
Habeas Corpus, N.O.S., Critical Attitude, Crankshaft, NO
FX, Penis Brigade, New Regime, Fatal Error, America's
Hardcore, Justice League, Sacred Cows, The O.D.'s, The
Micronotz, The Shemps, Sluggo, No Control, The Holly,
A.S.H., White Wreckage, Seizure, Subterfuge, Half Life,
O.N.S., Cancerous Growth, Seismic Waves, Caustic Cause,
The Grim, and SWA. With a cover featuring a dog in a party
hat this also came with a foldout newsprint poster with
band info, and hand scrawled notes for that D.I.Y. look.

WELCOME TO 1984 LP (MAXIMUMROCKNROLL)

"The hell with nationalism!" The second "Maximum Rocknroll
Presents..." compilation, and in keeping with the era, they
expanded their vision to the international hardcore scene
and it turned out to be one of the all-time greats. 23 bands
and songs from 17 countries, again no mean feat in the pre-
digital age. The countries being; Finland, Brazil, U.S.A.,
Denmark, W. Germany, France, England, Spain, Norway, Italy,
Sweden, Australia, Holland, Japan, Yugoslavia, Canada, and
Belgium. The bands being; Terveet Kädet, Olho Seco, The
Crucifucks, Electric Deads, Inferno, Kidnap, N.O.T.A.,
Icons Of Filth, R.I.P., Skjit-Lars, Rattus, Raw Power, The
Bristles, Depression, B.G.K., The Stalin, Frites Modern,
U.B.R., Mayhem, Red Tide, Moral Demolition, Huvudtvätt,
and Upright Citizens. With its 1984 themed cover art, liner
notes by Jeff Bale and inner sleeve with band info and
lyrics, to say this remains a spine tingling zeitgeist record
that will transport you back in time is an understatement.

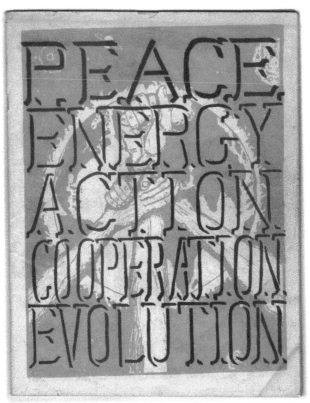

BOOKLET FOR "P.E.A.C.E." 2LP (R RADICAL RECORDS)

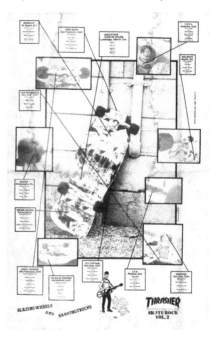

L: PROMO POSTER FOR "SOMETHING TO BELIEVE IN" LP (BYO)

R: INSERT FOR "BLAZING WHEELS AND BARKING TRUCKS" LP (THRASHER)

WHO? WHAT? WHY? WHEN? WHERE? LP (MORTAHATE RECORDS)

The first compilation on Conflict's Mortahate label that
read like a who's who of anarcho punk of the day with
eighteen bands and songs with contributions from; Conflict,
Anthrax, Karma Sutra, Moet The Poet, Sub Squad, Chaos,
Stigma, Toxic Shock, Vex, Exit-Stance, Poison Girls, Know
The Drill, Death Zone, Lost Cherrees, Sixteen Guns, Icons
Of Filth, The Mad Are Sane, and Hagar The Womb. With all
the Bands hailing from the U.K., and the majority from the
London area, this added to the feeling of uniformity of
approach of the increasingly militant anarcho movement of
the day, with a strong set of songs including Conflict's
"Cruise", Poison Girls "Offending Article" and "Stupid" by
Icons Of Filth. With a simple black and white sleeve to
accompany the Crass style title, with anarchist and animal
rights imagery on the rear, the album also came with an
inner sleeve that featured a graphic and lyric info box for
each band. Another snapshot in time captured for posterity.

YALTA HI-LIFE LP (BARABBAS RECORDS)

The second release and only compilation from the short-
lived Barabbas records from Oulu in Finland and it featured
six Finnish hardcore bands of the day (and thirty songs);
Terveet Kädet (four songs), Varaus (six songs), Äpärät
(four songs), Aivoproteesi (eight songs), Kaaos (three
songs), and Kansanturvamusiikkikomissio (aka KTMK with
five songs). As always the Finnish bands didn't mess
around with their no frills, fast and spiky punk approach.
All the bands seemed to take some kind of influence from
probably the most influential punk band ever: Discharge,
as well as inhabiting a similar sonic landscape as Finnish
legends Rattus. Named after the Yalta Conference of 1945
between the U.S., U.S.S.R. and U.K. to discuss the postwar
reorganisation of Europe, the album came in a Crass style
single-sided six panel foldout poster sleeve with info,
lyrics and graphics on all the bands. If you want an
unrelenting barrage of Finnish punk then look no further.

77 KK

TOLBIAC'S TOADS

MISSION IMPOSSIBLE

WARRIOR KIDS

YOUTH BRIGADE

TROTSKIDS

76 % UNCERTAIN

AL KAPOTT

WHITE CROSS

COLLABOS

GHOST WALKS

NEVROSE

RED TIDE

SNIX

D.O.A.

8 ESSENTIAL ATTITUDES

RED TAPE   exibit A   BEYOND WORDS   THEE KATATONIX
THE VIEW   MISSION   OFF THE WALL   CLEVER LINES

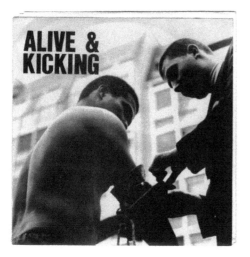

ALIVE & KICKING

ALLE 24 GOED!
ORIGINELE VERSIES

CAPITAL SCUM

KOYAANISQUATSI

VORTEX

WAR RISK 3

WULPSE VARKENS

ZYKLOME

PAY NO MORE THAN 500 BF

PUNK ETC

ATAQUE SONORO

1985

77 KK LP (77 KK RECORDS)

A collection out of France that was one side of French bands and one side of U.S. and Canadian bands. Compiled at a time when the bands from the other side of the Atlantic would've had no idea that a couple of the French bands were 'nationalist' (Snix and Tolbiac's Toads). The album opened with Snix and their Oi! followed by Trotskids with a more upbeat punk. Tolbiac's Toads then upped the pace a bit more in a UK82 fashion before Nevrose pumped out some gruff Mohawk hardcore. Al Kapott, Warrior Kids and Collabos (a stand out) saw off side one bouncing between hardcore, ska and Oi! while the U.S. and Canadian side brought us some great varied punk from; 76% Uncertain (Bridgeport, CT), D.O.A. (Vancouver, BC), Red Tide (Victoria, BC), White Cross (Richmond, VA), Mission Impossible (Washington, DC and featuring a young David Grohl), Youth Brigade (Los Angeles, CA), and Ghost Walks (Portland, ME). The cover art featured nothing but a skull and tracklist on the back.

8 ESSENTIAL ATTITUDES LP (FRANTIC RECORDS)

An area compilation of bands from Baltimore, Maryland, from this local label that released bands connected to the band herein Mission. The album opened with the mainstream radio rock of Red Tape before the all-female trio Exibit A with a catchy new wave. Beyond Words fronted by Lisa Mathews then supplied a very 80s new wave with sax and keyboard. The garage punk of Thee Katatonix finished up side one with an Aussie feel. The View opened side two with some more very 80s college rock with hints of Tommy Keene, before Mission supplied some synth new wave. Off The Wall then took the set off the wall with some swinging doo-wop before closer Clever Lines provided some atmospheric indie rock. The cover art depicted a can of 'Cream Of Baltimore' being poured onto a turntable with band info on the back.

ALIVE AND KICKING 7" EP (WGNS RECORDINGS/METROZINE)

A Washington DC/Virginia six band area compilation on 33 RPM put together by a teenage Scott Crawford (the "Salad Days" documentary) and Colin Sears (Dag Nasty) of MetroZine in conjunction with Bethesda studio WGNS (We Got No Station). The EP opened with a surprisingly straight forward sounding United Mutation (but with mandolin and sax) on "Sensations Fix" followed by Gray Matter and "Walk The Line". Beefeater closed side one with standout "Wars In Space" while the flip opened up with Dave Grohl's pre-Dain Bramage band Mission Impossible, and his first vinyl appearance alongside the Lünch Meat/Mission Impossible split EP (some of which was recorded at this April '85 Laundry Room session). Cereal Killer then took the stage with their catchy DC punk that featured Alec Bourgeois, later of Severin, and Emery Olexa of Slickee Boys. Closing play came Marginal Man with their signature theme song. The EP came in a fold over sleeve with photo by Tomas (Beefeater) and a folded insert.

ALLE 24 GOED! LP (PUNK ETC.)

The hardcore punk of 1980s Belgium was documented via Dirk Michiels' Punk Etc. label of Wolvertem just north of Brussels, with an album recorded at Soundworks Studio, Brussels. 6 bands and 24 "all good" songs that spanned over 45 minutes. Capital Scum got things started with 5 U.K. inspired speaker rattlers, before Koyaanisquatsi sped things up a bit with 5 more. War Risk 3 closed out side one with 4 UK82 inspired punk anthems, and fresh from their "Made In Belgium" LP, Zyklome A supplied 3 slow to fast songs. Vortex from the Wallonia region in the south provided 3 songs that were more in the vein of French style sing-along Oi!, and closing the LP with 4 songs were Wulpse Varkens and their chaotic barking hardcore. Wrapped in a six panel foldout poster sleeve with some basic cover art, the inside revealed panels on all six bands as well as big lists of Belgian band and fanzine addresses. On top of this there were a further 11 photocopied band sheets.

ANGLICAN SCRAPE ATTIC FLEXI (D.I.Y.)

At the time this was an early indication of the direction
the U.K. hardcore scene was heading - into metal territory.
Compiled by Dig (Earache Records) and Kalv (Heresy and In
Your Face Records) this 33 RPM flexi opened with the U.S./
Japan side and California's Hirax and "Destruction And
Terror", with Katon's metal vocals being of much amusement
to my teenage self ("Ooh, Can you feel the power, vibrating
all around?"). Execute then shredded through their Japanese
metal-tinged hardcore before their countrymen Lipcream
continued the sonic assault in a similar fashion to close
side one. Side two began with the crust metal of Concrete Sox
and "Eminent Scum" before Sacrilege battered the eardrums
with "Blood Run". This was one of two flexis compiled by
Kalv and Dig in 1985, the other being "Putrid Evil" that
came out in March, while this was pressed in October of
that year with a pressing of 5,000. My copy came with an
Earache insert and hype sticker on the poly sleeve.

ATAQUE SONORO LP (ATAQUE FRONTAL)

The second of two Brazilian punk compilations from Sao Paulo
label Ataque Frontal in 1985. Twenty songs from ten bands;
Vírus, Ratos De Porão, Garotos Podres, Espermogramix,
Auschwitz, Desordeiros, Cólera, Grinders, Armagedom, and
Lobotomia. Listening to this you could see why bands like
Rattus from Finland were being issued in Brazil around
this time, as the hectic and distorted hardcore on display
throughout had far more in common with the output of
countries like Finland than anything that had been coming
out of countries like the U.K. or U.S. Bands such as Ratos
De Porão, Cólera and Lobotomia soon became more well known
through international compilations, especially on cassette
from labels like Xcentric Noise and ROIR. With excellent
cover art depicting incoming U.S. and U.S.S.R. missiles
by Lobotomia guitarist Adherbal Billy Argel, the gatefold
opened to reveal the mushroom cloud and band photos, while
a soldier corpse observes the ruins on the back.

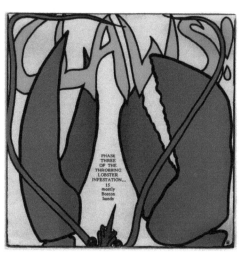

BANDS ON THE BLOCK LP (MATAKO MAZURI RECORDS)

A mixed bag of bands from Austin, Texas, compiled by Jeff Smith of the label and the Hickoids, as well as music writer, road manager and later future creative director of South By Southwest Brent Grulke. A whopping eighteen bands and songs showcased the local talent from; Doctor's Mob, The Wild Seeds, Go Dog Go, The True Believers, Zeitgeist, Pez, The Technicolor Yawns, Room City, Napalm, F.D.R., Meat Joy, Hickoids, Happy Death (hardcore), Not For Sale, Shockhead, Ideals, The Criminal Crew (punk), and The Jeffersons. This was one of those mid-80s U.S. compilations that for the most part marked a shift away from teenage hardcore and into a crossover towards college rock, the first handful of bands here leaning into 60s harmonies and clean guitars, while others had a definite roots/country feel (well it was Texas). The cover art by Smith depicted various photos of garages while the liner notes were handled by Grulke (also of The Austin Chronicle) and the insert supplied credits.

BIG CITY FIRST THREE LP (BIG CITY RECORDS)

As the title suggested, the first three out of print 7" releases from this Bronx, New York, label repackaged on an LP to keep them in circulation for less cost. First up was the "Big City Ain't Too Pretty" New York compilation EP that featured; XKI, Betrayed, Ultra Violence, Savage Circle, No Thanks, Armed Citizens, Fathead Suburbia, and Savage Circle. Next New York's Armed Citizens "Make Sense" 7" EP was split over two sides before the "Nice And Loud" New York/Connecticut compilation EP that featured; No Control, Disorderly Conduct and Ultra Violence (New York), and Reflex From Pain, Vatican Commandos, and C.I.A. (Connecticut). The style throughout was hardcore, and all from New York bar the CT bands, but from a time before the metal and uniformity crept in, meaning this was as varied in its approach to frantic street level punk as it is to production values. The sleeve featured the three EP covers front and back with the inserts recreated on one double-sided insert inside.

BIG CITY ONE BIG CROWD LP (BIG CITY RECORD)

One of the outstanding area compilations of the hardcore era from this New York City label that I bought new at a heavily reduced price back when they couldn't give this hardcore stuff away. This one had New York bands on side one and New Jersey and Connecticut bands on side two, totalling 20 bands. Side one featured; Unjust, Armed Citizens, Ultra Violence, Sheer Terror, Psychos, Shok, Krieg Kopf, Bloodlust and Javi And The Bastards (with Big City man Javi on vocals doing a cover of the Venus And The Razorblades' "Big City" that was also recorded by Dead Boys). The New Jersey bands on side two were; Pleased Youth, Sacred Denial, Bodies In Panic, Stetz, Bedlam, and Adrenalin OD (covering The Damned), while the Connecticut bands were; 76% Uncertain, Vatican Commandos, Chronic Disorder, Seizure, and Violent Children. Inside the crudely rendered cover came a 26 page booklet/zine with a page on each band, art by Sean Taggart and Brian Walsby and full of DIY charm.

CLAWS! LP (THROBBING LOBSTER)

The third and final installment of the Throbbing Lobster compilation LPs, this one containing "15 mostly Boston Bands". Throbbing Lobster inhabited a similar landscape to Ace Of Hearts with a definite garage punk theme. Opening up were the standout psych power pop band The Prime Movers, whose "Matters Of Time" 12" sadly went under most people's radar. Capture The Flag continued this theme before Turbines gave us a Cramps-ish rock'n'roll, The Primevals (The Real Kids minus one), Buzz And The Gang (outstanding pop punk fronted by the now VP of ASCAP Leslie Greene), Volcano Suns (Mission Of Burma), Classic Ruins, Unattached, Willie Alexander And The Jackals, Underachievers, Vandykes (ex-Unnatural Axe and La Peste), Last Stand (punk), New Parts From Old (ex-Sorry), Actual Size (ex-Ground Zero), and The Mighty Ions (with "Pedro Morales" a send up of "California über Alles"). The cover art continued the lobster theme while the liner notes on the rear supplied the info. A Stand out.

CLEANSE THE BACTERIA LP (PUSMORT)

"Pushead Presents..." One of the pinnacles of international hardcore compilations put together by Brian "Pushead" Schroeder for his Pusmort imprint and an introduction for thousands worldwide to the underground punk bands herein when this came out, which is when I bought it mail order. No less than 18 bands and a total of 34 songs were included; 7 Seconds, Civil Dissident, Instigators, Siege, C.O.C., Crude SS, Akutt Inleggelse, The Execute, Part 1, Poison Idea, Genocide Express, Inferno, Mob 47, Septic Death, Enola Gay, Holy Dolls, Zyklome A, and Extrem. With the bands hailing from 12 countries; USA, Japan, Finland, UK, Austria, Sweden, Australia, West Germany, Denmark, Belgium, Norway, and Netherlands, this was no mean feat for a solo operation in the pre-internet master tape era. Wrapped in Pushead art at the top of his game, the mail order version was on orange vinyl with a bonus 12" (with an extra song from 7 of the bands), a poster, sticker and insert.

CLOCKWORK ORANGE COUNTY LP (MYSTIC RECORDS)

"The electrifying cry of today's suburban youth"... or another Doug Moody compilation, this time zoning in on Orange County (the clue's in the title). Fifteen bands and songs from; Doggy Style, D.I., Psychotic Fungus, Just Because, Exobiota, Subculture, Large Hardware (covering Earl Vince & The Valiants aka Fleetwood Mac's "Somebody's Gonna Get Their Head Kicked In Tonight"), Bleeding Hearts, Love Canal, S.S. Nightmares, Scarecrows, Convicted, Partners In Crime, Blind Hatred, and Mind Over Four. Outside of Doggy Style, D.I. (covering The Stooges "Loose"), Love Canal, and rockers Mind Over Four, the vast majority of these bands did little else but that's not to say there's nothing here of merit, from the fast Mystic hardcore of Just Because, Convicted and Subculture, to the darker death rock edge of Exobiota, S.S. Nightmares and Psychotic Fungus, this is a varied and well recorded set. The cover featured a photo of a Mohawked youth, with two inserts supplying the info.

CONNECTICUT FUN LP (INCAS RECORDS)

The Constitution State put itself on the hardcore map with
this showcase of local regulars at punk run club The Anthrax
courtesy of Lost Generation vocalist Joe Dias' Incas label
and compiled by Anthrax promoter Brian Sheridan. First up
was the polka hardcore of Fatal Vision before End Product
from just over the state line in New York delivered some
punk rock featuring drummer Albert Brand of Rest In Pieces.
Contraband, Vatican Commandos, Seizure, and Bad Attitude
continued the hardcore for the rest of side one while side
two gave us C.I.A., Rude Awakening, Lost Generation, No
Milk On Tuesday, Youth Of Today (with five songs recorded
around the same time as their debut EP), 76% Uncertain,
and Punkestra (members of Seizure playing the album's
theme song). The cover art depicted the customary cop/
punk theme by Jim Martin, while the inserts supplied the
info including liner notes by James Spadaccini of Vatican
Commandos. A varied and memorable historical document.

COVERS LP (MYSTIC RECORDS)

"Mystic Radio Presents... Our favourite bands mutilate
your favourite songs" with Mystic studio engineer Phillip
Raves coming to the fore, "Covers" featured 20 bands and
songs from; Scared Straight, Idiot Pills, R.K.L., False
Confession, Sado Nation, Don't No, Acid Head, Love Canal,
Membranes, El Nirvana, Slaughterhouse Five, Ill Repute,
Party Doll, V.O.A., Government Issue, NOFX, Flower Leperds,
Stukas Over Bedrock, SWA, and Plain Wrap. Steppenwolf, The
Runaways, Heartbreakers, Devo, Aerosmith, Cheech & Chong,
The Supremes, The Eyes, Rick James, Iggy Pop, Status Quo,
Bachman-Turner Overdrive, Cream, David Bowie, The Seeds,
Black Sabbath, The Rolling Stones, Pink Floyd, and Disney's
"It's A Small World" all got the irreverent punk covers
treatment, all with that Mystic sound, varying degrees
of competence and tongues often placed in cheeks. The
cover art featured Raves in the DJ chair while a spoof
"Philboard" Top 20 on the rear presented the track list.

DIG THIS LP (FORWARD SOUNDS INTERNATIONAL LTD)

"A tribute to the great strike", this album was in posthumous support of the U.K. miners' strike that became the frontline for Margaret Thatcher's class war between March 1984 and '85. The LP evolved from a benefit gig at Southbank Poly in London, of which side one was gleaned (with side two being studio). Poison Girls opened up with two of their unique anarcho punk-funk songs, before Leeds alternative types the Mekons, and indie folk Londoners Men They Couldn't Hang. The second side began with the pop reggae of Akimbo before Steve Lake of Zounds and the Berlin based U.K. post-punk of Leningrad Sandwich. The album then took an anarchist turn with The Ex, Omega Tribe and Chumbawamba, with the latter's "The Police Have Been Wonderful" crediting vocals to Thatcher and guitar to then Labour leader Neil Kinnock. With striking cover art by artist Clifford Harper (see: Zounds and Poison Girls), "Dig This" was a document of a moment in time both musically and politically.

DRINKING IS GREAT 7" EP (FATAL ERECTION RECORDS)

"For best results, play this record DRUNK". The sole compilation on Malcolm Conover and Pig Champion's label and it was to highlight their alcoholism as well as local hardcore talent from their hometown of Portland, Oregon. This blink-and-you-missed-it EP got started with Champion's own band Poison Idea and blazer "Laughing Boy". E-13 (Ether Teen) were up next with the rocking hardcore of "Pancreatitis". The flip featured "You Dick" by belligerent hardcore types Lockjaw before Final Warning closed play with "I Quit". From a time when the geographic sound was still very much in play with hardcore punk, all the bands inhabited a similar plane on the sonic landscape that reinforced the feeling that you were listening to the product of a unified scene, even though that was no doubt not the case. With sharp hardcore cartoon art by Henry "Buns" Small, the glossy foldout insert featured a section for each band and a load of great local flyers on the reverse.

FALA LP (POLTON)

Fala or Wave was the first vinyl collection of punk and
ska/reggae bands out of Poland on this Warner Music Poland
subsidiary, that provided the first vinyl appearance for
many of the bands, who up until this point had only been
on DIY cassettes, many of which would be smuggled out of
the country. After a short intro by 12 Ra, the reggae of
Bakszysz was wiped away by the fast hardcore of Prowokacja
before Siekiera gave us two pacey songs from their punk
period, including theme song "Fala". Abaddon then took the
stage with more hardcore before Tilt and a live recording.
Dezerter then concluded side one in style while Kryzys
(later Brygada Kryzys) began the second side with low-
key ska while Kultura and Rio Ras provided more reggae
before Dezerter brought the punk back. Izrael then took up
8 minutes with their reggae and a strange outro by Józef
Broda concluded. The mysterious cover art with no tracklist
housed a label inner and a 4x12" foldout poster with info.

FLIPSIDE VINYL FANZINE VOL. 2 LP (GASATANKA RECORDS)

The second in this excellent series from legendary Los
Angeles fanzine Flipside that very much continued where
the first left off. Twenty one bands and songs from;
MIA, Decry, Outpatients, Naked Raygun, Roach Motel, JFA,
Massacre Guys, Vagina Dentata, Plain Wrap, D.I., Misfits,
Necros, C2D, Iconoclast, Cheetah Chrome Motherfuckers,
Disorderly Conduct, Catatonics, Braille Party, Germs, GKH,
and Agent Orange. With contributions mainly from around
the U.S., there were also submissions from Italy (CCM)
and Switzerlands (GKH) for this installment. A notable
entry was Vagina Dentata featuring Pat Smear (Georg Albert
Ruthenberg) of the Germs, as well as Darby's former girlfriend
Michelle Bell, with a version of unrecorded Germs song
"Golden Boys" that Smear also later recorded on his 1987
solo album "RuthenSmear". With cover art by Shawn Cowart
and John Crawford of "Baboon Dooley fame, the album came
with a giant eight panel newsprint poster with band info.

FOUND
OBJECTS

JOHANNA WENT / RASZEBRAE / BENT / DFO / SHUT-UP /
JOE BERARDI / D.O.M.E.S. / GREG BURK COMBO /
BROCK WHEATON / DWINDLE BROTHERS /
JOHN DENTINO / MARK WHEATON /
THE CHRISTIAN FLANGISTS

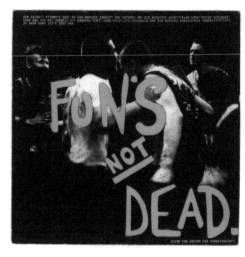

FUN'S
NOT
DEAD.

Hard-Core
LJUBLJANA

UBR

ToŽiBaBe

III.KATEGORIJA

LIMITED EDITION PUNK COMPILATION

HAVE A ROTTEN
CHRISTMAS
VOLUME
TWO

VARUKERS · ENGLISH DOGS · RATTUS
NO CHOICE · XTRACT · EXISTENZ
· SKEPTIX

GYRATIONS ACROSS THE NATIONS

HYBRID

INTRODUCING

THE BEASTS OF BOURBON
GUADALCANAL DIARY
THE LIME SPIDERS
SPIKES
THE VANDALS

IT CAME FROM THE PIT

FOUND OBJECTS LP (ATMOSPHEAR)

In its quest to cover as much ground as possible, Mystic Records created this subsidiary for "creative musicians and inter-media artists" and just this one release. Compiled by Mark Wheaton, the collection was an esoteric mix of soundscape projects on a variety of instruments; Joseph Berardi (The Fibonaccis), Johanna Went (Posh Boy Records), Brock Wheaton, Bent, Greg Burk Combo, D.O.M.E.S., John Dentino (The Fibonaccis), Mark Wheaton, Dwindle Family Orchestra, Shut Up, Raszebrae, Dwindle Brothers, and The Christian Flangists. The album is reminiscent of the art releases on San Francisco's Subterranean Records some years previous. There was straight up jazz (Greg Burk Combo, Dwindle Family Orchestra) but the album was saved from a punk perspective by the all-female Raszebrae featuring Janet Housden (Redd Kross, Love Dolls) on drums. The cover featured a photo of dolls heads with liner notes on the rear and a Mystic insert with info and 'upcoming releases'.

FUN'S NOT DEAD LP (MORE FUN RECORDS)

An all West German hardcore punk collection that featured eight bands; Ceresit 81, Boikottz, Rotting Carcass, Inferno, Sackgasse, Maniacs, ST-37, and Wut. Three of the bands contributed two songs, while Rotting Carcass submitted three, and Inferno, Sackgasse, Maniacs and ST-37 only one. The theme throughout was fast and straight forward West German hardcore with some lesser known names that provided some interesting songs such as ST-37 with their female vocals, and the darker feel of Wut and Ceresit 81. Inferno were an obvious standout here though with the ferocious "Ungewissheit". The production throughout was loud and clear with sharp performances. More Fun Records, the creation of Rüdiger Pfeiffer of Duisburg, only released this in a variety of pressings as well as volume two and a Rotting Carcass/Wut split LP. The album came on a variety of splattered coloured vinyl in DIY sleeves featuring a crowd shot, tracklist and a basic insert.

HARD-CORE LJUBLJANA LP (FV ZALOŽBA)

The second release on this (then) Yugoslavian indie label that was run by the band Borghesia, and it was the world's introduction to the punk output of the capital city of what would become Slovenia. The five band album began with five distorted hardcore songs from U.B.R. (Uporniki Brez Razloga aka Rebels Without a Cause) before Odpadki Civilizacije (Waste Of Civilisation) with four songs in a similar vein but more chaotic in an early 80s Bristol fashion. Side two brought the world the all-female Tožibabe who would record their own 7" EP for the label a year later. Tožibabe's five entries here were undeveloped and primitive but not without charm and sound somewhat polished compared to Epidemija's five attempts at recording an air raid. Finally III. Kategorija were probably the most realised here with six hardcore blasts akin to Siege. Hard-core Ljubljana came in a tri-fold black and white double-sided sleeve with band graphics and lyrics throughout.

HAVE A ROTTEN CHRISTMAS - VOLUME TWO LP (ROT RECORDS)

The second annual seasonal selection from Riot Squad's Rot Records to accompany a mince pie while relaxing in front of a log fire. The seven band and eleven song set began with the sing along '77 style punk of Xtract from Stoke-On-Trent before Finland's Rattus wiped the floor with them with the metallic "Will Evil Win?" Cardiff's No Choice then took things back down a notch with their melodic working class punk, before Varukers then ran through some Discharge homage followed by Sweden's Existenz and a galloping UK '82 style song. Side one closed with a crunchy plodder from Stoke's Skeptix while side two opened with Grantham's English Dogs who'd gone full-on noodling guitar metal by this point. One more song followed from; Xtract, Existenz, No Choice and Rattus, while Varukers, Skeptix and English Dogs all only contributed the one. The sleeve art of course was a snowy scene cut out of some Xmas wrapping paper with basic tracklist and band addresses on the rear.

HYBRID - GYRATIONS ACROSS THE NATIONS LP (HYBRID RECORDS)

A budget showcase sampler of London's Hybrid label run by
Laurie Dunn, also of Statik Records, who'd cut his teeth
working on the Guillotine punk compilation 10" for Virgin
in 1978 before starting Statik in 1980 with the Glasgow
compilation "Second City Statik". Five bands, three of
which were Australian, all with two songs apiece from
their Hybrid/Statik licensed releases. The Australian
bands; The Lime Spiders, The Beasts Of Bourbon and Spikes
all came from the rockin' garage/psych end of things with
contributions from their "Slave Girl", "The Axeman's Jazz"
and "6 Sharp Cuts" records respectively. The Los Angeles'
Vandals songs were gleaned from their "When In Rome Do As
The Vandals" album, while Georgia's Guadalcanal Diary were
from their "Walking In The Shadow Of The Big Man" LP with
the album closing with the excellent "Trail Of Tears".
With sci-fi B-Movie themed cover art and a back cover that
featured a tracklist and the relevant record covers.

IT CAME FROM THE PIT LP (PSYCHE INDUSTRY RECORDS)

The second Psyche Industry compilation following "Primitive
Air Raid" that expanded its remit to all across Canada for
this punk rock state of play for the mid 80s. Fourteen
bands covered all the punk bases; S.C.U.M., My Dog Popper,
Enigmas, Sudden Impact, Entirely Distorted, Count Down
Zero, Ruggedy Annes, S.N.F.U., Problem Children, League
Of Dead Politicans, Gassenhauer, October Crisis, Stretch
Marks, and Nomeansno, with one song each apart from My Dog
Popper and Sudden Impact with two. Smart arses My Dog Popper
had a pop at Jello Biafra in "Rock Stars Are Assholes",
S.N.F.U. covered "Poor Pitiful Me", Sudden Impact got in
early with their crossover, while Enigmas supplied some
post-punk featuring Randy Bowman of The Subhumans and Paul
McKenzie later of The Real McKenzies. This varied insight
into 1985 Canadian punk came with two slam pit photos front
and back by Android of the band House Of Commons, while a
simple insert supplied band addresses and not much else.

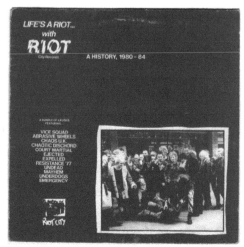

LIFE'S A RIOT...
with
RIOT
City Records
A HISTORY, 1980 – 84

A BUNDLE OF LAUGHS
FEATURING
VICE SQUAD
ABRASIVE WHEELS
CHAOS U.K.
CHAOTIC DISCHORD
COURT MARTIAL
EJECTED
EXPELLED
RESISTANCE 77
UNDEAD
MAYHEM
UNDERDOGS
EMERGENCY

RIOT CITY

MAKE
IT
WORK

MESSAGE FROM AMERICA

MENTAL ABUSE   BLACK OUT   VIOLENT IMAGE

AGNOSTIC FRONT   SUBURBAN   FLASHBACK   SEIZURE

HARDCORE HAS COME OF AGE

"MORE COFFEE FOR THE POLITICIANS"
(PHOENIX UNDERGROUND MUSIC COMPILATION #3)

PRESENTS
ALL HARD

The F.U.s   The Blackjacks
Prime Movers   Band 19
Gang Green   The Oysters
Johnny and the
Jumper Cables
                                 The Freeze
Scruffy   Last Stand
                                 Swinging Erudites

LET'S DIE LP (MYSTIC RECORDS)

It wasn't like Mystic was going to miss a trick on any sub-genre and this was their contribution to the death rock genre that was essentially goth from the Los Angeles area at the time. Not all of the bands herein were death rock and neither were they all from Los Angeles, but Mystic reached in and pulled out the darkest material from the cobwebs of these bands set lists. Sixteen bands and songs set the scene with spooky sounds between each tune from; False Confession, Subterfuge, A.W.O.L., Patrick Mata (Kommunity FK), Thieves Cross, Party Doll, White Pigs, The Mess, Ill Repute, Slaughterhouse 5, Burning Image, The Drab, Silver Chalice (Geza X, Don Bolles and Rob Graves of 45 Grave), Samson's Army (featuring early M.I.A. vocalist Todd Sampson), The Stain, and Flower Leperds. The result was a convincing hardcore era attempt at a death rock collection featuring Mad Marc Rude artwork on the cover and your typical skulls and gravestones on the rear.

LIFE'S A RIOT... WITH RIOT CITY RECORDS LP (RIOT CITY)

The last hurrah from Bristol's Riot City in the form of a singles compilation charting the label's catalogue and, judging by Simon Edwards liner notes, a swipe back at Garry Bushell's "Dustbin of punk" insult that he'd levied at the label. Compiled a year after the label had all but petered out, this collection featured thirteen bands and sixteen songs; Vice Squad ("Last Rockers"), Abrasive Wheels ("Vicious Circle"/"Burn 'Em Down"), Chaos UK ("4 Minute Warning"), Chaotic Dischord ("Never Trust A Friend"), Court Martial, Ejected ("Have You Got 1 0p?"), The Undead, The Expelled, Emergency, The Underdogs ("East Of Dachau"), Resistance '77, Mayhem ("Gentle Murder"), and Varukers ("Die For Your Government"). Every band had a song each apart from Vice Squad, Abrasive Wheels and Chaotic Dischord with two. The basic sleeve art by Shane of Vice Squad featured a shot from the famous photos of the punks outside Virgin Records in Bristol, songs and notes on the rear.

MAKE IT WORK 7" EP (RUN IT! RECORDS)

A Connecticut hardcore compilation that came with Run It!
fanzine that was put together by Dave Brushback, who's
still around today photographing gigs. First up of four
bands and seven songs was Darien, Connecticut's, Vatican
Commandos with two short youthful hardcore blasts followed
by Danbury's super youthful Youth Of Today and two of their
early straight edge outbursts. Side two gave us two from
South Windsor's Chronic Disorder including the tongue-in-
cheek "Unmoshable", a critique of the way hardcore was
going from the perspective of a band who'd been around a
while. Bridgeport's Seizure closed the EP with the longest
song here in the form of a live recording from a set in New
York of 50s song "Marylou" that they played to close their
set. 500 copies were pressed of this D.I.Y. Release, 300
with the zine and 200 with a cover. I sent off for this
when it came out but my money must've gone astray in the
mail and I never got over it at the time.

MESSAGE FROM AMERICA - HARDCORE HAS COME OF AGE LP (URINAL)

One of two releases on New Jersey's Urinal Records. This
compilation, all recorded at eight track studio Merlin
Music in Whippany, NJ, was mainly Jersey bands but New
York and Connecticut bands also made the cut. Opening
with local knuckle heads Black Out and Mental Abuse, the
majority of the rest of side one consisted of four songs by
Connecticut's Seizure. Side two began with two songs from
the stars of the show Agnostic Front with early song "United
Blood" re-recorded as well as an alternative version of
"Time Will Come". Recorded during their "Cause For Alarm"
period, an acetate 7" of these two songs was produced but
never released. The rest of side two consisted of three
songs by generic Jersey hardcore kids Violent Image and
two from more tuneful punks Suburban Flashback. The cover
featured a collage in black and white of the various
hardcore hooligans involved, with more photos on the rear.
"Message From America" received one press on blue vinyl.

MORE COFFEE FOR THE POLITICIANS LP (PLACEBO RECORDS)

The "Phoenix Underground Music Compilation #3" followed on from "Amuck" and "This Is Phoenix Not Circle Jerks" on local scene documentary imprint Placebo Records. The album began with a JFA instrumental that ended up on "Nowhere Blossoms" in 1988 before Sun City Girls, Mighty Sphincter and Ons then took things on a stranger turn before Zany Guys gave us a little hardcore punk fun with a frantic version of "Ballroom Blitz". The majority of the rest of the album could be filed under sun-baked art rock, post-punk and industrial, aside from Harvest (formerly Junior Achievement), who were still playing catchy hardcore but with a metal edge, and Dirt Clods with some catchy punk. The rest of the artists herein were; Bootbeast Carnival, Kill Everyone, Maybe Mental, Joke Flowers, Keening, Hellfire, Domino Theory, and Racer X. The cover art was on the politians and coffee theme. After this album Placebo turned its attention to industrial music with the Dry Lungs series.

MR. BEAUTIFUL PRESENTS ALL HARD LP (MODERN METHOD RECORDS)

The fourth and final compilation from Boston's Modern Method and this one was the brainchild of local producer Steve "Mr. Beautiful" Barry, who became known in hip hop circles via his radio show, but for now he was all rock. Twelve bands and songs that opened with The F.U.'s right before their transition to Straw Dogs with later Dogs song "In Deep". Following this were Prime Movers with some keyboard garage psych before thrashers Gang Green hit their standard theme with "Let's Drink Some Beer". The rest of side one came in the form of a Stooges style rock from Johnny And The Jumper Cables, some country punk from Scruffy The Cat, and The Dogmatics with a rock'n'roll standard changed to "Teenager On Drugs". Side two delivered more standard alternative rock from The Blackjacks, Band 19 and The Oysters before The Freeze and a different version of "Warped Confessional". Last Stand and Swinging Erudites concluded proceedings with a cover art theme of Mr. Beautiful in his Speedos.

MYSTIC SAMPLER #2 LP (MYSTIC RECORDS)

The second in the series of the full length Mystic samplers. Thirteen bands and songs from; Agression, The Grim, Rat Pack, Ill Repute, Slaughterhouse 5, Flower Leperds, Party Doll, Doggy Style, Dr. Know, Membranes, RKL, Corpus Delicti, and Subterfuge. The theme throughout as usual was full throttle hardcore with some death rock thrown in, and all the songs were taken from various Mystic releases. A lot of which here were compilations themselves. The Mystic skull adorned the front just to hammer the repeated image into the skulls of the hardcore generation for marketing purposes with the source record sleeves in question displayed on the back cover. Initially pressed on blue to match the sleeve.

MYSTIC SUPER SEVEN SAMPLER #1 & #2 7" EPS (MYSTIC RECORDS)

More label samplers from Mystic and this series was on the theme of 7 bands on a 7" with a song each from their individual Mystic 7" releases. R.K.L. opened up with some hyper fast Nardcore before Don't No bordered on Discharge homage. Scared Straight and Ill Repute then continued with some all out California hardcore. The flip began with False Confession before things took a darker turn with Flower Leperds, and the EP finished up with some raging hardcore by Manifest Destiny. Volume two opened with Party Doll setting out their stall with dramatic a death rock tune with female vocals from an EP that never happened. Dr. Know then livened up proceedings before Wall Flowers concluded side one with sax and an out of tune guitar from another EP that never happened, probably for good reason. Insolents then got things back on the hardcore track on side two before NO F-X, and a song from their very first EP. Doggy Style followed this with their poppy skate rock before Rat Pack closed the EP in a metal punk style. The cover art on both featured the Mystic skull with the individual 7" sleeves on the back, but you had to check the labels for the track lists. #1 came on black, purple or red vinyl while #2 was on black, white or blue.

NÅ ELLER ALDRI 7" EP (X-PORT PLATER)

The third release and only compilation from this Norwegian
label, and of course this was a showcase of Norsk talent
of the day titled "Now Or Never", that introduced the world
to some later well known names in hardcore punk circles.
Seven bands and songs, and Bannlyst opened the show with
a throaty Discharge inpired belter before Psykisk Terror
jumped on the stage for another galloping burner. Kafka
Prosess closed side one with something a little more U.S.
hardcore influenced. Side two introduced Siste Dagers
Helvete with a more rockin' hardcore approach before it all
went anarcho with Angor Wat and a scrappy song called "Bomb
Or Food". Landssvik continued the theme with "War" before
Akutt Innleggelse finished up with their snappy U.S. style
hardcore. Nå Eller Aldri, with simple cover art of just the
title, came in an oversized six panel foldout poster with
info on all the bands. Some copies also came with a Xerox
sheet with the lyrics translated into English.

NEW JERSEYS' GOT IT? LP (BUY OUR RECORDS)

The first compilation on this New Jersey label run by
members of Adrenalin O.D. and Bedlam so of course it was
a Noo Joisey area compilation. Nine bands and eighteen
songs with two each in neat order, the album kicked off
with Bedlam and Bodies In Panic, both with a unique very
punk take on hardcore. Cyanamid then took things in a more
chaotic direction, one hyper-speed and one slow burner,
before Pleased Youth and a more attitude filled hardcore.
Children In Adult Jails closed the first side with their
thumping but messy punk featuring long-time WFMU DJ Diane
Farris in their rank. The second side got going with Stetz
and their standard punk before My 3 Sons with their No Trend
style nihilistic thud. Sacred Denial then brought forth
their hardcore that bordered on crossover, before local
hardcore stars Adrenalin O.D. finished with two fuzzed up
blazers. The cover featured a photo of a Jersey garbage dump
and inside was a 16 page booklet with a page on each band.

OPEN MIND SURGERY LP (BLUURG RECORDS)

The second compilation on Dick Lucas' Bluurg imprint and this one reached into the international arena, as well as U.K. punk talent of the day, either connected to Bluurg already or presumably bands that were just on the radar. Nine bands with two songs each; Smart Pils, Culture Shock, Depraved, K4 (New Zealand), Civilised Society?, Freak Electric, Instigators, Steve L. (Dick's brother), and Scream (U.S. and fresh from their 1985 U.S. tour together). "Open Mind Surgery" provided a unique snapshot of the U.K. scene specifically as it moved in different directions in the mid 80s; from the more metal-tinged anarcho of Civilised Society?, to the more U.S. hardcore influenced anarcho of Instigators, the more festival ska anarcho of Culture Shock and the more post-punk anarcho of Freak Electric and Smart Pils. With a graphic of a face in an eye for the cover art, the back sported band photos while the 10 panel concertina insert provided a page on each band.

PANIC PANIC LP (PSYCHE INDUSTRY / PLANETARIUM)

The second compilation on this Montreal label after "Primitive Air-Raid" and this was a bit like a follow-up of Montreal bands that were generally less hardcore punk and more post-punk and experimental. Twelve songs from eleven bands with Biohazard (not the later hardcore band) having two songs, the rest one; Terapi, The Clicks, Susie Cue, Septyx, Monty Cantsin, Culture Shock, Charles Foucrault, Vomit And The Zits, Red Shift, and Wonderland And Lilyput. All sorts of styles of the era were present from funky post-punk to synthy new wave, some of it being an easier listen than others, but generally unique. The end result sounded like something that would've come out of San Francisco a good few years previous. Stand outs from a punk perspective were Vomit And The Zits and "Eyes" that twisted between post-punk and Dead Kennedys style hardcore. With typically mysterious cover art, the album came with a printed inner sleeve with black and white graphics for all the bands.

PARTY POOPING PUNK PROVOCATIONS LP (XCENTRIC NOISE RECORDS)

The second and final vinyl collection and last release from Hull's Xcentric Noise that was run by Andy "Shesk" Thompson. In spite of the label's history as a promoter of international hardcore, this one was an all U.K. affair featuring nine bands and eighteen songs with ridiculous samples between each song from; Stupids, The Samples, Death Zone, Quel Dommage, Self Abuse, Mizrabul Bar Stuards, Atrox, Protest, and Anihilated. There were two songs each for most of the bands but three songs from The Stupids and one from Anihilated. Another snapshot of the variety of styles emerging in the U.K. at the time from the U.S. hardcore inspired Stupids to the still UK '82 style of The Samples, Self Abuse and Death Zone, to the still very Joy Division style post-punk of Quel Dommage. With unique cover art by Charlie Mason of Atrox, the printed inner sleeve provided all the band info with a panel on each band all printed in blue to give it a real Xcentric Noise feel.

PUTRID EVIL E.P. FLEXI (D.I.Y.)

The first of two flexi discs compiled and issued in 1985 by Kalv (Heresy) and Dig, this being released in March, the other "Anglican Scrape Attic" released in October. Three bands and five songs on one side of this red flexi with a more metal title but less metal content than their other 1985 effort. The disc opened with Australia's Civil Dissident and "Tell Me The Solution" from their 1984 demo, followed by Septic Death from Idaho in the U.S. and the then unreleased "Poison Mask". The U.K.'s Stupids followed with three songs presumably recorded specifically for this release; "Sleeping Troubles", "This Is The Norm?" And "I Am Ill". As you can imagine it was all over in a flash. 3,000 copies were issued in a fold over sleeve with Nick Blinko inspired cover art by Shane and a panel for each band inside. Some copies also came with an alternative skate themed lyric insert. Dig soon went onto run Earache Records while Kalv played in many band and ran In Your Face Records.

RADIO TOKYO TAPES 3 LP (PVC RECORDS)

For the third and final installment in the series Ethan
James at Radio Tokyo Studio in Venice, California, amassed
this collection of sixteen acoustic recordings from; The
Knitters, Balancing Act, Kerry McBride, Revolver, Cindy
Lee Berryhill, Chris D. And The Divine Horsemen, Alisa,
Pop Art, Sandy Bull, Henry Rollins (like "Family Man" with
Tom Troccoli on guitar), Beefsisters, Carmaig de Forest,
Linda Albertano, The Minutemen, Phranc, and Drew Steele.
Minutemen covered Richard Hell & The Voidoids' "Time"
while The Knitters (members of X) covered two old Honky
Tonk tunes. A few of the songs definitely nodded back to
the Hollywood Hills of the 60s while other contributions
were more folk or country. The album sleeve featured a
cartoon strip by 'Teen Angel' depicting a call between
two female friends talking about the album and citing all
the artists. The back sleeve provides song and artist info
with an interview about the compilation with Ethan James.

REALLY FAST VOL. II LP (REALLY FAST RECORDS)

The second installment of this Swedish hardcore series and
it was much the same as the first with an all out assault of
fast and abrasive Swedish punk of the day. Thirty six songs
this time from fourteen bands; The Krixhjälters, S.O.D.,
Asocial, Tatuerade Snutkukar, Swankers, Nyx Negativ, Mob 47,
Bristles, Ab Hjärntvätt, Ingron Hutlös, R.T.S., Distrust,
Subway Army, and Sötlimpa. Album openers The Krixhjälters
were a stand out, probably as they didn't just go for the
throat, while the album also closed with the more punk
sounds of Sötlimpa. Familiar names provide some of the
fast hardcore, such as Asocial, and the blazing thrash of
Mob 47, while the UK '82 punk of The Bristles also made
the grade with varying recording quality throughout. The
cover featured an old experimental photo showing movement,
which expanded into a poster sleeve with graphics from all
the bands on one side, the track list and liner notes on a
relatively plain back sleeve.

RELYING ON US... 7" EP (ENDANGERED MUSIK)

For his third vinyl release Steve Beatty, later owner of Plastic Head Distribution and many bands, released this U.K. compilation featuring five bands and six songs. Opening proceedings were Stone The Crowz with two passionate anarcho songs; "No More Asking Nicely" and "Religion Only Exists" (featuring Mr. Beatty on the drums). H.D.Q. then "Take Control" with a song from the early line-up of the band, their debut LP being the next release on Endangered Musik. The flip continued with Oi Polloi and "Stop Vivisection Now!", Criminal Justice with "Overload" (featuring Xpozez drummer Brooky), and Depraved with "Resident President". A very D.I.Y. affair with some muddy sounding songs, the EP came with either a foldout sleeve or two pieces of paper forming the front and back cover, both with different artwork. The bottom of the front cover also states; "Unnecessary vivisection continues in British laboratories" making it look like a benefit but it probably wasn't at £1.10.

SHINDIG! LP (ZULUBIRD RECORDS)

Sub-titled; "Live at the Savoy" and "A compilation of six of Vancouver's most promising groups", this twelve song collection was the result of a collaboration between Vancouver record store Zulu Records and radio station CITR-FM, and contained the six winners of a battle of the bands competition called Shindig, held over eight months, whittled down from 60 entrants, and recorded on a 24 track mobile studio. The six bands were, Rhythm Mission, NG3, Red Herring, Nerve Tubes, My Three Sons, and Death Sentence. For the most part the bands here seemed to inhabit the same part of the sonic map as locals Nomeansno with chanting and bass-driven funky post-punk. Nerve Tubes picked up the pace a bit punk wise with "Things Break", a hectic keyboard infused punk, while of hardcore interest Death Sentence provided live versions of "Dawn Of The Dead" and "In Flames" from their debut LP. The sleeve featured live band photos, a shot of the stage on the back and a lyric inner.

SINGLE TICKET TO PARADISE 7" EP (NEG. FX RECORDS)

"The mini-sampler you'll die to play frisbee with". For his first release Gérard Miltzine, soon of Bunker Records (record store and distributor) and of Grenoble in France, released this D.I.Y. international hardcore compilation 7". Seven hardcore punk bands and songs from; Powerage (South Africa), Permanent Damage (Australia), Human Beings (France), T.A.S.K. (aka Tatuerade Snutkukar from France), Cancerous Growth (U.S.A.), Cheetah Chrome Motherfuckers (Italy), and Rattus (Finland). All seven played typical frantic but passionate mid 1980s hardcore to varying levels of proficiency and recording quality. The EP came in a fold over full colour printed sleeve depicting a blindfolded hostage about the get shot, with a photocopied lyric insert inside featuring a section for each band. Neg FX Records also released other records for Rattus and Powerage and Bunker released licensed French versions of Boneless Ones and Verbal Abuse records from Boner in the U.S.

SPEED TRIALS LP (HOMESTEAD RECORDS)

A live document of the "Speed Trials" five day festival that featured over 100 artists at White Columns gallery in New York between May 4th and 8th 1983. This eight band and nine song collection was notable as a new noise began to emerge out of the U.S. in the years when the dust of hardcore was beginning to settle. Opening with The Fall almost as a nod to inspiration of old, the album continued with Beastie Boys, Live Skull, Sonic Youth, Lydia Lunch, Carbon, Swans, and Toy Killers. Most of the bands and artists had been around a while but records like "Speed Trials" notified the world of the arrival of something that was coming at the post-punk era from a different angle than hardcore thrash or crossover. Even Beastie Boys "Egg Raid On Mojo" from their hardcore period was delivered as chaotic noise rock. The Sonic Youth track "Dig This!" was an edited collage of five songs. The cover featured a photo of Sonic Youth with more live photos on the rear. Released in the U.S. and U.K.

THE ENIGMA VARIATIONS 2LP (ENIGMA RECORDS)

A double sampler album of the then current roster of
Enigma artists, compiled by label owner William Hein and
A&R man Steve Pross. Twenty six band and songs from;
Screamin' Sirens, The Jet Black Berries, Naked Prey, Tex
And The Horseheads, Greg Sage, Chris D./Divine Horsemen,
John Trubee, Rain Parade, Plasticland, The Pandoras, Get
Smart!, The Leaving Trains, Green On Red, Game Theory, 45
Grave, The Effigies, Kraut, Redd Kross, TSOL, Channel 3,
Cathedral Of Tears, Passionel, The Untouchables, The Pool,
Scott Goddard, and SSQ. As should be apparent from the band
list, the label signings consisted of hardcore bands who
were branching out into a more rock direction, as well the
older punk, roots and garage rockers that had side-stepped
hardcore altogether. Housed in a typically enigmatic cover
with records on the back, and the inside of the gatefold
featured band photos and information. A snapshot of one
aspect of U.S. alternative rock in 1985.

THEM BONERS BE POPPIN' LP (BONER RECORDS)

Where else but Berkeley, California, would Boner Records
emerge to provide the world with their crossover, right at
the time that its more thrash metal cousins were gaining
momentum worldwide out of local clubs like Ruthie's Inn, a
melting pot for the purveyors of both hardcore and thrash
in the Bay Area. Featuring 6 bands and 15 songs from; Verbal
Abuse, Special Forces, The Boneless Ones, Fang, Blast, and
Tales Of Terror. Label owner Tom Flynn, who served time
in Fang and Special Forces (amongst others), was perfectly
positioned to put this compilation together, that featured
a goofy cover image but with a back cover containing six
action packed live shots of the bands by Murray Bowles.
Special Forces were fresh from playing the August 1984
'Eastern Front' in Aquatic Park, San Francisco, a two day
festival with hardcore on one day (Circle Jerks, F.U.'s,
Raw Power) and metal on the other (Suicidal Tendencies,
Exodus, Slayer). The LP was licensed to We Bite in Germany.

THE RETURN OF THE LIVING DEAD (ORIGINAL SOUNDTRACK) LP (ENIGMA RECORDS)

The soundtrack to the punk related comedy horror film that starred among others "Scream Queen" Linnea Quigley of The Skirts (see: The Sound of Hollywood: Girls) as Trash. The punk/death rock soundtrack began with The Cramps and "Surfin' Bird" followed by "Partytime" by 45 Grave, "Nothing For You" from TSOL, The Flesheaters, and Roky Erickson on side one. Side two began with a then exclusive song "Dead Beat Dance" by The Damned, notable as it was a reworking of a 1979 demo song "The Day I Met God" by Victimize from Barry in Wales, who'd featured then current Damned guitarist and bassist Roman Jogg and Bryn Merrick. The rest of the album consisted of Tall Boys, The Jet Black Berries and SSQ (closing with "Trash's Theme"). The album came with a variety of cover art depending on what country it was released in, but the original U.S. press came with the movie poster as the cover with stills on the back.

THE SOUND OF HOLLYWOOD - DU BEAT-E-O LP (MYSTIC RECORDS)

The soundtrack of a strange punk related film that was originally to be a day-in-the-life style film of The Runaways, but when the band split up it later morphed into this film about a director trying to get the film Finished. The film featured Joan Jett as well as other punk scene types; Derf Scratch (Fear), El Duce (Mentors), Texacala Jones (Tex And the Horseheads) and performance artist Johanna Went. A lot of this was made up of 'artists' here purely for this film with dialogue from the flick as an overdub; The M.G.B.'s, Rainbow Smith And The L.A. Girls, as well as individuals connected to the making of the film, but it also contained Social Distortion (three songs from "Mommy's Little Monster"), Tex And The Horseheads, Even Worse, Dr. Know, The Mentors, and Johanna Went. The cover featured stills from the film and back cover stated "Fifth In The Series" although this was the fourth and final, so it looks like a miscount took place. It came with a film synopsis insert.

274

THE VIKINGS ARE COMING LP (UPROAR RECORDS)

The first compilation and second vinyl release from Peter Ahlqvist, aka Babs, also of Uproar fanzine, and later owner of Burning Heart Records in the 1990s. Of course hailing from Sweden in 1985 this was a collection to promote seven Swedish bands, who seemed to be still largely looking to UK '82 for influence. Fear Of War kicked things off with three mid-tempo songs before Rescues In Future added a little melody with their four. Bedrövlerz were up next and took things in a more raw UK '82 direction before side one concluded with Rasta Boys with one reggae song that turned to punk. The second side began with two slow Ugly Squaw songs followed by three slightly faster tunes from Cruel Maniax, then three more tuneful Bizarr songs. The LP concluded with three standout Crude SS tunes, their "Who'll Survive" E.P. being the first Uproar release. The LP came in a foldout sleeve with rough cover art and a piece on each band. A copy of Uproar fanzine No.3 was also included.

THEY ONLY COME OUT AT NIGHT LP (CLAY RECORDS)

The first compilation from Mike Stone's Stoke-on-Trent based label, and curiously it featured no Discharge who largely managed to stay off compilations. A late in the day label sampler that featured fourteen songs from only four bands, all from records released in 1983 and 1984; The Lurkers, Abrasive Wheels, G.B.H., and English Dogs. The three Lurkers songs were from two Clay 7"s, the four Abrasive Wheels songs were taken from their more melodic second album and a B-side, the four G.B.H. Songs were from their second album "City Baby's Revenge" and a B-side, and the three English Dogs tunes were from the "Invasion Of The Porky Men" LP. The pencil cover art was handled by Mike Hannan, also of Discharge (see: "Warning: Her Majesty's Government Can Seriously Damage Your Health") and G.B.H. ("City Baby's Revenge") sleeve art, and depicted a late night punk, whose lengthening hair gave an indication of changes afoot. A simple black back cover supplied the tracks and credits.

THEY PELTED US WITH ROCKS AND GARBAGE LP (AFTER HOURS RECORDS)

The only compilation on this Cleveland, Ohio, label to promote Cleveland bands and compiled by Negative Print, WCSB radio, Fungus and Trans Dada Records. First up on this lost gem were Spike In Vain who by 1985 had taken a more tuneful direction, followed by the only band with two songs, The Offbeats, and their hectic catchy hardcore. The Dark followed with their bleak hardcore before Children's Crusade and Riot Architecture slowed things down in a post-punk way. The Guns then blazed some youthful hardcore before the death rock of Shadow Of Fear. Side two continued the death rock/post-punk theme with Death Of Samantha, Diffi-Cult, New Small Appliances, The Reactions (power pop that borrowed a Jam riff), the stand out punk of Idiot Humans with "Dressed In Green", and Faith Academy (with Pagans' Tim Allee). Titled after a Letterman catchphrase, the LP came with some unique cover art by Spike In Vain's Scott Pickering and two inserts with info on each band.

THEY SHALL NOT PASS LP (ABSTRACT SOUNDS)

A collection of CNT Productions, a label that was founded by The Mekons and producer Adrian Collins. As one of two verbose sub-titles stated; "This LP contains a selection of songs released by CNT productions of Leeds between September 1981 and October 1983. It was compiled during the tenth month of the British miners' strike and is dedicated to the striking miners and their families. Death to rock and roll monetarism". Featuring; Redskins, The Sisters Of Mercy, The Three Johns, The Mekons, Newtown Neurotics, Carlton B. Morgan, and Vicky Talbot. This overtly political album represented a loose group of bands who'd come out of punk over years previous but had floated around the weekly music press and presented varying styles that weren't post-punk or indie. This LP came about around the same time as the more mainstream Red Wedge, with this setting itself apart with some specific anti-fascist imagery. With art borrowed from the Spanish CNT, the LP came with a printed inner sleeve.

WE DON'T WANT YOUR FUCKING LAW! LP (FIGHT BACK)

Round two of the "We Don't Want Your Fucking..." collection (round one follows below alphabetically) and it was more of the same from this Mortahate subsidiary compiled by members of Conflict. This volume contained sixteen songs from even more mainly U.K. anarcho bands and some UK '82 hangers on; Karma Sutra, Arch Criminals, Vorkriegsjugend (West Germany), The Cause, The Insane (a stand out with the apparently older song "World's Going Insane"), Wardance, The Drill, Apostles, Rubella Ballet, The Partisans, Carnage, Vex, Positive Impact, Duet, Reality, and Upright Citizens (West Germany). With cover art soon adopted by Conflict as a logo of sorts, the back cover featured photos cut out of newspapers of the then very recent Miner's Strike, concentrating on the police violence obviously, and pasted down with a handwritten tracklist. The liner notes were absent on this one, as was a list of potential recipients or any insert. Again, a snapshot of a very specific time in punk history.

WE DON'T WANT YOUR FUCKING WAR! LP (FIGHT BACK RECORDS)

The first of three Mortahate related compilations with a running title theme (this being on the sub-label Fight Back). A set of anarcho centred punk with a U.K. emphasis. Nineteen bands and songs from; Broken Bones, Anthrax, Subhumans, The Soledad Brothers, Decadent Few, Dezerter (Poland), Potential Threat, Stalag 17, Lost Cherrees, Stigma, UK Subs, Admit You're Shit, Toxic Waste, Legion Of Parasites, Malinheads (West Germany), Instigators, The Varukers, Liberty, and State Hate. A strong line-up with some strong songs on the usual subjects of; war, animal rights, the state, racism, and class. With the usual stark black and white Discharge style war graphics, the somewhat vague liner notes on the back by "Someone Who Cares, London 84" about changing things, along with some equally vague causes that were going to benefit from the record. Another time capsule collection evocative of a time and place in punk rock history. Some copies came with a foldout insert.

WE WONT BE YOUR FUCKING POOR

THERE IS NO REASON FOR THIS LP TO COST MORE THAN £4.50 IF YOU ARE ASKED FOR MORE.
DON'T BUY IT.

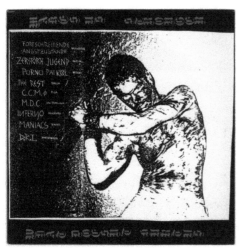

WHAT SURF II

AGENT ORANGE
DAVIE ALLAN and THE ARROWS
THE BURGLARS
THE HALIBUTS
SANDY NELSON
THE PANDORAS IV
THE PYRAMIDS
THE (ORIGINAL) SURFRAIDERS

When men were men... and sheep were scared

WELCOME TO VENICE LP (SUICIDAL RECORDS)

For the inaugural release on Suicidal Tendencies own imprint Mike Muir put together this showcase of Venice locals (only) with five bands and nine songs from; Suicidal Tendencies, Beowülf, Los Cycos, No Mercy, and Excel. Suicidal opened up the album with an exclusive song "Look Up..... (The Boys Are Back)", that at the halfway point between their first two albums, showed them heading directly into crossover metal territory. Beowülf continued, sounding a lot like classic Motörhead for two songs before Los Cycos (Suicidal's alter ego) then provided a six minute thrasher "It's Not Easy". Another Suicidal linked band, No Mercy, opened side two with two further thrash metal exercises; their theme song and "War Machine". Excel then closed the album with three speed metal songs, very much in keeping with the whole direction of this album and local scene, with ripping solos aplenty. The cover art by artist Michael Seiff and a Dogtown Skates insert completed the Venice thrash skate gang theme.

WE WONT BE YOUR FUCKING POOR 2LP (MORTAHATE RECORDS)

For the pièce de résistance in the "We Won't" series the release was shifted to parent label Mortahate and upgraded to a double album with a gatefold sleeve like a deluxe "Bullshit Detector" compilation. Featuring thirty two bands and songs from; Post Mortem, Political Asylum, Kulturkampf, Distrust (Sweden), Stagnant Era, Corpse, A.O.A., Conflict, Dirge, The Assassins, Vertical Hold, Nocturnal Emissions, K.C. & The Moonshine Band, The Fiend, Toxic Reasons (U.S.A.), Shrapnel, Revulsion, Nick Toczeck, Stone The Crowz, Death Sentance, Classified Protest, Systematic Annex, Fallout, D.O.A. (Canada), Miasma, Indian Dream, Sacrilege, Virus, Abreaction, The Waste, Diatribe (U.S.), and Oi Polloi. This mainly U.K. collection was given an international feel with the four overseas bands. Issued in an incredibly blank front cover with an image of the Ethiopian famine on the back, and band art and lyric boxes inside the gatefold (although some bands who have art aren't on the record).

WHAT DOESN'T HURT US MAKES US STRONGER LP (DESTINY RECORDS)

The second compilation on Destiny Records out of Berlin run by David Pollack of bands Porno Patrol and No Allegiance. Twenty one songs by ten hardcore punk bands, all German bar two U.S. bands thrown in for that international flavour; C.C.M. (Cheetah Chrome Motherfuckers), Porno Patrol, Zerstörte Jugend, The Rest, MDC (U.S.), Fortschreitende Angstzustände, Maniacs, D.R.I. (U.S.), Inferno, and The Rest. All the songs on the album were recorded in December 1984 at Musiclab Studios in Berlin except for the MDC ("Born To Die" and "Kleptomaniac") and D.R.I. songs ("Yes Ma'am"). Featuring a cover photo of C.C.M. Vocalist Syd Migx wielding something while covered in something equally unsavoury, the back was covered in live band photos while the insert supplied band graphics on one side and lyrics on the other. Originally issued with the title in gold ink in a barely readable Germanic font, it was corrected for the second press to a different font in white.

WHAT SURF II LP (WHAT? RECORDS)

The second installment of surf tunes from Chris Ashford's original 1977 punk label What? Records (that had started out by releasing the "Forming" 7" by Germs). This ten song instrumental album mixed some original surf bands of old with the then current crop of Eighties Californian surf bands. It is relevant for punk interest for the continued inclusion of Orange County surf punks Agent Orange, who supplied an updated "Surfbeat '85" for this second collection. The older bands included were; Davie Allan & The Arrows, The Pyramids and Sandy Nelson, while the then current bands were The Surf Raiders, The Halibuts, the all-female Pandoras and the very Agent Orange sounding The Burglars who featured two future members of Chemical People, Blair Jobe and Robert Asher. The surf themed (obviously) cover art was drawn by Marty Korth who was also responsible for artwork for The Ventures and The Halibuts, while the back cover featured photos and credits of all eight bands.

WHEN MEN WERE MEN... AND SHEEP WERE SCARED LP (BEMISBRAIN)

The third and final compilation on Jimmy Bemis of Modern Warfare's Bemisbrain Records of Southern Californian punk. This one was neatly put together with eight bands and sixteen songs, each with two each in order. Due to the label's hometown being Long Beach "When Men Were Men" concentrated on then local Long Beach talent; Rhino 39, The Vandals, Red Beret, The Crewd, Falling Idols, Secret Hate, Nip Drivers, and Target Of Demand. Notable here was that these were the last Vandals recordings before the line-up changed into the later version of the band with Dave Quackenbush of Falling Idols taking over vocals. Produced by Ron Goudie and Steve Sinclair, also of Modern Warfare, the cover featured art front and back by San Diego punk artist Mad Marc Rude (Misfits, Battalion Of Saints) featuring some famous types and sheep in lingerie, and due to John Wayne having his modesty revealed, a sticker was added to the shrink wrap falsely claiming it was a limited edition cover.

WILD RIDERS OF BOARDS: SKATE ROCK VOLUME 3 LP (THRASHER)

The first thing that struck you about this third episode in the 'Skate Rock' continuum was the unique cover of the underside of a skateboard cut into the shape of a board. First up on this ten band and seventeen song opus were Sweden's Slam with the title theme song, followed by a veritable hall of fame of hardcore and crossover; Boneless Ones, Christ On Parade, Septic Death, Slam, Beyond Possession, Corrosion Of Conformity, Accüsed, Gang Green, and No Rules. Compiler and designer Mörizen Föche (Drunk Injuns) knew what he was doing when bringing together songs like "Skate To Hell" by Gang Green, "Skater's Life" by Beyond Possession and "The Keg Kept A Flowin'" by Boneless Ones. Tapping into the whole skate punk crossover mentality throughout, and highlighting the role these Thrasher compilations played as intersection between skateboarding and hardcore punk. As well as the genius sleeve design, this came with the usual poster insert with skate photos and credits.

"BIG CITY'S ONE BIG CROWD" LP BOOKLET - ART BY BRIAN WALSBY

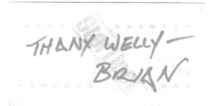

THANX WELLY —
BRIAN

ANTHRAX STICKER FROM CONNECTICUT FUN SIGNED BY BRIAN SHERIDAN

1986

A FAREWELL TO ARMS LP (SELFISH RECORDS)

The first compilation from Japan's Selfish Records and Chaos U.K.'s 1985 tour seemed to have seen the Japanese punks reach for their amps and turn everything up. Six bands and seventeen songs that opened with Lipcream and three swirling and chaotic thrash blasts. Outo followed with four salvos of polka hardcore fury in the Disorder vein, while Gastunk closed out side one with two more metallic thrash numbers with noodling guitars. Side two opened with four raging Gauze numbers that took no prisoners in a similar fashion to Septic Death, followed by two each from the much more metallic Ghoul and the searing din of The Execute. With a cover photo of Hiroshima by Mower of Chaos U.K. on their aforementioned tour, the insert offered lyrics in Japanese and English (The Execute). It was reissued in 1987 (pictured) and again in Germany in 1988 with different cover art.

ANOTHER SHOT FOR BRACKEN LP (POSITIVE FORCE)

The American hardcore punk scene was starting to change in myriad ways and this was one of those compilations that inadvertently documented that transition. Consisting of seventeen bands from all over the U.S. (and one from Canada) that presumably 7Seconds had played with and met on tour; Flag Of Democracy, Scream, Short Dogs Grow, Dissonance, Verbal Assault, Entirely Distorted (Canada), The Brigade, Outcry, White Flag, 7 Seconds, 5 Balls Of Power, Adrenalin O.D., Scram, Care Unit, Youth Of Today, Action Figure, and The Sins. Everything was covered here from the steadfast hardcore of Youth Of Today and Flag Of Democracy to the more progressive new rock direction of Scream and The Brigade (formerly Youth). By no means a dud this album had a varied mix of good songs. Only the compiler Kevin Seconds would know the meaning of the title and the strange cover art added little in the way of explanation.

"A Japanese punk compilation"
A Farewell to Arms
LIP CREAM
OUTO
GASTUNK

another shot for bracken

APATHY... NEVER!

THE BLASTING CONCEPT VOLUME II

SACCHARINE TRUST SAINT VITUS SWA
D.C.3 PAINTED WILLIE DUG OCTOBER FACTION
ANGST MEAT PUPPETS MINUTEMEN BLACK FLAG
GONE HÜSKER DÜ OVERKILL WÜRM
INCLUDES PREVIOUSLY UNRELEASED RECORDINGS

SPECIAL
LIST PRICE
$8.98

DEATH

DO YOU REMEMBER ROCK'N'ROLL?

A San Jose-South Bay Compilation

WITH:
STIKKY
NITEHAWKS
NO WARNING
FRONT LINE
THE FACTION
ORANGE CURTAIN
THE LIVING END
STEVE CABALLERO
JET CRASH MIRACLE

APATHY... NEVER! LP (OVER THE TOP)

The first release on this Guilford, Connecticut, label
and it showcased the international hardcore scene as the
mid 80s marched on with eleven bands and twenty songs
from; Depression (Australia), Half Life (U.S.), G.A.S.H.
(Australia), Mottek (Germany), Kauneus & Terveys (Finland),
Fair Warning (Canada), Fuck Geez (Japan), Sons Of Ishmael
(Canada), Dehumanizers (U.S.), So Much Hate (Norway), and
Raped Teenagers (Sweden). The transition of the hardcore
scene could be seen again here, but in a different direction;
no melodic college rock elements but a more metallic drift,
but not to crossover thrash, instead more of a precursor of
what would become the crust side of punk. The spiky artwork
by Australia's Tim 'Dognest' Coleman also reflected this
and "Apathy... Never!" came with a rough and ready twelve
page booklet with a band-supplied page for each band with
their own graphics, photos and lyrics.

BLASTING CONCEPT - VOLUME II LP (SST RECORDS)

A no frills label sampler from SST right down to the $3.49
list price on the plain front cover. Another album that
also highlighted the transition away from hardcore, and in
SST's case, towards 70s rock and extended stoner jams from
fifteen bands of the SST stable and Black Flag extended
family; Saint Vitus, D.C. 3, SWA, Black Flag, Gone, Würm,
Overkill, Saccharine Trust, Painted Willie, Angst, Meat
Puppets, Minutemen, Hüsker Dü, October Faction, and Tom
Troccoli's Dog. Hüsker Dü's "Flip Your Wig" era out-take
"Erase Today" remains a good song exclusive to this release,
but the majority of the rest of it was merely gleaned from
various SST releases, and the inclusion of Van Halen and
Foghat covers tells you everything you need to know about
where SST records were heading by this point (the bargain
bin). The plain green sleeve showed the amount of love that
went into this release and the only redeeming piece of
artistic interest was the photos of each band on the rear
by photographer Naomi Petersen.

EASTERN FRONT

EASTERN FRONT 3
Live At Ruthie's Inn

LIVE!

LIVE AT RUTHIE'S INN

THE WOUND DEEPENS

END THE WAR ZONE

FRESH SOUNDS FROM MIDDLE AMERICA #3

COMPLETE DEATH LP (DEATH / RESTLESS RECORDS)

The transition compilations were coming thick and fast
at this point and this was Death Records' (a subsidiary
of Metal Blade) time for the first showcase of their
roster of crossover hardcore/thrash bands aimed to harness
the emerging dual markets of both punks and metal heads
alike. Nine bands and ten songs from; D.R.I. (two songs),
Dr. Know, Mentors, Insolents, Corrosion Of Conformity,
Beyond Possession, Civilian Terrorists, Ugly Americans,
and Depression. This may have been intended as a label
sampler but Insolents never released anything with Death
Records (opting instead for Mystic Records) and neither did
Cleveland's Civilian Terrorists or Australia's Depression
(described as "Australia's biggest hardcore band"). The
album came wrapped in suitably metal art by Drew Elliott,
who at this time was also drawing art for many other thrash
releases, including False Liberty, from whom Greg Anderson
went onto co-found equally large metal label Southern Lord.

DO YOU REMEMBER ROCK'N'ROLL? LP (I.M. RECORDS)

"A San Jose-South Bay Compilation" from IM Records who were
largely responsible for bringing skate punks The Faction to
the world. Nine bands and thirteen songs from; The Living
End, No Warning, Orange Curtain, Stikky, The Faction, Front
Line, Jet Crash Miracle, Nitemare, and Steve Caballero (the
skater also of The Faction). The bands with two songs were;
The Faction, The Living End, Orange Curtain and Stikky,
the rest supplying one. This was across the board of styles
from the crossover thrash of No Warning to the synth new
wave of Orange Curtain, and the skate punk of The Faction.
This was also the vinyl debut of the goofy punk of Stikky
(pre-Chris Dodge) later of Lookout! Records. A stand out
song was "Here To Stay" from Front Line that featured
future members of 22 Jacks. Completed with some sharp
hardcore style graphics, replete with very early computer
typesetting, and band photos featuring the trademark mid
80s hair lengthening as the rock influence returned.

EASTERN FRONT 3 - LIVE AT RUTHIE'S INN 2LP (RESTLESS RECORDS)

Metal creep had even taken over this previously hardcore punk only festival and compilation series with this third installment. Mainly recorded at the festival, that had moved to Ruthie's Inn at 2618 San Pablo Avenue in Berkeley between December 26th and 31st 1985. This two record set was a mash of crossover and metal from; D.R.I., Stone Vengeance, Violence, Hexx, Sentinel Beast, Raw Power, Laaz Rockit, Fuhrer, Tyrranicide, Forbidden Evil, Morally Bankrupt, Sacrilege, Anti-Momb, Ruffians, Heathen, Death Angel, Chronic Plague, Legacy, Blood Bath, Messiah, Blind Illusion, and Aftermath. Most of the bands who played made the grade, with Raw Power being recorded at 1984's fest in Aquatic Park when it transitioned from hardcore to metal, with one day of each style but no record to document it (or 1983's hardcore only affair). At least the cover art was in keeping with the previous two volumes and there was an insert for the first time, a collage of horn-throwing metalheads of course.

EMMA 2LP (M.A. DRAJE RECORDS)

Meanwhile, in Europe the punks were still more concerned with squatting and building cultural centres to house their D.I.Y. ethics and punk scenes. This double album documented bands who'd played or supported the famous Emma squat in Amsterdam. Originally squatted on November 25th 1984, it became a venue, café-restaurant, rehearsal rooms for fifteen bands, and two recording studios. In total thirty bands contributed to the album; No Allegiance, Pandemonium, Tu-Do Hospital, BGK, Morzelpronk, Nog Watt, Impact, Deadlock, The Ex, Membranes, Kaki's, Vacuum, Zowiso, Sjako!, Zak In As, Sonic Youth, If, Svätsox & Dorpsoudste De Jong, Grin, The Gentry, Krapuul, Electric Hannes, No Pigz, Negazione, Indigesti, Hostages Of Ayatollah, Capital Scum, Combat Not Conform, Murder Inc. III, and UBCF. A fascinating document and insight into European punk and politics of the time, it came in a gatefold sleeve with a nicely designed 32 page booklet "EMMA De Provokatie" with a page on each band.

EMPTY SKULLS VOL. 2 - THE WOUND DEEPENS LP (FARTBLOSSOM)

The only vinyl compilation on Bob Durkee's (of Pillsbury
Hardcore) Fartblossom Enterprises that followed on from
volume one, that was a cassette only release put together
by Durkee, Justin Conlan and Tim Comiskey. An international
compilation in the Xcentric Noise tradition with twelve
bands and twenty one songs running in differing amounts
throughout; E.A.T.E.R. (Sweden), Stranglehold, Half Life,
Pillsbury Hardcore, White 'N' Hairy and Corrosion Of
Conformity (U.S.), Legion Of Parasites (U.K.), Justice
League (U.S.), Colera (Brazil), Pandemonium (Netherlands),
Crude S.S. (Sweden), and Ugly Americans (U.S.) This cross-
section of bands still largely resistant to the changes in
hardcore trends picked up a bit on side two with three prime
Corrosion Of Conformity Songs in a row. With incredible
hardcore cover art from Vince Ransid (MDC, Raw Power etc.)
on the front, something a bit simpler on the back from
Simon Bob Sinister of Ugly Americans, and a label insert.

END THE WAR ZONE 7" EP (ONE STEP AHEAD RECORDS)

The first release and a four band and seventeen song EP
from this short-lived (then Tarzana, later San Francisco)
Californian label that was also responsible for the Rest
In Pieces "My Rage" LP, Lärm's "Straight On View" LP and
False Liberty's "Silence Is Consent" 7" EP. This set opened
up with four Lärm blasts of ultra fast Dutch hardcore
before two Pillsbury Hardcore tunes, including a Negative
Approach cover. Following this, two thrashers from Attitude
Adjustment gave way to nine(!) swirling hardcore songs from
New York's Straight Ahead! Or the majority of their demo
tape. A curiously thrown together compilation from the era
when any teenage hardcore fan found that they could create
and operate their own D.I.Y. label from their bedroom and
somehow pull it off. The cover art covered the typical punk
anti-cop theme by Dave Moore, also responsible for the
Pillsbury Hardcore EP cover, while the flip of the folded
sleeve supplied the band photos, lyrics and credits.

gyrations volume II

HYBRID

INTRODUCING

THE WAYWARD SOULS
JON WAYNE
MULTICOLOURED SHADES
HONOLULU MOUNTAIN DAFFODILS
THE VOLCANOES

Life Is A Joke Vol. 2

16 BANDS FROM 10 COUNTRIES

LOVE DOLLS Superstar

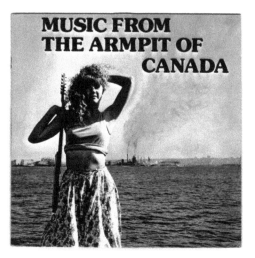

MUSIC FROM THE ARMPIT OF CANADA

MYSTIC SAMPLER #3

Ill Repute
Aggression
Psycho
Partners In Crime
Government Issue
Dr. Know
SLA
Mentors
Asbestos Rockpile
PTL Klub
White Flag
Faction
The Stain

N.Y. BEAT!

HIT & RUN

THIRTEEN NEW YORK BANDS

FRESH SOUNDS FROM MIDDLE AMERICA #3 LP (FRESH SOUNDS)

In conjunction with Redline Productions and local station
KJHK, this third compilation (the first two were cassette)
of mainly Kansas talent on Lawrence promoter Bill Rich's
label featured sixteen bands and songs from; Psychic Archie,
Von Bulows, Homestead Grays, Boxes Of Love, Yardapes, Lions
& Dogs, Thumbs, Hundreds & Thousands, Iguanas, Brompton's
Cocktail, Bum Kon, Near Death Experience, Micronotz, Short
Notice, Pedal Jets, and Rabbit Scat. Most of the bands did
little else outside of this and for the most part it was a
mix of new wave, college and roots rock. The bands of punk
interest; Micronotz were signed to Homestead by this point
and covered Iggy and the Stooges "Gimme Some Skin", while
Colorado's Bum Kon had a few records under their belt.
Other punk rock was provided by Near Death Experience
and Short Notice, with a poppier stand out came from Von
Bulows. The very Mid-West cover comic art by Brian Roberts
set the scene and a basic insert supplied the band info.

GOD'S FAVORITE DOG LP (TOUCH AND GO RECORDS)

Five years on from "Process Of Elimination" and things had
changed dramatically for Touch And Go Records. The hardcore
punk of 1981 was gone and a new different kind of noise
was on the rise, as documented here. Six bands and twelve
songs from; Butthole Surfers, Killdozer, Scratch Acid,
Hose, Happy Flowers, and Big Black. Whereas these bands
didn't conform to any particular style, they consisted of
musicians who had cut their teeth on hardcore punk but had
wandered off into new discordant territory. Unsurprisingly
the acid drenched Texan scene was well represented with
the Butthole Surfers and Scratch Acid, while Wisconsin's
Killdozer served up a drunken "Sweet Home Alabama". Steve
Albini and Big Black's exploits were legendary, while Happy
Flowers featured John Beers, formerly of Virginia punk band
Landlords and Catch Trout Records. Finally, Hose featured a
one Rick Rubin on guitar of Def Jam Records fame. Compiled
by Terry Tolkin with strong graphic design by Chris Gordon.

HYBRID - GYRATIONS VOLUME II LP (HYBRID RECORDS)

The second and final vinyl "Introducing" compilation from Laurie Dunn's London label (formerly of Statik Records). Five bands and ten songs from; The Wayward Souls (Sweden), Jon Wayne (U.S.), Multicoloured Shades (Germany), The Volcanoes and, Honolulu Mountain Daffodils (U.K.) The emphasis here was on jangling guitar garage meets alternative rock of the kind coming out of Australia at the time, but unlike volume one no Aussie bands were present here. Rather than a label sampler of purely licensed releases this one had some unreleased songs from the likes of The Wayward Souls and Multicoloured Shades. The Volcanoes had a heavy 60s garage psyche sound not unlike The Prime Movers out of Boston in the U.S., while Honolulu Mountain Daffodils went for a darker psychedelic noise. The cover art was a simple repeat of volume one in negative and different colours with the same sci-fi creature and band photos on the reverse. Both volumes were issued in Spain as a double album.

LIFE IS A JOKE VOL. 2 LP (WEIRD SYSTEM)

The second in this series of international LPs from Weird System and this time we got 16 bands from 10 countries; Blut & Eisen, Torpedo Moskau, Cyan Revue and Neurotic Arseholes (W. Germany), Angry Samoans, Corrosion Of Conformity and Fang (U.S.), Subhumans and The Depraved (U.K.), The Squirt (Switzerland), Siste Dagers Helvete (Norway), I Spit On Your Gravy (Australia), N.V.Boys (Holland), Kansanturvamusiikkikomissio (Finland), Fallout (Italy), and Some Weird Sin (Canada). A varied set as usual with the liner notes justifying the lack of unreleased material, although Subhumans "Human Error" was an alternate version. Some versions had a 12 bonus song LP with additional songs from; The Squirt, Angry Samoans, Blut & Eisen, Neurotic Arseholes, and Torpedo Moskau, as well as songs from; Ingron Hutlös (Sweden), Cretins and Der Riss (W. Germany), Kaaos (Finland), Special Forces and Medieval (U.S.), and Armatrak (New Zealand). Godzilla themed artwork and a printed inner.

293

LOVEDOLLS SUPERSTAR LP (SST RECORDS)

The soundtrack to David Markey's (Sin 34 and "We Got Power" zine) rock'n'roll chick flick sequel to "Desperate Teenage Lovedolls". Starring members of Redd Kross, as well as the brother and sister team of Jordan ("We Got Power" zine) and Jennifer Schwartz, there were special guest appearances from; Vicki Peterson (The Bangles), Jello Biafra (Dead Kennedys) and Sky Saxon (The Seeds). The soundtrack featured Redd Kross playing the theme song as well as The Lovedolls (the girls from the film backed by Redd Kross), Black Flag ("Kickin' N' Stickin'"), Sonic Youth, Painted Willie, Lawndale, Gone, Anarchy 6 (the Sin 34 related spoof hardcore band playing "Slam, Spit, Cut Your Hair, Kill Your Mom!"), Meat Puppets ("No Values"), and Dead Kennedys ("One Way Ticket To Pluto"). The artwork depicted the title as a star on the Hollywood "Walk Of Fame", stills from the film and some suitably tacky glam art from this group of friends who weren't taking themselves very seriously.

MUSIC FROM THE ARMPIT OF CANADA LP (PROBLEM CHILDREN)

Toronto's neighbour Hamilton was known as the 'Armpit of Ontario' due to the manufacturing industry located there, and so here was a showcase of bands from Hamilton, Toronto (and surrounding 'burbs) on the Problem Children's label (and one of only three releases). Twelve bands with a song each; Problem Children, Moon Crickets, Social Suicide, Trash And The Bags, Heimlich Maneuver, Hated Uncles, Condo Christ, Mean Red Spiders, The Dik Van Dykes, Drunk Dentist, A.K.S., and The Throbs. The style was mainly light-hearted catchy punk in a similar vein to Problem Children but there was also some hardcore, post-punk, garage and alternative rock in the mix. The short-lived Condo Christ's "Patriotic Fever" being a stand out with its distinct Canadian hardcore sound. With cover art depicting the manufacturing industry this benefit LP (for a local multi-service community organisation) also came with a neat insert with a graphic, lyric and info section for each band.

OUT OF THE FOG
THE HALIFAX UNDERGROUND 1986

PLAY NEW ROSE FOR ME ROSE 100

.ZOI.COCK ROACHS.DRAFT DODGERS.HEIMAT-LOS.SCRAPS.
.KONTINGENT SYPHILITIK.RAPT.KROMOZOM 4.BUTCHER.
.M.S.T.FINAL BLAST.

RAPSODIE

...LLY FAST VOL.
1986
SWE...
25 KR
BD 956

RED WAVE 4 UNDERGROUND BANDS FROM THE USSR

REMEMBER SOWETO★ -76-86 BULLETS WON'T STOP US NOW!★

MYSTIC SAMPLER #3 LP (MYSTIC RECORDS)

No change at Doug Moody's Mystic Records as it kept churning out the hardcore compilations of familiar punk names and songs from various other Mystic releases. Thirteen U.S. bands on this third and final installment in the series of one a year; Partners In Crime, Government Issue (" Understand" listed as "Dem Boots"), White Flag, PTL Klub, Ill Repute, Mentors, The Faction, The Stain, Aggression, Psycho, Asbestos Rockpyle, S.L.A., and Dr. Know. In a new creative low for Mystic three of the songs here (Partners In Crime, Asbestos Rockpyle and S.L.A.) were from other Mystic compilations, and it appeared that Psycho's "Hosebags From Hell" was originally to be released on Mystic but didn't happen. In the usual generic skull sleeve with relevant record covers on the back this showed Mystic to be in a downward slide, with the back cover announcement that "pregnant mothers listening to this record may give birth to a punker" only adding to the cringe.

N.Y. BEAT! - HIT & RUN LP (MOON RECORDS)

If you look up "third wave ska" you'll probably find these New York bands lumped in with cartoonish ska punk from the 90s but this had more in common with what came before than what came later. The first release on U.K. émigré Rob "Bucket" Hingley of The Toasters' label featured 13 bands and 14 songs from; The Toasters (two songs), Beat Brigade, The A-Kings, Cryin' Out Loud, City Beat, The Daybreakers, The Scene, The Press, Urban Blight, Second Step, The Boilers, Too True, and Floor Kiss. The Toasters served up some 2-Tone inspired ska, Beat Brigade went for the dancy edge of the The Beat, while The The Scene and The Press were more mod/street punk. With cartoon cover art by Bob Fingerman, it was reissued a year later as the first release on Roddy Moreno's (The Oppressed) Oi! Records subsidiary Ska' Records, Moreno later visiting N.Y. in 1989 to be inspired by the philosophy of "S.H.A.R.P." (Skin Heads Against Racial Prejudice) and taking it back to the U.K.

OUT OF THE FOG (THE HALIFAX UNDERGROUND 1986) LP (FLAMINGO)

With over one hundred days of fog or mist a year this showcase of bands from Halifax, Nova Scotia, on Canada's eastern fringe had its title ready made for the very first compilation of 13 bands from the city, mainly recorded at City Studios in Halifax in the summer of 1986. Opening with the melodic rock of Basic English, it continued with the Violent Femmes style acoustic rock of Mark Wellner. Jellyfishbabies then provided some catchy Replacements style punk before False Security and the stop'n'go hardcore of "Vietnam". the album continued with Karma Wolves (think The Smiths), Dogfood (Flipper style), Ridge Of Tears (dramatic synth), The Misery Goats and The October Game (goth), Roland Blinn & The Fishermen, I Want, as well as The Killer Klamz (indie rock) and finally The Lonestars (Johnny Cash style). Wrapped in some noir photography, the album came with a fold out insert with band info and photos. "Out Of The Fog Too" followed on CD and cassette much later in 1993.

PLAY NEW ROSE FOR ME - ROSE 100 2LP (NEW ROSE)

The 100th LP release on Paris label New Rose Records, created by Patrick Mathé and Louis Thévenon in 1980 to release The Saints. They released countless compilations but this double LP stood as a milestone celebration of the label with twenty six bands; Tav Falco's Panther Burns, Mudboy & The Neutrons, Alex Chilton, The Beatnik Flies, Divine Horsemen, Giant Sand, Dead Kennedys, Blood On The Saddle, Imitation Life With Eddie Munoz, The Bangsters, Sky S. Saxon, Dino Lee K.O.W.T., The Count, Dramarama, Willie Alexander, The Fortune Tellers, Mad Daddys, Reptiles At Dawn, Warum Joe, Psyche, Chris Bailey & Friends, The Slickee Boys, The Primevals, Sirens Of 7th Avenue, Charles De Goal, and R. Stevie Moore. The emphasis here was on garage rock (plus they licensed a few Dead Kennedys related releases). The records came housed in a simply designed and unique envelope sleeve with a foldout insert featuring band, song and release information. Also issued on CD and cassette.

RAPSODIE LP (JUNGLE HOP INTERNATIONAL)

A collection of eleven French bands on this former cassette label that was run by Hervé Lagille of the Paris commune Nogent-sur-Marne. The first compilation and second vinyl release on the label, nestled between the Flitox 7" and Scream's "Walking By Myself" 7", this album eschewed the traditional French Oi! theme and went instead for the jugular with the frantic French hardcore of; Zoi (three songs), Heimat-Los, Final Blast, Cock Roachs, Kontingent Syphilitik, Kromozom, and Scraps (two each), as well as M.S.T., Draft Dodgers, Rapt, and Butcher (one each) totalling 19 songs. "Rapsodie" proved that the French were very much up to speed with punk trends as the majority of this was blistering hardcore thrash with polka drums, no slow Oi! plod here. With cover art featuring a skull and splats it came with inserts or an inner sleeve depending on which press you saw, that came in a yellow, red or white sleeve also depending on which press.

REALLY FAST VOL. 3 LP (REALLY FAST RECORDS)

The third installment in the "Really Fast" series from this D.I.Y. label from Mjölby, Sweden that was run by Staffan Fagerberg, Patrik Jonsson and Peter Pinaitis of various bands. This time there were twenty nine songs from fourteen bands; Avskum, Discard, Von BΘΘm, DTR, S.S.S., Fear Of War, Existenz, Slam, Disarm, Dom Där, Svart Parad, The Bedrövlerz, Raped Teenagers, and Pöbel Möbel, with two or three songs each lumped together. The style, as the previous two, was primarily fast and rough Swedish hardcore punk from familiar names such as Avskum, Raped Teenagers and The Bedrövlerz, but some sonic diversions occurred in the form of the anthemic UK '82 style of Existenz, the melodic punk of Slam, and tuneful album closers Pöbel Möbel, who were a stand out. The sleeve, depicting a postage stamp, had the same simple foldout poster as the previous two, with band sections on the reverse and a plain back cover with the track listing.

Restless

V · A · R · I · A · T · I · O · N · S

SAN JOSE IS GROUND ZERO
WE'RE NUMBER ONE

THE
SOCIAL
CLUB

A GRUEL
HOAX

THE
KINGPINS

FRONTIER
WIVES

A SAN JOSE COMPILATION

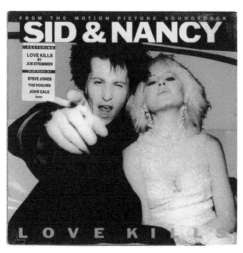

FROM THE MOTION PICTURE SOUNDTRACK
SID & NANCY

FEATURING
LOVE KILLS
BY
JOE STRUMMER

PLUS MUSIC BY
STEVE JONES
THE POGUES
JOHN CALE

L · O · V · E   K · I · L · L · S

SMASH

VOL. 4

SKATE

ROCK

INTERNATIONAL POP COMPILATION

SUB POP 100

RED WAVE: 4 UNDERGROUND BANDS FROM THE USSR 2LP (BIG TIME)

A double LP of four Soviet bands compiled by American singer
and actor Dianna Stingray and released on Australia's "Big
Time" in the U.S., Canada and Europe in the promotion of
peace. In 1984 Stingray had visited Leningrad with her
sister and while there she met Boris Grebenshchikov of the
band Aquarium at the Leningrad Rock Club and was introduced
to the underground scene. Impressed, she began smuggling
out recordings to the U.S. and by 1986 "Red Wave" was
born. "Red Wave" featured four bands with a side and six
songs each from; Aquarium, Kino, Alisa, and Strange Games.
While not strictly punk rock, "Red Wave" represented a
new wave that, while somewhat detached from the West,
was still experimenting with similar ideas. Issued in a
gatefold sleeve featuring photos of the band members, "Red
Wave" also came with two bilingual inserts. Soon Mikhail
Gorbachev got wind of the compilation and ordered the
minister of culture to initiate work with young artists.

REMEMBER SOWETO 76-86 - BULLETS WONT STOP US NOW! LP (KONKURREL)

One of two compilations on this Amsterdam label that were on
the same anti-apartheid theme, and specifically a benefit
for "Umkhonto We Sizwe", the paramilitary wing of the ANC
in South Africa at the time. An eclectic mix of Dutch
styles that opened with the Kwela of South African exiled
in Amsterdam Deezo (Dumayne) And The Bananabeats, followed
by the Poison Girls/Chumbawamba style pop of Dutch outfit
Max Gazolin Et Ses Pumps, while the first side concluded
with two songs from the Dutch Jazz/World Music of Lebombo.
The flip supplied some heavy hardcore punk in the form
of two live songs from Neuroot before the spoken word of
African exile Glenn Gibs, old Dutch punks Ivy Green, the
experimental sounds of Z'EV (originally from the U.S. but
living in Amsterdam) and the reggae of the Dam's Jah Sabi.
With strong sleeve design it also came with a spirited
12"x12" 24 page booklet with a history and photos of
apartheid and the beneficiary as well as band info.

RESTLESS VARIATIONS LP (RESTLESS)

A label sampler of this Enigma subsidiary showcasing their then recent signings, that opened with a trio of power pop from; The Neighborhoods, Get Smart! and Outlets. The Dead Milkmen then delivered some goofy punk with "Bitchin' Camaro" before the heavy psych-rock of Electric Peace. The first side concluded with the (former F.U.'s) Straw Dogs with former F.U.'s song "Young, Fast, Iranians". The second side providing some country from Mojo Nixon & Skid Roper before Lazy Cowgirls provided some rocking punk and 28th Day with some college garage rock. The Villanelles served up some more garage rock before the college rock of John Trubee & The Ugly Janitors Of America, and Fear concluded the record with LP title track "More Beer". The cover photo was peak mid 80s with a simple track list on the rear and the gatefold sleeve opened up to band photos, hype and info. The album was only released in the U.S. on vinyl and cassette with corresponding releases in Greece on Virgin.

SAN JOSE IS GROUND ZERO - WE'RE NUMBER ONE LP
(PETROLEUM BY-PRODUCTS)

As the title suggested, this was a collection of four bands from San Jose, California, that came around as a result of a benefit gig for the "Works" Gallery in San Jose. Despite the cover art featuring a nuclear explosion, the twelve song album wasn't an all out hardcore assault, but instead opened with the garage power pop sounds of A Cruel Hoax, followed by the mod-tinged alternative rock of The Social Club. Then came a change of pace in the form of rockabilly band The Kingpins (who'd also featured on "Blazing Wheels And Barking Trucks", the second Thrasher Skate Rock album in 1984). Finally, Frontier Wives, who featured Mike Donio, also of The Social Club, showcased their twanging country-edged college rock. In amongst the songs about love and broken hearts, A Cruel Hoax threw in some topical politics in the form of "Terroristas De Fortunada" about the Sandinistas on this area collection.

SID AND NANCY: LOVE KILLS LP (MCA)

The soundtrack for Alex "Repo Man" Cox's second film that
attempted to tell the tragic tale of the Sex Pistols' bassist
and his girlfriend. Joe Strummer supplied the opening title
track before The Pogues, Steve Jones, instrumentalists Pray
For Rain, and then Circle Jerks, who provided an alternative
"Love Kills" that later ended up on their "VI" album. More
soundtrack interludes followed from Pray For Rain and Joe
Strummer before some John Cale. More Pogues ensued before
Sid actor Gary Oldman's versions of "I Wanna Be Your Dog"
and "My Way" before Pray For Rain concluded in a style not
unlike Alex Gibson's soundtrack to "Suburbia". Much of the
rest of the soundtrack not on the album was composed by Dan
Wool (Pray for Rain) and Joe Strummer who, contractually
limited to contribute only two songs, continued to work
unpaid due to his interest in the film. The material was
credited to fictitious bands so as to keep Strummer's label
Epic in the dark. The sleeve was comprised of movie stills.

SMASH - SKATE ROCK VOL. 4 LP (THRASHER)

The last of the Eighties Thrasher compilations that made
it to vinyl before they returned to cassette only releases.
This was the weakest of the three vinyl Skate Rock offerings
and the subsequent sales figures probably helped with the
decision to stop pressing them to vinyl. The hip hop of
Skate Master Tate and the "Skaterock Rap" set the scene
before fellow skater Steve Caballero (Faction) and some
weird drum machine pop. McShred (McRad) sped things up in
a punk fashion before Tupelo Chain Sex and skate culture
originator Skip Engblom made things even weirder. The flip
opened with Philadelphia's Scram (BYO) and some ska punk
before Shredded Steale (Drunk Injuns or just compiler
MMörizen Föche?), and more McShred, before a highlight in
the form of Cargo Cult featuring Biscuit of Texas' Big Boys.
The all female Screamin' Sirens from Los Angeles closed the
album. The artwork as usual consisted of skate photos but
the lack of insert or any info must've helped seal its fate.

SMELLING JUST ANOTHER BAD BREATH LP (DOUBLE A RECORDS)

The second compilation on Double A run by Reiner Mettner
of Wuppertal after 1985's "Wie Lange Noch". The label had
a run of four compilations between 1985 and 1988 in the
era of internationalism in hardcore that spread the word,
and networked underground punk from all over the world to
the rest of the world. Eleven bands and eighteen songs
from; Psykisk Terror (Norway), Detonators (U.S.A.), Moskwa
(Poland), Instigators (U.K.), Z.S.D. and Sons Of Sadism
(West Germany) with two songs each, as well as; Angor Wat
(Norway), Blue Marbellas (Canada), Concrete Sox (U.K.),
and Billy & The Willies, Skeezicks, and EXXX (aka EA80,
all three of West Germany) with one song each. The style
throughout was hardcore punk with some gloomier and even
reggae moments. With an industrial themed cover photo the
back cover consisted of a hand written track listing, all
the band addresses, and another happy photo of a dead bird
on a railway. An eight page booklet supplied the band info.

SUB POP 100 LP (SUB POP)

After three issues of his early 80s fanzine "Subterranean
Pop", Bruce Pavitt shortened the name to "Sub Pop" and
began releasing alternate issues as compilation tapes.
After nine issues he teamed up with Jonathan Poneman and
turned it into a record label with this release "SP 10"
in 1986. Soon they would release records by; Green River,
Soundgarden and Mudhoney, and soon after the first 7"
by Nirvana, a band who would bring about seismic change
in the mainstream from the punk underground. After an
intro from Steve Albini, the album featured; Scratch Acid,
Wipers, Sonic Youth, Naked Raygun, U-Men, Dangerous Birds,
Skinny Puppy, Steve Fisk, Lupe Diaz, Boy Dirt Car, Savage
Republic, and Shonen Knife. A no doubt intentional mixed
bag of alternative and art rock that was developing out
of the underground punk scene as bands diversified in
different directions. With suitably deranged looking cover
art by Carl Smool the album received one pressing of 5,000.

THAT WAS THEN... THIS IS NOW 7" EP (PLUS RECORDS)

Philadelphia put itself on the hardcore compilation map
with this 4 band 4 song 7" EP on Plus Records that only stuck
around long enough for four releases (this, Homo Picnic,
Serial Killers and Legitimate Reason). Ruin opened up the EP
with their dirty punk on "By The By" followed by the almost
country punk of Electric Love Muffin with "Club Car". The
flip began with ska-tinged Scram (soon of BYO Records) and
"Something To Cling To", and the EP closed with F.O.D. (Flag
Of Democracy) with the ferocious "Meat Factory (Live)".
The cover featured a photo of the ruins of local venue Love
Hall. After a fire in 1983 at the building next door the
punk club had suffered water damage and became unstable
when its neighbour was demolished and it only lasted another
six months of gigs before it was condemned and demolished
not long before this EP. The back cover featured a photo
of the local scenesters while the insert provided the info
and it came with five stickers, each band and the label.

THE POWER OF LOVE LP (STARVING MISSILE)

The sub-title "International Hardcore Compilation" turned
out to be slightly disingenuous from this collection
released by Mike Just of Starving Missile, a label set up
via a bootleg Dead Kennedys album ("Skateboard Party").
As it turned out seven of the ten bands were from West
Germany, two were from the U.S.A. and one from Netherlands.
The bands were; Toxic Reasons and Artless (U.S.A.), Frites
Modern (Netherlands) and Mottek, Z.S.D., R.a.f.gier, Cocks
In Stained Satin, Smarties, K.G.B., and Toxoplasma (West
Germany). This didn't detract from the high quality of this
compilation and its recording quality though, that was put
to tape at Masterplan Studio by engineer Stephan Grujicof of
Mottek (the sleeve sharp sleeve being designed by Margret,
also of Mottek, suggesting heavy Mottek involvement). The
Artless songs were later released on 7" by Artless, while the
Toxic Reasons songs were more dynamic versions of "Bullets
For You" songs "Never Give In" and "Party's Over".

THERE'S A METHOD TO OUR MADNESS LP (PHANTOM RECORDS)

This album marked the transition from cassette to vinyl compilations for this South Carolina label (formerly "Wally And The Beaver" run by Wally Kustreva vocalist of Fear Itself) that had previously released the "War Between The States" and "Bleeding Between The Lines" tape compilations. This was a varied set of then current underground U.S. hardcore bands (and one from Canada) that proved it was in no way all over by 1986, but still reverberating around the States. Nineteen bands and twenty songs from; Ludichrist, P.T.L. Klub, Legion Of Doom, Sacred Denial, Sloppy Seconds, Damage, The Burnt, Vatican Commandos, Life Sentence, Disorderly Conduct, Amazing Grace, Direct Action (Canada), Dead Silence, Psycho, Born Without A Face (two songs), Ultra Violence, Bored Suburban Youths, Assault, and Sacrilege. With great hardcore cover art by R.K. Sloane of New Mexico, this was the first of only three releases on the label, along with the Fear Itself album and another compilation in 1988.

THE SAVAGES ARE LOOSE LP (MYSTIC RECORDS)

Sub-titled "A Washington D.C. Band Compilation" this was a new series for Mystic Records called "Sound of U.S.A. Cities", this being #1. A set of fourteen bands, all essentially from Maryland; Motor Morons, Phlegm, The Thing That Wouldn't Leave, The Platinum Slugs, The Receptacles, Bad Vibes, Asbestos Rockpyle, Roadside Pets, Sybil, Madhouse, Painkillers, Pure Evil, Christian Nightmare, and Sarcastic Orgasm. Seeing as you'd probably heard of three of those bands from the legendary D.C. area punk scene at its peak, it should've told you everything that you needed to know; that this is a patchy lack-lustre affair. It was compiled by Paul R.W. Clark of Asbestos Rockpyle, who also supplied the hand-written liner notes, suggesting he approached Mystic with the idea for the collection. Wrapped in some fittingly amateurish artwork, that served as more of a caveat emptor than an invitation to listen, this would've better served everyone as a local cassette only compilation.

THIS IS OI! (A STREETPUNK COMPILATION) LP (OI! RECORDS)

A nine band and eighteen song set of Oi! bands at a
time when the youth trend had pretty much had its day of
mass popularity and was heading underground, seeing most
skinheads morphing into scooterists, psychobillies or far
right hooligans. Roddy Moreno of Cardiff's The Oppressed
fought on though, with his label and this set that would see
the likes of anarcho lefties Oi Polloi share a vinyl stage
with the questionable Condemned 84. The nine band roster
consisted of; The Oppressed, Vicious Rumours, Section 5,
Complete Control, Feckin Ejits, Barbed Wire, Condemned 84,
Societys Rejects, and Oi! Polloi, and was mainly a bouncy
'82 style punk affair with the odd song that sounded like
borderline mod, and of course the strange drum sound that so
many of these bands ended up with in search of the 'tribal'.
With a cover photo that had been previously used on the back
of The Oppressed album and a less than imaginative title
on "Oi! Records" you knew what you were going to get it.

THRASH TIL DEATH LP (SELFISH / PUSMORT)

The second 1986 compilation from Selfish Records, this
"Japanese Punk Sampler" compiled by Naoki of Lip Cream
featured four bands and twenty one songs from; Lip Cream,
Systematic Death, Gauze, and Outo. Lip Cream opened up the
thrashing with a cacophonous fury not unlike Italy's Raw
Power. Systematic Death then upped the pace significantly
into frantic snare popping hardcore that left you in no
doubt as to where bands like Septic Death were getting
their inspiration from. Gauze kicked off the thrashing on
side two with five ferocious shouty blasts, before Outo
continued the blazing thrash theme with yet more relentless
intensity. The cover art was split into four panels for
the four bands front and back (with the back cover art of
Lip Cream changed for the reissue). Originally released in
Japan in 1986, this was licensed by Pushead for Pusmort in
1987 (pictured) when it was released internationally and
put this compilation on the map.

U-BOATS ATTACK AMERICA!!! LP (FLIPSIDE / WEIRD SYSTEM)

Sub-titled; "Germany Invading Your Household... 15 Tough Tracks Out Of Deutschland's New Music Underground In The Mid-80's!" This was a powerful showcase of German hardcore talent from some Weird System releases for the U.S. punk market, and a departure for Flipside Fanzine. A seven band and fifteen song collection that featured; Blut & Eisen (four songs), Neurotic Arseholes (three), Torpedo Moskau (three), Razzia (two), Daily Terror, Upright Citizens and Cretins (one each). If you'd never heard German hardcore punk of this period then this was a great place to start as it was a high quality selection and presented with some typical Flipside style artwork and a minimalist insert. Weird System would soon license the third Flipside compilation for a German release as well as a best of their first two collections titled "Paranoia You Can Dance To". The back cover also featured liner notes by Weird System explaining what it was all about for the American audience.

WE CAN DO WHATEVER WE WANT LP (BC TAPES AND RECORDS)

Sub-titled "Best of BCT #1" this ended up being one of only two vinyl compilations from probably the most prolific of the 80s underground tape labels Bad Compilation Tapes aka Borderless Countries Tapes (BCT) from Chris Chacon and Dave W. of San Diego, with this international (U.S., Italy and Finland) collection. Seventeen hardcore bands gleaned from 12 hours of tapes (twenty seven cassettes) they'd released on tape and tidied up at Radio Tokyo in Venice, California. The 29 songs were from; Raw Power, Traumatic, I Refuse It, War Dogs, Shockin' TV, Wretched, Peggio Punx, and Cheetah Chrome Motherfuckers (Italy), Eat The Rich, Psycho, Violation, Snufflex, Detention, Suburban Decay, and No Response (U.S.), and Rattus and Terveet Kadet (Finland). The quality was good with a little tape hiss and some live Distortion. The cartoon cover art by "J.T." couldn't have been more representative of the attitude on display here: total hardcore punk rock D.I.Y. independence.

WE DON'T NEED NUCLEAR FORCE LP (MÜLLEIMER RECORDS)

The third and final Mülleimer compilation after "Ultra
Hardcore Power" and "Hardcore Power Music Part 2" and it
was a true international compilation that initially came
with a bonus 7" EP. Twelve bands and sixteen songs from;
Maniacs, Ausbruch, Boskops and Normahl (West Germany),
Appliances, Toxic Reasons and White Flag (U.S.), Uproar and
Varukers (U.K.), The Bristles (Sweden), Rattus (Finland),
and H.H.H. (Spain). A varied set of punk styles with an
emphasis on West German and U.S. bands, a standout being
Madison, Wisconsin's Appliances (SFB) with their Nomeansno
meets Dead Kennedys style quirky art punk. The bonus EP
featured six extra songs from; Ausbruch, Boskops, Toxic
Reasons, Varukers (two songs), and Rattus. With airbrush
cover art depicting the dinosaur apocalypse as early man
looked on. The rear featured a map of European based nukes
and a barely legible tracklist. The insert and printed
inner sleeve provided further information.

WELCOME TO AX/CTION ISLAND 7" EP (AX/CTION RECORDS)

The fifth release and first vinyl compilation from Boston's
Ax/ction run by members of Psycho that was split into
Charlie's side (drums) and Johnny's side (guitar). Seven
bands and songs from; Cancerous Growth (Boston band with
Charlie Infection of Psycho also on drums), Stupids (U.K.),
and G.G. Allin on Charlie's side, as well as Psycho,
Spastic Rats, PTL Klub, and The Scam on Johhny's side. The
EP was a mixed bag of good quality hardcore of the day
with G.G. Allin of course managing to be as obnoxious as
possible (Psycho were soon his backing band on "Freaks,
Faggots, Drunks & Junkies"), while Psycho continued the
theme with some creepy misogyny. Spastic Rats had just
released their debut EP on their own label Vermin Scum,
run by drummer Kenny Hill also of the Hated, who went onto
release The Hated and Moss Icon. With excellent cover art
by R.K. Sloane depicted Johnny as a pirate and Charlie as
a cannibal by a cauldron, and it also came with an insert.

ISSUE №1

FUTURE—NOW !

PRICE £1·00

Includes FREE Flexi

UNRELEASED
DEPRAVED
STUPIDS
HERESY

B.G.K

Warhol

Japan Report

Head of David

Mass Murders

Splatter Movies

Record Reviews

Visions of Change

Nottingham Scene

Amsterdam Report

Skating and Dave Ross

and more...

"INCLUDES FREE FLEXI": "FUTURE-NOW!" FANZINE, U.K., 1987

WORLD WAR III? LP (ROT RECORDS)

The third 1986 budget compilation from the highly prolific
Rot Records and after this, along with the "What Are You
Doing About That Hole In Your Head?" and "Religious As Hell"
LPs, only a final best of double LP compilation followed.
"World War III?" was an international collection featuring
ten bands and eighteen songs from; Threats (U.K.), Crude SS
(Sweden), Tin Can Army (West Germany), Raw Power (Italy),
Zyklome A, Wulpse Varkens and Vortex (Belgium), Rövsvett
(Sweden), Rattus (Finland), and Jonee Jonee (Iceland).
Whereas some of the Rot Records could be patchy quality-
wise, this one was consistently good throughout with
standout songs from; Threats, Crude SS, Raw Power, Zyklome
A, and Rattus (the latter two supplying only one song each).
In keeping with the label house style the cover featured
a photo, this time of a woman being showered by someone
in a hazmat suit, a simple track list on a black back
cover. The album received one pressing of 1,000 copies.

YOU ARE NOT ALONE! 7" EP (WORDS OF WARNING RECORDS)

The year ended with a special compilation for me as W.O.W.
Records of Newport in South Wales was the first label that
I ended up doing my first record cover artwork for in 1987
as I met label owner Karl Horton at a gig in September 1986
just after buying this record. This was the first release
on the label and consisted of a band from each part of
the United Kingdom; Hex (England) with "Is This To Be?",
Stalag 17 (Northern Ireland) with "Harmless Fun", Oi Polloi
(Scotland) with "Nuclear Waste", and Symbol Of Freedom
(Wales) with "Suffering Persists". The EP had a strong
anarcho punk feel that was very much still representative
of how a large part of the U.K. punk scene still sounded
in the mid 80s, and was reflective of Karl's tastes with
animal rights and anti-nuclear lyrics. With some Nick Blinko
(Rudimentary Peni) inspired cover art on both sides of the
folded sleeve, it also came with a folded insert with a
section for each band featuring lyrics, info and graphics.

1987-1989: HARDCORE EVOLUTION

Margaret Thatcher's Conservative government is re-elected for a third term in 1987, and Michael Ryan carries out the Hungerford massacre, killing sixteen, while Peaceville Records begins releasing its first records. British work place radios play the hits of the day by Rick Astley, Pet Shop Boys and T'Pau, as British cinemas show Hellraiser, Predator and Dirty Dancing.

Ronald Reagan declares, "Mr. Gorbachev, tear down this wall!" during a speech at the Brandenburg Gate in West Berlin as Funhouse Records releases its first records. Canada introduces a $1 coin, commonly called a "Loonie" while Cargo Records begins trading in Montréal, soon opening an office in the U.S.

The Dow Jones Industrial Average falls 22.6% in a single session on Black Monday before Reagan and Gorbachev sign the Intermediate-Range Nuclear Forces Treaty at the White House, while Revelation and Lookout! Records both press a slew of initial 7" releases. U.S. cinema goers marvel at Fatal Attraction, The Untouchables and Full Metal Jacket, while U2, Bon Jovi as the Bangles blare from teenage stereos country wide.

As Soviet forces begin pulling out of Afghanistan in 1988 "groups of drug pushers, homeless, squatters and punks" protest a police curfew of Tompkins Square Park in New York, sparking two nights of riots as Hawker Records begins documenting the New York hardcore scene.

Arizona Governor Evan Mecham is impeached and removed from office as local Fanzine, Hippycore also starts releasing records as a label. MTV rotates videos by Tiffany, INXS and Guns'n'Roses, while theatre attendances swell for Rain Man, Beetlejuice and Who Framed Roger Rabbit?

313

The Berlin Wall falls and the San Francisco Bay Area rocks to the Loma Prieta earthquake in 1989, injuring 3,757 and killing 63, as Very Small Records presses it inaugural release, and Squat Or Rot out of New York continues the conversation about gentrification with its new fanzine and label.

George H.W. Bush is sworn in as president and declares a "War on drugs" as Merge Records inks its first record in North Carolina. Theatre seats fill for Bill And Ted's Excellent Adventure, When Harry Met Sally and Born On The Fourth Of July, while the Billboard charts see Paula Abdul, Bobby Brown and Poison do the most damage.

As the U.K. parliament is televised for the first time and British Muslims demonstrate against Salman Rushdie's "Satanic Verses", further South in Devon the label Hometown Atrocities sets up shop while faces in the cinema rows flicker to A Fish Called Wanda, Dead Poets Society, and My Left Foot, while the U.K. chart shows danced along to Jive Bunny, The Bangles and Jason Donovan.

BACK COVER OF "MAGGIE, MAGGIE, MAGGIE;
OUT! OUT! OUT!" LP (ANAGRAM) 1987

1987

4 BANDS THAT COULD CHANGE THE WORLD! / 5 BANDS THAT HAVE CHANGED THE WORLD! LPS (GASATANKA/P. FORCE/BUY OUR/FUNHOUSE)

A collaborative effort between White Flag's, 7 Seconds', and A.O.D.'s labels to bring together their bands as well as F from Florida. 7 Seconds opened with five songs, the first two recorded at Inner Ear and out-takes from the "Walk Together" 12", followed by two live songs and a practice jam. White Flag followed with five; two live and two covers (Generation X and Dr. Seuss), while side two featured four F songs, all studio, and four from Adrenalin O.D. with three covers (Sex Pistols, Kiss, and Bay City Rollers) and a live original. The album was licensed to German label "Funhouse" with different art and Flag Of Democracy added to make five bands and a tweaked title. Each of the original band's contributions were then trimmed to make way for F.O.D.'s three songs, two of which were live. The patchy end result was each LP ended up with eighteen songs.

AT DIANNE'S PLACE LP (PENULTIMATE/EMPTY RECORDS)

A document of Santa Cruz venue "Dianne's" that only existed for six months in 1986 but left enough of a mark on the locals for this vinyl commemoration. Dianne Van Eron's bar was failing when she took the advice of booking local bands and turned it into a happening joint before the police, fire marshals and the Alcoholic Beverage Commission, had other ideas and then the landlord decided not to renew the lease for unspecified "business reasons." Fourteen bands and songs from notables Camper Van Beethoven, as well as; Nimoys, Ten Foot Faces, Catheads, Spot 1019, Nice Guys, Donner Party, Raining House, Barnacle Choir, Thongs, Carmaig De Forest, Wrestling Worms, Holy Sisters Of The Gaga Dada, and Vomit Launch, with a variety of punk, garage and alternative rock. The cover featured a photo of the owner and venue, and the album came with a 12 page booklet with band info.

BURNING BRIDGES

featuring

CIVILISED SOCIETY?

Why !

INSTIGATORS

The Blood is on your Hands

MAD PARADE

Prisoner

PAGAN BABIES

Dirty Knees on Black Slacks

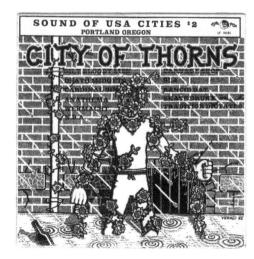

SOUND OF USA CITIES #2
PORTLAND OREGON

CITY OF THORNS

H.R. scythian press mob i.n.i.c.u. outrage + dave

a compilation of dc area artists

DISORDER CHAOS UK THE STUPIDS DEPRAVED GENERIC

DIGGINGINWATER

OI POLLOI EXTREME NOISE TERROR RIPCORD POTENTIAL THREAT

CONCRETE SOX CIVILISED SOCIETY? CCM VICIOUS CIRCLE

BAD DRESS SENSE EYES ON YOU DR & THE CRIPPENS ELECTRO HIPPIES

THE ORIGINAL MOTION PICTURE SOUNDTRACK ALBUM

DUDES

Featuring the
Track and Video By
REEL
"Rock 'N' Roll Outlaw"
AND
A Brand New Version of
"These Boots"
By
MEGADETH

FEATURING:
Charles Bernstein
Jane's Addiction
Keel
The Leather Nun
Lord Tracy
W.A.S.P.

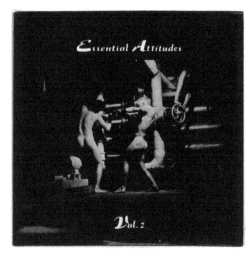

Essential Attitudes

Vol. 2

BORDER RADIO (ORIGINAL SOUNDTRACK RECORDING) LP (ENIGMA)

The roots rock slash country soundtrack to the film that depicted "the last days West Coast punk rock" following two musicians and a roadie who haven't been paid so they steal money from a club, one fleeing to Mexico leaving his wife and daughter behind. The film starred Chris D., Chris Shearer, Dave Alvin, John Doe, Luanna Anders and Texacala Jones among others. As for the soundtrack; The Tonys (Chip and Tony Kinman of The Dils/Rank & File) opened up with their version of The Blasters title track before Dave Alvin and Steve Berlin (Blasters) handled the soundtrack work on "La Frontera I", "Burning Guitar" and "Driving To Mexico", with atmospheric drums not unlike the "Suburbia" score. The Lazy Cowgirls punked things up in a garage style before Dave Alvin (Blasters), John Doe (X), Chris D. (Flesh Eaters) and the Divine Horsemen, as well as Green On Red all contributed. The sleeve art features a border map and the original LP came with a cool 8" slice of 16mm film from the movie.

BREAKING THE SILENCE 7" EP (ARTCORE RECORDS)

The second 7" compilation and final vinyl release on this short-lived West German label Artcore (nothing to do with the zine of the same name) run by Guido Heffels of Mönchengladbach. Four bands on this international compilation; Homo Picnic (U.S.), Kazjurol (Sweden), Quod Massacre (Yugoslavia, now Slovenia), and Instigators (U.K.). Homo Picnic opened up with two of their Philadelphia hardcore songs before Kazjurol supplied some metallic hardcore. The flip side then gave us Quod Massacre and something a little more melodic akin to Asta Kask from Sweden. Finally Instigators, who were everywhere at this point, provided their usual live track in the form of "Not Free" recorded live in Berlin in 1986. With a typically odd punk cover illustration of the era, the foldout sleeve featured a neat pre-computer layout with lots of backgrounds, photos of the bands, lyrics and liner notes. Pressed on two colours and numbered, my copy being 1131, I presume there were a couple of thousand.

BURIED ALIVE LP (SMOKE 7 RECORDS)

Sub-titled "The Best Of Smoke 7 Records 1981-1983" this was
a collection of this Canoga Park label's output gleaned
from its early releases by label owner Felix Alanis of
RF7. Featuring eleven bands and nineteen songs from; Redd
Kross, MIA, Bad Religion, RF7, Sin 34, Youth Gone Mad,
JFA, Genocide, Circle One, Sacred Order, and Ten Minute
Warning. Four Redd Kross songs came from "Born Innocent"
and the "Sudden Death" compilation, there was a song each
from the MIA/Genocide split LP, the Bad Religion and Circle
One songs were from the "Public Service" compilation, the
Sin 34, JFA and Youth Gone Mad were from the "Sudden Death"
compilation, and Ten Minute Warning and Sacred Order were
taken from "Lung Cookies". Finally the RF7 songs were from
their "Fall In" 12" and "Submit To Them Freely" 7". For
the most part this was a compilation of compilations, the
sleeve featured some ghoulish photos and an unreadable
track listing. Reissued on Bomp in 1995 with different art.

BURNING BRIDGES 7" EP (WEAR & TEAR)

The only release on this label from Buxton in Derbyshire,
U.K. The EP opened with Mad Parade and their '77 inspired
melodic Southern Californian punk on "Prisoner" followed
by the metal-tinged anarcho punk of Civilised Society? From
West Yorkshire and "Why?" The flip side opened with West
Yorkshire's The Instigators recorded live (of course) in
Germany in June 1987 with "The Blood Is On Your Hands", and
the EP closed with Pagan Babies from Philadelphia and the
fast positive hardcore of "Dirty Knees On Black Slacks".
Still somewhat of a mystery, this varied EP came with very
simple artwork with the track list on the front on a plain
black background, a photo of an old couple on the back,
and a folded A4 insert with an A5 section supplied by each
band. Little else is known about this possibly partially
unofficial EP outside of an address of a suburban flat in
Buxton on the back cover and that it was distributed by
Red Rhino/Cartel.

319

CITY OF THORNS LP (MYSTIC)

The second in Mystic's "Sound Of USA Cities" series and this time "The City Of Roses" aka Portland, Oregon was the city of choice. Eleven bands and nineteen songs from; Cardinal Sin, Death Midgets, Anathema, N.R.A., Wehrmacht, Oily Bloody Men, Carnage Shop, SLA, Rancid Bat (Vat), Skate Drunx, and Tradition Dictates. This was a far better effort than the first in the series "The Savages Are Loose" (Washington D.C.) in that it was far more fast and aggressive and harked back to the older Mystic compilations and other underground cassette compilations from around this time. There was a definite Portland feel to the music, with a predominance of muscular and throaty hardcore with some crossover elements. The strange cover art by Vernon somewhat disguised the quality herein and as a result "City Of Thorns" remains a forgotten nugget of hardcore history from the Pacific Northwest that can still be found brand new and sealed in bargain bins the world over.

DC ROX LP (WETSTPOTS RECORDS/OLIVE TREE RECORDS)

"A compilation of D.C. area artists" and one of two H.R. of Bad Brains' "Olive Tree" releases (along with Beefeater's "Need A Job" 12") that was licensed by Johnny "Jabbs" Barry of Nottingham (and bands Eyes On You and Filler) for a U.K. release. Initially a cassette on "Olive Tree" this was the vinyl version of seven bands and twelve songs of D.C. bands who shared a similar area on the sonic landscape as late 80s Bad Brains; H.R., Scythian, Press Mob, Revelation (featuring Skeeter Thompson from Scream), Outrage, and I.N.I.C.U. The existence of "DC Rox" stood as an example of how much attention was being bestowed on Washington D.C. post "Revolution Summer", whether it was warranted or not, and even though it didn't contain a "Dischord" logo it no doubt sold to many a D.C. hungry punk who were then left scratching their heads at the funk rock and Rastafarian gibberish herein. The sleeve layout was by John of Wetspots who later went on to be label manager at Earache Records.

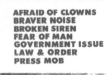

AFRAID OF CLOWNS · SCHMOVIE
BRAVER NOISE · SCREAM
BROKEN SIREN · SHUDDER TO THINK
FEAR OF MAN · STRANGE BOUTIQUE
GOVERNMENT ISSUE · UNDECIDED
LAW & ORDER · UNKNOWN
PRESS MOB · (F-R-5)

GEYSER

ANTHOLOGY OF THE ICELANDIC INDEPENDENT MUSIC SCENE OF THE EIGHTIES

GEYSER

KUKL
BUBBI & DAS KAPITAL
ÞEYR
MEGAS & ÍKARUS
HÖH
SVEINBJÖRN BEINTEINSSON
JONEE JONEE
PURRKUR PILLNIKK
STANYA
VONBRIGDI
MICKEY DEAN & DE VUNDERFOOLZ

DIGGING IN WATER LP (MANIC EARS/CHILDREN OF THE REVOLUTION)

A joint release from two Bristol labels and primarily a
U.K. compilation made international with the inclusion
of Vicious Circle (Australia) and CCM (Italy), both with
releases on the above labels. Mastered and edited at
Emergency Plus Studio in Bristol on 18th March 1987 with
a release date of 24th April, it included seventeen bands
and songs; Disorder, Chaos UK, Concrete Sox, Ripcord,
Vicious Circle, CCM, E.N.T., Electro Hippies, Generic,
The Stupids, Depraved, Bad Dress Sense, Dr & The Crippens,
Civilised Society?, Eyes On You, Potential Threat, and Oi
Polloi. "Digging In Water" was the perfect document of the
U.K. scene at this time, highlighting the cross-section
of styles that came together to form one scene with all
these both older and newer bands playing gigs alongside
each other. With punk cover art by Stel it was originally
intended to come in a gatefold sleeve but instead ended up
with a regular sleeve and band info insert.

DUDES (THE ORIGINAL MOTION PICTURE SOUNDTRACK ALBUM) LP (MCA)

The soundtrack to Penelope Spheeris' punk-related flick
that starred Jon Cryer, Flea and Daniel Roebuck as three
punks who decided to leave New York and headed out west but
it all went south when they encountered Lee Ving's character
Missoula in Arizona. Primarily a metal album, the inclusion
of a different version of "Urban Struggle" by The Vandals
warranted its inclusion, its "I Want To Be A Cowboy" line
being part of a pivotal scene of the film (and could've even
been the inspiration for its idea). The rockers also present
were; Keel, W.A.S.P., Simon Steele & The Claw, Megadeth,
Legal Weapon, The Leather Nun, Jane's Addiction, The Little
Kings, Charles Bernstein & Co. and Steve Vai. The Little
Kings, who featured Gore Verbinski on guitar and vocals,
would soon record an album for Epitaph before he turned
his hand to videos for NOFX and Bad Religion and ended up
directing films in the "Pirates of The Caribbean" series.
The cover art featured the customary stills from the film.

322

ESSENTIAL ATTITUDES VOL. 2 LP (FRANTIC RECORDS)

The second installment of this series of late stage Maryland "new wave" bands that skirted a little too close to mainstream rock with ten bands and songs from; Jim Ball and the Suits, Beyond Words, Exibit A, Sunday Cannons, Two Legs, Thee Katatonix, Red Tape, The Last Picture Show, When Thunder Comes, and Tangled Hangers. Four of the bands also appeared on volume one (Red Tape, Exibit A, Beyond Words and Thee Katatonix) as well as When Thunder Comes who were originally called Mission but changed their name into their album title. All of the releases on "Frantic" were from Mission, When Thunder Comes and the 1980 punk band with the same members; The Accused, so the label was connected to the band and the band repeatedly changed their name. A pretty mainstream, pedestrian compilation, even former punks Thee Katatonix had slowed down their 1983 song "Joie Du Vivre" here. With a typically 80s arty cover it also came with an inner sleeve with band info.

FLIPSIDE VINYL FANZINE VOL. 3 LP (FLIPSIDE/GASATANKA)

The final episode in the Flipside Vinyl Fanzine story, and as usual this reflected the punk scene of the time from a mainly U.S. perspective, with a couple of Canadians, a Swiss and one Japanese band thrown in. Nineteen bands and songs from; Adolescents, 76% Uncertain, Slapshot, The Brigade, Mad Parade, Bulimia Banquet, Shonen Knife, 7 Seconds, Copulation, Tesco Vee & White Flag, C.O.C., Lemonheads, Circle Jerks, Problem Children, Vatican Commandos, MIA, Little Gentlemen, SNFU, and Doggy Style. The German press on Weird System included additional songs from; Celebrity Skin, Ruthensmear and ROTA, rendering that vinyl version lower in quality. A stand out here was Tesco Vee & White Flag's rendition of Blue Öyster Cult's "Hot Rails To Hell" with a hilarious intro from Tesco. The Brigade entry "Living With The Bomb" with vocals handled by Bob Gnarly Stern (formerly of Plain Wrap) was unreleased, as was Slapshot and others. With cartoon and computer colliding cover art.

F-R-5 LP (FETAL RECORDS)

A collection of bands on Fetal (The Baltimore label run by members of Law And Order and The Bollocks) of bands from Washington D.C., Maryland and Virginia that somehow flew under the radar despite containing some popular bands from the D.C. punk scene. Fifteen songs from thirteen bands; Undecided, Afraid Of Clowns, Schmovie, Government Issue, Shudder To Think, The Unknown, Fear Of Man, Press Mob, Scream, Broken Siren, Braver Noise, Strange Boutigue, and Law & Order. Government Issue's "Public Stage" was recorded live in Maryland in 1987, while Scream's "Solidarity" was an unreleased version from a 1981 Inner Ear session, and Shudder To Think's "Too Little Too Late" was gleaned from their then new first demo. Strange Boutique featured Monica Richards from Madhouse and Hate From Ignorance, Danny Ingram from Madhouse and Youth Brigade (DC) and Fred "Freak" Smith from Beefeater. The cover was a mysterious Dischord style photo with band info and photos on the back.

FUTURE-NOW! PRESENTS: FLEXI (FUTURE NOW!)

A flexi that came with issue #1 of the short-lived zine of the same name that was "putting Nottingham on the map" by John March, vocalist of Heresy and friends. Three U.K. hardcore bands on one side; Nottingham's Heresy with "Make The Connection", Leamington Spa's Depraved and "Reciprocate", and Stupids from Ipswich with "I'm So Lazy", a page of the A4 zine performing the task of accompanying lyric sheet. The zine itself featured; B.G.K., Head Of David, Visions Of Change (The Depraved's then new name), Nottingham, Amsterdam and Japan reports, skating, reviews and other fanzine fare. A nicely put together litho printed zine with a spot colour on the cover sheet, as well as a full page advert on the back cover for their friend Dig's then new label "Earache" and his first three releases proper from Accüsed, Heresy/Concrete Sox and Napalm Death, simply titled "Mosh!" highlighting the U.K. scene's further slide towards American hardcore and crossover thrash.

LET'S GET PISSED - IT'S CHRISTMAS
VOLUME TWO

LIMITED PUNK SAMPLER ONLY 3-99

LIFE IS A JOKE
Vol. 3

MAGGIE, MAGGIE, MAGGIE; OUT! OUT! OUT!
16 TRACKS OF SUBTLE AND INFORMED POLITICAL COMMENT

MENTAL FLOSS

PUNK LIVES - LET'S SLAM 2

Limited Edition Only 1.000

PAY 3-99 U.K.

GEYSER LP (ENIGMA RECORDS)

Sub-titled "Anthology of the Icelandic Independent Music
Scene of the Eighties" this showcase of eleven Icelandic
bands was compiled by Reykjavik's Gramm Records and
featured; Þeyr, Purrkur Pillnikk, Bubbi & Das Kapital,
Megas & Íkarus, Vonbrigði, Jonee Jonee, HÖH, Kukl, Mickey
Dean & De Vunderfoolz, Stanya, and Sveinbjörn Beinteinsson.
The predominant sound and approach was driving but quirky
post-punk but there was also the odd outburst of fast
punk rock and even straight forward atmospheric Eighties
rock not unlike what Killing Joke were doing at the time.
Kukl recorded two albums for Crass Records and featured
Björk Guðmundsdottir who went onto a solo career, their
submission here being "Man on the Cross". If music from
off the beaten path is your thing you probably already had
this fascinating document. With cover graphics depicting
volcanic activity, the back cover featured band photos and
liner notes from Einar Örn Benediktsson (of Kukl etc.)

I'VE GOT AN ATTITUDE PROBLEM 7" EP (B.C.T./ LOONY TUNES)

The more D.I.Y. hardcore became throughout the Eighties
the more 7" compilations appeared and this Transatlantic
collaboration between Scarborough's Loony Tunes and San
Diego's B.C. Tapes featured seven bands and eleven songs
from; Wretched and Raw Power (Italy), Psycho (U.S.),
Satanic Malfunctions (U.K.), Mob 47 (Sweden), Quod
Massacre (Yugoslavia), and Funeral Oration (Holland). With
a running time of nearly thirteen minutes on 33 RPM this
was surprisingly loud and clear and the emphasis was on
all-out fast hardcore, but you could tell just by holding
the vinyl that this was a U.S. press, so avoiding the
typical muddiness of 33 RPM U.K. pressings of the time.
In fact B.C.T. had also used the same pressing plant, Bill
Smith Custom Records of El Segundo, California, for their
previous compilation "We Can Do Whatever We Want". The cover
art depicted a punk flying over a map and came in a typical
photocopied foldover sleeve with band info on the inside.

JAK PUNK TO PUNK LP (TONPRESS)

"If it is punk, then it is punk", a cohesive document of Polish underground hardcore punk finally arrived in 1987 on government controlled imprint Tonpress, a part of the KAW (Krajowa Agencja Wydawnicza aka The National Publishing Agency). This seven band and fourteen song set became the discovery point for a lot of people outside Poland and the Eastern Bloc looking to hear what was going on behind the iron curtain. Armia, Dezerter, Rejestracja, Tzn Xenna, Siekiera, Abaddon, and Processs, all with two songs each except for Armia with three, and Processs with one. The style was fast punk and post-punk with good production recorded in 1986 at the KAW studio in Warsaw. A stark image of a sawblade adorned the cover designed by Tomasz Jagodzinski in cold black and white, the title in red, while the tracklist was hand written on the back, the sleeve torn to reveal the sawblade as the vinyl record inside. An essential document of Cold War punk from the Eastern Bloc.

LET'S GET PISSED - IT'S CHRISTMAS VOLUME TWO LP (CULT RECORDS)

Continuing the annual "Have A Rotten Christmas" series on Rot Records, sub-label Cult run by members of Riot Squad, came this similarly themed budget international "limited punk sampler" set featuring nine bands and eighteen songs with two songs apiece from; Killroy (U.S.A.), U.B.R. (Yugoslavia), Rattus (Finland), Normahl and Maniacs (West Germany) and Colera (Brazil), three songs from Fear Of War (Sweden), and only one song each from Rappresaglia and Pedago Party (Italy). Notable here was the complete absence of U.K. bands from a U.K. label, and also only one band from the U.S. This one didn't suffer the overloaded low volume of some Rot compilations and the quality remained good throughout. They eschewed their usual theme of cut up Christmas wrapping paper for cover art though and went inside with an image from "The Pope Speaks: The Teachings of Pope Pius XII" from 1957. This was the fourth and last in the "Christmas" series 1984-87.

327

LIFE IS A JOKE VOL. 3 LP (WEIRD SYSTEM)

"Further fast uprockers and adventures in punkland"...
The third and final installment in this series of
international punk compilations with eighteen bands from
six countries; M.I.A., Hell's Kitchen, Government Issue,
Fearless, Iranians From Hell, Doggy Style, The Freeze,
The Conditionz and White Flag (U.S.), Tu-Do Hospital,
Challenger Crew and Circle Of Sig Tiu (West Germany),
L'Attentat (East Germany), Culture Shock and Instigators
(U.K.), Brain Death and Junk Schizo (Japan), Dream Police
(Denmark), and Indigesti (Italy). Typically for a German
label the majority of this was comprised of U.S. and German
bands but it remains a good example of the international
punk scene at the time with a mix of punk styles that also
crossed over into metal territory in places. The cover
graphic featured pill bottles and pills spilled over,
possibly indicating the last in the series, and the back
cover featured the info. On black or mint splatter vinyl.

MAGGIE, MAGGIE, MAGGIE; OUT! OUT! OUT! LP (ANAGRAM)

With the sub-title; "16 tracks of subtle and informed
political comment", this late in the day Anagram rehashed
collection of UK82 punk seemed like both a hangover from
the past and a timely reminder that nothing had changed in
five years, and that the Conservatives were still in charge
in the U.K. A song each from various releases from; The
Violators, Angelic Upstarts, Chaotic Dischord, UK Subs,
Vice Squad, Red Alert, The Expelled, Discharge, The Dead
Kennedys, The Samples, Abrasive Wheels, Peter And The Test
Tube Babies, The Varukers, The Partisans, One Way System,
and Action Pact! The tongue in cheek credits said everything
here claiming the album was apparently compiled by "A.
Scargill" with photos by "D. Healey" and sleeve design by
"K. Livingstone". Cover art that depicted Margaret Thatcher
as Hitler in the John Heartfield photomontage tradition,
while the inventive back cover featured all the songs
as tabloid headlines finished the concept off in style.

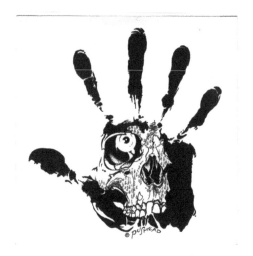

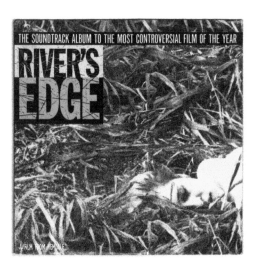

MENTAL FLOSS LP (WRSU RECORDS)

A showcase of talent from the New Brunswick, New Jersey, area compiled by DJs Bryan Bruden and Ethan Stein of the late night show "Overnight Sensations" on student-run radio WRSU at Rutgers University, a show that had started in 1984 and also featured later MTV VJ Matt Pinfield. Fourteen bands and songs from; TMA, Catharsis, Need State, Outdoor Minor, Opium Vala, P.E.D., Spiral Jetty, The Blasés, The Plague Dogs, Third Party, Vendettas, Wooden Soldiers, Destroy All Bands, and Tom's Electric Tombstone. Hardcore band TMA had two albums out and provided "Miserable" from their second album, while P.E.D. (Post Ejaculation Depression) released an album on New Red Archives a year later. A standout here was the crossover of Destroy all Bands with "No Time Left", and perhaps surprisingly for an area compilation, half of these bands released records. Mike Demko of Genocide and TMA handled the cover art and the album also came with a sixteen page newsprint booklet with a page on each band.

OVERSEA CONNECTION LP (DOUBLE A RECORDS)

If you were in any doubt that we were still in the era of the international compilation in 1987, here is yet another from West Germany's Double A records (compiled by label owner Reiner Mettner) to prove it. The "Oversea Connection" here was essentially U.S. and Australia (with a little Canada and New Zealand thrown in). Twenty bands and songs from; Fear Itself, Life Sentence, Attitude, Psycho, Agent 86, Dead Silence, A.P.P.L.E., Hated Principles, Th'Inbred, Accelerators and Pinewood Box (U.S.), Civil Dissident, G.A.S.H, Arm The Insane, Depression, Vicious Circle, Extremes and Nobody's Victim (Australia), Random Killing (Canada) and Compos Mentis (New Zealand). The age of crossover hardcore was very apparent here with the majority being fast thrash, but there were some great songs with a unique version of "Plain Speaking" by Th'Inbred. With well executed cover art by Didie it also came with a large insert with band info.

PUNK LIVES - LET'S SLAM 2 LP (SLAM RECORDS)

The second and final in the series from another Rot Records
sub-label and this one was an all U.K. budget compilation
of largely melodic punk that could've just as easily come
out five years earlier. Six bands and twelve songs; Jive
Turkey, Sad Society, Atrox, The Disturbed, Perjury, and
Rejected. The theme here was mid-tempo anthemic British
punk that at the time was being largely left behind in
favour of hardcore, crossover and thrash, but could still
be found lurking on pretty much every bill of U.K. punk
gigs alongside all those other styles. With cover art
probably cut out of a comic the sleeve info on the rear was
sparse to say the least. Limited to 1,000 copies.

PUSMORT SAMPLER 7" EP (PUSMORT)

Three years into Pushead's label Pusmort this was only the
second 7" release, a label sampler to showcase existing and
upcoming releases, some of which didn't end up happening.
Featuring six bands and six songs, Pushead's own band Septic
Death opened up with "Insanity" from the "Burial Mai So"
7", followed by Vancouver's Fratricide and "Going Under"
from an intended split LP with Holland's Neuroot that only
reached the test pressing stage. Side one closed with Japan's
Corruption Of Peace and "Bleeding Children" from their
"Confusion" LP that was never reissued on Pusmort. The flip
began with Long Beach's Final Conflict with "Constant Fear"
from their "Ashes To Ashes" LP, before Toronto's Negative
Gain and "No Life At All" from the "Back From The Dead" LP.
Ghoul from Japan then closed play with "Jerusalem" that only
appeared on the 1986 Japanese compilation LP "A Farewell
To Arms". The mailorder version of the EP came with a
bonus flexi featuring two blazing Japanese hardcore bands;
Outo and S.O.B. (Sabotage Organized Barbarian), as well as
Ghoul Squad featuring two former members of The Freeze,
their Pusmort album also going unreleased. The EP featured
Pushead's skull hand art on the cover that was soon globally
recognisable, and became many a t-shirt and tattoo.

331

RAT MUSIC FOR RAT PEOPLE VOL. III LP (CD PRESENTS)

As with most of many other punk compilation series ending in 1987 this too was the final episode for the "Rat Music" set that documented the San Francisco area gigs of Paul Rat with high quality live albums. Reflecting the gigs of the day were the thirteen bands and fifteen songs from; D.I., Corrosion Of Conformity, Doggy Style, Raw Power, Attitude, Naked Raygun, Verbal Abuse, Mojo Nixon & Skid Roper, White Flag, Sacrilege, Adrenalin O.D., Frontline, and Adolescents, with one song each, except for D.I. and White Flag with two. The Naked Raygun entry "Rocks Of Sweden" was unreleased and the album opened and closed on cover versions; "Ballroom Blitz" (D.I.) and "All Day And All Of The Night" (Adolescents). The addition of some crossover via C.O.C., Verbal Abuse and Sacrilege was in keeping with its release date. With cover art continued "The Council of Rats" theme by recycling the Gustave Doré etching from the back of volume one but colourised.

RIVER'S EDGE - SOUNDTRACK LP (ENIGMA/METAL BLADE)

"The soundtrack album to the most controversial film of the year" that starred Crispin Glover, Keanu Reeves, Ione Skye Leitch, Daniel Roebuck and Dennis Hopper. The story of a group of teens in a Northern California town (although primarily filmed in the foothills of Sunland-Tujunga in Los Angeles), their friend's murder of his girlfriend and the disposal of her body on a River's Edge. Primarily a metal album featuring four Slayer songs (three from "Show No Mercy" and one from "Haunting The Chapel"), along with Hallows Eve and Fate's Warning, you got the impression that Metal Blade definitely won out over Enigma here, but it also featured a song each from Agent Orange and Wipers, both from their Enigma albums "This Is The Voice" and "Land Of The Lost" respectively. Just for a change of pace, signing off the soundtrack was the reggae of Burning Spear. The cover art featured the movie poster with band photos, song titles and movie credits on the back.

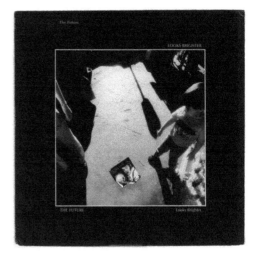

SCREAM - THE COMPILATION LP (GEFFEN RECORDS)

The document of the Los Angeles goth, death rock and hard
rock club "Scream" that called various locations home until
they were closed down and moved on throughout the mid-late
Eighties. The gay club "The Probe" was one, the Embassy
Hotel another and the Park Plaza Hotel another. The club
featured in a few films including the club scene in "Less
Than Zero", and bands such as; Christian Death, Jane's
Addiction, Sonic Youth, X, Iggy Pop, Soundgarden, The
Sugarcubes, and Firehose all graced the stage at one point.
This album though featured ten bands; Jane's Addiction,
Caterwaul, Human Drama, Francis X and the Bushmen, TSOL,
Delta Rebels, The Hangmen, Tender Fury, Abecedarians, and
Kommunity FK. "Scream" all has that very Eighties echoing
production when the style was very dramatic with big hair.
The cover and inner sleeve art was handled by punk artist Mad
Marc Rude and club promotion was based on his illustrated
flyers he left on store counters throughout Hollywood.

SHALL WE DANCE LP (MEANTIME RECORDS)

A collection of four underground U.K. punk bands on Ian
Armstrong's (of the bands Dan and Sofahead) label that was
complimented by all the bands touring the U.K. with each
other to promote the release at the time. The album opened
with four songs from Leamington Spa's The Joyce McKinney
Experience who would soon release their album of great
punk rock (with two female vocalists) on Meantime. J.M.E.
were followed by three complex Subhumans (U.K.) influenced
songs from Ledbury's Decadence Within that featured in
their ranks a one future punk author Ian Glasper. Side two
opened with three songs from Southampton's anarcho punks
Nox Mortis before a whopping seven songs from Leeds squat
punks Incest Brothers (don't Google that) with song titles
like "Dungarundies" and "Do Silly Dances". With cover art
by Mick of Chemical Warfare zine the album came with a 4x12"
foldout poster with two panels per band for lyrics and art
full of twisted plants, barbed wire and wacky cartoons.

STONEHENGE 7" EP (BLUURG RECORDS)

The anarcho punks had always had a connection to the ancient site of Stonehenge that dated back to the roots of Crass history and the Wallies, but when the "Battle of the Beanfield" took place (1st of June 1985), when Wiltshire Police prevented The Peace Convoy of several hundred New Age travellers from setting up the 1985 Stonehenge Free Festival, this was further galvanised. Here was the vinyl document of the event (and another offshoot of U.K. punk) where dozens were injured and 537 arrested (one of the largest mass civilian arrests in U.K. history), a benefit EP compiled by Dick Lucas of Subhumans/Bluurg that opened with his then relatively new band Culture Shock and the title track. This was followed by more reggae from Rhythm-Ites, Hippy Slags and Military Surplus (vocalist Chris Bowsher was also interviewed as a witness to the Hungerford Massacre on BBC News in August of this year). The four panel fold out sleeve very much in keeping with the Bluurg house style.

SUPER SEVEN SAMPLER LP (MYSTIC RECORDS)

The Mystic vinyl landfill machine fired up once again for this collection of songs from various Mystic "Super Seven" budget releases. A pretty much all-Californian affair with a few others thrown in, "Super Seven Sampler" featured fourteen bands and songs from; NOFX, Scared Straight, Agression, RKL, Social Spit, Battalion Of Saints ("Second Coming"), Ill Repute ("In Society"), The Grim, P.T.L. Klub (Massachusetts), Identity Crysis, Instigators (U.K.), The Stain (Ohio), Insolents, and Dr. Know (with Brandon Cruz). Despite appearances, this was a decent enough quality set of pretty much all frantic hardcore that was over in a flash, and if you'd never heard a Mystic record in your life then this could've been a place to start. The cover featured a goofy cartoon strip about the record penned by Dennis Worden who was also responsible for artwork for everyone from Rancid Vat to The Doughboys and Mutha Records. The back cover featured the track list and the original 7" EP covers.

THE BIG APPLE ROTTEN TO THE CORE VOL. 2 LP
(RAW POWER RECORDS)

Sub-titled "Sin City... 5 Years Later" this was the second and final in the series of New York punk compilations that were compiled by Ism's manager Bob Sallese, who also handled sleeve design with some help from Ism vocalist Jism. Ten bands from the late 80s CBGB's scene that weren't New York Hardcore but instead continued the original rockin' punk sound of New York City. A total of sixteen songs from; Ism, Norman Bates & The Showerheads, Bunker's Boys, Six & Violence, Ed Gein's Car, and Slime Puppies (all with two songs), and U.F. Omer Band, The Headlickers, Butch Lust and The Mob (all with one song). Four of the bands returned from volume one; Ism, The Mob, The Headlickers, and Butch Lust (of The Hypocrites). The end result was a well recorded and consistent collection reflecting the time and place, while the cover art matched volume one but was yellow instead of red, and an insert supplied band info.

THE ENIGMA VARIATIONS 2 2LP (ENIGMA RECORDS)

The second and final chapter of this Enigma Records budget sampler series. Twelve bands and twenty two songs, with two each on this double album from various Enigma releases, as well as its Restless subsidiary; Mojo Nixon And Skid Roper, T.S.O.L. ("Revenge" period), The Dead Milkmen ("Eat Your Paisley!" period), Agent Orange ("This Is The Voice" period), Plan 9, Wire, Don Dixon, Wednesday Week, Game Theory, and Peter Hammill, as well as one song each from John. St. James and SSQ. Interestingly the first disc featured songs from the bands' other releases while the second disc was mostly unreleased or at least unreleased versions from seven of the bands including; The Dead Milkmen, T.S.O.L. and Agent Orange, giving it at least something different than the standard budget sampler fare. With its peak Eighties cover graphics, the double album came housed in a gatefold sleeve with the Enigma house style band info and photos inside.

THE INCREDIBLE POWER OF DARKNESS

Accused
Manson Youth
Stupids
Velocet
Capital Scum
Inferno
No Allegiance
Damage
Maniacs
G.B.B.

THE BEST OF WORLDWIDE HARDCORE! VOL.1

WAILING ULTIMATELY

Antietam
Big Black
Dipper
Breaking Circus
Death Of Samantha
Dinosaur
Great Plains
Live Skull
Naked Raygun
Phantom Tollbooth
The Reactions
Salem 66
Squirrel Bait
Volcano Suns

X-MIST & REMEDY-RECORDS present:

TRUST

VINYL-COMPILATION

Challenger Crew
Unwanted Youth
Jump for Joy
Anti-Toxin
Spermbirds
Skeezicks
P.M.A.

MAXIMUM ROCK N ROLL PRESENTS

The Gilman Street Project Double 7" Compilation

12 S.F. Bay Area Bands

TURN IT AROUND!

VIVA UMKHONTO!

·BENEFIT· COMPILATION

SCREAM · MORZELPRONK · B.G.K. · DEPRAVED · RHYTHM PIGS ·
· SOCIAL UNREST · THE EX · VICTIMS FAMILY · KAFKA PROSESS ·
· EVERYTHING FALLS APART · CHALLENGER CREW · '96% UNCERTAIN · S.C.A.

WGP #3

THIS RECORD CONTAINS 41 BANDS

WE GOT PARTY

SOCIAL SPIT
DEHUMANIZERS
NO WE'RE NOT
THE MESS
STUPID LITTLE RUBBER HAT
PTL KLUB
IDENTITY CRYSIS
PLUS IN WONDERLAND
ABUSIVE ACTION
DEFECTIVE INFANTS
SOCIAL DISEASE
HATED PRINCIPALS
TOXIC NOISE
PUB 1
FILE
WITHDRAWN
LIKE SCHTEIN
CONFLICTING INTERESTS
YOUTHFULL AGGRESSION
TOXIC PETS
FCC
YOUTH IAM
HAMSTER
POSITIVE ACTION
THIRSTY BRATS
SYRINGER
THE WORM
MANIFEST DESTINY
THE ROMULANS
THE SHEMPS
CANCEROUS GROWTH
ACTIVE INGREDIENT
FOLLOW FASHION MONKEES
TRANSGRESSION
THIRD FORCE
LIKE A HORSE
PSYCHO
ASBESTOS ROCKPYLE
SKULLBUSTERS
PEASANTS WITH PITCHFORKS

THE FIRST CUTS ARE THE DEEPEST 7" EP (WORDS OF WARNING)

After "You Are Not Alone" Karl W.O.W. wanted to release an all-Welsh compilation but was stuck on a title and cover, and my dad actually came up with the title after I told him about it, based on the fact that bands were mainly new to vinyl and it was the title of a Rod Stewart single that kept "God Save the Queen" by Sex Pistols from the U.K. number one spot. Six Welsh bands and songs; Blaina's Classified Protest were the street punk band that soon became Rectify, while I Mobster was an instrumental project by members of Soldier Dolls before they became Slowjam. The Bugs were a Newport minimalist art-punk band, while Yr Anhrefn and Elfyn Presli were Welsh language bands from North Wales. The EP closed with my friends Cardiff's tuneful punks The Heretics. This was the first record I did the artwork for, a suited record label executive monster's talons making those first cuts, a horrified punk on the back. The eight page booklet's inner pages were by the bands themselves.

THE FUTURE LOOKS BRIGHTER LP (POSH BOY)

The 1981 Posh Boy and SST split radio promo LP and general release cassette "The Future Looks Bright" reworked as a Posh Boy only release with five bands and seventeen songs. Side one remained the same as the original Posh Boy side with Shattered Faith, T.S.O.L., Social Distortion, and CH3, while side two added three more songs each from Shattered Faith and Social Distortion, as their 1981 Posh Boy 7"s were originally intended as 12"s, so the other "lost" songs that didn't make the 7" cuts were here, adding four non 7" songs, to a total of six each. Symbol Six filled out the centre of side two with two songs including "Box Of Bones" that didn't make their Posh Boy 12" in 1982. The updated sleeve art featured a photo with the original sleeve placed within it, while the back cover featured some band photos and liner notes by label owner Robbie Fields. As good a cross-section of Posh Boy and early eighties Southern Californian punk rock as you were going to get.

THE INCREDIBLE POWER OF DARKNESS LP (RISE AND FALL)

Sub-titled "The Best Of Worldwide Hardcore", the transition of hardcore into crossover appeared complete with this international (half West German) compilation put together by Inferno's label Rise And Fall. Ten bands and fifteen songs from; Vellocet, Inferno, No Allegiance, Manson Youth and Maniacs (West Germany), Accüsed (U.S.), Damage (Finland), Capital Scum (Belgium), Stupids (U.K.), and G.R.B. (Spain). Opening with the "Teutonic Speedcore" of Berlin thrash exponents Vellocet to set the tone, and the Accüsed providing different versions of "Open Casket Funeral" album tracks, "Power Of Darkness" was a mix of released, unreleased and different versions of songs with an emphasis on speed rules, with Stupids briefly lightening up the darkness. A cartoon of a devil adorned the cover and became the theme throughout, while a nice litho-printed twenty four page booklet had two pages on each band. The cover stated "Vol. 1" but a volume two never materialised.

THE WAILING ULTIMATE LP (HOMESTEAD)

The bubbling up of college rock over a number of years from college towns such as Boston was presented here as fully formed on this showcase of label talent of Gerard Cosloy's Homestead (formerly of Conflict Fanzine, and later of Matador Records). The second Homestead compilation after "Speed Trials" featured fourteen bands and songs from; Dinosaur, Volcano Suns, Phantom Tollbooth, Squirrel Bait, Breaking Circus, Big Black, Salem 66, Death Of Samantha, Antietam, Live Skull, Naked Raygun, The Reactions, Big Dipper, and Great Plains. The overwhelming approach here was a loose-riffed almost Sixties psyche-tinged melodic rock made by bands largely moving on from the confines of their punk and post-punk pasts and ending up at a sort of mid-point between the hardcore era and what would later evolve into something dubbed grunge. With a somewhat enigmatic cover photo with an American flag, the gatefold sleeve opened to reveal band photos and info.

TRUST VINYL-COMPILATION 7" EP (X-MIST/REMEDY)

An all-German hardcore showcase promoting West Germany's Trust Fanzine, the now third longest running punk zine in the world (after the oldest Suspect Device, followed by Artcore) released by Armin Hoffman's (bassist of Skeezicks) X-Mist imprint and its only compilation. Seven hardcore bands and angry songs from; Challenger Crew, Unwanted Youth, Spermbirds, Jump For Joy, Skeezicks, P.M.A., and Antitoxin. The EP was a cohesive set of fast hardcore in the American vein with standouts from Challenger Crew, Spermbirds and Skeezicks. The cover featured the typically bad punk art (theme and execution) common at this time and it came with a randomly folded double-sided insert with photos and info on both sides. With different record speeds stated on the cover and label this compilation definitely had a slapped together feel.

TURN IT AROUND! 2 X 7" EP (MAXIMUMROCKNROLL)

Maximum Rock'n'Roll's third compilation and first for three years came about to document the bands playing its then new project; the D.I.Y run club 924 Gilman Street in Berkeley. Featuring twelve bands and seventeen songs from; Corrupted Morals, Sweet Baby Jesus, Isocracy, No Use For A Name, Crimpshrine, Operation Ivy, Stikky, Nasal Sex, Yeastie Girlz, Rabid Lassie, Sewer Trout, and Buggerall. Isocracy, Operation Ivy, Sweet Baby Jesus, Crimpshrine and Stikky all contributed two songs, the rest one. The vast majority of these bands would soon make up the roster of Lookout! Records, some becoming legendary, others sinking without a trace, but all taking part in the Bay Area club and its goofy antics. Housed in an impressive gatefold sleeve, that incorporated a twelve page booklet with a page on each band, it had liner notes by Tim Yohannan, David Hayes and Martin Sprouse, while the cover featured MRR contributor Walter Glaser pulling a goofy face. 2,000 copies were pressed in October 1987 and it was later reissued on David Hayes' Very Small Records, paid for by MRR as a benefit for Gilman St.

ABOVE: BOOKLET FROM: "MENTAL FLOSS" LP (WRSU)
BOOKLET FROM: "THE INCREDIBLE POWER OF DARKNESS" LP (RISE & FALL)

BELOW: NEWSPAPER & BOOKLET FROM: "VIVA UMKHONTO!" LP (KONKURREL)

VIVA UMKHONTO! LP (KONKURREL)

The second Konkurrel benefit compilation LP for Umkhonto
We Sizwe, the military wing of the ANC in South Africa, the
first being "Remember Soweto" In 1986. Thirteen bands from
five countries and thirteen songs from; Scream, Social
Unrest, Victims Family, Rhythm Pigs and 76% Uncertain (U.S.),
Morzelpronk, The Ex, B.G.K. and S.C.A. (Netherlands),
Challenger Crew and Everything Falls Apart (West Germany),
Depraved (U.K.), and Kafka Prosess (Norway). A varied set
of songs from bands who were touring Europe at the time or
local to Konkurrel at a time when horrifying images of the
apartheid regime were regularly broadcast by news media
worldwide. With the same strong graphic design as "Remember
Soweto", "Viva Umkhonto!" came with a twenty page litho-
printed booklet and a large four page newsprint foldout,
both bearing the album's title and featuring articles and
lyrics. The album was actually pressed and distributed in
the U.S. by Mordam Records of San Francisco.

WE GOT PARTY LP (MYSTIC RECORDS)

With the involvement of "We Got Power" fanzine way off
in the rearview mirror, Mystic continued the 'borrowed'
theme with this third and final forty one band and
song compilation of largely generic teen thrash from;
Social Spit, No We're Not, Stupid Little Rubber Raft,
Youthfull Aggression, P.T.L. Klub, Phallus In Wonderland,
Skullbusters, The Romulans, Peasants With Pitchforks,
Asbestos Rockpyle, Cancerous Growth, F.C.C., Life Sentence,
Pus 1, The Shemps, Like A Horse, Psycho, The Mess, Identity
Crysis, The Dehumanizers, NOFX, Abusive Action, Defective
Infants, Social Disease, Toxic Noise, Vile, Withdrawn,
Toxic Pets, Conflicting Interests, Thirsty Brats, Cringer,
Positive Action, Youthquake, I Am The Hamster, Active
Ingredients, The Grim, Manifest Destiny, Follow Fashion
Monkeys, Transgression, Third Force, and Hated Principles.
With a photo of a dog on the cover to tie it in with "We
Got Power #2: Party Animal", this was one for completists.

NEW RELEASE

ARTIST: VARIOUS

TITLE: DIGGING IN WATER

FORMAT: LP

LABEL: MANIC EARS

CATALOGUE NUMBER: ACHE 3   **DEALER PRICE:** 3.05

RELEASE DATE: 24/4/87   **SHIPPING DATE:**

ADDITIONAL INFORMATION:
THE ULTIMATE HARDCORE COMPILATION IS THIS
CO-RELEASE FROM MANIC EARS/C.O.R.
GATEFOLD SLEEVE WITH FULL BAND INFORMATION.
TRACK LISTING OVER.

SPECIAL INSTRUCTIONS:

REVOLVER DISTRIBUTION
The Old Malt House, Little Ann St., BRISTOL BS2 9EB.
0272 540004 FAX: 0272 540013

EVERY FRIDAY **SCREAM** WILL BE AT

836 N.HIGHLAND AVE

2 VIDEO ROOMS—DANCE ROOM—GAME ROOM

FREE ADMISSION 10—11 W/MEMBERSHIP CARD

HAPPY HOUR 10—11   5 CENT BEER

21 & OVER W/I.D.

SAT.26

SONIC YOUTH

fIREHOSE

SANDBOX

607 S.PARKVIEW   18 & OVER W/I.D.

INFO:213 650—5600   818 843—6676

TOP: "DIGGING IN WATER" RELEASE INFORMATION FROM TEST PRESSING
BOTTOM: "SCREAM" CARD FLYER (FRONT AND BACK) BY MAD MARC RUDE

WILL EVIL WIN? FLEXI (PEACEVILLE)

Signalling punk and metal slowly becoming indiscernible from
each other in the U.K. at this time, for the first release
on his then new label, Hammy (formerly of Instigators,
then of Civilised Society?) Released this four band and
song flexi disc on his newly forged Peaceville Records
in February 1987. With a title referring to the raging
punk versus metal debate at the time, the flexi opened
with crossover band Annihilated and "Inferno" before the
evermore thrash metal sounding Civilised Society? Followed
with "Star Wars". The flip provided Lord Crucifier and
"Deserter To Freedom", an overly long tinny metal song,
before Desecrators (featuring members of Destructors and
later Monks Of Science) closed play with "Ban On Impurity"
with a confused mash of thrash metal and anarcho punk
vocals. With typically crust meets metal Dungeons And
Dragons cover art, the sleeve folded out to reveal band
artwork and lyrics and an anti-vivisection leaflet.

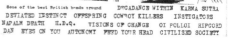

1988

THE 11 YEARS ON 'ZINE FAREWELL FLEXI (11 YEARS ON)

The flexi that came with the final issue of 8/9/10/11 Years On fanzine that was created by Graeme Price of County Durham, UK. The zine with a name change every year (that he no doubt soon regretted) ran for ten issues covering the international hardcore punk scene between 1984 and 1987. Two issues of the zine came with flexis and Graeme then started up Real World Records between 1987 and 1988. Three bands and songs from; Blood And Thunder with "Cities Of Fire", a very GBH inspired song, Heavy Discipline and "Symbol Of Capitalism", a metallic anarcho hardcore song, and Instigators with "The Church Says", recorded live, of course, with Andy Turner on vocals. The flexi came with no sleeve, the zine supplying the info.

AIRSTRIP ONE U.K. LP (MYSTIC RECORDS)

A showcase of a cross-section of the U.K. hardcore punk scene as it stood in 1988 put together by Andy Turner of Instigators for Mystic Records with the amusing sub-title; "The Sound Of U.S. Colonies". Sixteen bands and seventeen songs from; Visions Of Change, Oi Polloi, Napalm Death (the only band with two songs), H.D.Q., Deviated Instinct, Offspring (U.K.), Cowboy Killers, Decadance Within, Karma Sutra, Instigators, Ripcord, Dan, Eyes On You, Autonomy, Feed Your Head, and Civilised Society. This remains one of the most accurate reflections of how the punk gig circuit looked in the U.K. at a time when it was at its most active yet fading from international attention in favour of the increasing popularity of American bands. That U.S. influence could also be heard here with bands like H.D.Q. and Visions Of Change, but mixed in with all the styles prevalent at the time. With a cover cartoon, no doubt cut out of a newspaper, with Ronnie and Maggie of course, the back cover a collage of band photos enhancing the tracklist.

ATTACK IS NOW SUICIDE LP (DOUBLE A / PHANTOM RECORDS)

By 1988 Wally of Phantom had relocated from South Carolina
to Alaska and had run into some financial difficulties, so
in stepped Reiner of Double A Records to help out. Twenty
three international bands and songs from; US.Distress,
Vatican Commandos (& Dusk), Stikky, No Fraud, Rancid Decay,
Dresden 45 and Fear Itself (U.S.), Sic Boy Federation and
Deviated Instinct (U.K.), O.H.M. (Denmark), S.H.Draumur
(Iceland), I Deny (Italy), Dawn Of Liberty (Belgium),
Extrem (Austria), Collaps (West Germany), Raped Teenagers
and Asocial (Sweden), Terveyskeskus and Damage (Finland),
Problem Children (Canada), Subterranean Kids (Spain), Pin
Prick (France), and Afflict (Netherlands). Although seven
of the bands were from the U.S. the album was a good cross-
section of crossover era hardcore. With great cover art
by R.K. Sloane, the back featured liner notes from both
labels and a foldout lyric insert. Phantom unsurprisingly
folded after this LP while Double A continued until 1991.

BARK! BARK! BARK! LP (DEAD ISSUE RECORDS)

A collection of New Jersey and New York bands compiled by
members of The Dream Smashes who ran the label. Eleven
bands and fourteen songs from; False Prophets, The Burnt
(two songs), Under Control, Stetz (two songs), Sinister
Reflections, Twisted World View, Fragrant Moth (two songs),
The Dream Smashes, Ugly Rumors, This Ordeal, and Van Gogh's
Ear. Opening with a great False Prophets song "Destructive
Engagement" it was followed by The Burnt and a punked up
"Bad Moon Rising" (both their songs were unique to this
release) and the unknown NJHC of Under Control. Despite its
artistic cover, the album was predominantly hardcore and
post-punk from quite a few bands who did very little else,
and as a result it remains a largely forgotten artefact. The
aforementioned cover art was designed by Patty Mooney who
cut her teeth on Dag Nasty and Verbal Assault sleeves before
working with Sepultura, Type O Negative and Motörhead. A
double sided insert supplied the info and band photos.

BEAUTIFUL HAPPINESS LP (SOUNDS AND SHIGAKU LIMITED)

While U.K. music weekly Sounds had been relatively dismissive of a lot of US hardcore early on, by the late eighties hardcore's pre-grunge "noise rock" hangover had become far more palatable to its tastes. They teamed up with Shigaku here, the UK distribution for Dutch East India Trading (its own label being What Goes On) responsible for Homestead Records. A fourteen band and song showcase of what the arbiters of good taste had decided the fashionable kids were now going to listen to; Art Phag, Expando Brain, Halo Of Flies, Shadowy Men On A Shadowy Planet, Iowa Beef Experience, Disappointments, Live Skull, D. J. Lebowitz, Naked Raygun, Elvis Hitler, Bastards, Stikky, Bullet Lavolta, and Drunk With Guns. A solid album with insert liner notes by Sounds' Ralph Traitor (aka Jeremy Gluck) that may have featured the first use of the idiotic term "post-hardcore", while the sleeve featured artwork by Brian Bolland (of 2000 AD) and an extra insert advertised What Goes On releases.

DIAMONDS AT A DISCOUNT LP (FRONTIER RECORDS)

Sub-titled "Tower Records and Pulse Presents" this $1.99 Frontier sampler documented how far they'd drifted from their original roster of Southern Californian hardcore classics to alternative/college radio rock. Nine bands and songs from; E*I*E*I*O*, The Pontiac Brothers, Young Fresh Fellows, Flying Color, Thin White Rope, American Music Club, Mallet-Head, Circle Jerks, Naked Prey, and Young Fresh Fellows. Saved by the somehow surviving Circle Jerks and "Wild In The Streets", the rest of the album was just a good example of how former punk labels were floundering at this point, unsure of what, if anything, was coming next. The result was a set of songs that sounded like latter day discarded Replacements demos. With a garish cover design and back cover liner notes from J.B. Griffith desperately trying to make it seem like these bands were the future of rock, it was like "new wave" was happening all over again. Oh well, at least it was only $1.99.

GERM'S CHOICE (A KUSF COMPILATION) LP (GERM RECORDS)

A collection of songs that had received airplay on KUSF's (Uinversity Of San Francsico radio) hosted by DJ Germ, hence the title. Twelve bands with a song each; Capture The Flag, Monks Of Doom, Carnival Law, M-1 Alternative, Denim T.V., Sordid Humor, Shiva Dancing, Primus, Mud Puppies, Eskimo, Mood Swing, and Shower Scene. Being from the era of college rock before it morphed into "grunge", the vast majority of this reflected that with multiple bands playing R.E.M. style indie rock. Most of the bands herein also did little else but it was notable for the inclusion of the first vinyl appearance from Primus with a demo version of "Tommy The Cat", as well as an early entry from Camper Van band side project Monks Of Doom, while Sordid Humor featured Tom Barnes later of Engine 88. With sleeve artwork by David Cooper the back cover featured a tracklist, the station's skull and crossed microphones logo, as well as brief liner notes from Cary Tennis of Calendar Magazine.

GRUESOME STAINS LP (WORKERS PLAYTIME)

An interesting budget compilation named by Klaus Fluoride of Dead Kennedys, and containing a seemingly random set of underground bands housed in a newsprint sleeve with a flexi disc. The only compilation on Workers Playtime (a subsidiary of Nick Garrard's Upright Records) that primarily released records by Snuff, Crane and Bivouac. Eleven bands and songs; Dan, Gold Frankincense & Disk Drive, Bad Beach, Well Phead, Grateful Def, Visions Of Change, Doctor And The Crippens, Death By Milkfloat, Jailcell Recipes, The Joyce McKinney Experience, and Mute Drivers. The bonus flexi featured The Reverend Jimmy Creamjeens & The Sweetcorn Ministry Of Faith playing a country version of Dead Kennedys' "Too Drunk To Fuck". "Gruesome Stains" was all over the map style-wise from hardcore to hip hop, the cover and centre spread design handled by emerging graphic designer John Yates, while the delicate newsprint booklet revealed sixteen pages with one for each band.

350

HAMBURG '88 LP (BITZCORE RECORDS)

For its first compilation, Juergen Goldschmitt's Bitzcore stepped outside its then recently forged sphere of reissuing U.S. hardcore classics with this eight band and sixteen song set from Hamburg locals; Destination Zero, C³I, Emils, Omicidio, 100% Diskretion, Angeschissen, The Legendary Nice Boys, and Erosion. With bands' hair everywhere getting ever longer and riffs getting ever more complicated, a notable exception here was opening song "Kicks" by Destination Zero, who while sounding like L.A.'s Youth Brigade, also seemed to accurately predict what was yet to come from Nineties Southern Californian before it happened. Other bands here such as Emils and Omicidio presented their overly complicated and unlistenable thrash metal while the likes of C³I and Angeschissen harked back to earlier Deutsch punk. With cover art depicting metal dinosaurs about to enter the city by thrash artist Helmut Kettner, the inner sleeve provided the band photos and lyrics.

HARDCORE HOLOCAUST (87-88 SESSIONS) LP (STRANGE FRUIT)

A compendium of abridged John Peel sessions trimmed down onto one handy album at the height of what the U.K. music press stupidly tried to dub "Britcore '88". Twenty five songs from nine bands; Stupids, Electro Hippies, Extreme Noise Terror, Bolt Thrower, Intense Degree, Unseen Terror, Napalm Death, Doctor And The Crippens, and Doom. All of these sessions were released on their own Peel Sessions 12"s but at some point Strange Fruit must've realised that the lengths of some of these songs didn't really warrant all that vinyl, and as a result the Doctor And The Crippens 12" was never released and the second Napalm Death session here was later issued on an LP of both sessions. The styles spanned hardcore to crust to thrash to death metal, from a time when these bands almost inexplicably received their moment in the sun thanks to old Peely. The sleeve featured typical "grind" cover art from "Rot Flesh" accompanied by some basic computer text and an insert.

INVASION 88 LP (RADIO TRIPOLI RECORDS)

Outside of early major label "new wave" compilations of non-Argentinian bands, little punk rock was released in Argentina until Walter Kolm (now CEO of Walter Kolm Entertainment in Miami) and Sergio Fasanelli (of Comando Suicida) founded Radio Tripoli and put together this compilation of ten bands recorded between 1982 and 1988. With two songs each to a total of twenty songs from; Los Laxantes, Attaque 77, Division Autista, Flema, Exeroica, Comando Suicida, Defensa Y Justicia, Rigidez Kadaverika, Conmocion Cerebral, and Los Baraja. The recordings were live and studio and the approach was primarily a well executed and overly excited UK '82 or Oi! approach with some 1977 style punk for good measure. A stand out among the sneering punks and skinheads was the equally menacing all-female band Exeroica and their Slits-like punk. With striking comic cover art, the album came with a booklet with band info and was originally issued on clear vinyl.

IT'S SO HARD TO BE COOL IN AN UNCOOL WORLD LP (I WANNA)

The only compilation from this Dayton, Ohio, label of a set of garage roots rock'n'roll bands that also documented what a few old punks were up to by 1988. Twelve bands and songs; The Human Switchboard, The True Believers, The Reducers, The Highwaymen, Tall Lonesome Pines, The Schramms, The Obvious, Randy X With The McQuires, Truckadelics Featuring Frankie Camaro, The Libertines, Go To Blazes, and Mecca Normal. While the Obvious handled the punk rock here in a driving Ramones fashion, The True Believers' blues slash garage rock featured the Escovedo brothers (The Nuns and Zeros) and Connecticut's The Reducers had gone full garage rock. The Highwaymen featured Mark Thomas Patterson, the original drummer of Toxic Reasons, and guest guitarist Jon Dee Graham of Texas punks The Skunks, while Truckadelics featured Randy Ochsenrider of The Slammies (see: "Master Tape"). I have no idea what's going with the cover art but the back cover photos and insert supplied all the info.

KILLED BY DEATH: RARE PUNK 77-82 LP (REDRUM RECORDS)

The moment that punk rock's journey into retrospection began with this series of bootlegs compiled by Sweden's Johan Kugelberg (the first drummer of Action Swingers) who'd emigrated to New York. The theme was a collection of old and rare early (mainly U.S.) punk 7" A and B sides thrown together in a random fashion (with the majority of the bands having one song each, and in some cases more) inspired by Tesco Vee's 1984 "Collecting" article for Maximum Rock'n'Roll and the "Back From The Grave" series. Seventeen bands and twenty three songs from; The Mad, Hollywood Squares, Slugs, Vox Pop, Controllers, Dogs, Gasoline, Beastie Boys (six songs), Kraut, Child Molesters, Cold Cock, Authorities (two songs), Nuns, Users, Wipers, Vicious Visions, and F.U.2 (unlisted). The first volume was the only one with original cover art by Swedish comic artist David Nessle with some of the covers thrown on the back with; "It's the same music, and you'll afford food."

LIVE FROM LAWRENCE LP (FRESH SOUNDS)

A showcase of talent from Kansas and Missouri bands put together by Fresh Sounds owner Bill Rich in conjunction with local station KJHK. Recorded live at a March 1988 three day festival at the Bottleneck in Lawrence called "Quest For Vinyl" that was promoted by Fresh Sounds, the album featured fourteen bands and songs from; Sin City Disciples, Ultraviolets, Rhythm Kings, Random Aztech, Common Ground, Lonesome Houndogs, Mudhead, Homestead Grays, No Difference, Todd Newman Band, Parlor Frogs, Bangtails, Drowning Incident, and Moving Van Goghs. The style throughout was essentially alternative rock with some swing, reggae, college rock and a hardcore punk entry from No Difference, whose only recorded work was here. The cover featured a painting in the Meat Puppets style by Jana Erwin (now apparently the Head of Education at Ulrich Museum of Art in Wichita) and a letter-sized insert with info on the bands.

METAL GIVES US A HEADACHE 7" EP (HIPPYCORE RECORDS)

The first release from the Mesa, Arizona, fanzine of the same name run by Jack Kahn and Joel Olson. An all U.S. band set from six bands with a song each from; Subvert, Dissent, Desecration (with Jack Hippycore on vocals), Dead Silence, Cringer, and Stikky. A perfect snapshot of the peace punk end of the U.S. hardcore scene of the late Eighties where anarcho punk crossed over into thrash while remaining political and optimistic, highlighted by each band's earnest spoken intros to their songs. In a litho-printed foldover sleeve, the EP came with a twenty page photocopied booklet with band pages and liner notes. Despite the joke title and intro notes about the metal attitudes creeping into the hardcore punk scene, the EP was a benefit for a local Arizona animal rights charity. The cover art featured a photo of the Hippycore Krew goofing off, while the booklet featured art by Missouri punk artist Morbid Mark (Cancerous Growth, Stikky, Desecration).

MUTINY ON THE BOWERY LP (MYSTIC RECORDS)

Despite being sub-titled "Sound Of USA Cities #6 - New York City" this was the third and final in this Mystic series, and one of its last compilations ever before the label became inactive around 1990. Recorded live at CBGB's in 1986, rather than relative unknowns like the rest of this series, this volume featured eight New York, New Jersey and Connecticut bands and twenty songs from some well known names such as; Adrenalin O.D., Children In Adult Jails, Chronic Disorder, Damage, Seizure, 76% Uncertain, Sharkey's Machine, and Stisism. Featuring the usual high quality CBGB recording quality this was a snapshot of hardcore punk two years previous, and was produced by the Alternative Press & Radio Council (APRC) for Greater New York and contained an insert with band photos and lyrics titled "Alternative Info: The Newsletter of the APRC". The cover art was executed by Gary Tse Tse Fly ("Big City's One Big Crowd", Straight Ahead) and Patty Mooney (Dag Nasty, Verbal Assault).

NEW YORK HARDCORE - THE WAY IT IS LP (REVELATION RECORDS)

For the seventh release and second compilation on their label Revelation Records, Jordan Cooper and Ray Cappo (Youth Of Today) compiled this showcase of the new breed of NYHC bands. Emblematic of a period when hardcore punk really began to segregate, seeing these largely straight edge inspired bands set themselves apart with their own identity, uniform, sound and aesthetic. Twelve bands and seventeen songs from; Bold, Nausea, Warzone, Gorilla Biscuits, Trip 6, Breakdown, Youth Of Today, Sick Of It All, Krakdown, Side By Side, Youth Defense League, and Supertouch. The inclusion of crust peace punks Nausea showed that the separation was yet to be fully complete though and the sound throughout was the trademark dense, fast and tough hardcore punk that New York became known for. The sleeve featured photos of crowd shots, while the 12"x12" 8-page booklet provided the band info and liner notes, while a separate insert supplied the label and band photos.

ODD MAN OUT 7" EP (D.S.I. RECORDS)

The only compilation on this Washington D.C. area label, with a set of five D.C. area bands; Government Issue with "Forever", Fun Junkies and "Hardcore Hotel", Black Market Baby with "Back Seat Sally", M.F.D. (Music For the Deaf) and "Minutes To Go", and finally Shudder To Think with "Touch". All but ignoring the post-Revolution Summer Dischord bands, maybe the "Odd Man Out" title was a reference to the bands herein all largely being outside of that Dischord sphere, as even Shudder To Think weren't on the label yet, while Black Market Baby and Government Issue had both existed since 1980 and yet had only largely remained in its orbit, releasing albums on local labels such as Fountain Of Youth instead. With a cover photograph fitting the title by Hajime Sawatari, the EP came in three forms; green vinyl and purple sleeve, blue vinyl and black sleeve, and black vinyl and black sleeve, with two differing inserts. A distinctly D.C. EP but on a slightly different path.

OOPS! WRONG STEREOTYPE

An ALTERNATIVE TENTACLES Compilation

POLKA SLAM

INSTIGATORS   BOLT THROWER

CULTURE SHOCK   H.D.Q

Crisis point

R E A L L Y F A S T

VOL.4

25 KRONOR

RESISTE CROS '10

L'ODI SOCIAL   X ANTI·MANGUIS X   anti DOGMATIKSS

INCLUVE FANZINE

AZAGRA

REVENGE OF THE STEGOSAURUS
FROM OUTERSPACE!

SPLEURK!

IF YOU THINK YOU ARE FREE THINK AGAIN!

CHOPPER
CITY INDIANS
COLD VIETNAM
COWBOY KILLERS
DOOM
EXIT CONDITION
GOLD, FRANKINCENSE AND DISK DRIVE
H.D.Q.
INSIDE OUT
NOX MORTIS
SOFA HEAD
SORE THROAT
TRENCHFEVER
UPSET TUMMY
WHY?
SHRUG

22 TRACK ALBUM & BOOKLET   4·99

OOPS! WRONG STEREOTYPE LP (ALTERNATIVE TENTACLES)

For its first compilation in five years Alternative Tentacles ushered in the return of the budget label sampler with this nine artist and eleven track showcase compiled by Gary Strasburg and Jello Biafra. Nomeansno, False Prophets, The Beatnigs, Tragic Mulatto, Alice Donut, Christian Lunch, Stickdog, Jello Biafra, and Klaus Flouride all made the cut with songs from various Virus releases. As you'd expect this was an eclectic mix of A.T. signings that swung from the pounding post-punk of Noemeansno on "Love Thang" to the nearly twelve minute rant "Love American Death Squad Style" from Jello Biafra, while Christian Lunch survived all the way from 1981's "Let Them Eat Jellybeans". With a trademark Winston Smith cover collage, the back cover featured track list, the bands' record sleeves, liner notes by Jello, as well write-ups on the bands. A large label catalogue was also included so you knew what else was available. The album was released in the U.K./Europe and U.S.

POLKA SLAM/CRISIS POINT 7" EP (SISTERS OF PERCY RECORDS)

A U.K. compilation that came with the Polka Slam (issue #2) and Crisis Point (issue #3) split fanzine, by two zines from Surrey in the U.K. The EP featured four bands that were very much staples of the U.K. gig circuit, the "Crisis" side featured; Culture Shock with "Upside Down" and H.D.Q. with "Looking Back", while the "Polka Slam" side had Bolt Thrower with "Drowned In Torment" and Instigators with "Disorder By Design". Covering some distinct bases of where the British underground scene was at at this point, with the American influenced melodic hardcore of H.D.Q. and Instigators, the anarcho ska-punk of Culture Shock and then the all-out dirge metal of Bolt Thrower. With cover graphics by Steve Throb of Crisis Point zine, the double sided litho printed sleeve by zine/sleeve printer Juma had the requisite band info inside. I remember being impressed by this as they had record shop distribution for this release, no mean feat for D.I.Y. zines at the time.

REALLY FAST VOL. 4 LP (REALLY FAST RECORDS)

The fourth in the series of hardcore punk from this Swedish
label that continues to this day. The usual fourteen bands
provided twenty six songs this time; Wounded Knee, Strebers,
D.T.A.L. (Dr Tjock Och Atomligan), Filthy Christians, Röten
Tandkräm, No Security, Kazjurol, Fred & Frihet, G-Anx,
Puke, Dross, Svart Snö, Rövsvett, and Otakt, with between
one and three songs each all placed together band by band.
Things were definitely changing by 1988 with Wounded Knee
adding some funky slap bass into their hardcore, D.T.A.L.,
Kazjurol, G-Anx and even Rövsvett all adding some crossover
metal crunch into their thrash punk. Strebers provided
some fast and catchy Trall Punk while Fred & Frihetfast
played a slightly Dead Kennedys influenced (in places)
hardcore. The cover image this time depicting speed was a
wasp and the standard foldout poster template was employed
with band graphics on the reverse, but this time a band
photo was added to the track list on the back sleeve.

RESISTE CROS 10 7" EP (PENETRACIÓN / N.D.F)

Outside of "Locos Por La Música" and "Punk Que Punk?" a
surprisingly small amount of vinyl compilations came out
of Spain in the Seventies and Eighties, the favoured format
being the more affordable cassette compilation (another
book entirely) to get the word out. This set of three
Barcelona bands was put together by Joni Destruye's N.D.F.
fanzine and Penetración Records in 1988. With two songs
each by; L'Odi Social ("No Olimpica" and "Veinte Anos"),
Antidogmatikss ("Alerta" and "La Diferencia La Marca El
Color De La Piel"), and Antimanguis ("Acero Y Hormigon" and
"Tu Mujer Se Fue"). The style was hardcore punk with some
metal tinges typical of the late Eighties and a slightly
muddy sound due to the length of the music pressed onto the
vinyl to maximise its potential. With unmistakeably Spanish
cartoon cover art by Carlos Azagra the record also came
with a twelve page copy of N.D.F fanzine on thick newsprint
paper with info on all the bands and their politics.

REVENGE OF THE KAMIKAZE STEGOSAURUS FROM OUTERSPACE! LP
(AX/CTION RECORDS)

For their second and final vinyl "intergalactic compilation" Charlie and Johnny of Psycho went full length with this mainly U.S. set, with a few foreign entries thrown in. Eighteen bands and twenty songs from; No Fraud, Wretched (Italy), XYZ, Rise (Canada), P.T.L. Klub, Prong, Bulge, Ripcord (U.K. with two songs), GG Allin & The Scumfucs, The Stain, Psycho (two songs), Damage (Finland), Afterbirth, Phobia (France), Cancerous Growth, The Freeze, Mentors, and The Scam. The style throughout was hardcore punk, some metal elements common at the time, some scum punk in the form of Bulge, GG Allin and Mentors, and even the more melodic in the form of Canada's Rise. With excellent full colour punk art from R.K. Sloane on the front and back, the album came with a printed inner sleeve with info on all the bands, while a label insert provided all the releases, cassettes and shirt available from Ax/ction.

SPLEURK! LP (MEANTIME RECORDS)

Meantime Records, that was run by Ian Armstrong of Darlington and the bands Dan and Sofahead, issued three compilations; 1987's "Shall We Dance" and two volumes of this mainly U.K. punk showcase. Sixteen bands and twenty two songs from; Exit Condition, G.F.D.D., Cowboy Killers, Sore Throat (four "songs"), Cold Vietnam (two songs), Trenchfever, Sofa Head (two songs), Chopper (two songs), Why?, Shrug, Doom, City Indians, Upset Tummy, Nox Mortis, H.D.Q., and Inside Out (U.S.) The over-riding style was the fast but tuneful American inspired hardcore that was at its peak in the U.K. around this time. With a cartoon cover by Dillon, the minimal printed inner looked like it belonged on a Touch & Go record, while the sixteen page booklet provided a page on each band with liner notes indicating that this came out very late in 1988. The back cover was dedicated to Simon Gregory of Nox Mortis who'd passed away earlier in the year. Spleurk*2 followed in 1990.

THE NOT SO LUCKY COUNTRY 2LP (REACTOR RECORDS)

The only compilation on Phil MacDougall of Melbourne's Reactor Records that documented Australian hardcore punk between 1984 and 1988, and the label's penultimate release. Thirty five songs from thirty three bands; Arm The Insane, Where's The Pope?, Nobody's Victim, End Result, Fear And Loathing, Internal Haemorrhage, Gash, Permanent Damage, Cosmic Psychos, Massappeal, Condemned Attitude, Renegade, Aardvarks Afterbirth, Septic Saw Blades, The Fester Brothers, Death Sentence, Slub, Depression, Civil Dissident, Hard-Ons, Alligator Parade, Filthy Scumbags, Utter Stench, Bad Ronald, Death Sentence, Venom P. Stinger, Vicious Circle, Hard Corpuscles, Extremes, Mental Hellth, No Control, Be Kind To Beavers, Crucified Truth, Psychotic Maniacs, and Permanent Damage. A true labour of love, look no further than here for a comprehensive document of Eighties Aussie punk. The cartoon cover art by Ben Brown revealed a gatefold sleeve and an incredible thirty page booklet.

THE THING THAT ATE FLOYD 2LP (LOOKOUT! RECORDS)

For Lookout's first and only Eighties vinyl compilation David Hayes compiled this vast array of Bay Area bands who frequented the Gilman Street era punk scene. Thirty four bands and songs from *deep breath*; Skin Flutes, East Bay Mud, Corrupted Morals, Neighborhood Watch, Tommy Rot, Cringer, Boo! Hiss! Pfftlb!, Eyeball, Isocracy, Kamala & The Karnivores, Bitch Fight, Plaid Retina, Neurosis, Complete Disorder, Well Hung Monks, Swollen Boss Toad, Vomit Launch, Relief Society, The Mr. T Experience, Sewer Trout, Vagrants, Sweet Babys, Stikky, No Use For A Name, Surrogate Brains, Lookouts, Capitol Punishment, Crimpshrine, Spent, Raskul, Tribe Of Resistance, Nuisance, Operation Ivy, and Steel Pole Bath Tub. The style throughout was the tongue-in-cheek punk you'd have expected from this label. With cover art by Hayes the double LP also came with a twenty four page litho printed booklet with band pages and liner notes from Hayes and Lookout! co-conspirator Lawrence Livermore.

THE WORLD'S IN SHREDS VOLUME ONE - EAST BAY 7" EP (SHREDDER)

For its second release Mel Cheplowitz' Shredder Records
of San Rafael, California, began this series of 7"
compilations that ended up running for five volumes between
1988 and 1991. Four bands and songs, this time from from
San Francisco's East Bay; Gail & The Fudgepackers with
"Head In A Bag", Bo and "The Wonder Of You", Crimpshrine
"Pick Up The Pieces", and Special Forces with a cover of
"Blitzkrieg Bop". Gail & The Fudgepackers members went
onto form The Happy Clams, and along with Bo shared members
with The Jars (Subterranean Records, 1980). Crimpshrine
had recently released their first 7" EP "Sleep, What's
That?" while hardcore veterans Special Forces had somehow
survived since 1983, with a variety of members over the
years, providing this Ramones cover from their then recent
album for New Wave Records of France. The cover featured
various local flyers and a now very dated Mac computer
font, while the insert provided info on all the bands.

VIRUS COMPILATION JAP LP (JUNGLE HOPE INTERNATIONAL)

A seven band compilation album of Japanese hardcore punk
bands compiled by Hervé Lagille of Jungle Hop International
for European release that came after a 1987 7" he'd put
together in Japanese that roughly translated as "Rusu
Attack". Seven bands and sixteen songs from; Sic, Lip Cream,
Fuck Geez, FVK (Fearless Vampire Killers), Systematic
Death, Mad Conflux, and Don Don. Most of the bands provided
two songs each apart from Systematic Death and Mad Conflux
with three each. The theme for the majority of this was of
course the trademark Japanese relentlessly fast hardcore
with throaty yelped vocals and it did not disappoint in
that department. Essentially like a "Thrash Til Death"
volume two, only Fuck Geez slowed proceedings a little,
but not too much. With suitably chaotic cover art by
"Succullus" and "Philukiyukrus", the album came with a
printed spot colour insert with band photos, contacts and
thanks list with art by "Blahblablus".

X-MIST RECORDS SOLD-OUT EP'S RE-RELEASE RIP-OFF LP (X-MIST)

After the initial presses sold out, X-Mist Records owner
and Skeezicks bassist Armin Hofmann reissued the Spermbirds
and Die Walter Elf "Don't Forget The Fun" five song split
7" EP and Skeezicks "There's A Charlie Brown In Every One
Of Us" seven song 7" EP all on this one LP with typically
punk title. The original twelve songs by the three bands
were reissued as well four bonus live songs; "4 Bier Right
Here" and a cover of "1-2-XU" by Spermbirds, "Provinc"
by Die Walter Elf and "Nothing" by Skeezicks. Spermbirds
played an American influenced hardcore made all the more
authentic by their immigrant American vocalist Lee Hollis.
Spermbirds' alter ego (everyone on different instruments)
Die Walter Elf (The Walter Eleven) played a more melodic
football inspired punk rock, while Skeezicks were overtly
U.S. hardcore inspired with Brian Walsby art. The cover
art featured the original front covers with track list on
the rear, the insert with lyrics and other releases.

YOU'RE SOAKING IN IT! LP (APEX)

Sub-titled "(Music From Philadelphia & N.Y.)", this
Skyclad subsidiary released this fourteen band fifteen
song album that featured; Electric Love Muffin, Nixon's
Head, Ornamental Wigwam, Gus Cordovox Quintet, 7 Dancing
Etruscan Slaves Of The 4th Dimension, Wishniaks, Baby
Flame Head, The Things That Creeped-N-Crawled Right Out-O-
The Ground, Dr. Bombay, Da Willys, Kenn Kweder, Wack Mags,
Mick Cancer, and Buddhist Delite. The predominant style
here was the jangle-guitar college rock of the day with
some dirty garage rock, and a stand out came in the form of
the catchy "What Kind Of Trip Are You On?" by Dr. Bombay.
Ornamental Wigwam were a Joe Genaro and David Schulthise
of The Dead Milkmen side-project, while Da Willys' Peter
Landau had been the first drummer of White Zombie. With a
simple cover graphic photo of a girl with an umbrella, the
back cover was just a track list, while the foldout insert
provided band photos and info.

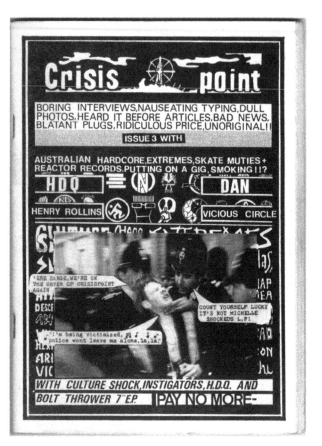

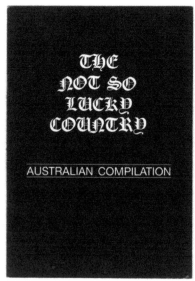

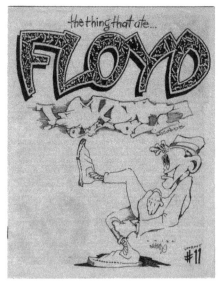

TOP: "CRISIS POINT" SIDE OF THE SPLIT ZINE WITH "POLKA SLAM"
BOTTOM: "THE NOT SO LUCKY COUNTRY" 2LP (REACTOR) AND "THE
THING THAT ATE FLOYD" 2LP (LOOKOUT!) BOOKLETS

1989

BLITZ HITS 2LP (BLITZ)

A double album of bands who played the Blitz cultural centre in Oslo, Norway, so the vast majority were Norwegian bands. Thirty bands and songs from; Ø.B.K., Villsvin, Disorder, Fire Fæle Fyrer, Daggers, Lesbian Cowboys, T-Zers, Data Morgana, Seppo Goes To Holocaust, Within Range, Stengte Dører, Hjerterått, Black & Decker, Behind Bars, Life But How To Live It?, So Much Hate, Junkfood Society, T.H.C., Tremulators, Nemlig Hemlig, Bøyen Beng, Septique, Ym-Stammen, Asod Dvi, Gaia, Fat Molly, Karin Wright, Ane, Pretty And The Tenders, and Libido Link. The first record was predominantly hardcore punk while the third side was mostly experimental and the fourth predominantly female bands. With a cover spray stencil of a fist delivering the Blitz Hits, the gatefold opened to reveal a colour collage featuring the squat, and some copies contained a special edition of the "Smørsyra" twelve page newspaper.

CRUNCHOUSE LP (GLITTERHOUSE RECORDS)

A twelve band and song showcase from this West German label run by Reinhard Holstein, formerly of the fanzine of the same name, that became the European conduit for Sub Pop and Amphetamine Reptile licensed releases when grunge and noise rock were in the ascendency. This was just one of a few compilations on the label ("Sub Pop Rock City", "This House Is Not A Motel" and the "Howl" series being others) around this time, but this stands as a good example with hard, heavy and often repetitive songs from the above labels (as well as Treehouse, Circuit and Whitewurst Records) of bands that seemed to owe a lot to the likes of Big Black; Tad, Halo Of Flies, Bastards, Helios Creed, Unsane, Boss Hog, God Bullies, Mudhoney, Cows, Surgery, First Things First, and The Thrown Ups. The cover art was by Mark Dancey (then of Big Chief, earlier of Born Without A Face).

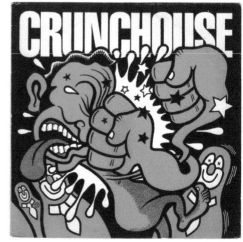

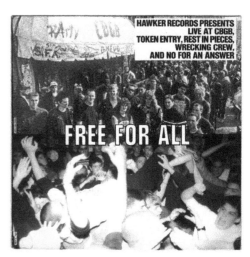

EARTH RAPERS AND HELL RAISERS 2 X 7" EP (HIPPYCORE)

For their second and final compilation the Hippycore krew out of Mesa, Arizona, brought us this double EP benefit for Phoenix Earth First, which was very much in keeping with the punk conversation at the time when environmental activism became a hot topic. Twelve bands and songs from; Sins Of The Flesh, Bent!, Jesters Of Chaos, Pissed Happy Children, Reality Control, Conspiracy Of Equals, Machine, Samiam, Pleasant Valley Children, Pollution Circus, Seein' Red, and Christ On A Crutch. The style was mainly overtly political peace hardcore with a slight metal crunch so typical of the time, and mainly from the western U.S., with the exception of Pleasant Valley Children from the U.K. and Seein' Red from the Netherlands. With a cover theme revolving around pollution and Jack Hippycore holding a stein of beer, the double EP came with a forty page 7"x7" booklet/zine with band pages, political thought and art by Morbid Mark. On green (of course) or black vinyl.

FREE FOR ALL LP (HAWKER RECORDS)

An introductory showcase from this short-lived Roadrunner hardcore subsidiary. Legend has it that Roadrunner founder Cees Wessels' heavy Dutch accent would apparently mean he pronounced "Hardcore" as "Hawker", hence the name. 4 bands and 12 songs recorded live at CBGB's on the 9th April 1989 featuring three songs each from; Token Entry, Wrecking Crew, Rest In Pieces, and No For An Answer. Three of the bands released albums with Hawker, while Rest In Pieces' second album came out on other Roadrunner subsidiary Roadracer in 1990 after Hawker became inactive. Token Entry and Rest In Pieces were New York locals while Wrecking Crew hailed from up the road in Boston and N.F.A.A. had travelled all the way from Orange County, California. The style throughout was the then relatively new more metallic take on the straight edge of hardcore that ended up becoming what hardcore meant to a lot of people who came later. The cover featured the typical crowd shots while the rear had band photos.

HARDCORE EVOLUTION LP (JUNGLE HOP INTERNATIONAl)

A collection of thirteen French bands of the day with one song apiece; Les Gnomes, Original Disease, Parkinson Square, Apologize, Oncle Slam, Endless Diatribe, MST, Smegmatics, Brainwashers, Infected Youth, Flitox, Nomed, and Krull. In keeping with the times, the 'hardcore' herein tended to nod more in the metal direction, or was influenced by the North American sound with intricate structures. Parkinson Square had a rapid approach somewhere between SNFU and RKL, while Apologize were more U.K. via American sounding such as Instigators or Heresy. "Hardcore Evolution" was similar to what was coming out of Italy, with a fast crossover that would go on to form the metallic hardcore they became known for. With computer-generated cover art that seemed influenced by New York hardcore compilations such as "Free For All", with its crowd shot (plus skating) themes, the album came with a folded insert with a small section for each band and a label advert.

HOMETOWN ATROCITIES 7" EP (HOMETOWN ATROCITIES)

Devon in southern England put itself on the punk map with this four band and song EP that featured three Exeter bands and one from Plymouth, all Recorded At Daylight Studios in Honiton, Devon. The EP opened with Plymouth's charmingly named Jackson Penis with "Who Cares?", a riffed up vitriolic punk song, followed by Beaver Patrol and "No Respect" with a more fuzzed out indie punk feel. The flip opened with Mad At The Sun with "This Could Be...", a faster punk tune with members who would go onto Wordbug and Annalise. The EP closed with the decidedly more indie-fuzz, but highly catchy "I Don't Want To Go To Woodstock" by Headless Chickens, notable for featuring a one Thom Yorke on guitar and backing vocals a few years before Radiohead. With a nicely designed sleeve by Mad At The Sun bassist, Hometown Atrocities owner (with Martin Edmunds), and man responsible for gigs at the Cavern in Exeter to this day, Dave Goodchild. The EP also came with three inserts.

KILLED BY DEATH #2 LP, #3 LP & #4 LPS (REDRUM RECORDS)

Johan Kugelberg's bootleg series of "Raw Rare Punk Rock 77-82" went into overdrive in 1989 with three further volumes in the series. Each album with a seemingly random selection of 7" songs from mainly early U.S. punk bands with the odd U.K. or European selection thrown in. The underlying theme being riffs, snot and sneer, and a definite garageland punk edge.

#2 featured sixteen bands and songs from; Freestone, Freeze, Chain Gang, Mad, Machines, Vains, S'Nots, Rude Kids, Nervous Eaters, Detention, Eat, Cheifs, Mentally Ill, Really Red, Psycho Surgeons, and Child Molesters. The sleeve art from here on in became a reworked version of one of the 7"s featured, this one being the cover of Detention's "Dead Rock & Rollers" 7", which was from 1983 despite the cover legend of "77-82".

#3 featured fourteen bands and seventeen songs from; The Lewd, Defnics, 84 Flesh, The Plugz, The Eat (two songs), Shock, Sods, Ambient Noise, The Queers (three songs), Ebenezer & The Bludgeons, NY Niggers, Screamin' Mee-Mees, Violators, and John Berenzy Group. The cover this time taken from The Eat's "God Punishes The Eat" 7".

#4 featured thirteen bands and seventeen songs from; Zero Boys (four songs), Rotters (two songs), Really Red, Filth, Kaos, Heart Attack, Brülbåjz, Zero Boys, Huns, Subhumans, Victims, Mad Virgins, Ism, and Jerks. The cover this time taken from The Jerks' "Get Your Woofing Dog Off Me" 7".

These three volumes were presumably released at the same time as they all received pressings of 700 with the same yellow labels. After the first four volumes the label became inactive, until after a four year gap to sow the seeds, the baton was taken up by others who wanted to make their own bootlegs, and after #7 the numbering turned to chaos and over forty more were issued between 1993 and 2018.

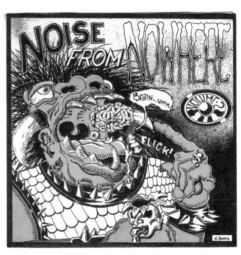

MAKE THE COLLECTOR NERD SWEAT 10" (VERY SMALL RECORDS)

Just prior to his announcement that he would be departing
Lookout! Records on January 1st 1990, David Hayes began his
newly coined Very Small Records. He issued two compilations
in 1989, this being the second in December, right on
the cusp of the Nineties. Featuring ten bands and songs
from San Francisco Bay Area bands; The Mr. T Experience,
Crimpshrine, Crummy Musicians, Lookouts, Coffee & Donuts,
The Wrong (originally from Hawaii), Samiam, Jawbreaker,
The Offspring, and Plaid Retina. With a mix of bands,
some of whom would soon see commercial success, you could
hear punk knocking on the door of the Nineties without a
hint of 'grunge' present. With cover cartoon art by Sergie
Loobkoff of Samiam, a soon to be graphic designer in his own
right (from 1992 on with Sergie Graphics). The foldout 10"
sleeve folded out to reveal a chaotic set of band designs
and a zine style booklet. Issued on five colours to a total
of 1512 copies in 1989, 2300 copies were reissued in 1994.

NO FRONTIERS 7" EP (LOONY TUNES)

Compiled by Graeme Price formerly of 11 Years On and
Real World Records, for Active Minds' label Loony Tunes,
came this mainly U.K. six band and song EP featuring;
Debauchery, Advance Warning, Bad Attitude (West Germany),
T.W.E.R.P., Chaotic Subversion, and Neighbourhood Watch
(Canada). The third compilation 7" from Loony Tunes opened
with two longer songs on side one; Debauchery, a metallic
hangover from the days of GBH, before Advance Warning who
sped things up a bit (before becoming Oi! band Boisterous
in the early Nineties). The flip offered four shorter songs
of the hardcore variety that were more fitting for short
attention spans. Due to the fact that I was writing to
Graeme at the time and had done some artwork for his zine,
I ended up doing the appalling front cover art for this,
but the less said about that the better. Finland's Jouni
Waarakangas handled the rear cover art while a folded A4
printed insert provided the band info.

NOISE FROM NOWHERE VOLUME 2 7" EP (TOXIC SHOCK RECORDS)

Six years after the first volume, Bill Sassenberger and Julianna Towns (both of the band Peace Corpse) moved their Toxic Shock record store and label from Pomona in California to Tuscon in Arizona in 1988. The theme this time around was cover versions of non-punk songs, with four bands and tunes; Massachusett's Hullabaloo did a crunchy and throaty noise version of Deep Purple's "Highway Star", while Texas' Hickoids performed their a cowpunk reimagination of the theme from "Green Acres". On the B-Side Iowa's House Of Large Sizes punked up Cher's "Half Breed", while Indiana's Sloppy Seconds did their pop punk rendition of Sammy Davis Jr.'s "Candy Man". With cannibalistic punk cover artwork by Kevin Bakos (D.R.I., S.N.O.T. etc.), the back and inside cartoons of Eva Gabor (Green Acres actress), Ian Gillan, Cher and Sammy Davis Jr. were drawn by Davy Jones of Hickoids (as well as The Next and Ideals). The series continued as split 7"s until 1992's final #10 compilation.

PEACE THROUGH CHEMISTRY LP (ALCHEMY RECORDS)

A label sampler from this San Francisco label set up by Captain Beefheart's cousin Victor Hayden along with Clown Alley guitarist Mark Deutrom in 1985. Eleven bands and eighteen songs gleaned from the twelve Alchemy releases to date; Clown Alley, Paranoia, Melvins, Guillotine, The Grim, Poison Idea, Rich Kids On LSD, Virulence, Neurosis, Spiderworks, and Sacrilege (B.C.) Most of the bands had two songs while Clown Alley, Guillotine, The Grim, Virulence and Spiderworks only provided one, and The Melvins supplied three. At this point the hardcore punk and metal scenes were undergoing a merging and slowing down into what would become grunge and sludge. The album saved from this sludge induced sleep by Poison Idea, RKL and Neurosis. Clown Alley also featured vocalist David Duran formerly of New Mexico's Jerry's Kidz, and bassist Lori Black the daughter of Shirley Temple. The artwork was simply the label logo, with the covers on the back and an inner with the lyrics.

PROGRAM: ANNIHILATOR II LP (SST RECORDS)

Sub-titled "A Soundtrack For Destruction" this was the second installment of an SST sampler series that, due to a twist of format fate, features here while volume one doesn't, due to it being a 1986 CD and cassette only release that didn't see a vinyl pressing until 1991, while this one did upon release in 1989. Sixteen songs from eight SST recording artists with two songs each bunched together; Soundgarden, Saint Vitus, Sylvia Juncosa, Descendents, Bad Brains, SWA, Bl'ast, and D.C. 3. Seeing as it was the end of the decade the emphasis here was on the pre-grunge hard rock and stoner side of the label. To prove this even the Descendents more rocking songs "Hurtin' Crue" and "Iceman" here weren't representative of the more melodic majority of their back catalogue, while the Bad Brains songs "The Regulator", "Coptic Times / F.V.K." were earlier material from a later live album. The sleeve art featured simply red text on black with a message from "The Programmer".

SOUNDS BLASTS! EP2 7" EP (SOUNDS)

An example of the three sampler EPs issued with U.K. weekly music paper Sounds for three consecutive weeks in March 1989 that highlighted the music paper's then current interest in all things alternative rock, especially of the U.S. variety. This second EP featured "Silver Rocket (Take 6)" (live in New York) by Sonic Youth, Prong with "You Fear" from the "Beg to Differ" album, Pailhead and "Don't Stand In Line" from the "Trait" 12", and Thin White Rope with "Munich Eunich", a bonus track on the CD and cassette of the U.S. version of their "In The Spanish Cave" CD And Cassette. The first "Sounds Blasts!" had featured; Iggy Pop, Fishbone, Dan Reed Network, and Blue Aeroplanes, while the third installment featured; The Perfect Disaster, Mega City Four, Cerebral Fix, Killdozer, and Pussy Galore. Each cover featured the same cover illustration by Simon Cooper in a different colour scheme with band photos and track list on the back.

374

SQUAT OR ROT 7" EP (SQUAT OR ROT)

A five band and song inaugural release from this New York
fanzine and label that came out of the squat punk scene
that was moving away from the traditional local CBGBs to
soon coalesce around the club and space ABC No Rio at 156
Rivington Street on Manhattan's Lower East Side. The 7"
came in a plain white sleeve inside issue one of a large
format newsprint zine and featured; SFA with "Gyroscope",
Resisturz and "Nazi Bullshit", Nausea with "Productive Not
Destructive", Public Nuisance and "Dead End Street", and
Radicts with "6 Of Them". The style throughout had that
distinctive New York punk sound reminiscent of earlier in
the Eighties on labels like "Big City". Five gritty malt
liquor punk blasts, with a layer of crust, by squat kids in
the yet-to-be-gentrified ruins of New York, encapsulated
perfectly here by Public Nuisance. The zine featured a page
for each band, animal rights, and artwork by John Guzman of
Nausea. Volumes two and three followed in 1990 and 1992.

STATE OF THE UNION LP (DISCHORD)

A lot had changed in the Washington D.C. punk scene since
1982's "Flex Your Head"; the "Revolution Summer" had come
and gone and the scene had grown more political with the
entry of Mark Andersen and Positive Force, benefit gigs
and anti-apartheid drum protests. The intention of this
"DC Benefit", compiled by Andersen in conjunction with
Dischord, was an alternative "State Of The Union" message
with proceeds going to the "A.C.L.U & The Community for
Creative Non-Violence". With material recorded between
1986 and 1988, this sixteen band and song LP featured
songs by; Scream, Ignition, Soulside, Broken Siren, Christ
On A Crutch, King Face, Rain, 3, Marginal Man, One Last
Wish, Fugazi, Thorns, Fire Party, Fidelity Jones, Red
Emma, and Shudder To Think. With a cover photo of homeless
men in shadow of the U.S. Capitol by Jimmy Hubbard, the
enclosed twelve page booklet primarily focused on politics
(apartheid, anti-war) with band photos in the centre spread.

TASTE TEST #1 2LP (NEW ALLIANCE RECORDS)

The fifth and final Eighties compilation from New Alliance
run by Minutemen and friends and this one was a "Collection
of live performances on Spat Wingers's "Brain Cookies", as
broadcast from the studios of KXLU-FM, Los Angeles". Twenty
one artists and twenty five songs from; fIREHOSE (two
songs), Deborah Exit (two songs), Roger Miller, Screaming
Trees, Paper Bag (two songs), Cat's Cradle, Brother A. West
(two songs), Crimony, Lawndale, Skinhorse, Overpass, Always
August, 5uu's, D. Boon, Wanda Coleman, Question Mark, Red
Temple Spirits, Universal Congress Of, Abominable, Freshly
Wrapped Candies, and D. Boon And The Stone Puppies. The
results were in keeping with the label's back catalogue
with both driving songs from the likes of Firehose and
Deborah Exit, the art-rock side of Roger Miller (Mission Of
Burma) and some beat-poetry. With Oingo Boingo-esque cover
art by Brother A. West, "Taste Test #1" was engineered
by Phil Newman (Sin 34), and came with two inserts.

TERMINAL CITY RICOCHET LP (ALTERNATIVE TENTACLES)

The soundtrack to the Canadian indie dystopian comedy
film directed by Zale Dalen and starring Peter Breck,
Germain Houde, Jello Biafra (Dead Kennedys) and Joe
Keithley (D.O.A.). Named after hockey team "the Terminal
City Ricochets" and the prescient tagline; "When real life
is a television show, you can't change the channel", this
twelve song LP featured; D.O.A. (two songs), The Beatnigs,
Jello Biafra and Nomeansno, I, Braineater, Gerry Hannah
(Canada's Subhumans and Squamish Five), Art Bergman (Young
Canadians), Jello Biafra and D.O.A., Evan Johns and The
H-Bombs, Nomeansno, The Groovaholics, and Keith LeBlanc with
Jello Biafra. D.O.A. covered Subhumans "Behind The Smile"
(Subhumans vocalist Brian Goble had joined D.O.A.), while
Beatnigs continued the film's theme with "Television". The
sleeve design featured stills from the film put together
by John Yates and David Lester, the liner notes handled by
David's brother and D.O.A. manager Ken Lester.

THE NORTH ATLANTIC NOISE ATTACK 2LP (MANIC EARS)

Originally intended as an all U.K. compilation, this double album's gestation period of eighteen months saw it morph into a twenty three song U.K. album with a 'bonus' eight song 12" of U.S. bands. Ten U.K. bands made the cut that very representative of what was going on in the British underground scene at the time; Ripcord, Intense Degree, Visions Of Change, Jailcell Recipes, Civilised Society?, Doctor And The Crippens, Extreme Noise Terror, Heresy, Napalm Death, and Concrete Sox. While six U.S. bands were also included; Septic Death, Transgression, Adversity, Fear Itself, No Fraud, and Desecration, some of which had Manic Ears releases. The style of the U.K. bands was fast hardcore very much influenced by U.S. hardcore, while the U.S. bands at this point were leaning more into crossover metal. With cover art in the Maximum Rock'n'Roll style, the back cover featured a collage of band photos while the insert featured a Brian Walsby cartoon, liner notes and more photos.

THE WORLD'S IN SHREDS VOLUME TWO & VOLUME THREE 7" EP (SHREDDER)

The second and third volumes of this area series from Mel Cheplowitz' Shredder Records, by now in San Francisco (formerly of the North Bay Area San Rafael) to get in the thick of the action. Volume Two covered "U.S.A." with four bands; Crimpshrine (Bekreley, California), Jawbreaker (still then based in Los Angeles), Moral Crux (Washington State), and A Priori (New Jersey), while Volume Three highlighted "Fresno" with six bands; S.A.D. Boyz, Capitol Punishment, Slut Vinyl, Plaid Retina, Kondom-Nation, and Abducted Children. Both volumes showcased, the then still underground, scrappy but tuneful punk at the turn of the decade, mixed with hardcore veterans such as Capitol Punishment. Both came with the same house-style flyer collage cover art surrounded by early computer fonts, in folded sleeves with inserts. Volume Four and Five followed in 1990 and 1991 before Shredder turned to CD for the "Shreds" series.

ORIGINAL MOTION PICTURE SOUNDTRACK

JELLO BIAFRA • D.O.A. BEATNIGS • KEITH LeBLANC

TERMINAL CITY
RiCOCHET

WHEN REAL LIFE IS A TELEVISION SHOW
YOU CAN'T CHANGE THE CHANNEL

MANIC EARS RECORDS PRESENTS

the NORTH ATLANTIC NOISE ATTACK

WORLD OF MUSIC ARTS DANCE

SHREDDER PRESENTS the WORLDs iN 8hrEDs

VOLUME TWO

USA

CRIMPSHRINE - JAWBREAKER
MORAL CRUX - A PRIORI

SHREDDER PRESENTS the WORLDs iN 8hrEDs

VOLUME THREE

FRESNO

S.A.D. BOYZ - CAPITOL PUNISHMENT
PLAID RETINA - KONDOM-NATION
SLUT VINYL - ABDUCTED CHILDREN

MAXIMUMROCKNROLL PRESENTS

THEY DON'T GET PAID,
THEY DON'T GET LAID,
BUT BOY DO THEY WORK HARD!

WHAT ARE YOU POINTING AT?

ECONOCHRIST
SCHIZOID
VAPOR LOCK
SCREECHING WEASEL
BAZOOKA JOE
DISSENT

THEY DON'T GET PAID, THEY DON'T GET LAID, BUT BOY DO THEY WORK HARD! LP (MAXIMUM ROCKNROLL)

The fourth "M.R.R. Presents" compilation from Berkeley California's Maximum Rock'n'Roll zine and radio station to see out the Eighties, the theme here being the North American D.I.Y. punk scene featuring fourteen bands and ten fanzines, compiled by Lance Hahn of Cringer and J Church. The LP featured a song each from the more political peace punk to the more personal melodic punk; The Detonators, Amenity, Christ On A Crutch, Nausea, Apocalypse, Conspiracy Of Equals, Screeching Weasel, Jawbox, Dissent, Downfall, Dead Silence, Cringer, Bazooka Joe, and Libido Boyz. The enclosed twenty four page copy of "MRR #79.5" featured the following zines; Absolutely Zippo, Dead Jesus, Endless Struggle, Hippycore, Nomadic Underground, No Answers, Profane Existence, Time To Unite, Tunga Tunga, and Village Noize, with a page on each zine and half a page on each band as well as liner notes from Tim Yohannan. The sleeve was sharply designed by U.K. émigré John Yates.

WHAT ARE YOU POINTING AT? 10" (VERY SMALL RECORDS)

Just prior to the "Make The Collector Nerd Sweat" 10" came this introductory compilation from David Hayes' Very Small just as he was planning on leaving Lookout! Records in September 1989. Six U.S. bands and sixteen songs from; Econochrist (California via Arkansas), Screeching Weasel (Illinois), Vapor Lock (California), Schizoid (Nevada), Dissent (South Dakota), and Bazooka Joe (South Carolina). A mix of poppier side of punk of the time as well as the more political, very much like the M.R.R. compilation above, of bands that were much active on the U.S. D.I.Y. punk scene in 1989. With a straight edge mocking cover cartoon by "Otto", the foldout sleeve revealed a chaotic collage of band graphics. The 10" was initially pressed on eight different colour variants to a total of 1,071, and Hayes reissued 1,700 copies on his later Spokane, Washington, based Too Many Records five years later.

380

TOP: "SQUAT OR ROT" FANZINE, ISSUE #1, NEW YORK CITY, 1989
BOTTOM: "STATE OF THE UNION" LP (DISCHORD) AND "THEY
DON'T GET PAID, THEY DON'T GET LAID" LP (MRR) BOOKLETS

KILLED BY DEATH

At the beginning of the Nineties punk's evolution saw it splinter off into distinct rock sub-genres with an increasing eye on commercial appeal. Aspects of hardcore punk had morphed first into 'noise rock' and then 'grunge', while fusions of funk, metal and hip hop became a new bandwagon to jump on.

The volume of compilations began to drop and it wasn't long before they started to shift back to being mere label samplers with the rapid rise of the compact disc. 1990 however, still brought us punk vinyl compilations such as; "A Compilation Of Deleted Dialogue" LP, the "Beautiful Music For Beautiful People" 10", "Built On Blood" LP, "Can You Break Through?" LP, "City Of L.A. 1990" LP, "Forever (A Hardcore Compilation)" 7" EP, "Hardcore Breakout USA" LP, "If You Can See Through It It Ain't Coffee" 10", "More Songs About Plants And Trees" 7" EP, "Murders Among Us" 7" EP, "No Control At The Country Club" Live 7" EP, "Satyricon ...The Album" LP, "Spleurk*2" LP, "What Stuff" LP, and the "You're Going Home" 7" EP.

But by the time Nirvana and grunge hit big between 1991 and 1994, compilations increasingly began to look back with the first "Dangerhouse" label retrospective, the 1982 cassette only compilation "New York Thrash" was reissued on vinyl, the "Reagan Regime Review" hardcore 7" EP, the "Smash The State" Canadian punk series, and the "Bloodstains" series of LPs. Covers and tribute compilations also began to appear such as the "Under The Influence" covers 7" EP, the "Virus 100" Dead Kennedys tribute, the "Surprise Your Pig" R.E.M. tribute, and the "From Home Front To War Front" Discharge tribute.

Labels such as Ebullition, Allied and Simple Machines did start the new decade with their new labels' first releases as compilations though; the "Give Me Back" LP, the "Emergency Broadcast Systems" series of 7" EPs, and the "Simple Machines" series of 7" EPs respectively.

One place where compilation activity continued into
the 1990s unabated was the San Francisco Bay Area with
compilations such as the "Brouhaha" 7" EP, "Sasquatch:
The Man, The Myth" double 7" EP, "The Mission District:
17 Reasons" triple 7" box set, Allied's triple 7" box set
"Sign Language", and the "Misfit Heartbeat" double 7" EP.
The emphasis shifting to multiple 7" releases. Lookout!
also continued with the "Can Of Pork" double LP and the
"Punk USA" LP. Coincidentally, this continued compilation
activity in the San Francisco Bay Area would soon also see
locals Green Day smash into the mainstream in 1994, around
the same time as Kamala of the Karnivores and Jesse of
Blatz' label Zafio released the "This Is Berkeley Not West
Bay" 7" EP featuring future stars AFI.

Ironically, it was the commercial success of Green Day that
launched a major label feeding frenzy of new Nineties pop
punk, as well as an international tidal wave of bands playing
this more polished style. The ensuing influx of cash and bands
would see compilations return to being samplers, switching
to the compact disc format. These samplers were cheap or free
and filled to their seventy minute brim with new bands, all
vying for the attention of a new generation of punk kids.

This glut of lower quality compilations on this new format
saw the punk vinyl compilation record take a nose dive in
both quantity and quality, as any label samplers that did
make it to vinyl were largely just afterthoughts. The punk
compilation never recovered and to this day exists as a
diminished format. It still makes underground appearances
of course, though largely as one-off or anniversary projects
of a format largely viewed as an obsolete anachronism in a
streaming internet age of algorithmic playlists.

The punk compilation records collected herein stand as a
testament to the creative explosion of a generation, from the
birth of the punk rock compilation in 1976 to it's commercial
rebirth nearly two decades later, that ultimately saw the
compilation become the victim of punk rock's newfound success.

FOUND OBJECTS

1977

A REVISTA POP APRESENTA O PUNK ROCK LP
CE N'EST PAS DE LA COUILLE, VOICI LA NEW WAVE GREATEST HITS LP
LA BOITE PUNK! OUVREZ OU CA VA SAUTER! 16 X 7" BOX SET
NEVER MIND OTHER LABELS - HERE'S CHISWICK 10"
PUNK MIX, ROCK MIX LP
WE ARE PUNK GENERATION LP

1978

BLUB KRAD LP
ENGLISH WAVES! LP
FROM PUNK TO NEW WAVE LP
KYLMÄÄ JOULUA! LP
LE ROCK D'ICI À L'OLYMPIA LP
LJUD FRÅN FRIBERGA LP
NEW WAVE PUNK LP
PUNK COLLECTION VOL. 2 LP
PUNK OFF! LP
PUNK ROCK '77 NEW WAVE '77 LP
SKYDOG COMMANDO LP
THE NEW SOUNDS ARE ON SIRE RECORDS LP
THE NEW WAVE PUNK ROCK'S GREAT GROUPS 2LP
THE SIRE RECORDS STORY LP
WISH YOU WERE HEAR (JEM IMPORT SAMPLER NO. 6) LP

1979

7000 RIFF LP
COMPILATION I. THE VOXHALL TRACKS. LUTON. 7" EP
EAST WEST '79 2LP
GO GO 7"
KNUCKLE SANDWICH LP
L.A. RADIO 2LP
OVERSELL LP

PERMANENT NEW WAVE LP

SPECTACULAR COMMODITY 7" EP

THAT SUMMER! LP

THE BOSTON BOOTLEG LP

TOKYO NEW WAVE '79 LP

VAULTAGE 79 (ANOTHER TWO SIDES OF BRIGHTON) LP

WEIRD NOISE 7" EP

WHO PUT THE BOMP? 2LP

ROCKERS TOKYO ROCKERS LP

1980

3 VUOTTA MYÖHEMMIN LP

8 FROM '80. A CARLISLE COMPILATION. 7" EP

A FACTORY QUARTET 2LP

A FASHIONABLE COLLECTION 7" EP

A TRIP TO THE DENTIST LP

ALIVE ROCK CITY LP

ANDRA BRANDEN 7" EP

BELFAST LP

BELIEBTE MELODIEN AUS DEUTSCHEM SÜDEN 7" EP

BOYS AND GIRLS COME OUT TO PLAY 7" EP

BRITANNIA WAIVES THE RULES 12"

BRUM BEAT LIVE AT THE BARREL ORGAN! 1 & 2 2LP & LP

CLEVELAND CONFIDENTIAL 7" EP

CONCERT OF THE MOMENT: LIVE I SALTLAGERET D. 9-11/79 3LP

DENK DARAN! LP

DOKKIRI RECORD LP

E(GG)CLECTIC 1 LP

FIRST OFFENDERS LP

GERÄUSCHE FÜR DIE 80ER LP

HAKOZAKISAI ROCK FES. LIVE LP

HANNOVER FUN FUN FUN LP

HELLÄÄ TERRORIA KORVILLE 7" EP

IN DIE ZUKUNFT LP

KAUGHT AT THE KAMPUS 12"

KELLERROCK 7" EP

KLART FÖR LADDNING! LP

LOGICAL STEPS LP

LONDON 1980 - NEW WAVE LP

MAPS TO THE STARS' HOMES 7" EP

MARTY THAU PRESENTS 2X5 LP

MELL SQUARE MUSICK 7" EP

METROPOLIS 3LP

NEW WAVE DISCO D'OURO LP

NO-COWBOYS LP

PORDENONE / THE GREAT COMPLOTTO LP

PRESAGE(S) 12"

ROCK' 80 LP

ROUGH CUTS 7" EP

SCHALLMAUER SAMPLER LP

STANDARDEVIATION LP

STREET LEVEL 7" EP

THE ART OF SOLVING PROBLEMS LP

THE BUNTINGFORD LONG PLAYING RECORD LP

THE CLASS OF '81 (MUSIC FOR THE UPPER CLASSES TO SOMETHING TO ...) LP

THE NEW WAVE TIMES LP

UNZIPPING THE ABSTRACT (MANCHESTER MUSICIANS' COLLECTIVE) LP

UTREG PUNX 7" EP

VAULTAGE 80: A VINYL CHAPTER LP

WHERE THE ACTION IS LP

1981

5 MILES TO MIDNIGHT 12"

A SPLASH OF COLOUR LP

A SUDDEN SURGE OF SOUND LP

AN X-TRA FOR X-PERTS LP

ANDRA BRÄNDER LP

ARTISTIĐKA RADNA AKCIJA - BEOGRAD '81 LP

CABARET FUTURA - FOOLS RUSH IN WHERE ANGELS DARE TO TREAD LP

CLASS OF '81 LP

DIE TÖDLICHE DOSIS LP

H'ARTCORE LP

HACKNEY MUSICIANS COLLECTIVE LP

HEAT FROM THE STREET LP

HITS & MYTHS LP

KATASTROPHE PROVINCE 2 X 7" EP
KZ 36 II LP
LIEBER ZUVIEL ALS ZUWENIG (ZICKZACK SOMMERHITS 81) LP
LIVE AT LE DISQUE LP
MAKING WAVES - A COLLECTION OF 12 WOMENS BANDS FROM THE UK LP
METHODS OF DANCE LP
MODERN DANCE LP
MRS. WILSON'S CHILDREN LP
MUENCHEN: REIFENWECHSEL LEICHT GEMACHT LP
MUND-ART LP
NEW ACCOUNTS 7" EP
NEW ROCK CHAMPIONS LP
NEWSLINES VOLUME 1 & 2 7" EPS
NICE NO. 4 4 X FLEXI 7"
NO ONE WITH A BULLET (AN ENDURANCE SAMPLER) LP
NOVI PUNK VAL 78-80 LP
NOVI VAL LP
PALACE OF LIGHTS 7" EP
PALLADIUM LP
PERSPECTIVES AND DISTORTION LP
ROCK TEGEN DE ROLLEN LP
ROUGH MIXES FROM SWITZERLAND 10"
ROUGH TRADE RECORDS COMPILATION LP
RUPERT PREACHING AT A PICNIC LP
SAD DAY WE LEFT THE CROFT LP
SCHAU HÖR MAIN HERZ IST RHEIN LP
SHAKE TO DATE LP
SUOMI - ILMIÖ LP
SVI MARŠ NA PLES! LP
TEN FROM THE MADHOUSE LP
THE RECORDER LP
THE THING FROM THE CRYPT LP
TUSEN OCH EN NATT... (EN EP FRÅN LINKÖPING) 7" EP
TV RÄJÄHTÄÄ! LP
VINYL VIRGINS LP
WE COULDN'T AGREE ON A TITLE LP
WOOL CITY ROCKER #14 FLEXI 7"

1982

4 AD DARK PATHS LP

A DROP IN THE OCEAN 12"

ABGWÜRGT - ZONE TIROLMUSIK LP

ALS JE HAAR MAAR GOED ZIT LP

BURST CITY / O.S.T. LP

COLOR THE REALITY LP

CRUISIN' ANN ARBOR LP

DAS ABENDPROGRAMM LP

DEUTSCHLAND (A COMPILATION OF "NEW" GERMAN MUSIK) LP

DIE DEUTSCHEN KOMMEN LP

DIE NEUE DEUTSCHE WELLE IST DA DA DA LP

DIRT COMPILATION VOLUME 1 LP

DOOBIE DO DISC LP

EFFENAAR 7" EP

FLEXIPOP! (THE FLEXIPOP ALBUM) LP

GATHERED LP

GOATS MILK SOAP LP

GÖTEBORGSROCK / YTTERROCK LP

HEIMAT BIST DU GROSSER SÖHNE LP

IT HAPPENED... BUT NOBODY NOTICED LP

LEPO JE ... LP

MURDERED BY THE MUSIC LP

MUSIC AND RHYTHM LP

NEUEDEUTSCHEUNTERHALTUNGSMUSIK(ROCKINDEUTSCHLAND,VOL.3)2LP

NEW ROSE 82 LP

NO FUTURE LP

NO PLATFORM FOR HEELS LP

NOSFERATU FESTIVAL LP

OVERLOAD LP

PANGKAKA LP

PAPI, QUEENS, REICHKANZLERS & PRESIDENNTI 7"EP

PRIMA TANZMUSIK 10"

PUNK LIVE IN BROUWERSHOECK LP

REBEL STREET LP

ROKK Í REYKJAVÍK 2LP

SCHIAVI NELLA CITTÀ PIÙ LIBERA DEL MONDO 7"EP

SING AS WE GO LP

STABS IN THE DARK LP

STERKT STOFF LP
SYSTEEMI EI TOIMI 7" EP
T.M.I. 015: A COMPILATION LP
UNITED SKINS LP
VOICES OF THE ANGELS (SPOKEN WORDS) 2LP
YOUR SECRET'S SAFE WITH US... 2LP

1983

1. 2. 3... START LP
ALS JE HAAR MAAR GOED ZIT... NR.2 LP
AMERICAN UNDERGROUND 3LP
BLENDER MIX LP
BLOOD ON THE ROQ! LP
CHOM L'ESPRIT '83 LP
DANSA MED FIG.13. LP
DER 8-EP-SAMPLER 2LP
DESPUES DEL HOLOCAUSTO - UNA OFENSIVA MUSICAL DRO 83 LP
ENGLISH AS A SECOND LANGUAGE (TALKING PACKAGE) 2LP
FIESTA INDEPENDIENTE LP
FROM MONTREAL... 7" EP
G-FORCE 7" EP
MONDO MONTAGE LP
NEW GENERATION - ROCK AGAINST RACISM LP
NEW PERFORMANCES FOR SOUNDPROOF ROOMS LP
NEW ROSE RECORDS LP
O COMEÇO DO FIM DO MUNDO LP
RAPTUS LP
ROCK & DOLE 7" EP
SEATTLE SYNDROME TWO LP
SKINS E PUNKS = T.N.T. 7" EP
SON OF OI! LP
SWISS WAVE ALBUM 2 LP
THE BEERDROP EXPLODES LP
THE REBEL KIND LP
VÄGRA FÖR HELVETE LP
VALLADOLID 83 LP
VENTILATOR 202 DEMO TOP 10 LP
VI FESTIVAL ROCK VILLA DE MADRID LP
WATERKANT-HITS LP

1984

84 LP
4 PER TUTTI 7" EP
AO VIVO NO ROCK RENDEZ VOUS EM 1984 LP
ASLEEP AT THE WHEEL LP
BIRDSKIT I LP
CAPITOL KAOS LP
CHAOS EN FRANCE - VOLUME 2 LP
DAFFODILS TO THE DAFFODILS HERE'S THE DAFFODILS LP
DON'T LET THE HOPE CLOSE DOWN LP
EAT YOUR HEAD 2 X 12"
ENEMIES OF THE STATE LP
EVERYTHING 7" EP
FINNISH SPUNK / HARD BEAT LP
GIVE ME SOME CHERRY LP
HARDCORE UNLAWFUL ASSEMBLY LP
HOLD UP OMNIBUS 8" EP
HOLLOW WEINERS 7" EP
HYVINKÄÄ 7" EP
INNER MYSTIQUE #3 7" EP
JOBS FOR THE BOYS LP
LA MOVIDA MADRILEÑA DE MUSICRA RECORDS LP
LASTA 7" EP 1 & 2
LET'S CUT A RUG LP
MADE IN FRANCE LP
MUTTI'S MUNTERE MELODEI LP
N-340 LP
NOGET PÅ DANSK 7" EP
NOT SO HUMDRUM, THE 2ND ABERRANT SYDNEY COMPILATION LP
ON THE STREET LP
PERSONALITY CRISIS LP
PROPAGANDA LIVE LP
ROCK A ROUEN LP
THE LIVES OF LHASA LP
THE OI! OF SEX LP
THE QUAKE FM99 PRESENTS THE ROCK OF '84' LP
TRACKS ON THE GREEN
TRANSMISSION SAMPLER 01 7" EP
TWO NINETY NINE LP
WET DREAMS LP

1985

1984 THE SECOND 2LP
A KICK UP THE ARSE - VOLUME ONE LP
AT THE FUHRERS REQUEST... LP
BABYLON: BLEIBT FAHREN LP
BACKLASH! (ORIGINAL FILM SOUNDTRACK) LP
BITES & STABS LP
CHAOS IN EUROPE LP
COMMUNICATE!!!! LIVE AT THAMES POLY 2LP
COMPULSORY OVERTIME LP
DRY LUNGS LP
.EP. 7" EP
EXPLOSIVE LP
HEAT FROM THE WIND CHILL FACTORY LP
IT CAME FROM CANADA LP
LE CIMETIÈRE DES PASSIONS LP
LET'S HAVE MORE FUN LP
MONTREAL NEW YORK CONNECTION 85 LIVE LP
MORE MONDO LP
NÃO SÃO PAULO LP
NEVER MIND THE JACKSONS... HERE'S THE POLLOCKS LP
NO VISIBLE SCARS 7" EP
OI OF JAPAN LP
PINCH AND OUCH! LP
PLOW! LP
QUELLI CHE URLANO ANCORA... LP
QUESTIONABLE: THE COMPILATION LP
SF UNSCENE LP
SMUTSIG JUL 7" EP
SPIN RADIO UNDERGROUND 2LP
SUB LP
SYSTEMBEAT & SYSTEMBEATWO LPS
SZTUKA LATANIA LP
THE TROUSERS IN ACTION 7" EP
THE VINYL SOLUTION LP
ULTIMATUM LP
V.I.S.A. PRÉSENTE LP
VERY SCARY CEMETERY 7" EP
VIVA LA REVOLUTION! 2LP
WHEN MONKEYS WERE GODS! LP
WHY MARCH WHEN YOU CAN RIOT?! LP
WIE LANGE NOCH... LP

1986

77 RECORDS PRÉSENTE... LP

AFFLICTED CRIES IN THE DARKNESS OF WAR LP

BIG HITS OF MID AMERICA 4

BLOODSUCKER 7" EP

BRITISH FRONT LINE LP

BURNING AMBITIONS LP

CALGARY COMPELATION LP

CHEMICAL IMBALANCE #4 7" EP

CHRW COMPILATION LONDON UNDERGROUND LP

COMPILEATION LP

¡CONDENADOS A LUCHAR! BOROCKARI LOTURIK! LP

D.O.A. AND FRIENDS: EXPO HURTS EVERYONE 7" EP

DECLARATION OF FUZZ LP

DEEP SIX LP

DESTROY THE WORLD 7" EP

DRY LUNGS II LP

EAST COAST 60'S ROCK & ROLL EXPERIMENT LP

EASTERN SHORES - AN AMERICAN COMPILATION LP

END OF THE WORLD A GO-GO LP

FIGHT BACK 7" EP

FLOWERS FROM THE DUSTBIN LP

FUTURE TENSE LP

GÄRDESFEST 12"

GBG PUNK 77-80 LP

HERE'S EGG ON YOUR FACE! LP

IT CAME FROM CANADA VOLUME 2 LP

IT CAME FROM THE GARAGE! LP

KULTURSCHOCK ATTACKE VOL.1 LP

LET'S GET PISSED - IT'S CHRISTMAS LP

MARYLAND MUSICIANS FOR MUSIC LP

MUSIC FROM EARTH LP

MÚSICA MODERNA PORTUGUESA 1 & 2 LP

NOBODY'S PERFECT LP

ON OUR WAY TO FOOLS PARADISE LP

PARANOIA YOU CAN DANCE TO LP

PUNK LIVES! - LET'S SLAM LP

QUEEN CITY ROCKER SOUNDTRACK LP

RADIO ACTIVE LP

RELIGIOUS AS HELL LP

ROCK AT THE EDGE LP

ROCK REBEL QUALITY (BEST BRITISH PUNK ROCK) LP

SHADES OF THE FUTURE LP

SKALHERRIA PUNK LP

SPLITTING HEADACHE ON A SUNDAY AFTERNOON! 7" EP

STRICTLY TABOO LP

SUTURA ETERNA LP

THE DEADLY SPAWN LP

THE RISE AND FALL OF OMA HODEL - ORIGINAL SOUNDTRACK 7" EP

THERE IS NO REASON TO BE HAPPY 7" EP

TORN IN TWO LP

TROUSERS IN ACTION 2 7" EP

VIVA LOS ANGELES LP

WE ARE BEAT CRAZY LP

WHAT ARE YOU DOING ABOUT THAT HOLE IN YOUR HEAD? LP

WOODSHOCK 85 2LP

1987

1984 THE THIRD 2LP

A MINUTE TO MIDNIGHT... LP

A VILE PEACE LP

ACRES FOR CENTS LP

ALL WASHED UP...THE LAST DAYS OF THE LAUNDRY WORKS 2LP

ANIMAL LIBERATION LP

ATTACK 7" EP

BIG NOISE FROM BIG TIME LP

BRITTLE BLACK FRISBEE LP

BUY OR DIE 14 7" EP

BUY OR DIE 14 1/2 7" EP

CENSORSHIP SUCKS! LP

CITY HISTORY 2LP

CONSOLIDATION 7" EP

CRAWLING FROM WITHIN LP

DIE, JERRY, DIE LP

DRY LUNGS III LP

EVIL I DO NOT TO NOD I LIVE 5 X 7" BOX SET

FEAR • POWER • GOD LP

FOR NO APPARENT REASON LP

FOR FRANCE PROFONDE VOL. 2 LP

GOD SAVE US FROM THE USA LP

HAPPINESS IS DRY PANTS 7" EP

HEAD OVER EARS (A DEBRIS COMPILATION) LP

I AM THE FLY 7" EP

INDESTRUCTIBLE LP

I WAS A TEENAGE ZOMBIE (ORIGINAL MOTION PICTURE SOUNDTRACK) LP

IT CAME FROM CANADA VOLUME 3 LP

IT CAME FROM THE GARAGE II! LP

KULTURSCHOCK ATTACKE VOL. 2 LP

LA NOUVELLE FRONTIÈRE... PAS DE FRONTIÈRE LP

MASH IT UP! LP

MINDLESS SLAUGHTER LP

MOM 7" EP

MY MEAT'S YOUR POISON LP

NEW YORK CITY HARDCORE 1987 - TOGETHER 7" EP

NEW ZEALAND 7" EP

NO AGE - A COMPILATION OF SST INSTRUMENTAL MUSIC LP

NUREMBERGA IN VERTEBRIS LP

OMLADINA '87 - NAJBOLJI UŽIVO LP

RECORDED LIVE OFF THE BOARD AT CBGB LP

RIJEKA-PARIS-TEXAS LP

ROCK DO ABC LP

SCHMURZ-PILATION LP

SENSELESS DEATH LP

SENSELESS DEATH 7"

SHODOKU GIG (STERILIZATION GIG) LP

SIX DISQUES BLEU 6LP

SKA-VILLE USA VOLUME-2 (A BOSTON SKA COMPILATION) LP

SON OF HUDSON ROCK LP

SORORITY SAMPLER LP

STILL THINKING PRESENTS: PROGRESS ?! 7" EP

STRANGE BABIES WHO CRY ROCK LP

THE A.L.F. IS WATCHING AND THERE'S NO PLACE TO HIDE... LP
THE IOWA COMPILATION LP
THESE DOGS LIVE IN THE GARAGE (THE ARF ARF MUSIC SAMPLER II) LP
THE VIEW FROM HERE: THE SAN FRANCISCO COMPILATION LP
THIS IS THE LIFE (MCR COMP LP VOL.2) LP
TSJERNOBILLY BOOGIE LP
VANITY! 7 DEADLY SINS 15 DEADLY SONGS LP
WHAT IS THIS PLACE? (A NEW PLYMOUTH COMPILATION ALBUM) LP
WRITING ON STONE: THE ALBERTA COMPILATION LP
Z SIEGE 7" EP

1988

A BAS TOUTES LES ARMÉES LP
A CONSONANT VOWEL LP
ALBANY STYLE HARDCORE 7" EP
ASSORTED DESECRATIONS AND MAGNIFICENT MUTATIONS LP
BETTER YET... CONNECTICUT HARDCORE 7" EP
BRITISH AIRWAVES 2LP
CAUTION 7" EP
COMPLETE DEATH II LP
CONTRA ATAQUE LP
DON'T ENFRCE YOUR VLUES ON ME! FLEXI 7"
DON'T LET THE FRUIT ROT ON THE TREE LP
DOPE-GUNS-'N-FUCKING IN THE STREETS VOLUME ONE 7" EP
EDGE OF THE ROAD (MEDIUM COOL SAMPLER) LP
ENJOY YOUR YOUTH BY THIS HARDCORE SAMPLER LP
ESSENTIAL ATTITUDES VOL. 3 LP
EYE OF THE THRASH GUERRILLA LP
FOLK SONGS FROM THE TWILIGHT ZONE LP
FOUR, WHOM THE BELL TOLLS 7" EP
GDYNIA LP
GIMME THE KEYS!! LP
HANG THE SUCKER VOL.1 7" EP
HARD-CORE FOR THE MASSES LP
HARDCORE VOL. I LP
HOWL 1 7" EP
HUMAN MUSIC 2LP

IN BETWEEN THE LINES LP
IT CAME FROM CANADA 4 LP
IT'S ANOTHER IOWA COMPILATION (UNCHARTED TERRITORIES) LP
LOKALE LEIDENSCHAFTEN VOL. I 2 X 7" EP
MAS QUE PUNK... PUNK BAINO GEHIAGO LP
MOTOR CITY MADNESS LP
NO TWO FLAKES THE SAME LP
ÓDIO MORTAL LP
OIHUKA - 88 LP
OVERLY-ANXIOUS CELEBATE PRIEST 7" EP
REBEL INCORPORATED 2LP
ROCK TURNS TO STONE LP
RONDA ALTERNATIVA LP
SAN JOSE ROCKS! VOLUME ONE LP
SKA FACE: AN ALL AMERICAN SKA COMPILATION LP
SKULLFUCK VOL. 1 7" EP
SUB POP 200 3 X 12"
SUB POP ROCK CITY LP
SUFFER THIS... A COMPILATION OF BOSTON'S BACKWASH LP
SWEDISH EXOTICA VOLUME ONE LP
THE ANDREW NOEL LIN MEMORIAL TRAILER PARK 7" EP
THE END OF AN ERA - THE BEST OF ROT RECORDS LP
THE MELTING PLOT LP
THE PEEL SESSIONS - THE SAMPLER LP
THE U.S. OF OI! LP
THE WATER MUSIC COMPILATION ALBUM LP
THIS IS MY LIFE NOT YOURS 7" EP
THRASHOLD LP
TIME BOMB! FLESHTONES PRESENT: THE BIG BANG THEORY LP
UNDERGROUND ROCKERS LP
VOICE OF EUROPE 7" EP
WAASA 7" EP
WAR 7" EP
WHAT'VE YA BROUGHT ME THIS TIME? 7" EP
WHERE THE HELL ARE THE GOOD SCISSORS? LP
WIPE OUT! PRESENTS 12 RAW GREEK GROUPS LP & 7" EP
X MARKS THE SPOT 7" EP

1989

A GIANT LEAP OF FAITH - THE PALINDROME COMPILATION LP

À SOMBRA DE DEUS - BRAGA 88 LP

AVALANCHE SWISS UNDERGROUND LP

BEAT OF THE STREET 7" EP

BOMBARDIRANJE NEW YORKA LP

BRAIN FOOD LP

CHEMICAL IMBALANCE 1 & 2 7" EP

CHOP CHOP 7" EP

COMPOSITE DRAWING LP

CZERWONA FALA - EPOKA DLA NAS LP

DEVOURING OUR ROOTS LP

DOKUMENTTI TODELLISUUDESTA LP

DOPE-GUNS-'N-FUCKING IN THE STREETS VOLUME 1 - 3 7" EPS

DRY LUNGS IV LP

EAT ME TENDER 7" EP

EVERY BAND HAS A SHONEN KNIFE WHO LOVES THEM LP

EXCLUSION LP

GARÁZS LP

GO AHEAD MAKE MY DAY - SMASHING ODDS NESS 2 LP

HANG THE SUCKER VOL.2 LP

HARD ON... 7" EP

HIATUS LP

HOWL 2, 3, 4, 5 7" EPS

I COULD'A BEEN A CONTENDER LP

IT CAME FROM CANADA #5 LP

JAROCIN'88 3LP

JUSTICE IS OUR CONVICTION LP

KYOTO CITY HARDCORE FLEXI 7"

LA RELEVE. MON PETITE FRERE EST UN ROCKER LP

LETNIA ZADYMA W ĐRODKU ZIMY 2LP

LIFE IS CHANGE LP

MAANALAINEN VUOSIKERTA 1989 LP

MASHIN' UP THE NATION BEST OF U.S. SKA VOL. 1 LP

MUST GET TO THE POWER OF THE DEFENCE FOR... FLEXI 7"

NARDWUAR THE HUMAN SERVIETTE: "OH GOD, MY MOM'S ON CHANNEL 10!" LP

NEW YORK HARDCORE - WHERE THE WILD THINGS ARE... LP

NOTES FROM THE UNDERGROUND: AN ICON RECORDS COMPILATION LP

NOTHING SHORT OF TOTAL WAR (PART ONE) LP
PANX VINYL ZINE 01 / 02 / 03 7" EPS
PRINZEN DER PROVINZEN - LAUT! LP
RADIO TOKYO TAPES VOLUME 4 WOMEN 2LP
REARGARDE PRESENTS THE EN GARDE COMPILATION LP
REGISTOS - 5º CONCURSO DE MÚSICA MODERNA PORTUGUESA LP
SCREAMING FOR A BETTER FUTURE LP
SCUMBAIT #1 7" EP
SKATE'N ROLL! LIVE AUF DEM WINTERFELDTPLATZ / BERLIN LP
SMALL BANDS BIG SOUND 7" EP
STÅKKÅLMSJÄVLAR 1978-1981 LP
STEP BY STEP 7" EP
SWEDISH EXOTICA VOLUME TWO LP
TERIYAKI ASTHMA 1 & 2 7" EPS
THE PLEASURES IN LIFE 2LP
THERE'S A FUNGUS AMOUNGUS 7" EP
THIS HOUSE IS NOT A MOTEL LP
THRESHOLD COMPLICATION LP
TOUR DE FARCE PART 3 LP
TRIPLE CROSS COUNTER 7" EP
UNDERGROUND ROCKERS VOLUME 2 LP
VOLNITZA (WORST OF THE 1 IN 12 CLUB VOL 6/7) 2LP
WE'VE GOT YOUR SHORTS 7" EP
YUP IN FLAMES LP

...among others.

CATALOGUE NUMBERS

403

ALSO BY THE AUXTHOR

"Directions To The Outskirts Of Town - Punk Rock Tour Diaries From Nineties North America"

Earth Island Books (2021)

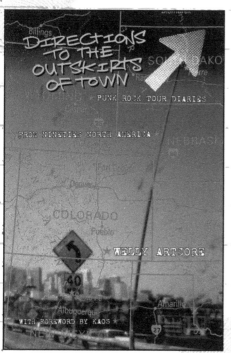

"Down all the years of DIY punk touring, there will be countless stories like this. Most remain mouldering in fading grey matter, all but lost in a pickled stew of alcohol abuse, sanity-destroying drives, and endless half-sleeps on rough floors. Thankfully, this one escaped the fate. Along with in-the-moment photography, diary entries are polished with desert-dry sarcasm and whiplash wit, often prosaic stories rendered dryly caustic, frequently absorbing, and occasionally poignant. There is no attempt to dress them up as glamorous, rock n' roll adventures, or hardcore baptisms of fire - though they undoubtedly are the latter. Descriptions of long drives, stunning views, eye-opening encounters with the best and worst that life on the road throws up - pun intended - are as compelling as scuffles, arguments, and encounters with egos and cops. Writing blunt prose with the ability to propel you into the moment is an often unacknowledged skill. Whether in a cramped, stinking van after a seven-hour drive, down the front at a sweaty gig, at a punk house full of pissheads or as an onlooker during an awkward moment. I wasn't there - but it almost felt like I was."

STEVEN MIDWINTER, PERSONAL PUNK

ABOUT THE AUTKHOR

Welly Artcore is a graphic designer, fanzine editor, and punk vocalist from Cardiff, Wales, U.K. Creator of Artcore Fanzine since 1986, graphic designer and illustrator for independent vinyl, CD and merchandise since 1987, he studied Graphic Design at Cardiff University. He was also vocalist and lyricist for Four Letter Word, State Funeral, Violent Arrest and Signal Crimes between 1991 and 2018. He is also the author of "Directions To The Outskirts Of Town" (2021). He relocated with his family to the outskirts of Phoenix, Arizona in 2018.

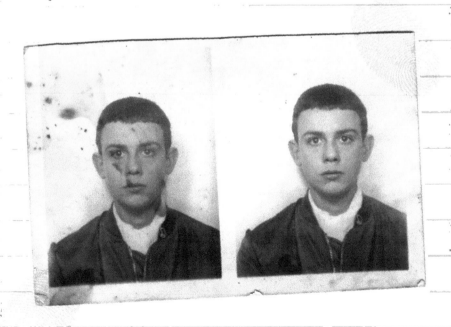

THE AUTHOR CKIRCA 1981